HISTORIC PHOTOS OF
HUNTSVILLE

TEXT AND CAPTIONS BY
JACQUELYN PROCTER REEVES

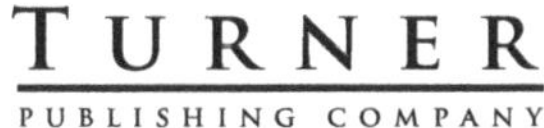
TURNER
PUBLISHING COMPANY

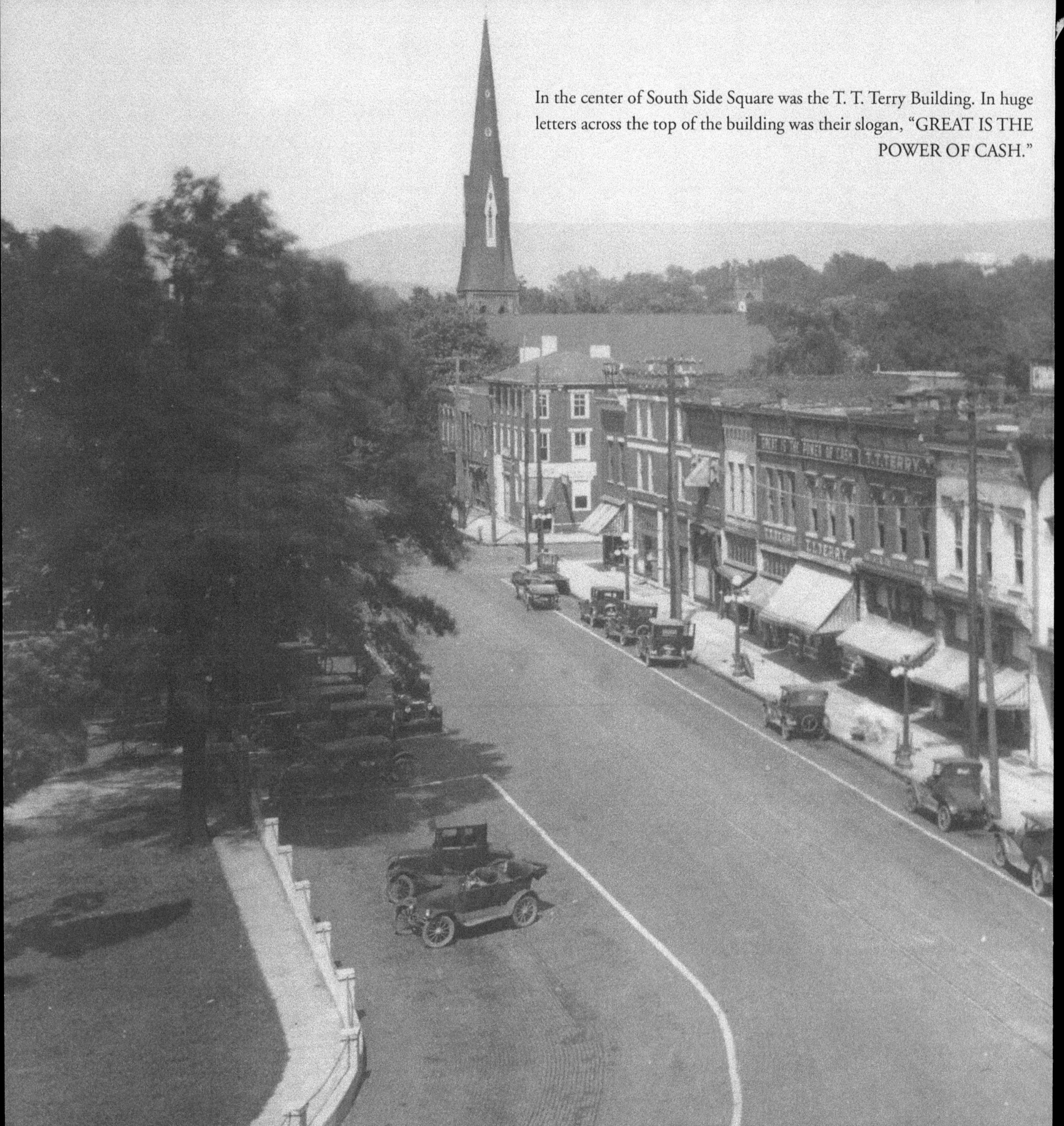

In the center of South Side Square was the T. T. Terry Building. In huge letters across the top of the building was their slogan, "GREAT IS THE POWER OF CASH."

HISTORIC PHOTOS OF
HUNTSVILLE

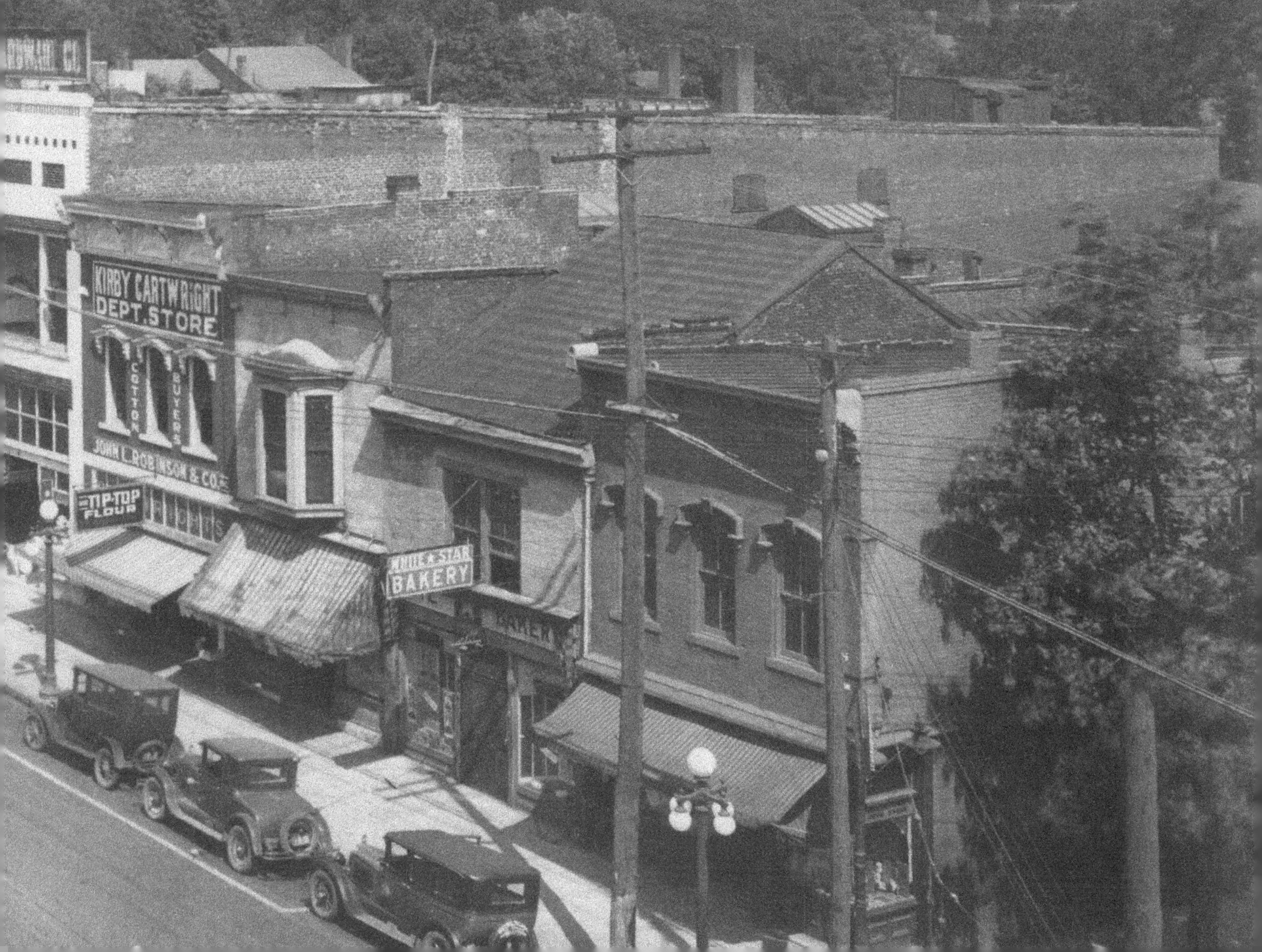

Turner Publishing Company
www.turnerpublishing.com

Historic Photos of Huntsville

Library of Congress Control Number: 2007923673

ISBN: 978-1-59652-372-2

ISBN 978-1-68336-959-2 (hc)

Contents

John Stallworth, third from left, is honored by his college alma mater, Alabama A & M University. John went on to become a pro football player (wide receiver) with the Pittsburgh Steelers before returning to Huntsville to become a successful businessman. After a stellar career, he was named to the NFL Hall of Fame. He still holds Super Bowl records.

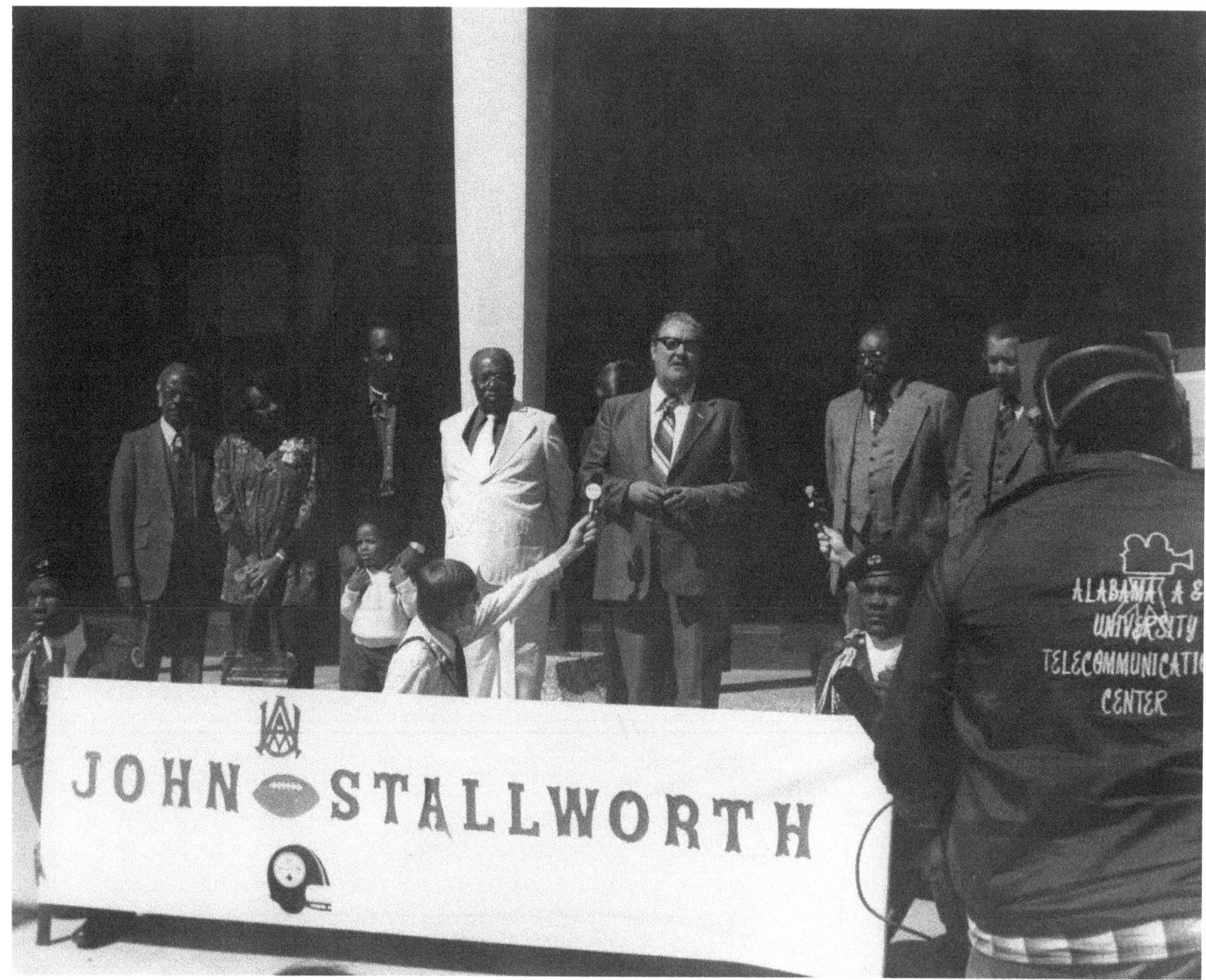

Acknowledgments

This volume, *Historic Photos of Huntsville* is the result of the cooperation and efforts of many individuals, organizations, and corporations. It is with great thanks that we acknowledge the valuable contribution of the Huntsville Public Library staff for their generous support.

We would also like to thank the following individuals for valuable contributions and assistance in making this work possible:

Tim Griffin, Historian
Thomas Hutchens, Heritage Room, Huntsville Public Library
Jim Maples, Historian and Editor
Mona Mitchell, Technical Processing, Huntsville Public Library
Raneé Pruitt, Archivist, Huntsville Public Library
Robert Reeves, who identified the dates of many photographs by the automobiles in them

This project represents countless hours of review and research. The researchers and writer have reviewed thousands of photographs. We greatly appreciate the generous assistance of the archives listed here, without whom this project could not have been completed.

The goal in publishing the work is to provide broader access to a set of extraordinary photographs. The aim is to inspire, provide perspective, and evoke insight that might assist officials and citizens, who together are responsible for determining Huntsville's future. In addition, the book seeks to preserve the past with respect and reverence.

With the exception of touching up imperfections caused by the vicissitudes of time and cropping where necessary, no other changes have been made. The focus and clarity of many images is limited to the technology of the day and the skill of the photographer who captured them.

We encourage readers to reflect as they explore Huntsville, stroll along its streets, or wander its neighborhoods. It is the publisher's hope that in making use of this work, longtime residents will learn something new and that new residents will gain a perspective on where Huntsville has been, so that each can contribute to its future.

—Todd Bottorff, Publisher

Preface

What is a photograph? More than ink on paper, a record of the past, or an image in time, a photograph captures a moment that can never be recreated, a moment forever recorded that sparks the imagination not only of those who lived it but of those not yet born when the shutter was clicked.

Look into these images of the past and see the muddy streets, feel the chill that comes with the winter snow, listen to the brass band of a 4th of July parade, and cheer for the success of the moon landing. Imagine the wariness of the Union soldiers who occupied a Rebel town, as well as the fear of the residents under that occupation. We read about the many events in our history, but words are not enough to describe the joyous smiles on youngsters or the lined and weathered faces of veterans who saw war so many years before. We are fortunate to see these captured moments in time.

No images exist from 1805, when pioneer John Hunt established his home at the Big Spring, a body of water under a bluff that has served as the heart of this ever-changing community for more than 200 years. The town of Hunt's Spring became Twickenham for a brief period, before being permanently named Huntsville in honor of its first white settler. The first Constitutional Convention was held here in 1819, making Huntsville the provisional capital as well as the county seat. Cotton thrived in the rich soil. It represented a source of wealth for some but back-breaking labor for the large number of slaves brought here to harvest the "white gold."

A few of these images may look familiar to Huntsvillians and former residents, but many are of places lost to the ravages of fire and urban renewal. Our structures of 150 years ago dictated taste and refinement, an ideal now overshadowed by cost and efficiency. Few of us can comprehend the hustle and bustle of our downtown in past decades, before television drew us inside and shopping malls pulled customers and stores to the suburbs. Many of these pictures from the past, never before published, are now available for the first time to new generations.

Many people helped create this book. Without their expertise and enthusiasm, we could not offer this treasure. We appreciate their willingness to share their knowledge.

Millions of photographs are taken every day—for a special occasion or no particular reason at all. In our distant past, however, very few pictures were made and even fewer have survived. Look at the faces of those long gone and feel their pride and their heartaches and imagine their everyday lives. Will future generations wonder about our own lives, long after we are gone, as they gaze into our eyes captured in photographs? Of course they will! Though buildings come and go, our images, and perhaps even a smidgen of our personalities, will remain in each and every timeless photograph.

—Jacquelyn Procter Reeves

Architect George Steele designed this Greek Revival bank in 1835. His highly trained slaves were the artisans who constructed it. The oldest bank in continual use in the State of Alabama, it is presently home to Regions Bank.

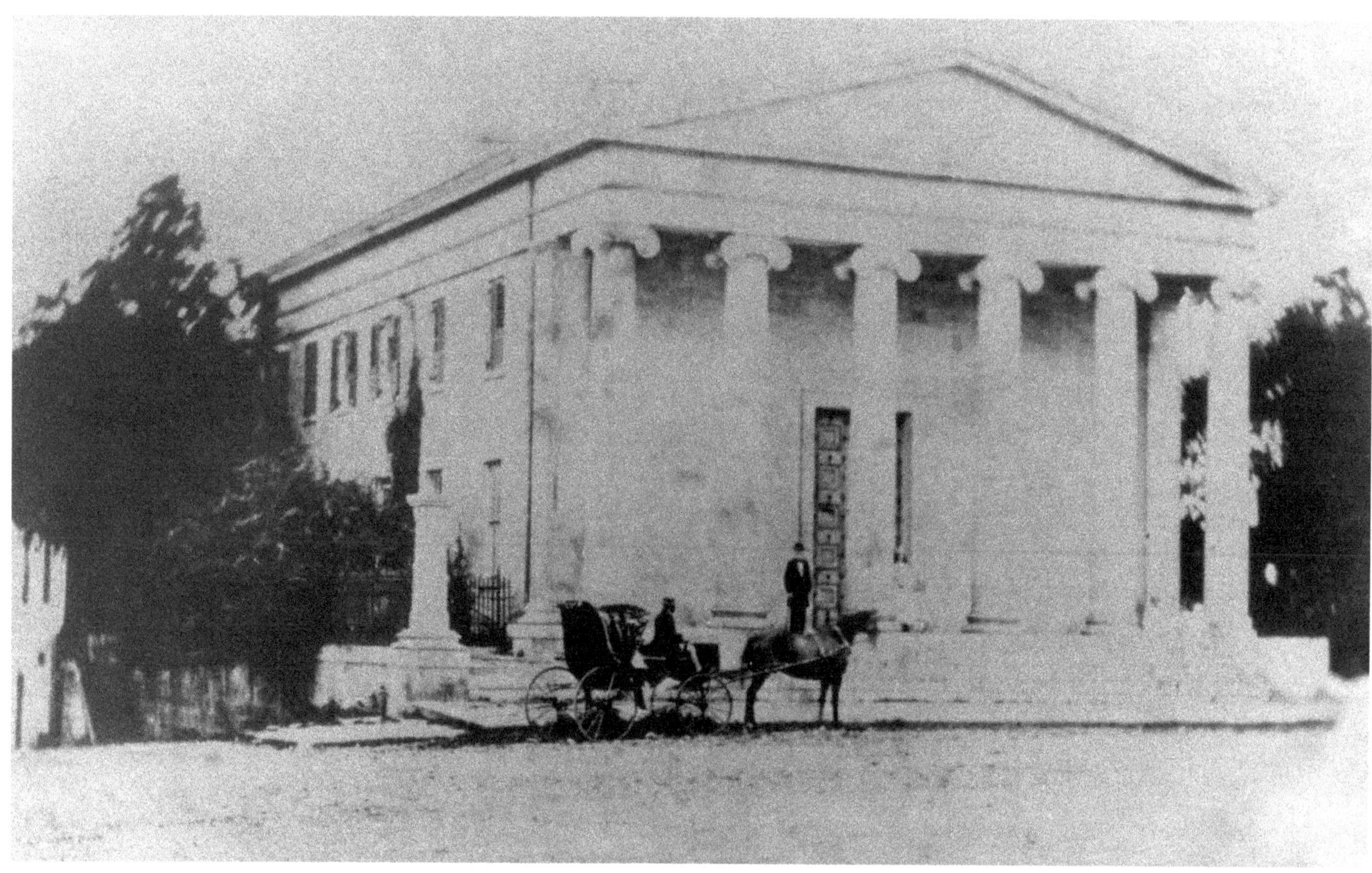

War and Reconstruction

(1850–1899)

In April, 1861, Huntsville native Leroy Pope Walker, as secretary of war for the newly formed Southern Confederacy, sent orders to fire on Fort Sumter in the harbor of Charleston, South Carolina, the action that began the Civil War. One year later, Union soldiers marched into Huntsville, surprised its inhabitants and captured the town. In retrospect, Huntsville fared better than most of its neighboring cities. Because there was neither time nor men available to provide resistance, it was not laid to waste, and for that reason, many of our beautiful antebellum structures still exist.

For the remainder of the war, Huntsville was occupied, off and on, by Union soldiers who pitched their tents on the courthouse square or at Maple Hill Cemetery (then known simply as "the burying ground"), or they took up residence in one of the many spacious homes in the historic Twickenham District.

The conflict finally ended in 1865, after four years of lost lives and bloodied fields. Weary soldiers came home to begin again in a country transformed by war. Former slaves struggled to find their new place in the changed world. In time, fields of fluffy, white cotton once again stretched as far as the eye could see. In the late 1800s, money began to flow into the area from Northern investors—"Yankee money"—and cotton mills were established to provide thousands of jobs, albeit low-paying ones, to those anxious for work. Mini-towns sprang up around each mill, and although citizens of those "mill towns" were all considered residents of Huntsville, they found themselves in competition and sometimes in conflict with each other.

The end of the century found Huntsville once again full of soldiers, after the brief Spanish-American War; as many as 15,000 came here to recover from the effects of yellow fever before mustering out. The 10th Cavalry Regiment—African American troops known as Buffalo Soldiers—were among those who stayed briefly in Huntsville. They were encamped at what is still known today as Cavalry Hill. Future World War I commander John "Black Jack" Pershing stayed in Huntsville during that period, and the city enjoyed several visits from U.S. Major General Joseph Wheeler, formerly a brilliant Confederate cavalry leader.

Madison County's second courthouse was designed by architect George Steele. This beautiful Greek Revival structure was built in 1835 and torn down in 1914. The dome was copper-clad. A sign at the gate states, "Five dollar fine for hitching within ten feet of this gate."

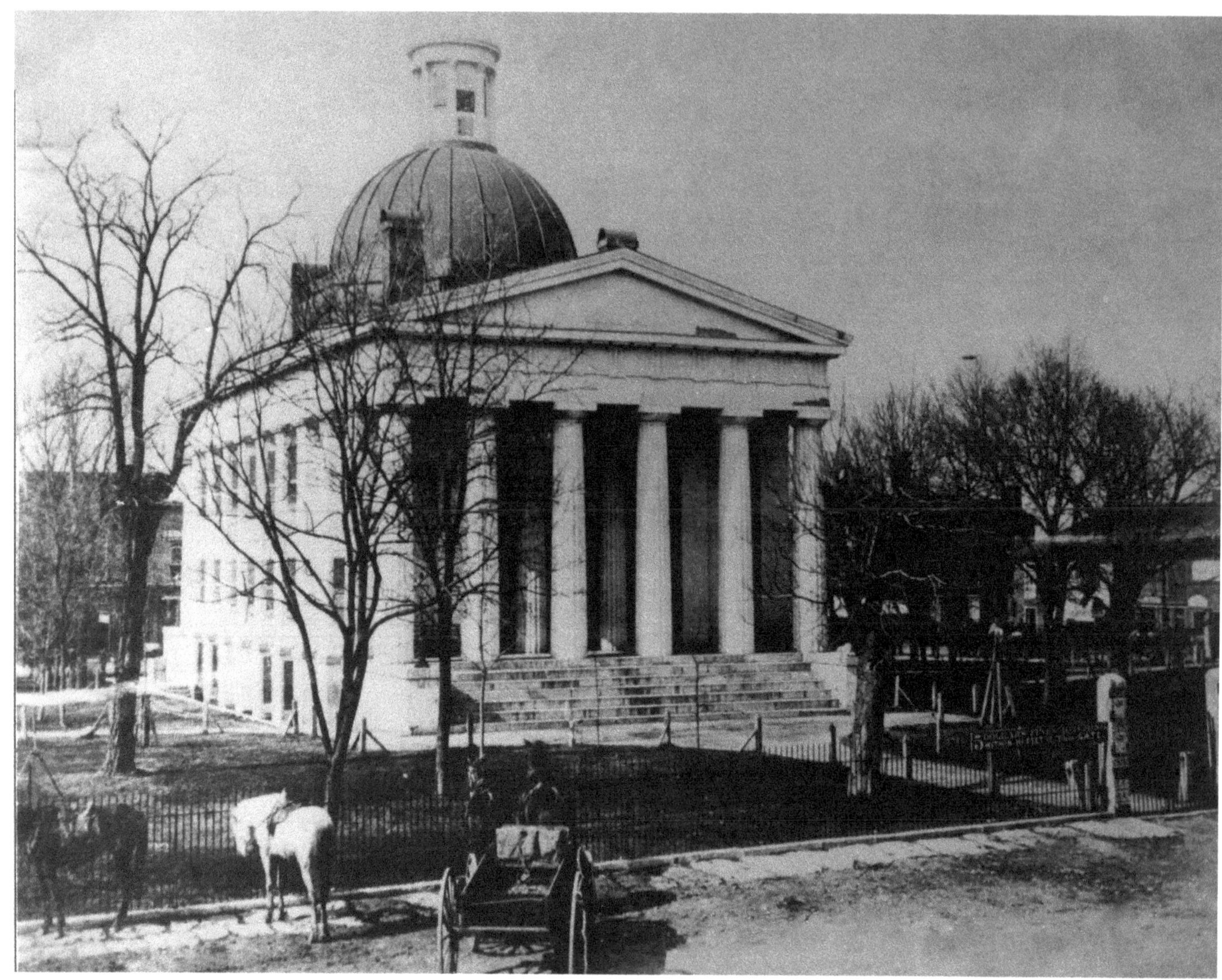

Bringing cotton into town to sell was a big event for farmers and spectators, as seen in this 1860 photograph.

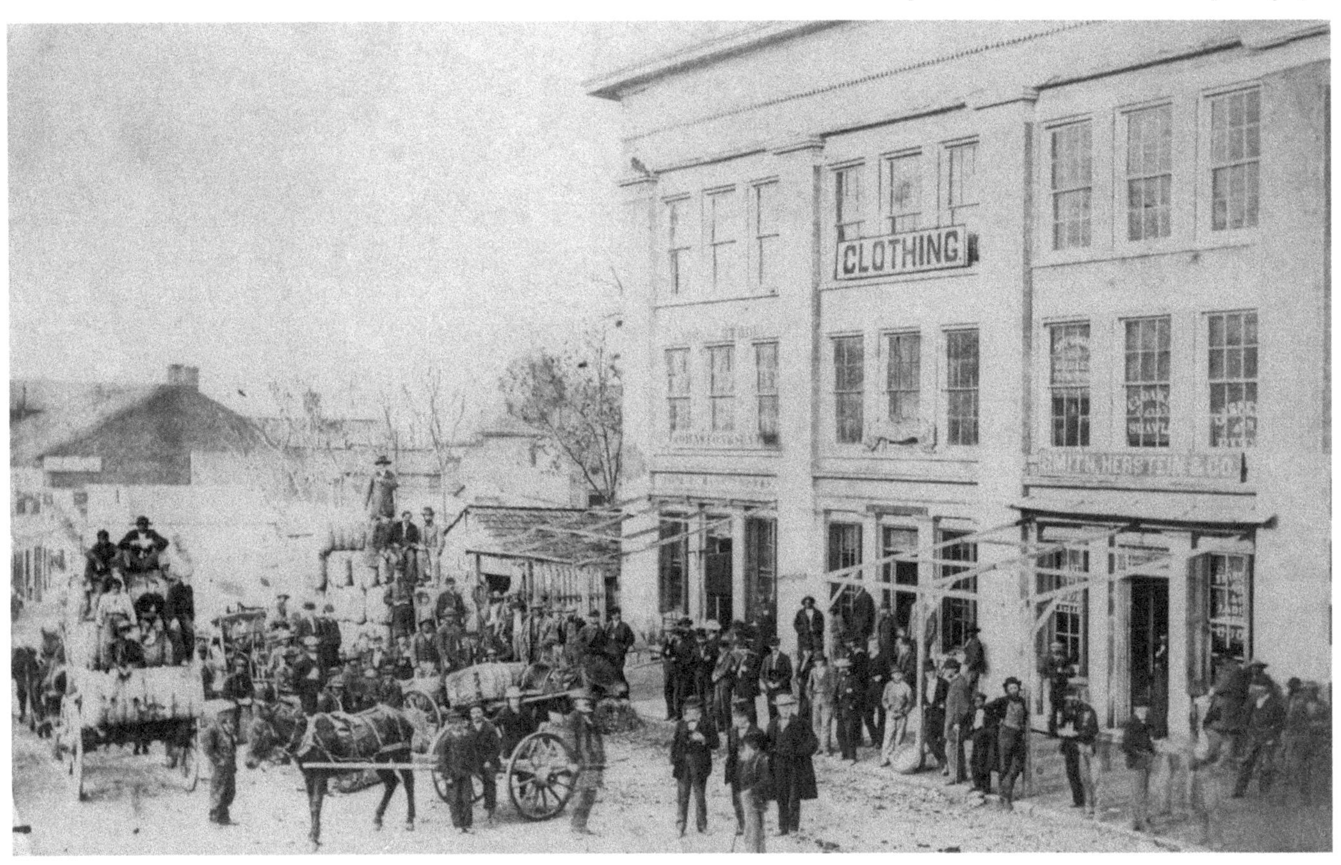

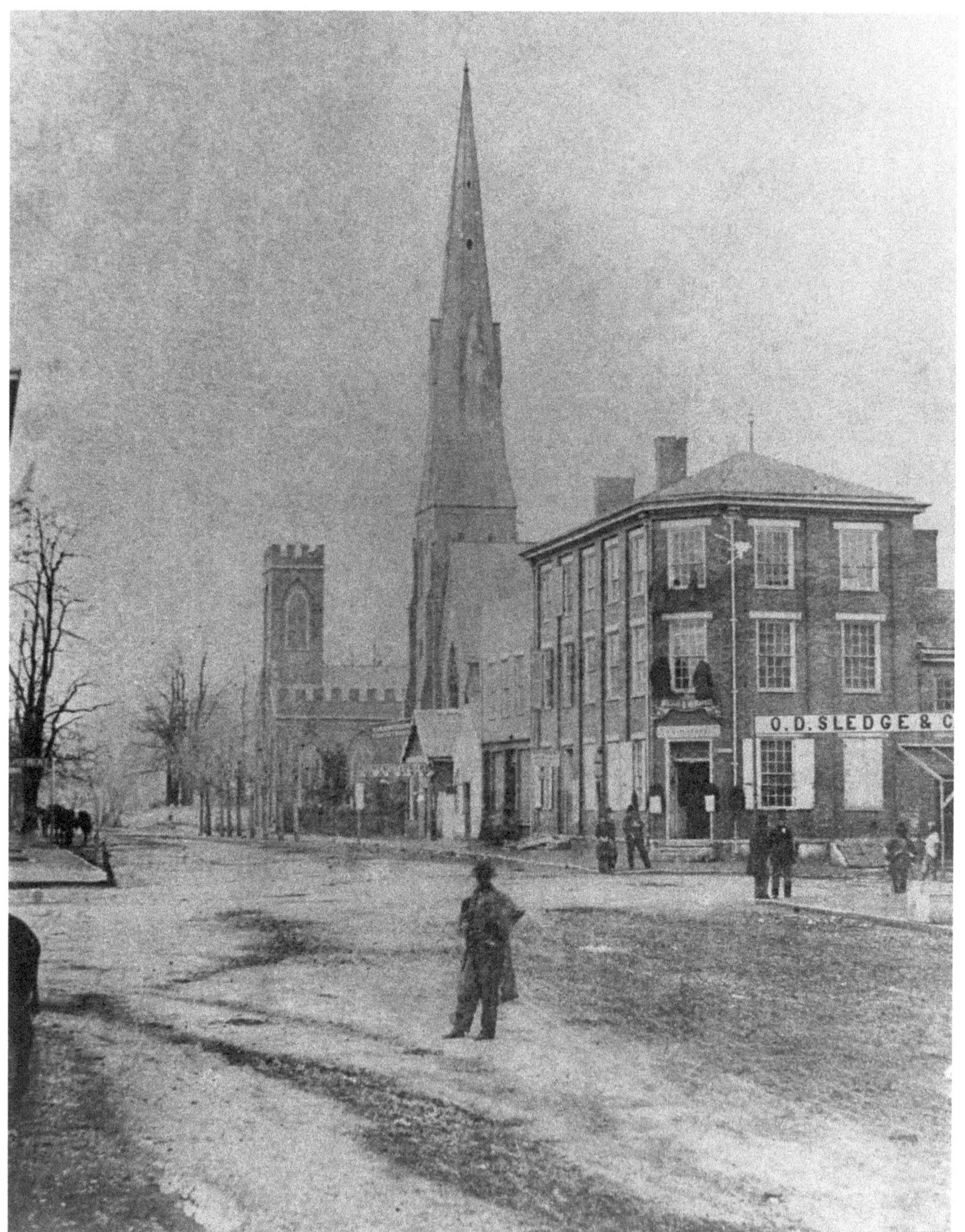

The towering steeple of the Church of the Nativity Episcopal soars above the buildings on Eustis Street from the southeast corner of the courthouse square. The castle-like church to the left was also an Episcopal Church. This appears to be around the time of the Civil War.

Two tents occupy the open lot on East Side Square, known as Cheap Side Row. Churches in the background are the Presbyterian Church, the old Episcopal Church, and the Church of the Nativity. There is speculation that the tents belonged to Union soldiers who occupied Huntsville during the Civil War. Barely visible in the upper left side of the picture is the partially obscured front of LeRoy Pope's mansion on Echols Hill. He was the grandfather of LeRoy Pope Walker, first secretary of war for the Confederate States of America.

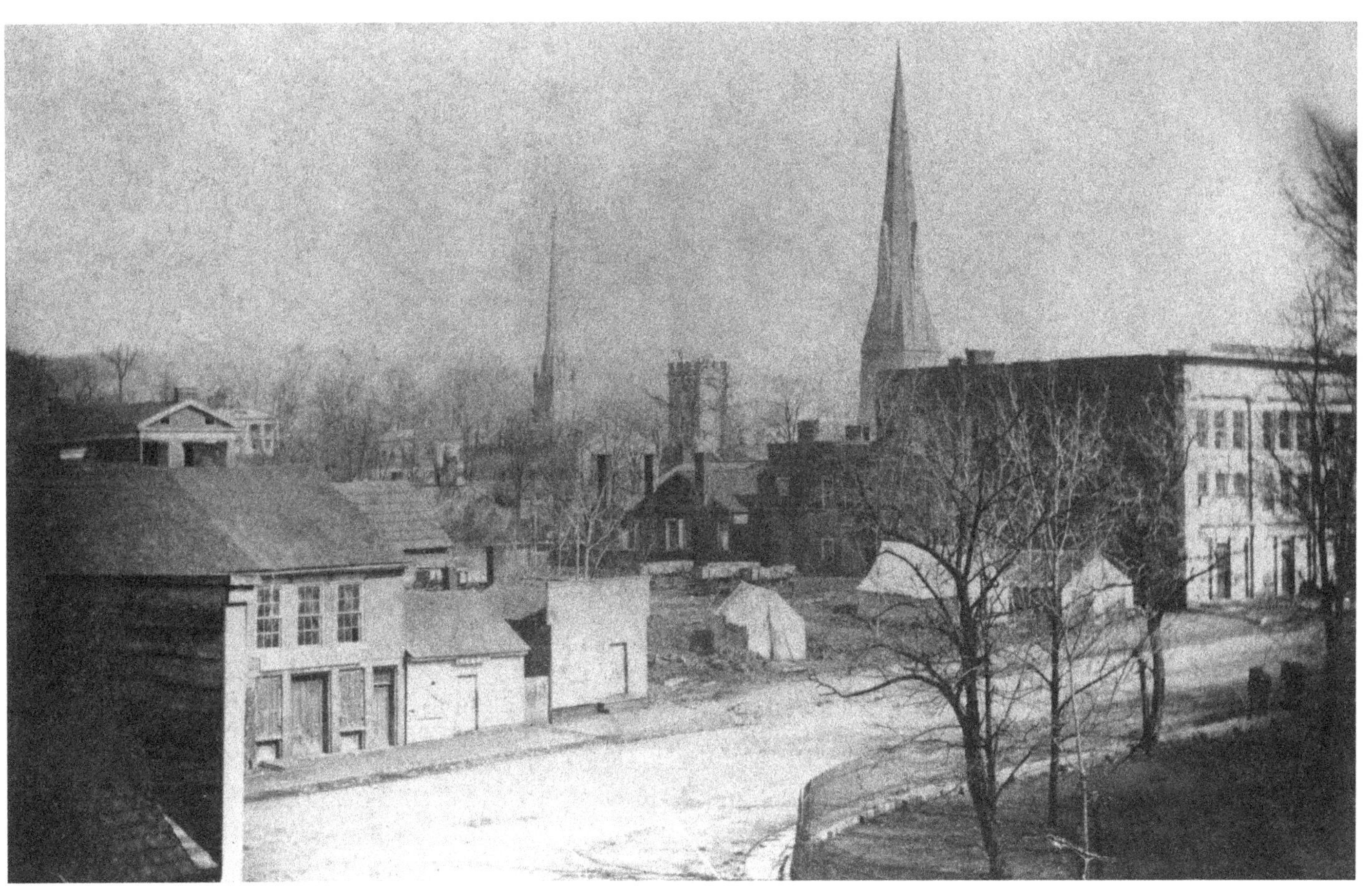

Huntsville was captured by Union soldiers in April 1862 and occupied, off and on, throughout the war. This photograph shows the Union tent city erected around the courthouse.

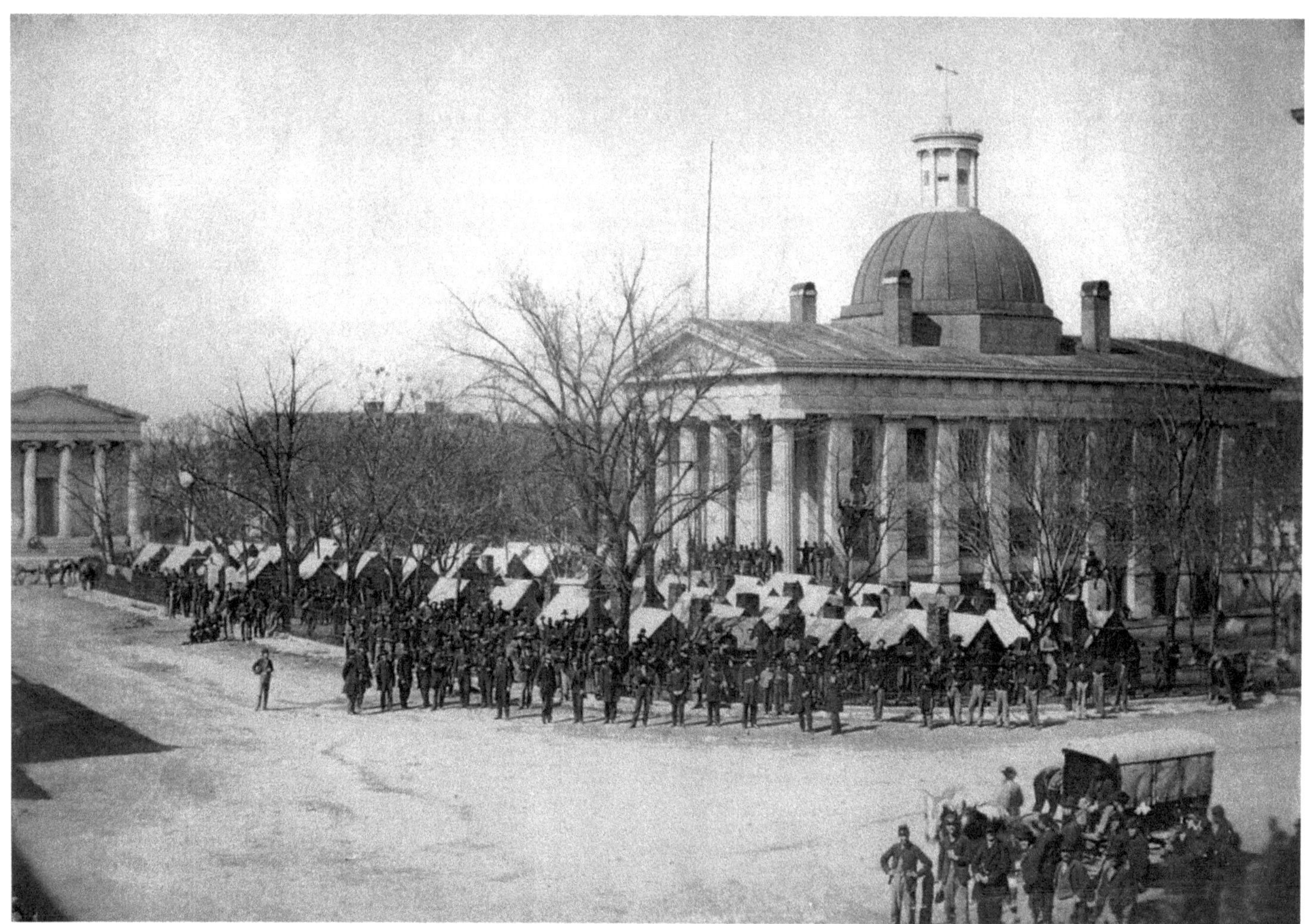

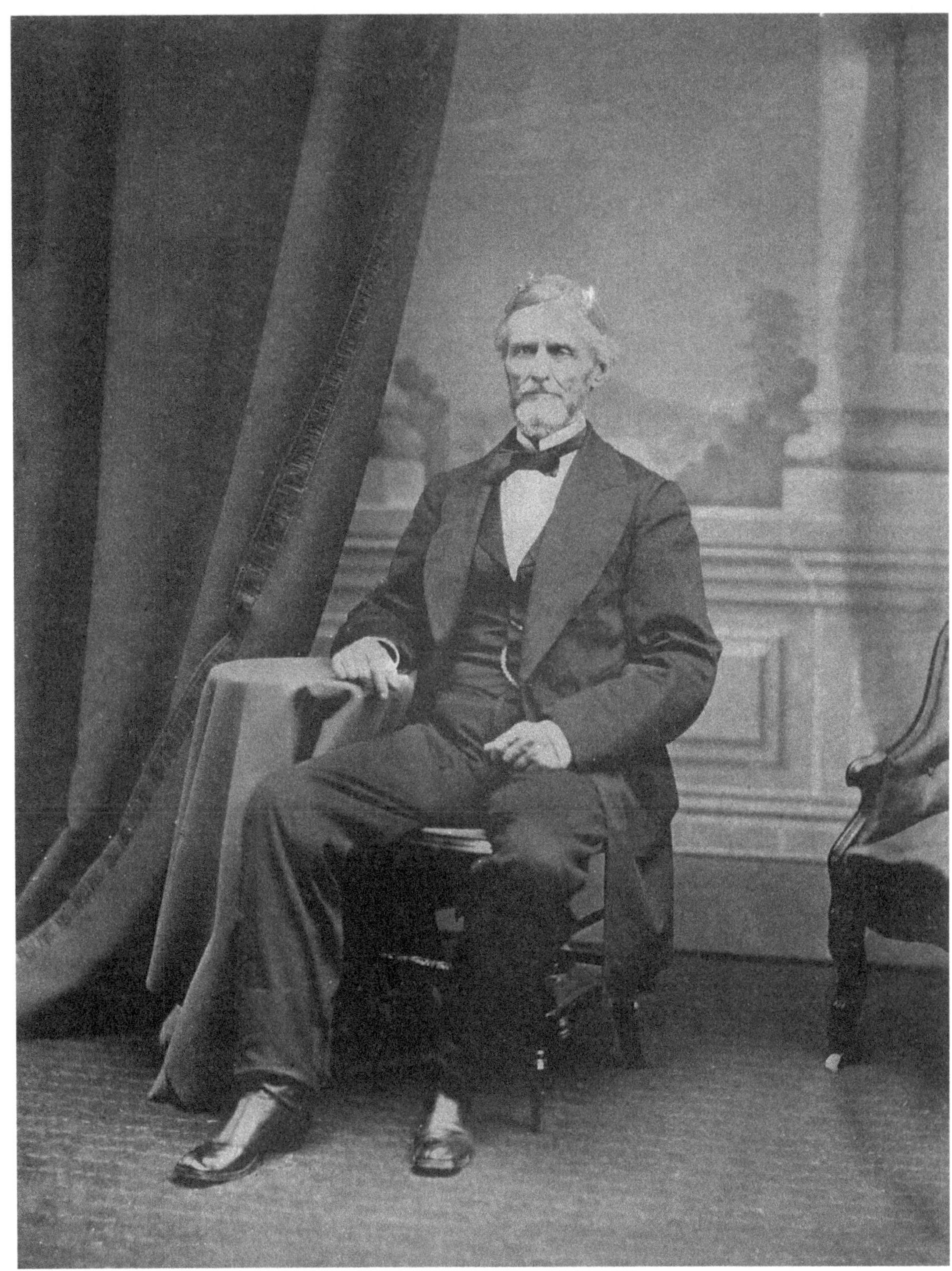

Jefferson Davis, former president of the Confederacy, visited his many friends in Huntsville following his 1867 release from Fortress Monroe, Virginia. Huntsville native Clement Claiborne Clay was imprisoned at the same time. Both were accused of being part of the conspiracy to assassinate President Abraham Lincoln. Clay, son of Governor Clement Comer Clay, was released in 1866 and spent the remainder of his life in nearby Gurley.

This 1867 photograph of the South Side Square suggests a slow business day. Horses are tethered at the iron fence surrounding the courthouse. None of the original buildings constructed on this block now exist.

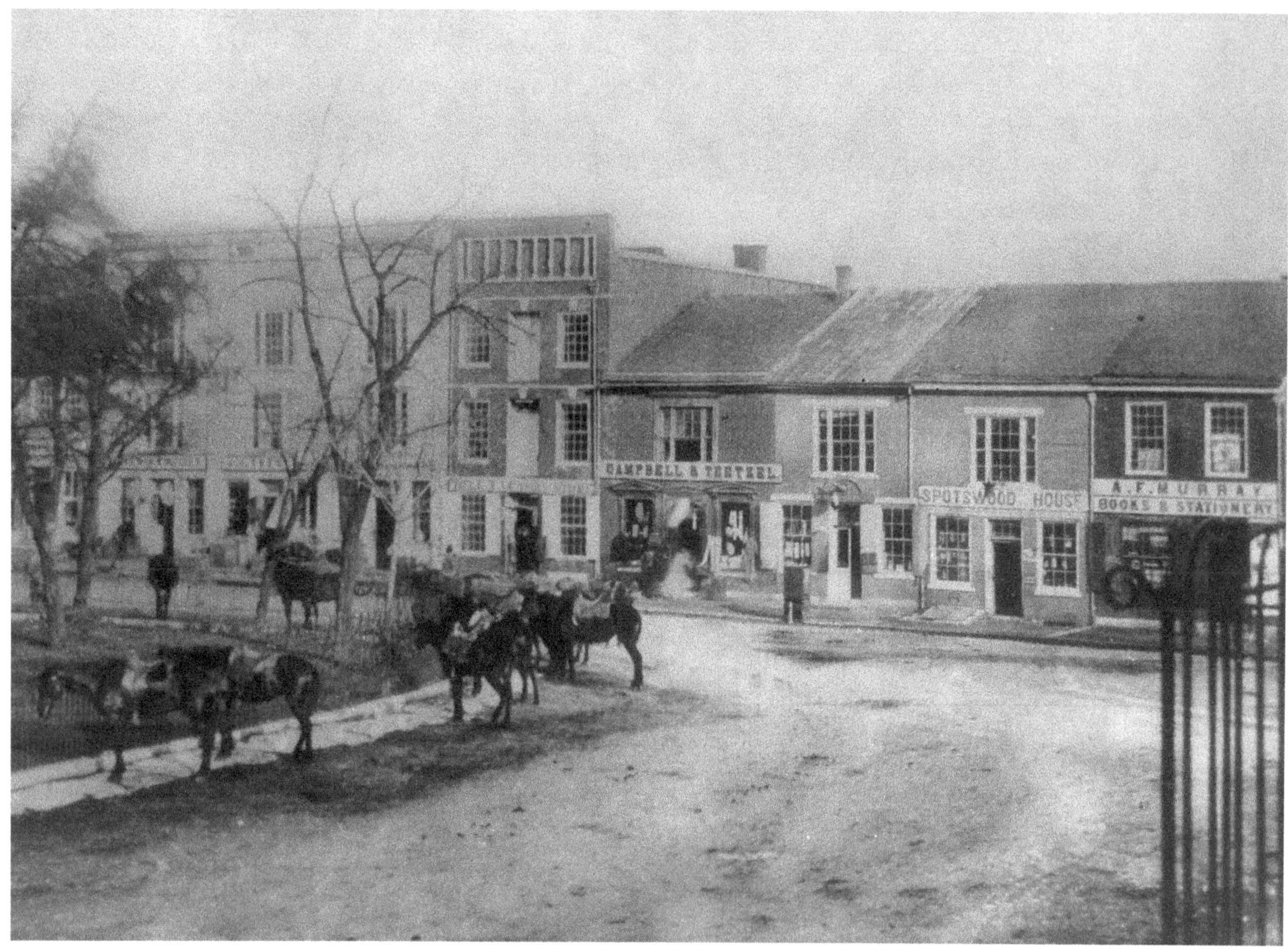

This photograph taken around 1870 shows the Market House at the southwest corner of Washington Street and Clinton Avenue. The city hall behind it was torn down and replaced by the Twickenham Hotel. Today a parking garage occupies this site.

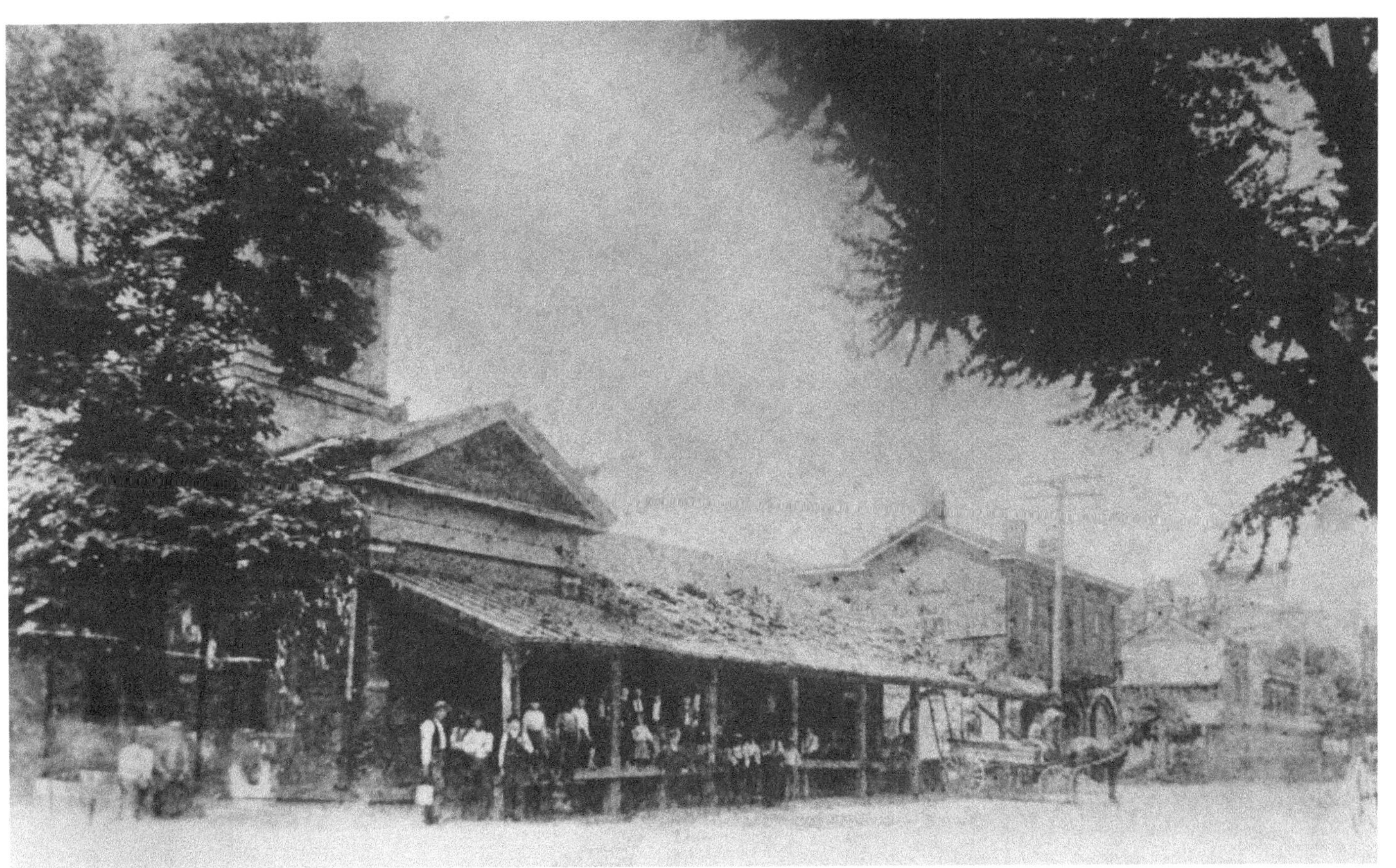

North Side Square appears shut down due to a rare blanket of snow in 1876. Unseen at the left and inside the fence is the Madison County Courthouse.

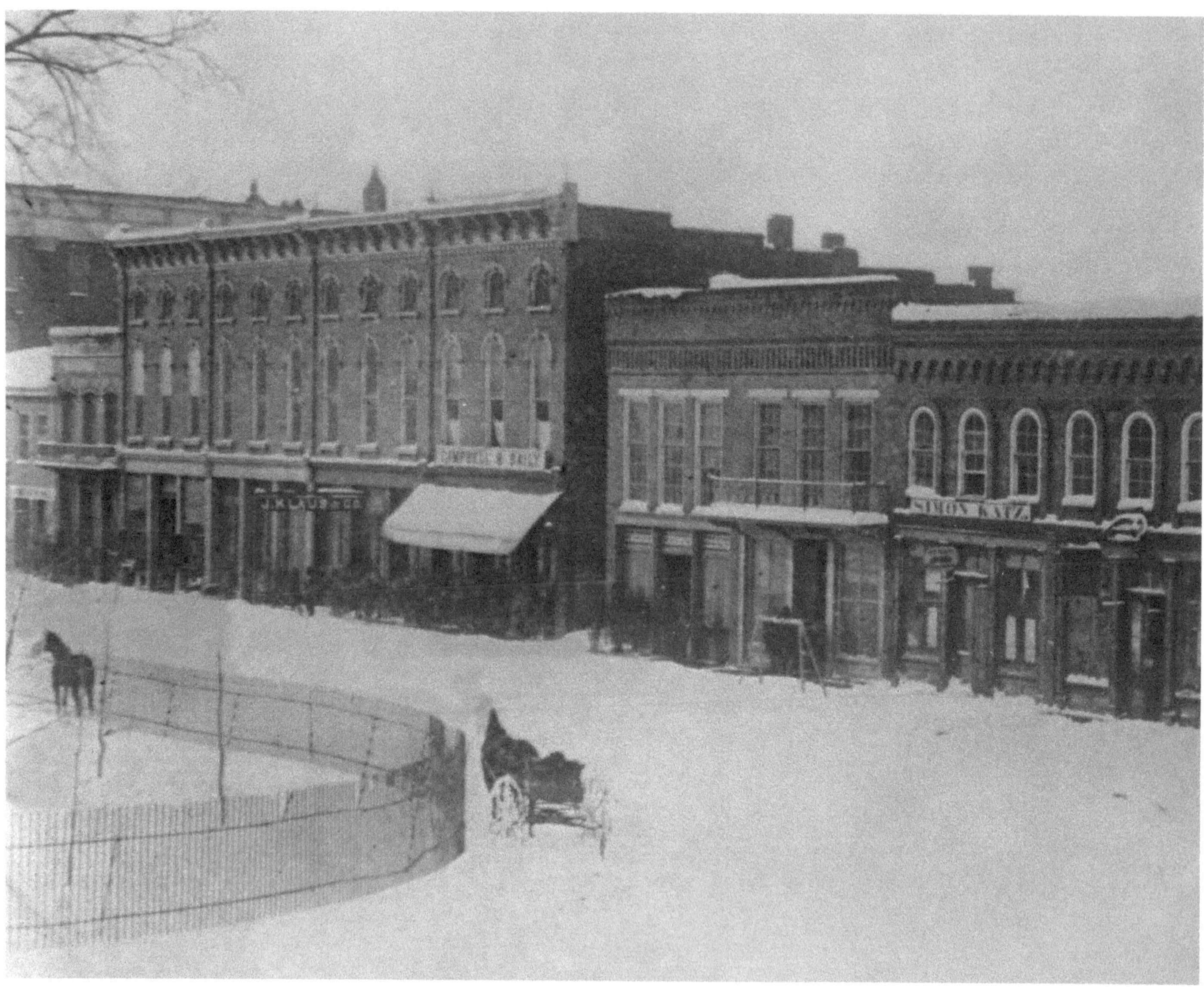

History has not recorded the reason why these wagonloads of timbers were brought to the Square.

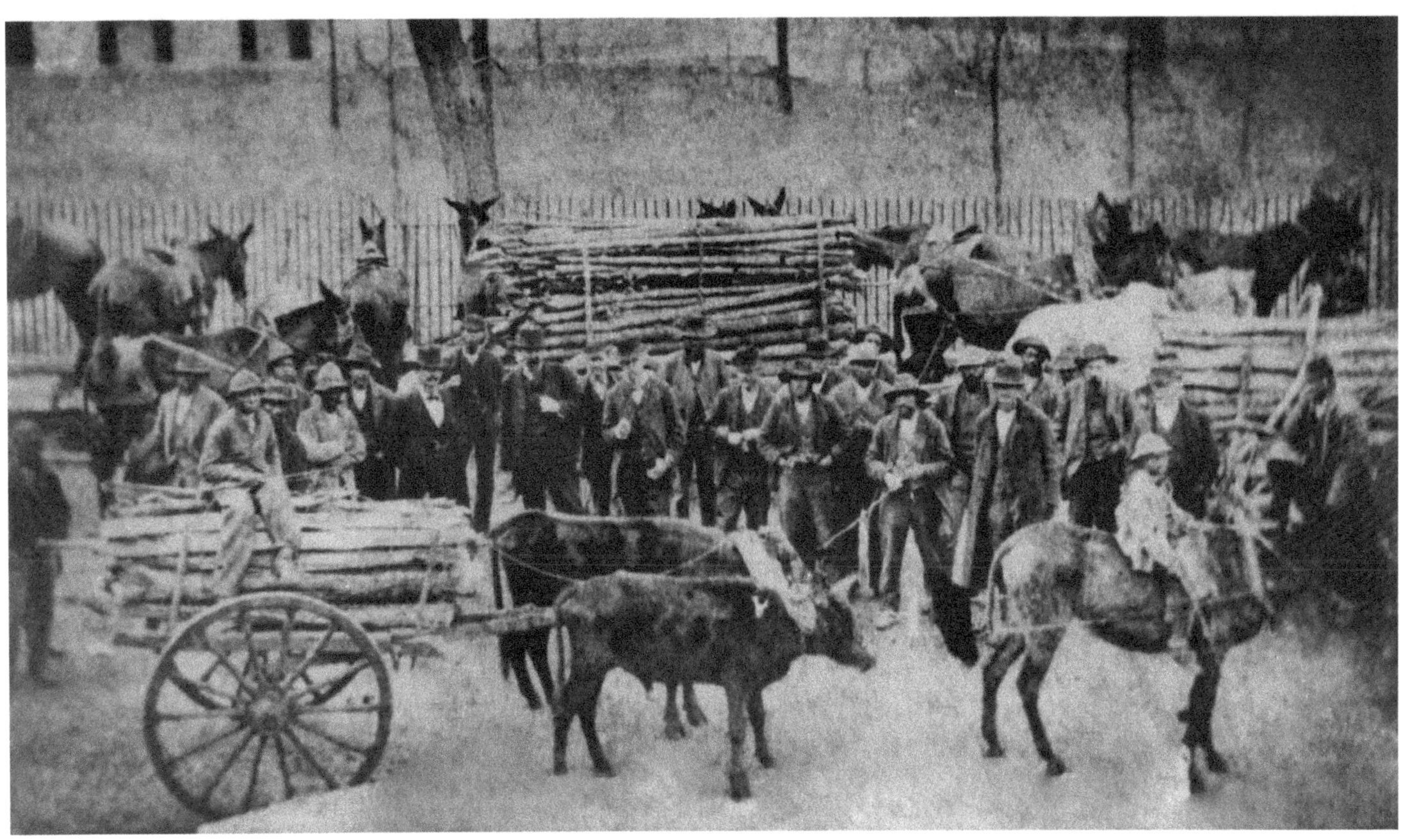

Wagons of cotton clogged the Courthouse Square while residents came to enjoy an eventful day in town.

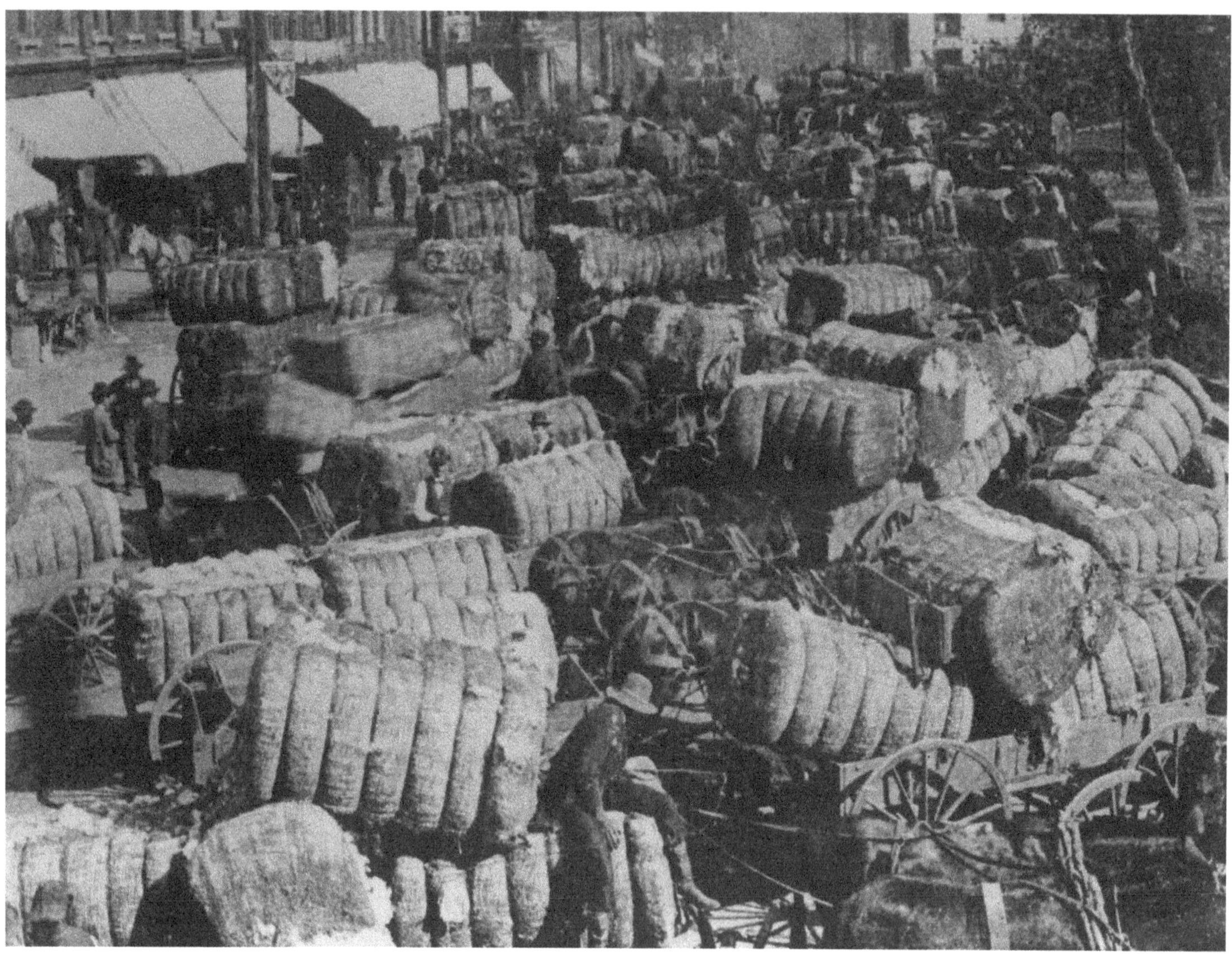

East Side Square is bustling with activity after a heavy rain. What a sloppy mess!

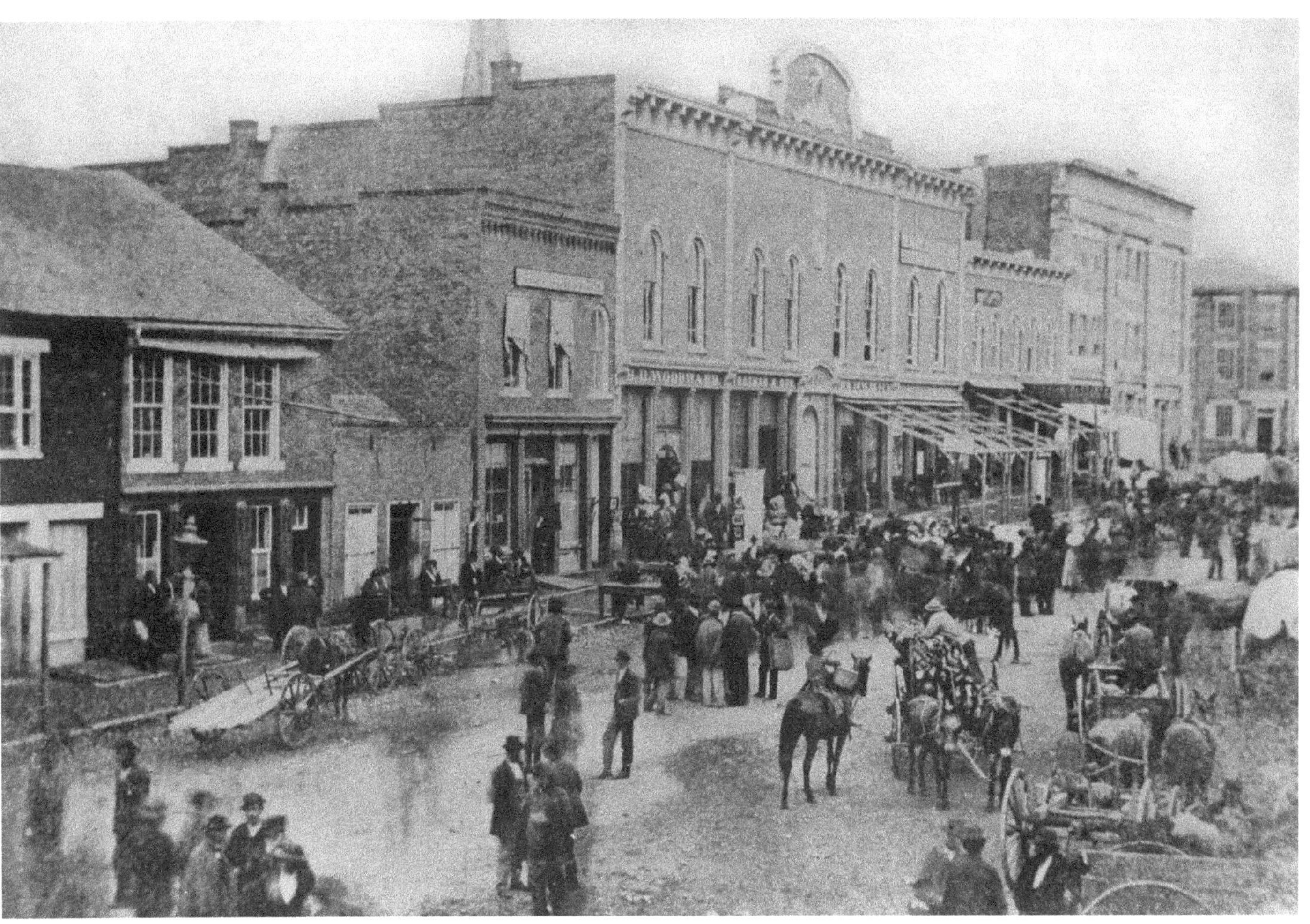

A cow meanders down the street in front of the Presbyterian Church. This was the second Presbyterian Church on this site, finished and dedicated in 1860. It was said to have "the handsomest building, the tallest spire, the biggest bell, the finest organ, the four richest bronze chandeliers, and the highest-priced pews in the city." The spire was blown down by a storm in 1878.

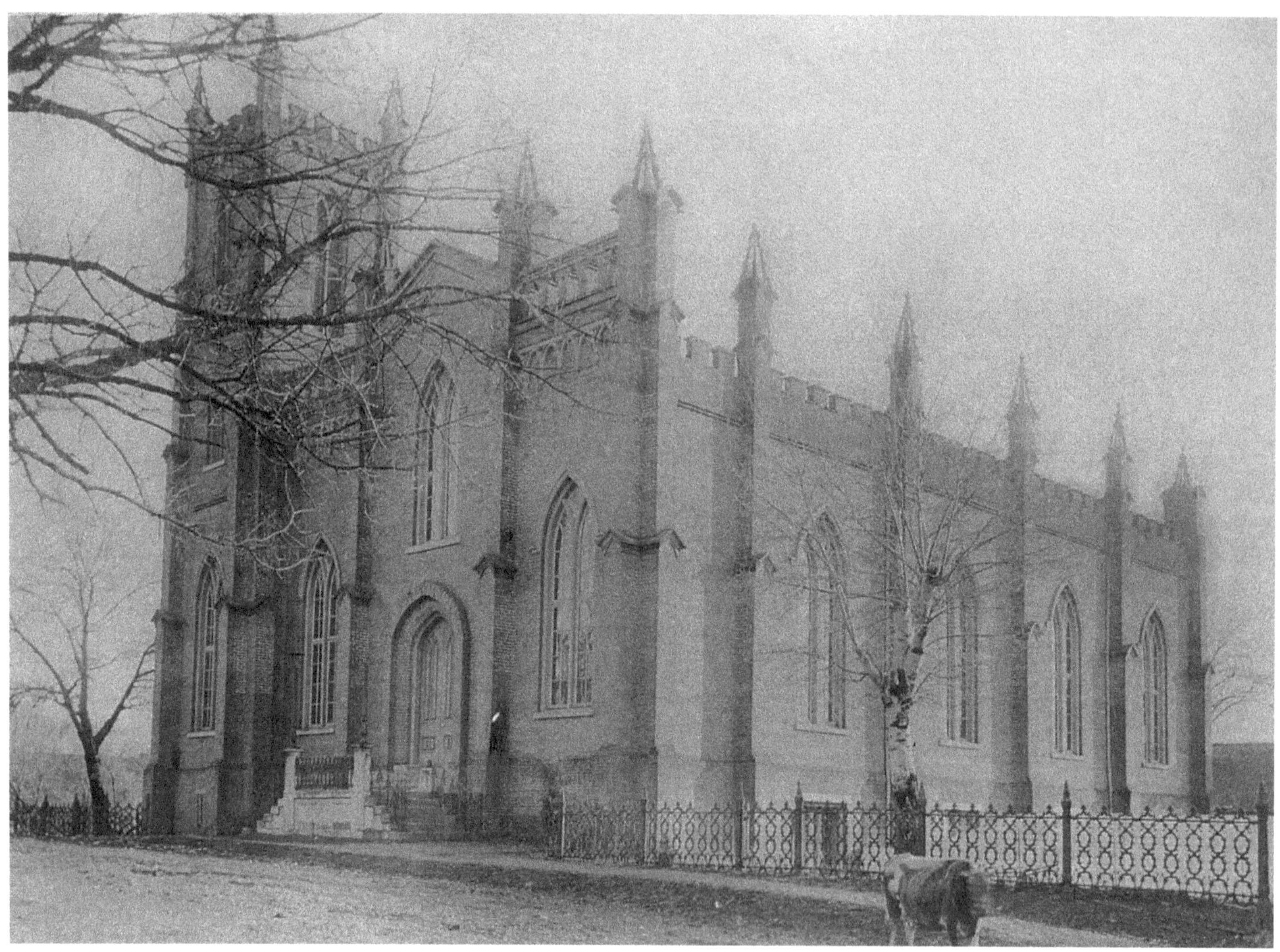

A boy crosses the street at the corner of East Side Square and North Side Square on a slow business day. The toy horse on the sign probably advertises a tack shop. This picture was taken around 1880.

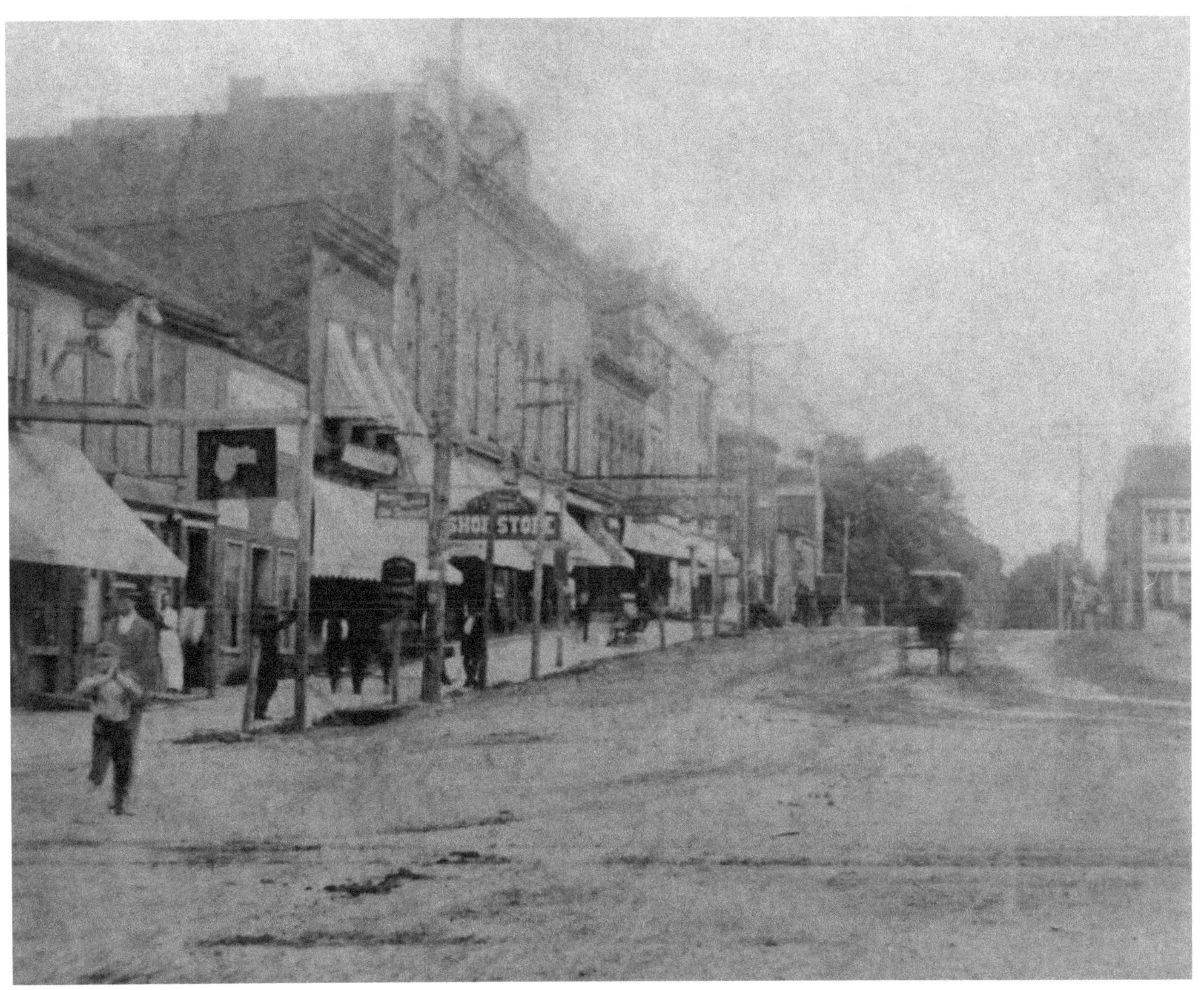

This photograph, taken about 1880, is of Engine House No. 1 and the City Scales, located between Washington and Jefferson streets.

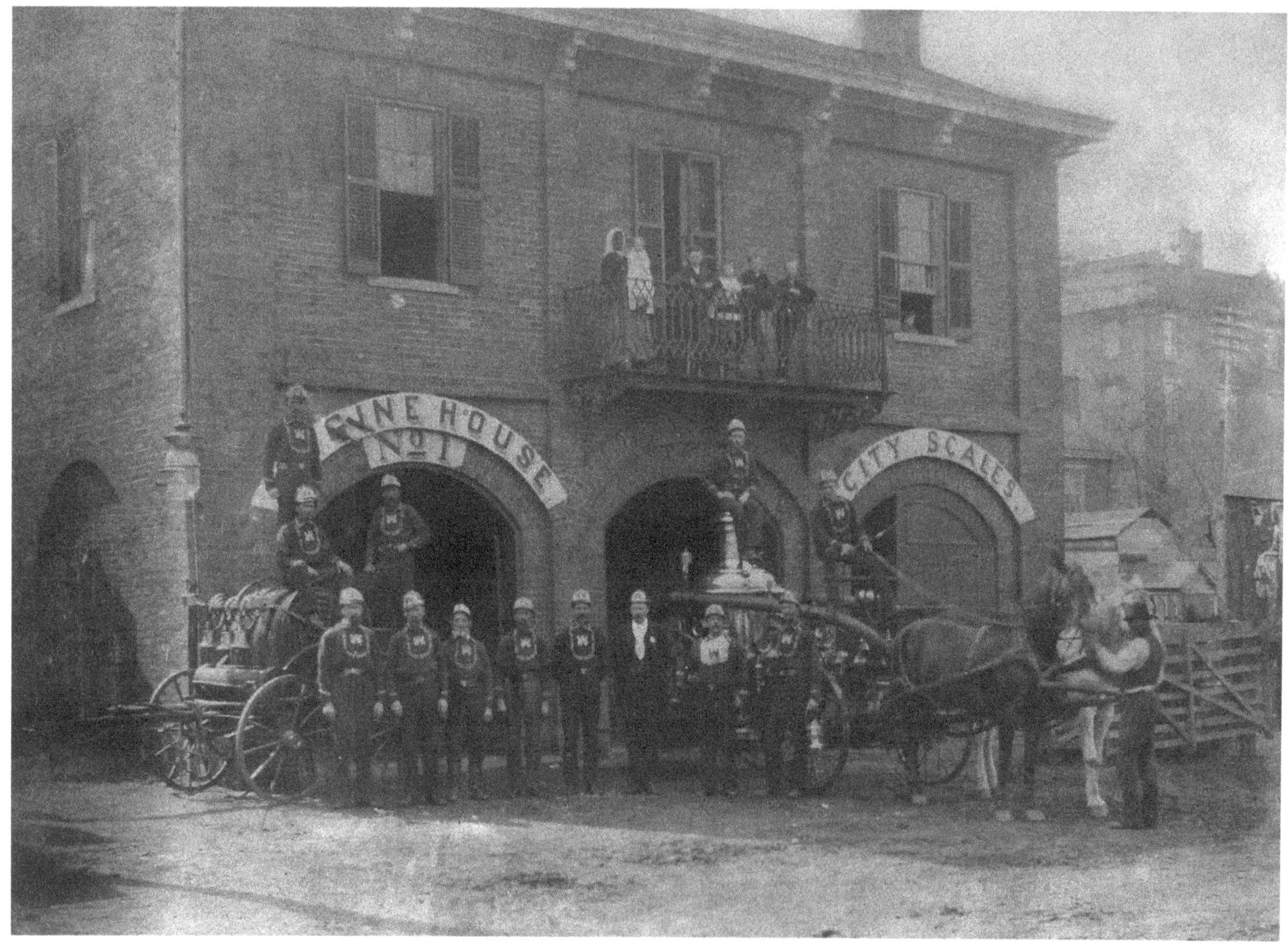

Completed in 1872, the magnificent city hall building on the corner of Jefferson Street and Clinton Avenue burned down in 1911. This photograph was taken in 1882.

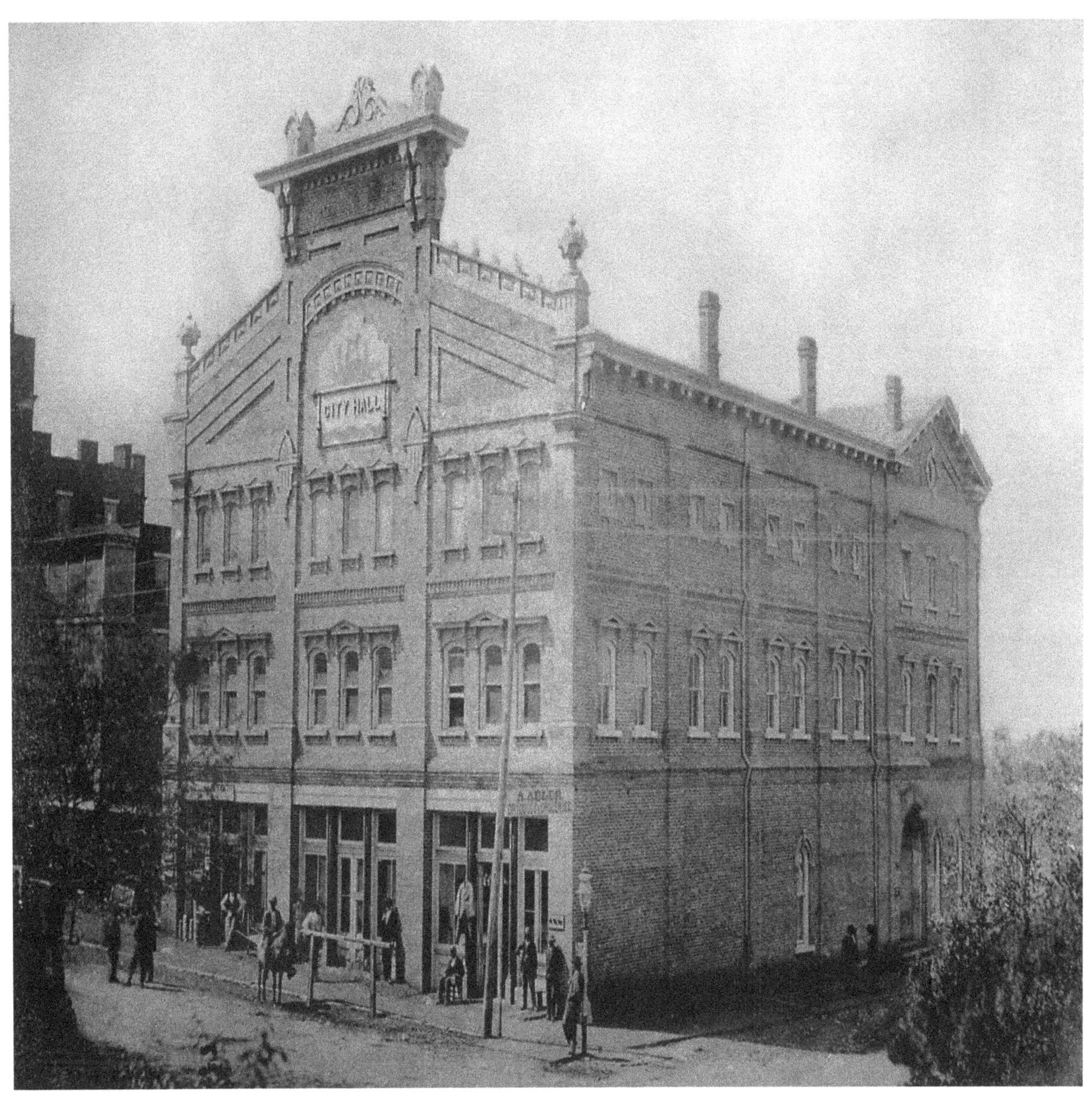

Thompson Land & Investment Co. specialized in buying and selling farm land in and around Huntsville. Their advertisement boasted they were "one of the most progressive and widely known Real Estate Companies in the South."

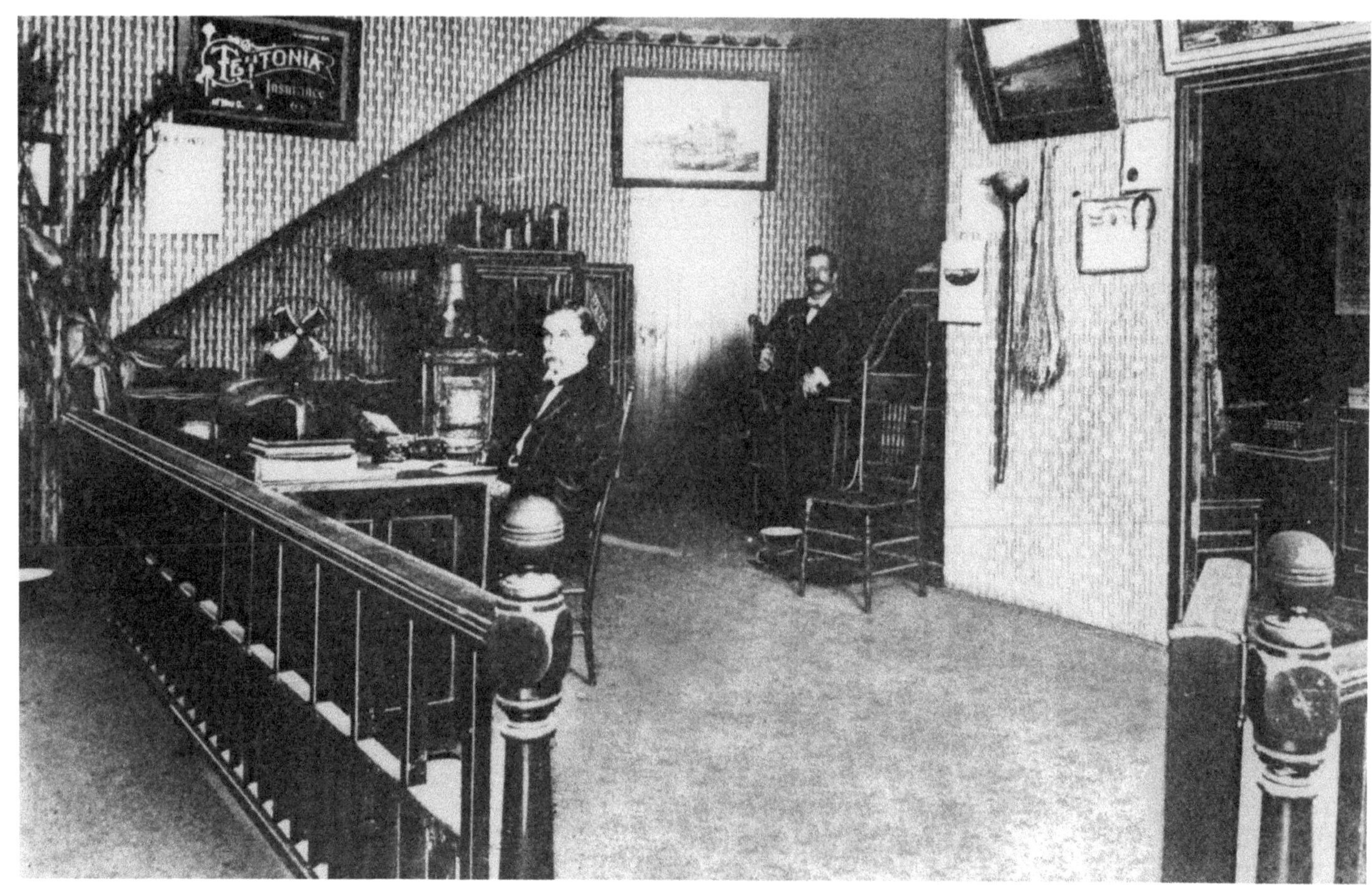

There were several bars in Huntsville, though mostly associated with hotels. J. E. Payne and Company was located on Exchange Row. Buckets underneath the foot rests served as spittoons.

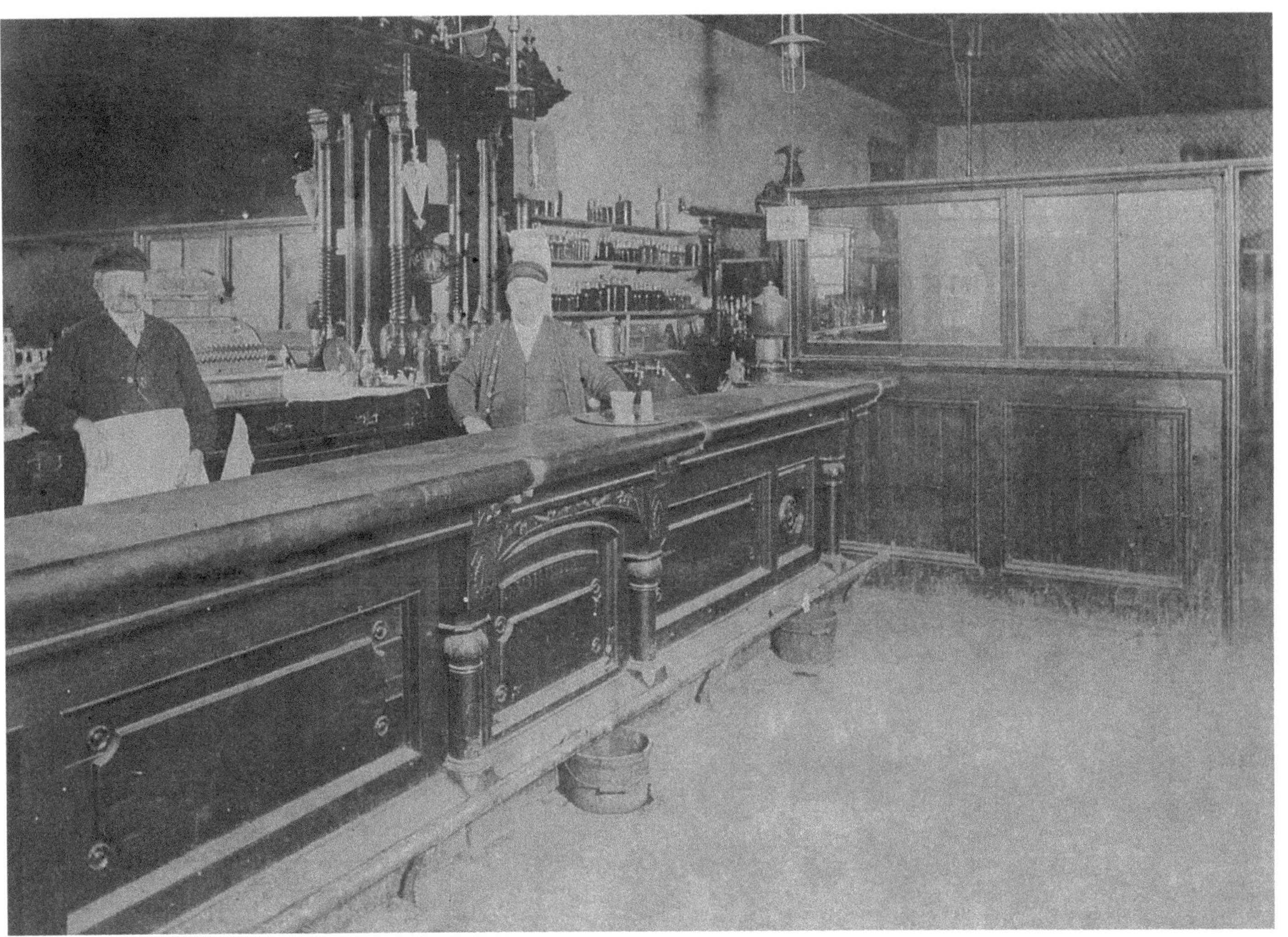

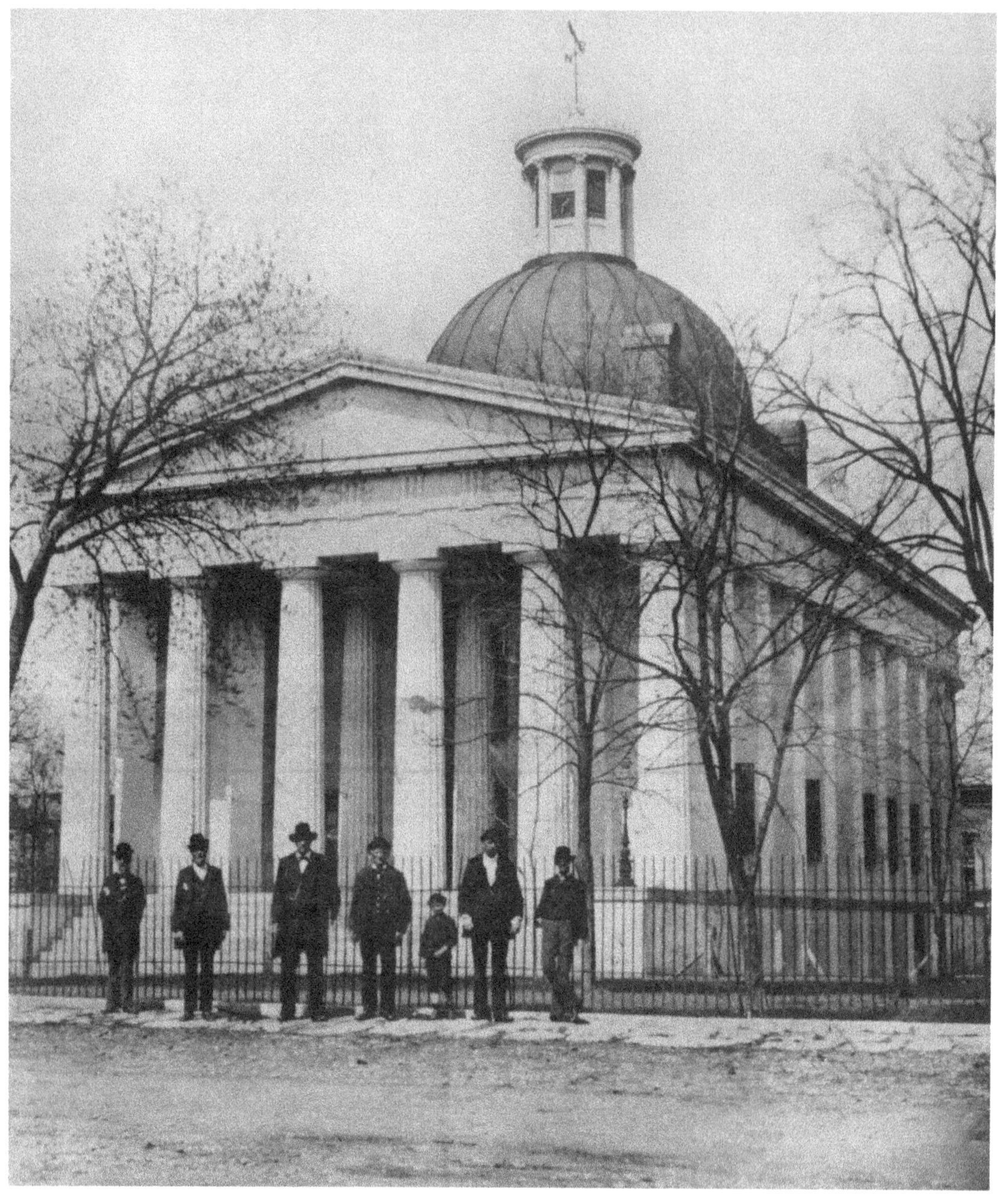

Six men and one youngster pose in front of the second Madison County Courthouse. The fence now borders the back of Maple Hill Cemetery.

A light dusting of snow didn't keep Huntsvillians away from downtown on a busy Saturday afternoon. This view is taken from the corner of Jefferson Street and North Side Square looking toward East Side Square.

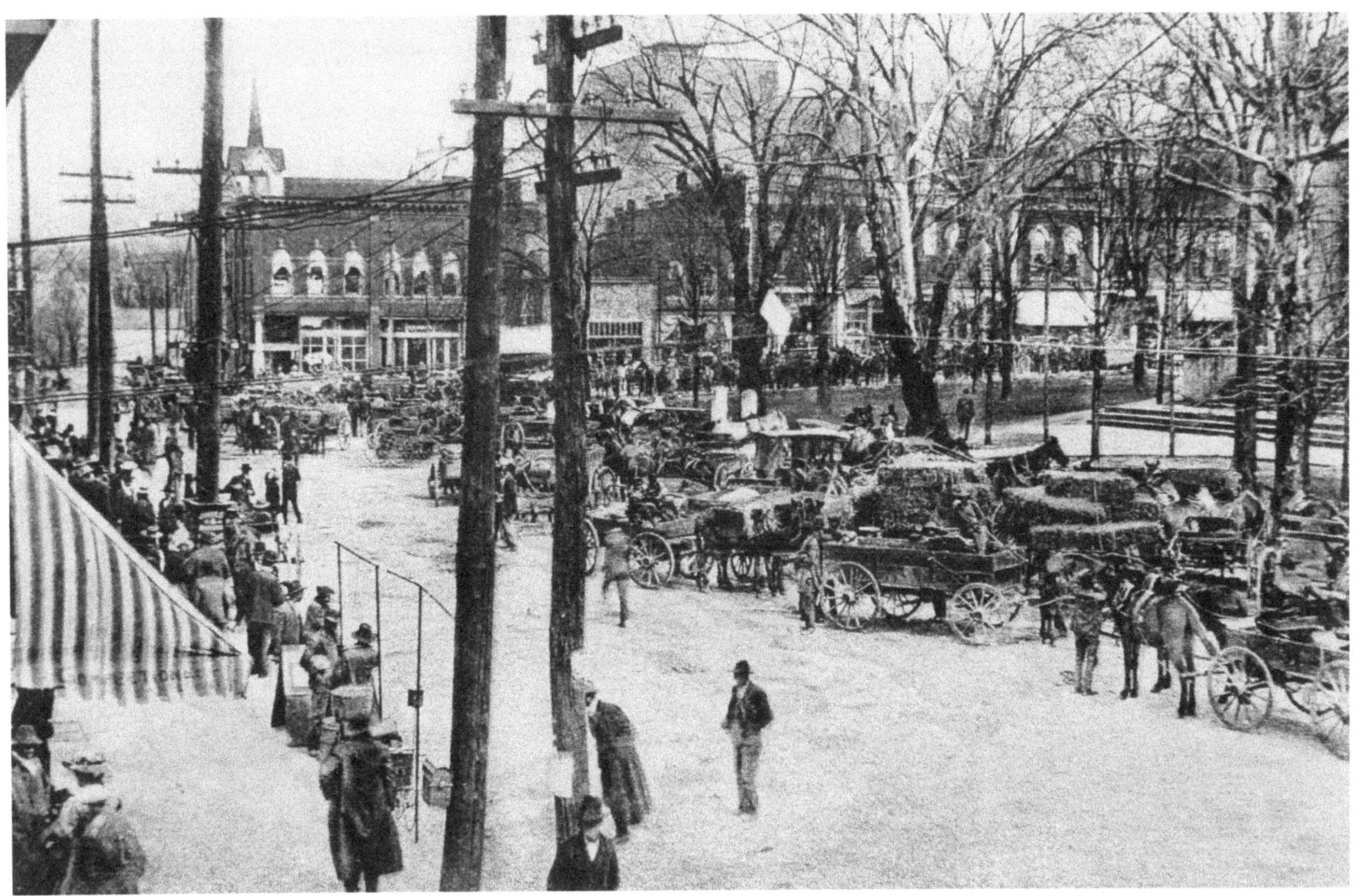

The livery stable, a place to board and rent horses, was the precursor to the modern-day parking garage. Gentlemen knew that while they spent the day doing business, their horses would be well tended by W. J. Bennett & Co. Livery.

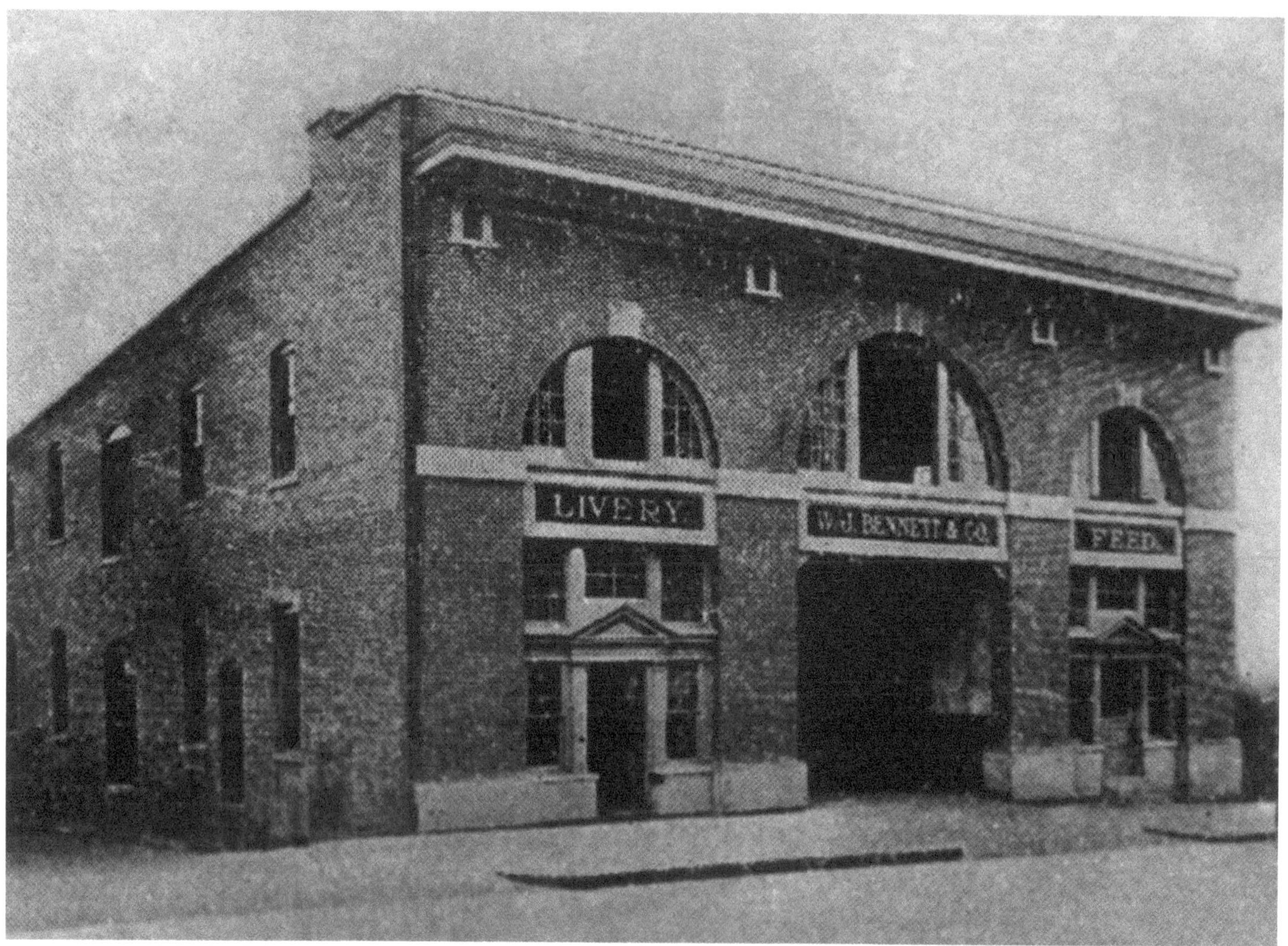

A dam and city waterworks were built at the Big Spring. The bluff overlooking the spring is at the left.

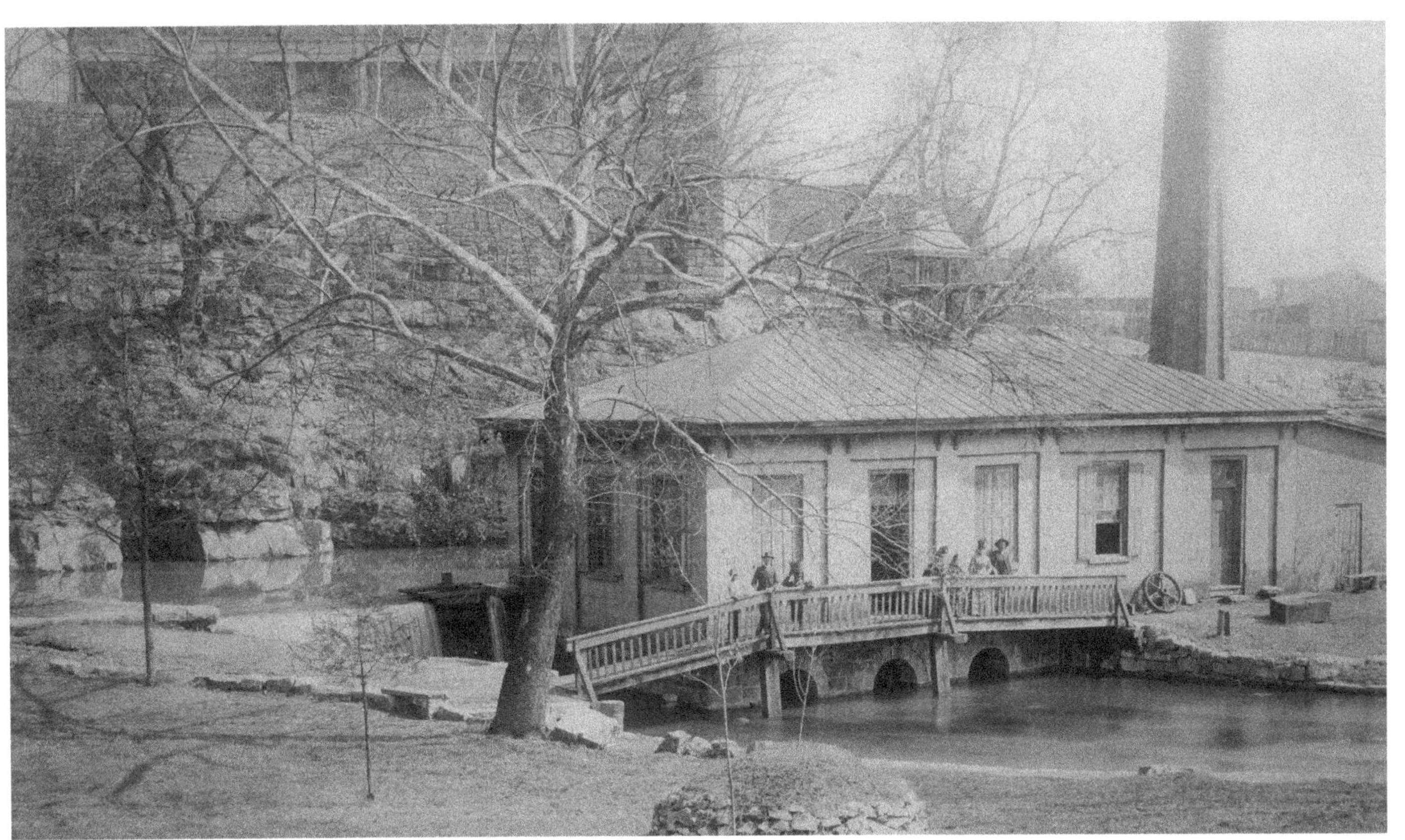

This photograph, taken in the late 1800s, may be of a funeral. Legend says Union soldiers refused to stable their horses inside the Church of the Nativity Episcopal even though they were ordered to do so during the Civil War. The reason? Over the entrance of the chapel are the words, "Reverence My Sanctuary."

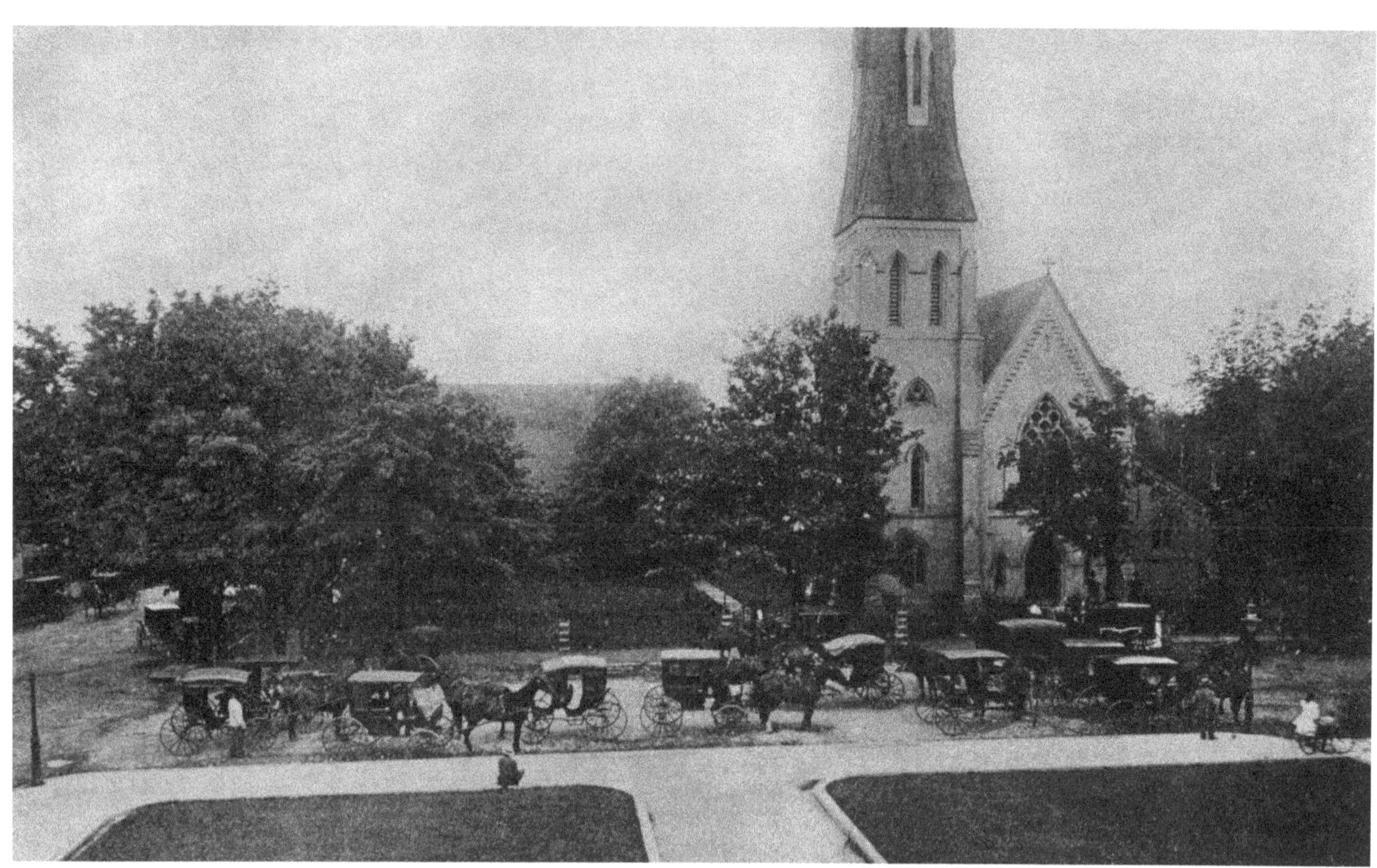

The Federal Courthouse, an imposing and impressive structure built on the corner of Eustis and Greene streets in 1890, was torn down in 1954.

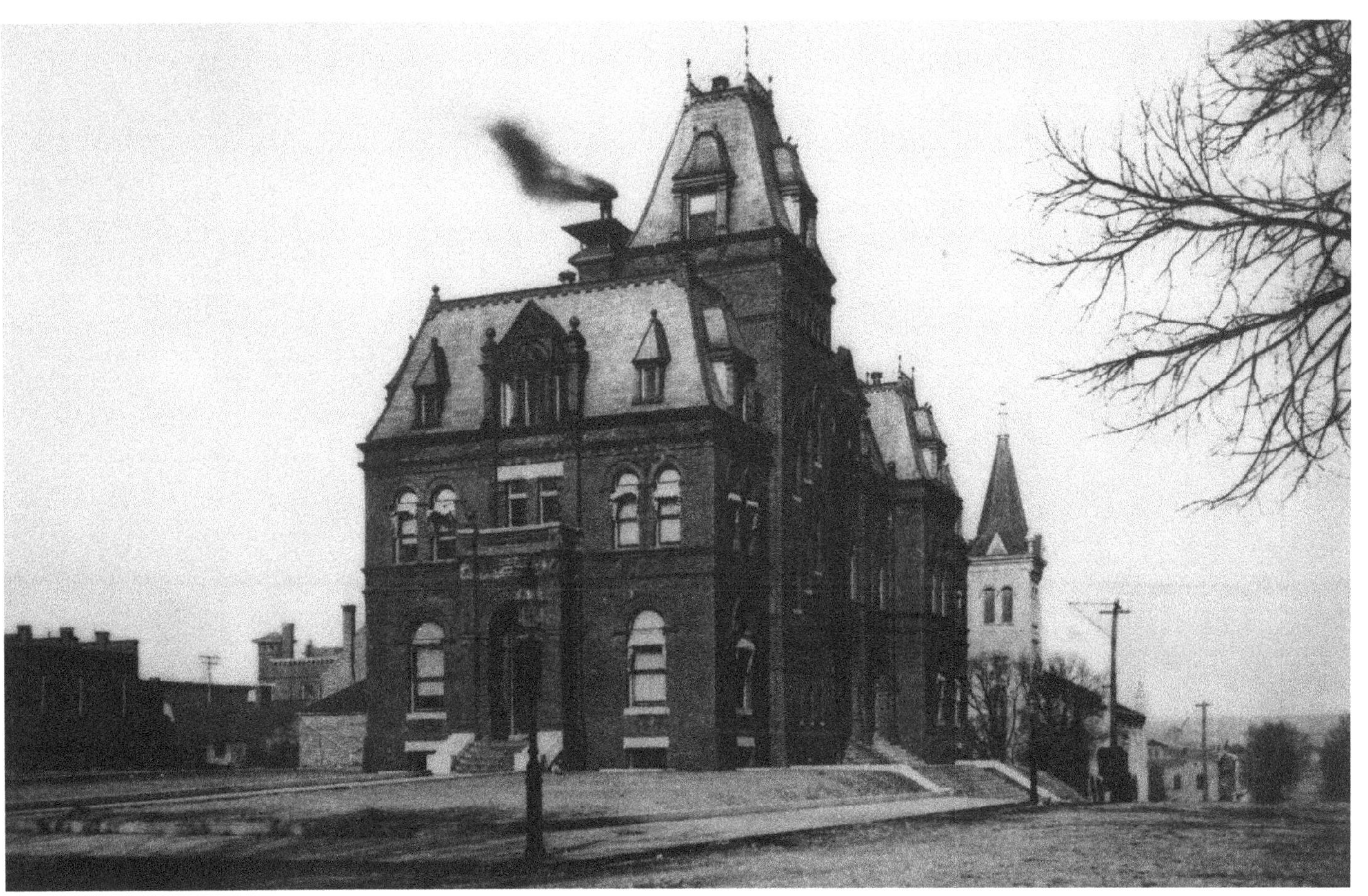

E. C. Yarbrough, center, and Joe Yarbrough, right, stand in front of the E. C. Yarbrough Grocery and Feed Store in this 1890 photograph. It was located on the corner of Washington and Randolph streets.

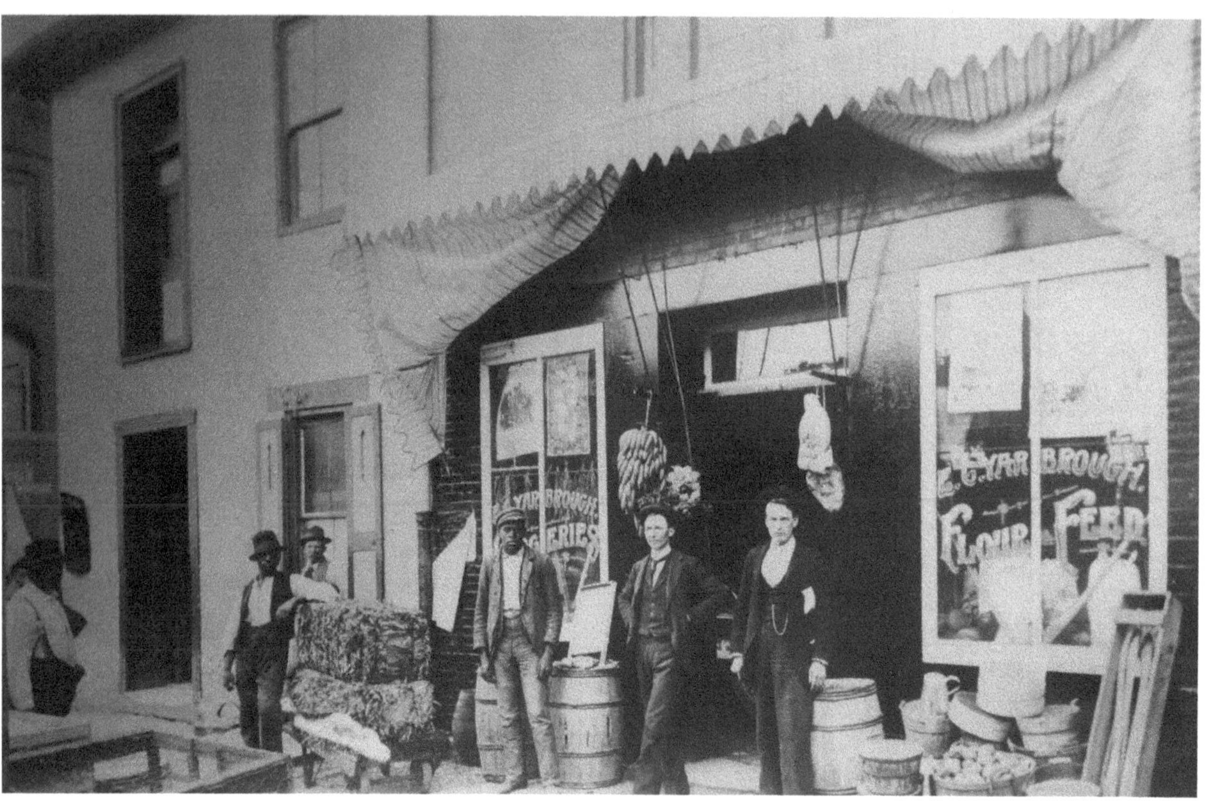

Wages were low for mill workers. Unions stepped in to help improve working conditions, but mill owners usually responded by temporarily shutting down operations, throwing employees out of work while negotiations were going on.

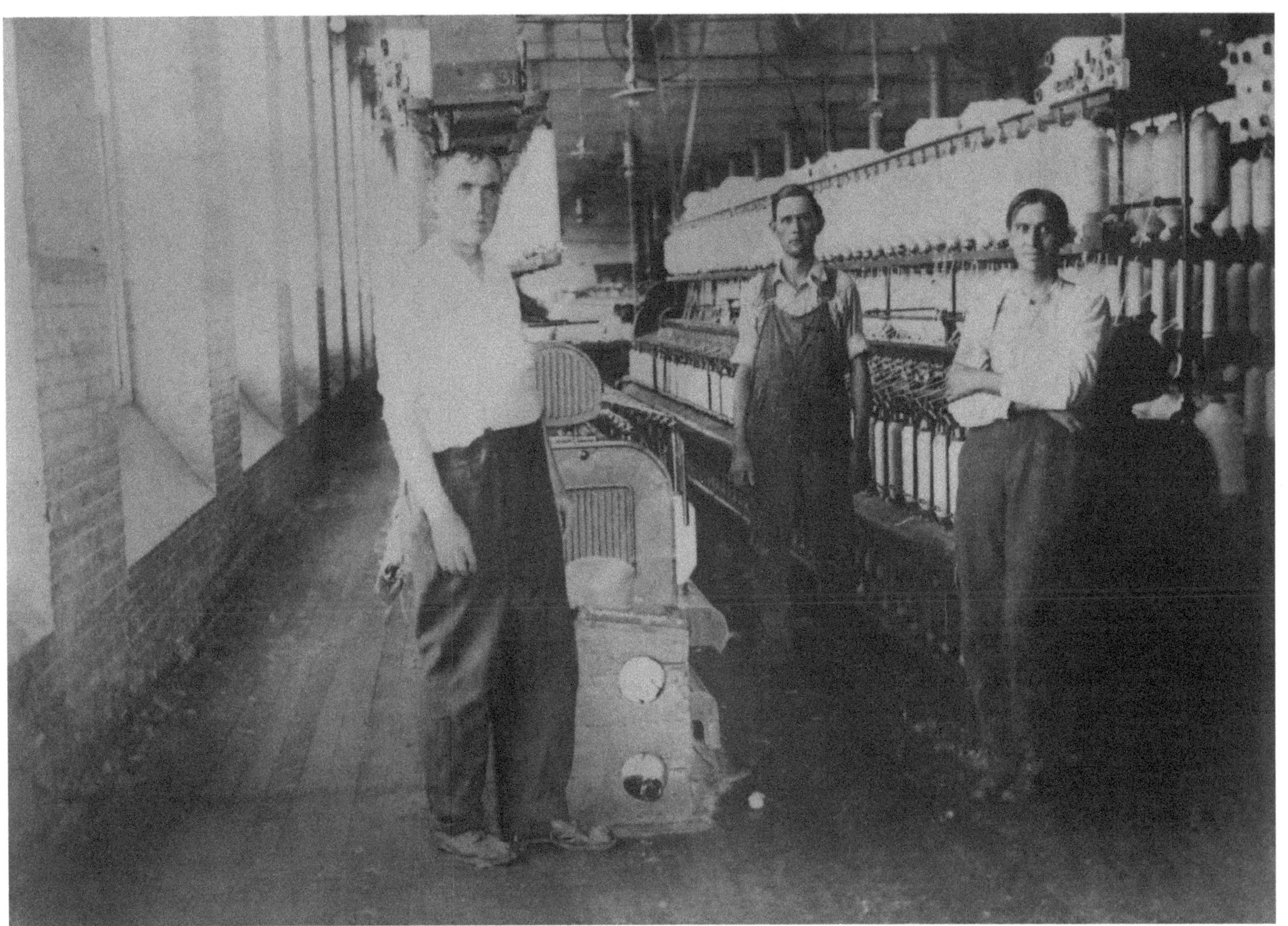

The sign at the left says it all: "This is not the place for the first Quarrel." The young boy appears deep in thought as the man in front walks across a precarious plank with a bucket of water. Note the man sitting cross-legged on the bluff. Cold Spring was located on Monte Sano Mountain.

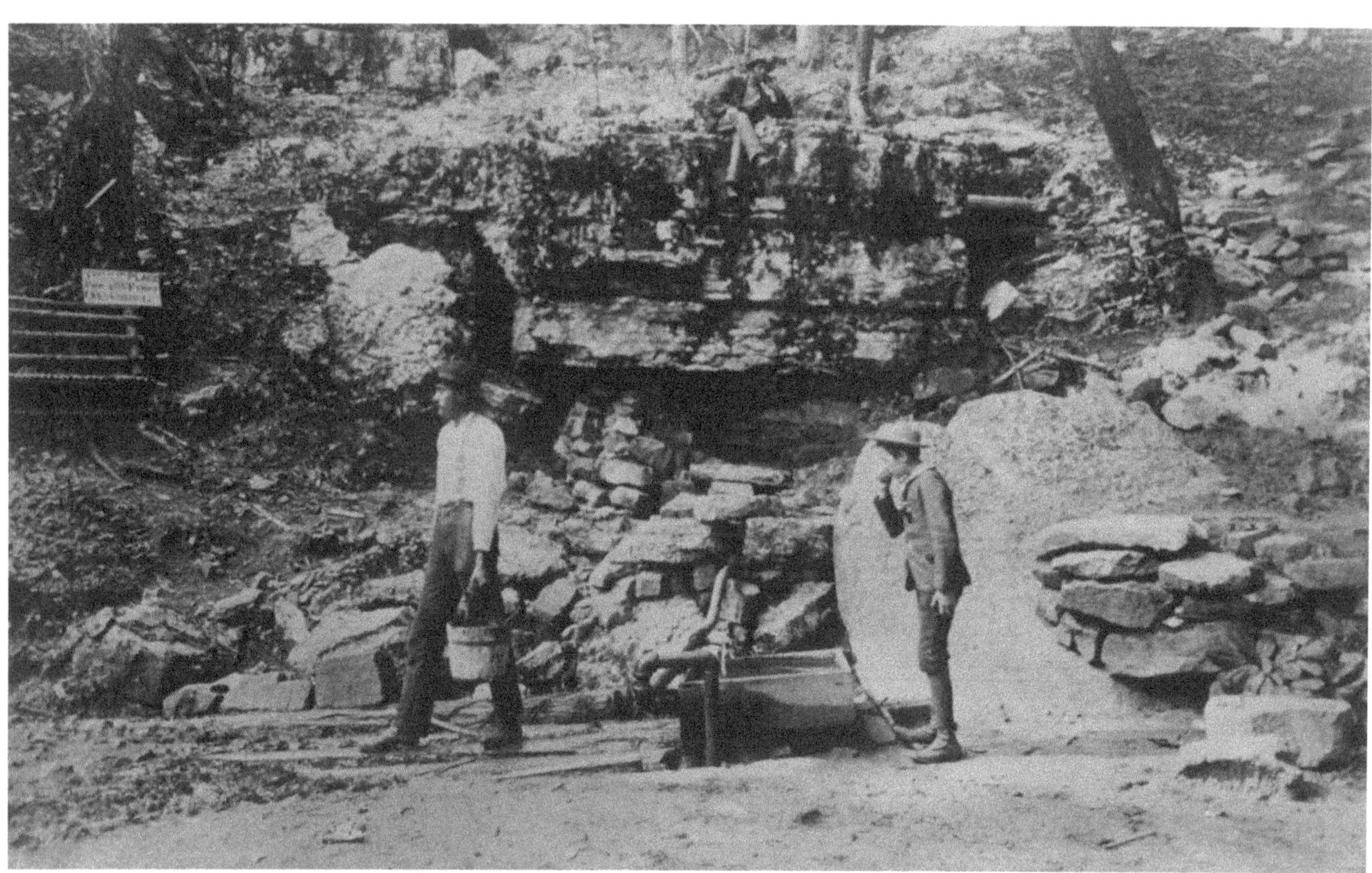

Dignitaries and workers pose while construction continues on the Monte Sano Railroad. Note the heavy pick-axes the workers are holding.

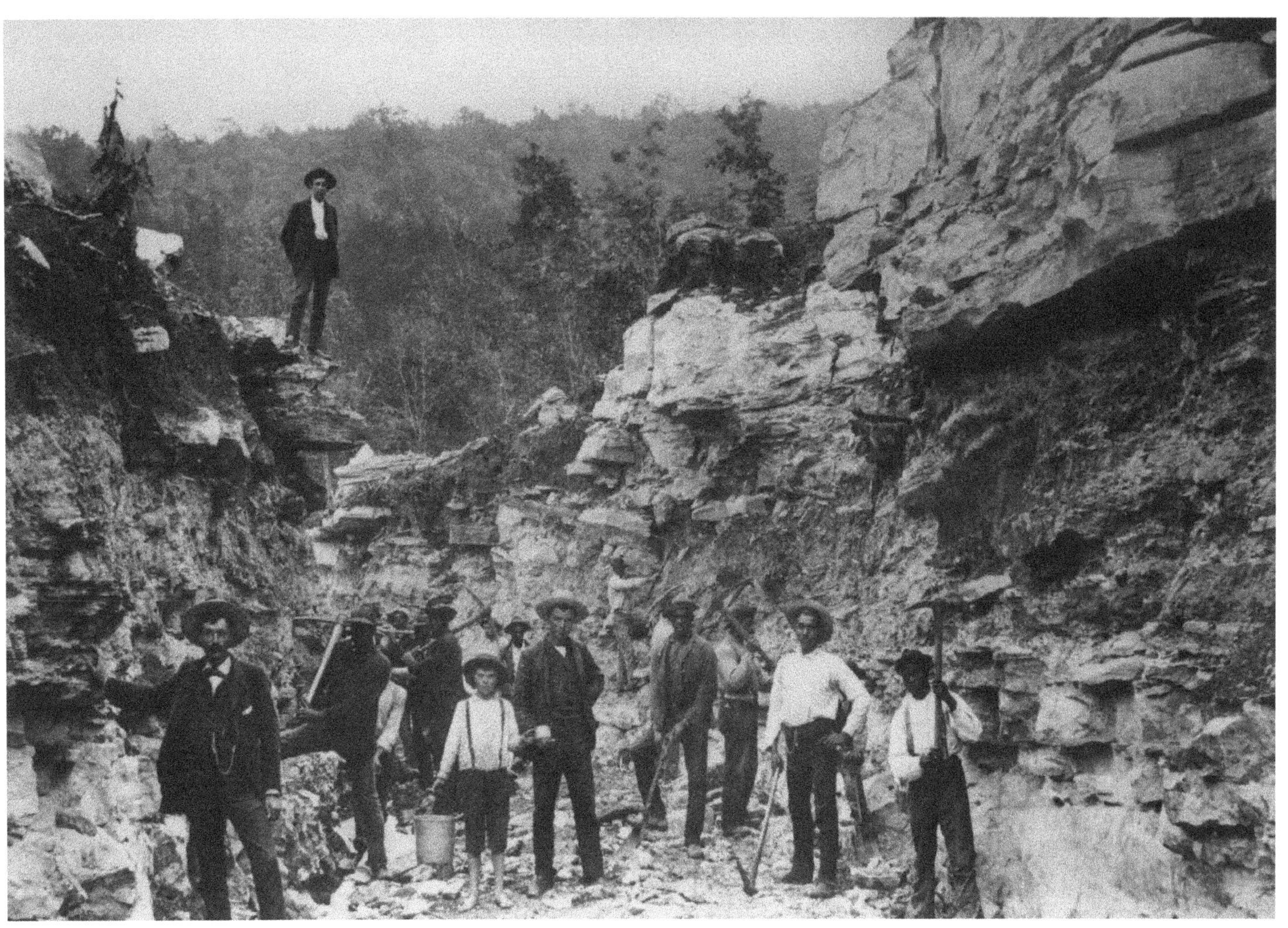

The Monte Sano Hotel was built as a health resort, but traveling the primitive road in a Tally-ho coach was tedious. For easier access from the downtown Huntsville depot, a dummy-line railway was constructed. This 1890 photograph shows the impressive engineering design of its trestle. "Dummy line" in this case refers to a private rail line not maintained by the railroad company, in essence, a dead-end line.

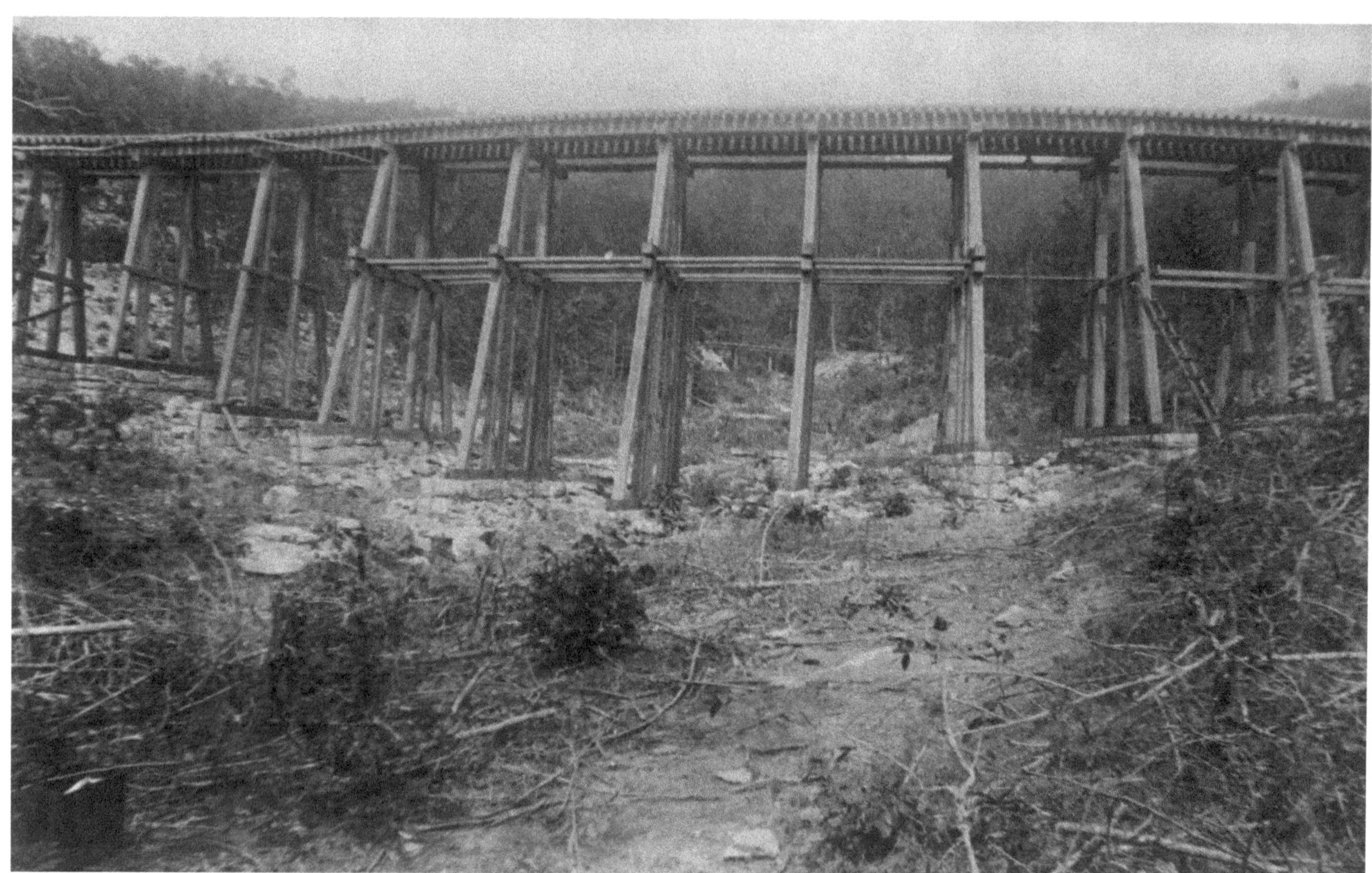

A rock crusher at work on the Monte Sano Railway. Fliers advertised "For pleasure, convenience, safety and beautiful scenery, take the Monte Sano Standard Gauge Railway." Unfortunately, the railroad up to the resort was full of hairpin turns and frightened many tourists.

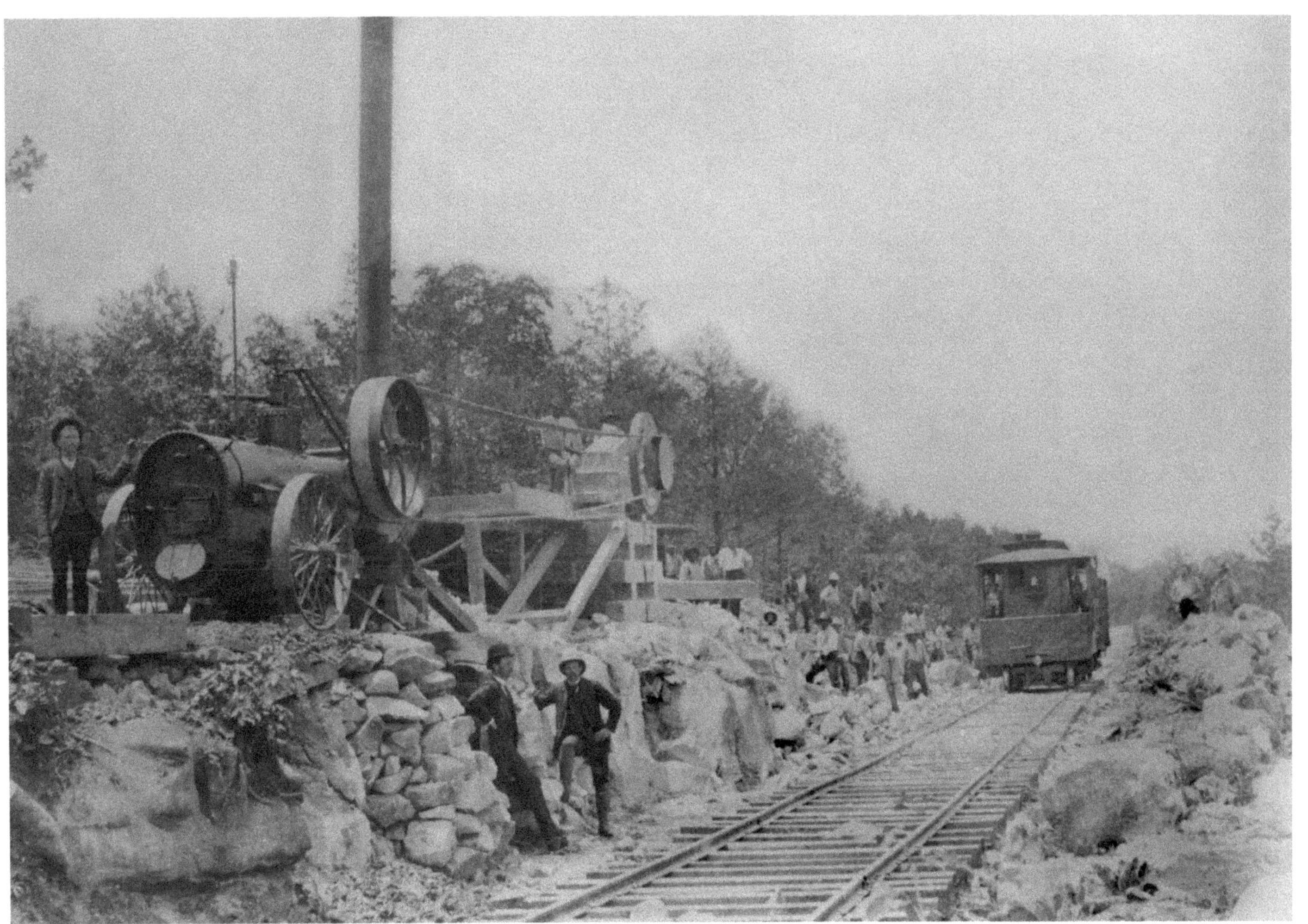

The Monte Sano Hotel was built atop Monte Sano Mountain, known as the "Mountain of Health." The luxury resort was visited by guests from all over the world, as shown in this 1891 photograph. It closed down in the early 1900s and became a private home for the Garths, a wealthy couple from New York. It was dismantled in the 1940s. A single chimney is all that remains.

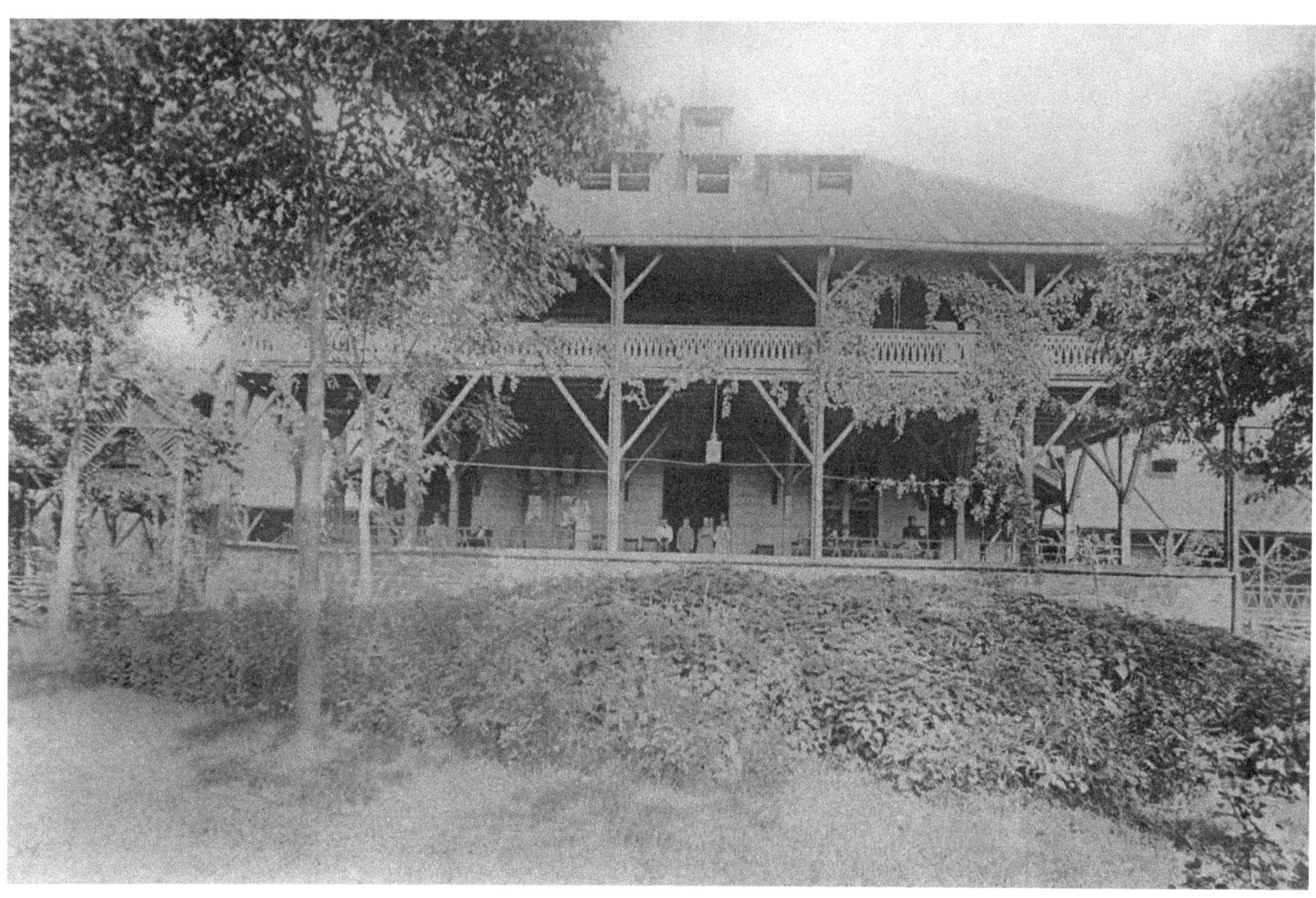

Built in 1892, the Dallas Cotton Mill was a huge employer. More than 1,000 workers operated 1,500 looms and 59,000 spindles. The Dallas Mill ceased operation in 1952, and the vacant building burned to the ground in a horrendous 1991 fire.

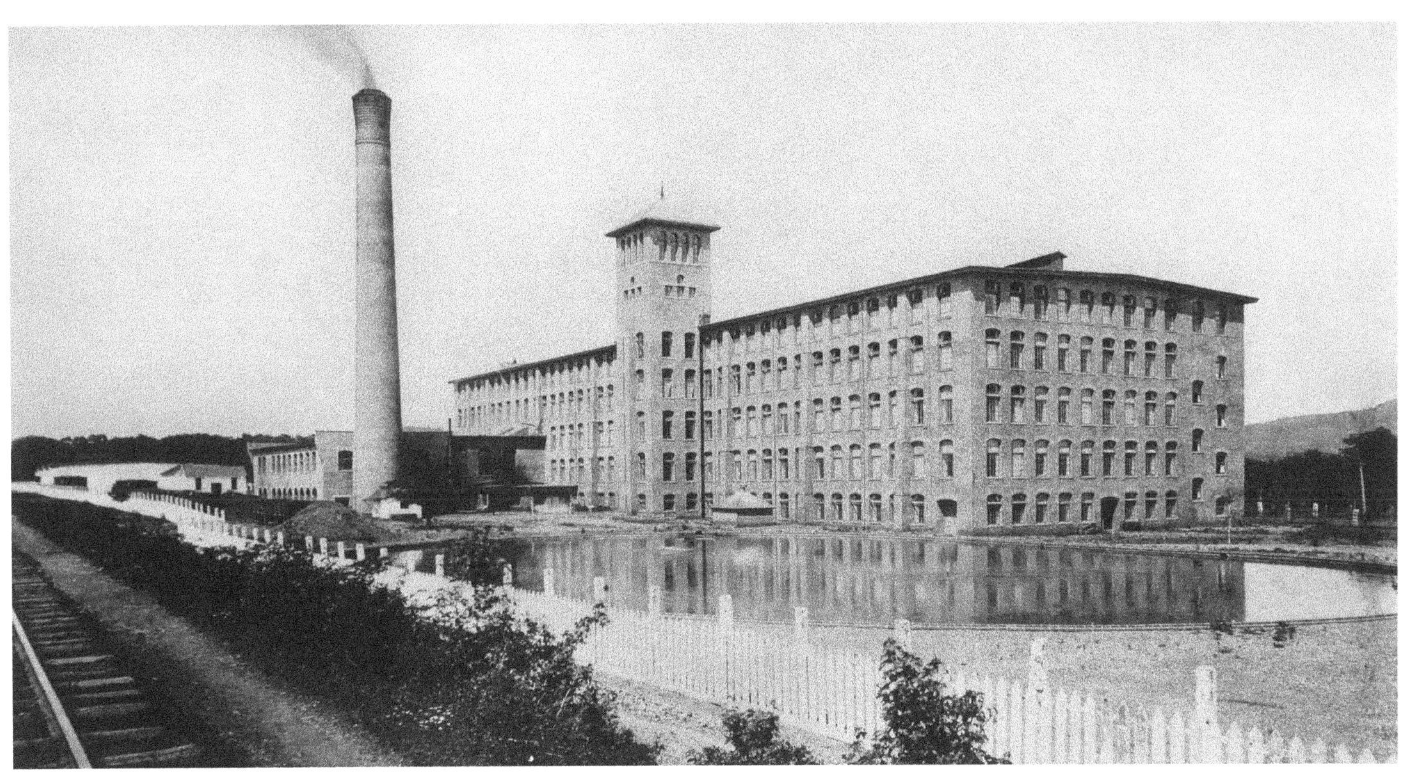

The Dallas Mill was the center of the mill village that grew up around it. Even children worked at the local mills under terrible conditions until Child Labor Laws came into effect in the twentieth century.

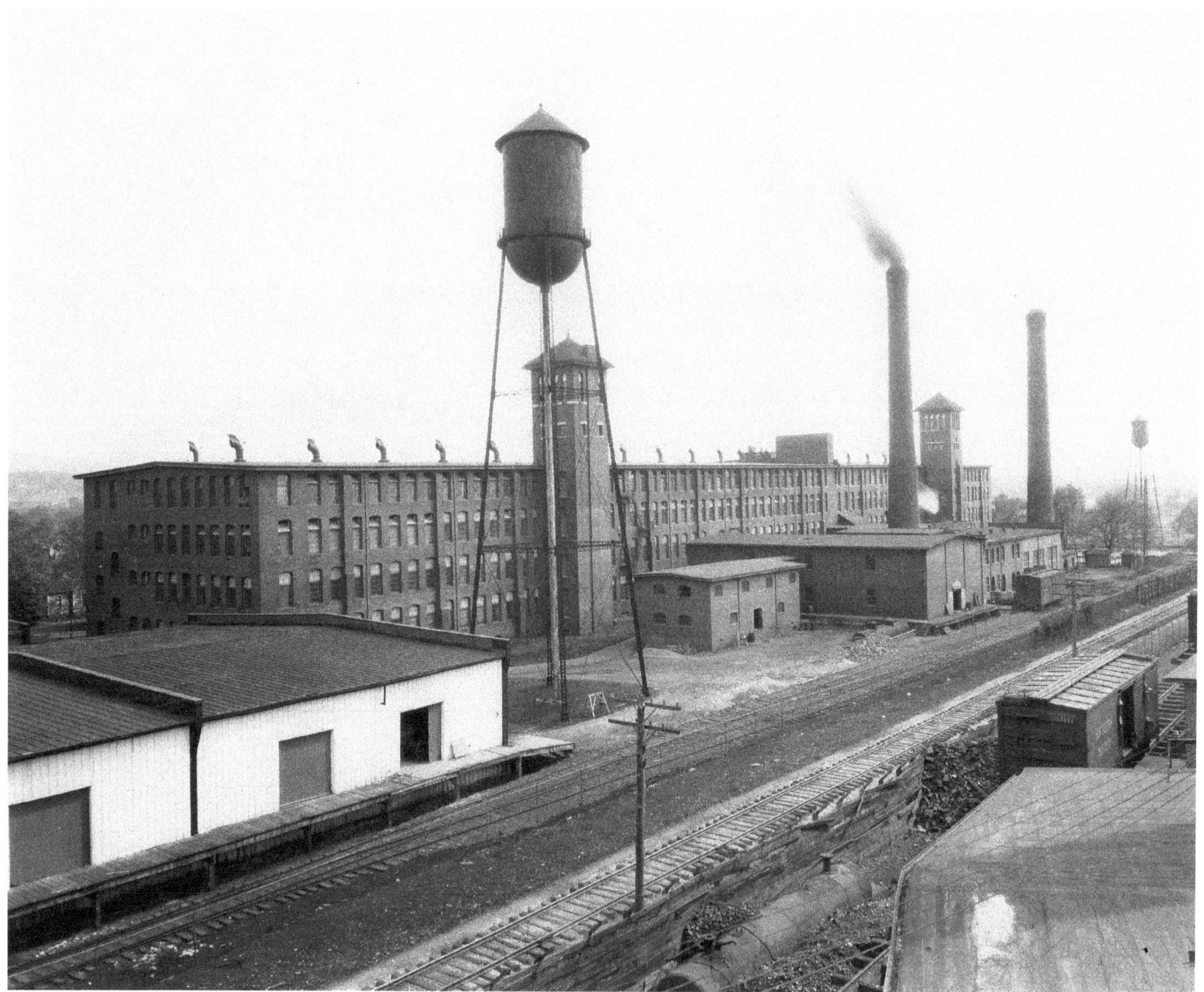

This building, finished in 1892, was the second city hall on this site at Washington Street and Clinton Avenue. The beautiful structure was built of limestone and brick.

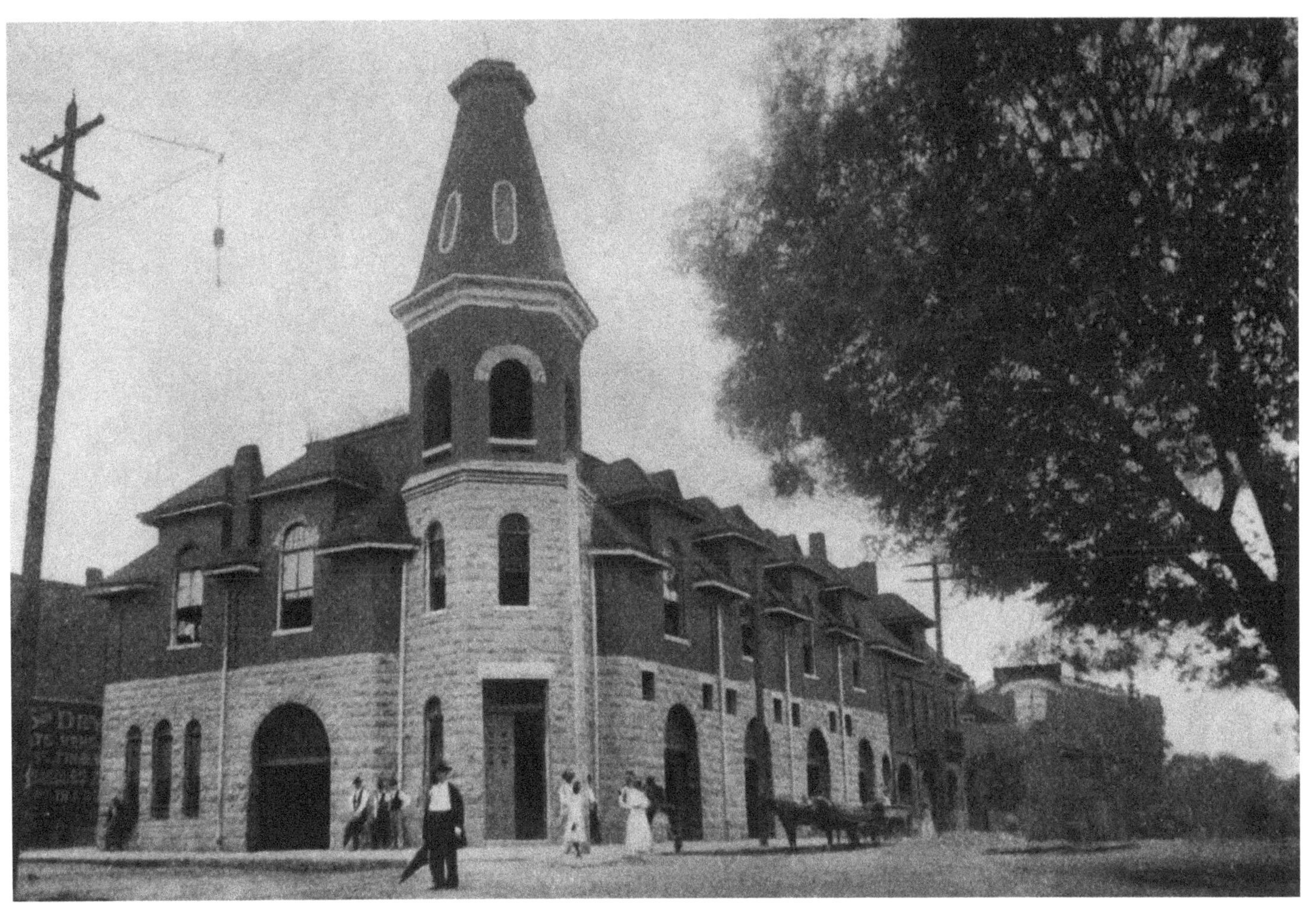

The gatekeeper lived in this house at the tollgate to Monte Sano Mountain. Note the richly upholstered horse carriage to the right. Present day Tollgate Road retains the name of those long-ago days.

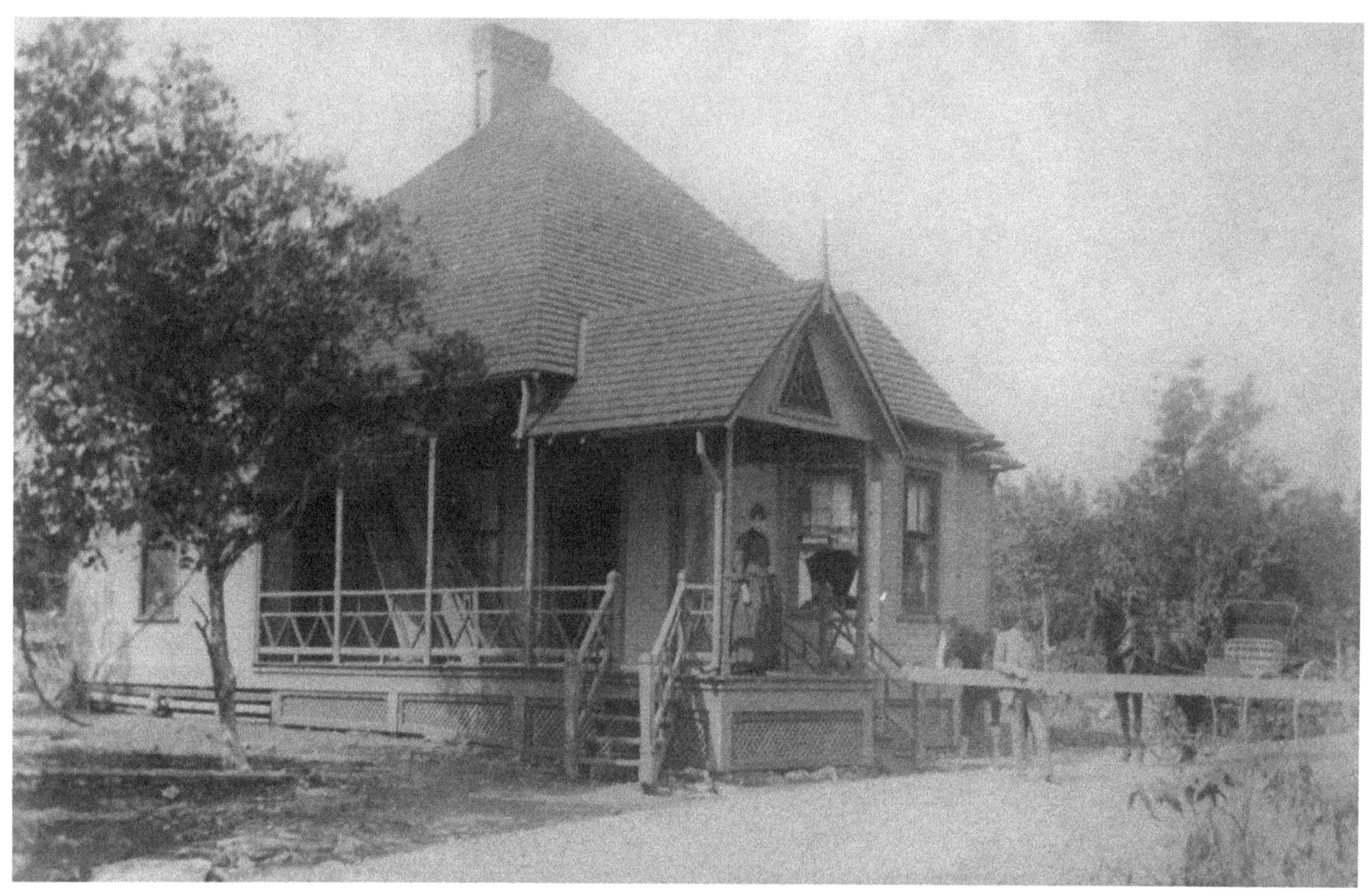

Some of the finest carriages in the South could be bought from J. W. Skinner Carriage Factory, formerly known as Columbus Buggy Company, located on the corner of Greene Street and Clinton Avenue. The business burned in 1883 and was rebuilt in 1893. This photograph shows several different types of buggies.

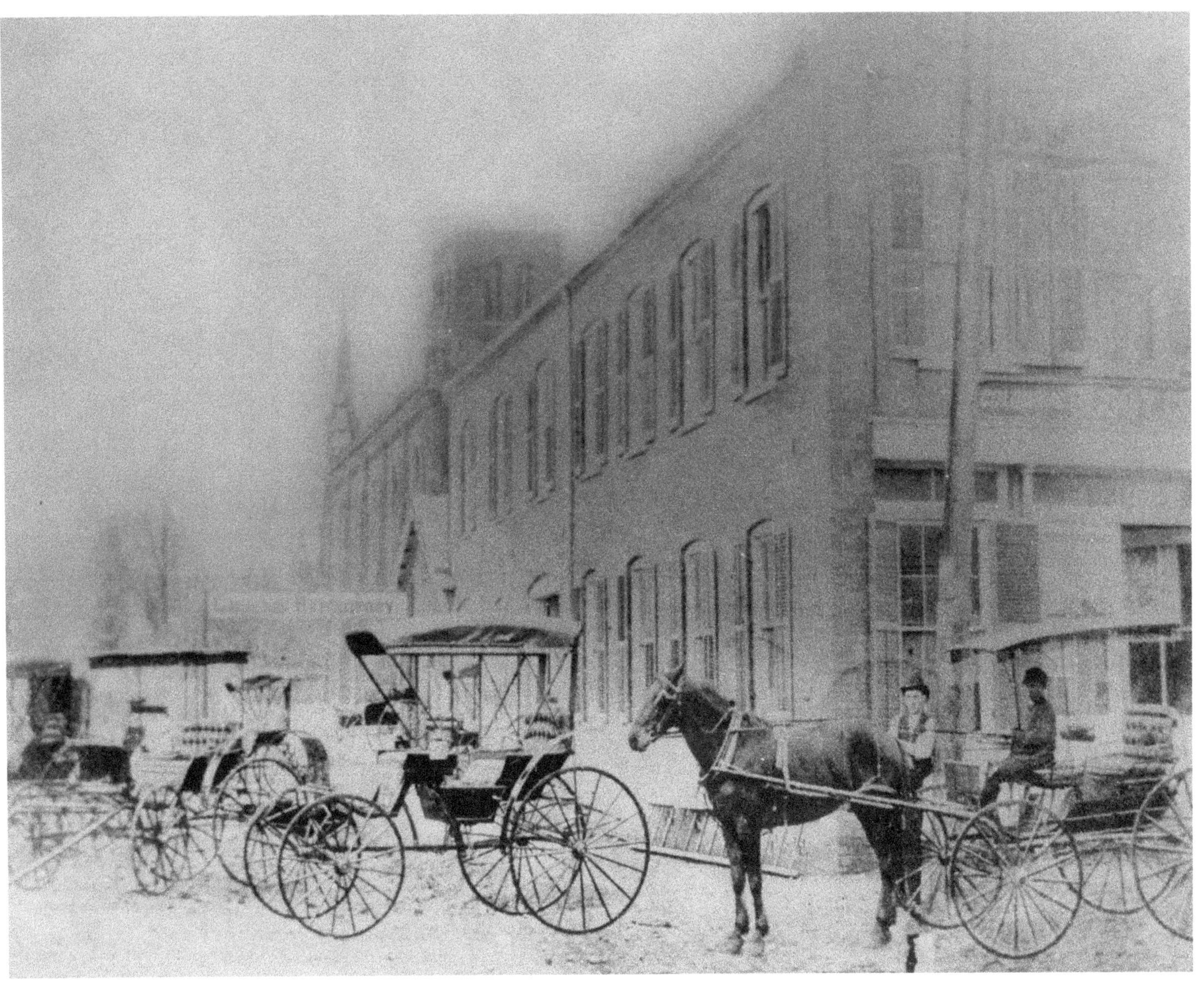

This photograph of the S. Schiffman & Co. store on the courthouse square was taken around 1893. The name of the man on the far left of the front row is unknown, but the others pictured here have been identified as: (front row, left to right), unknown; Solomon Schiffman; Bob-Lee Schiffman as a child; Israel Schiffman; Albert Jacoby; Sam L. Garner; Will Falk; Ike Schiffman; Sam Weil as a boy; (back row, from left) John F. Smith; Leon Lehman, behind Schiffman child; Jessie C. Va—(last name illegible).

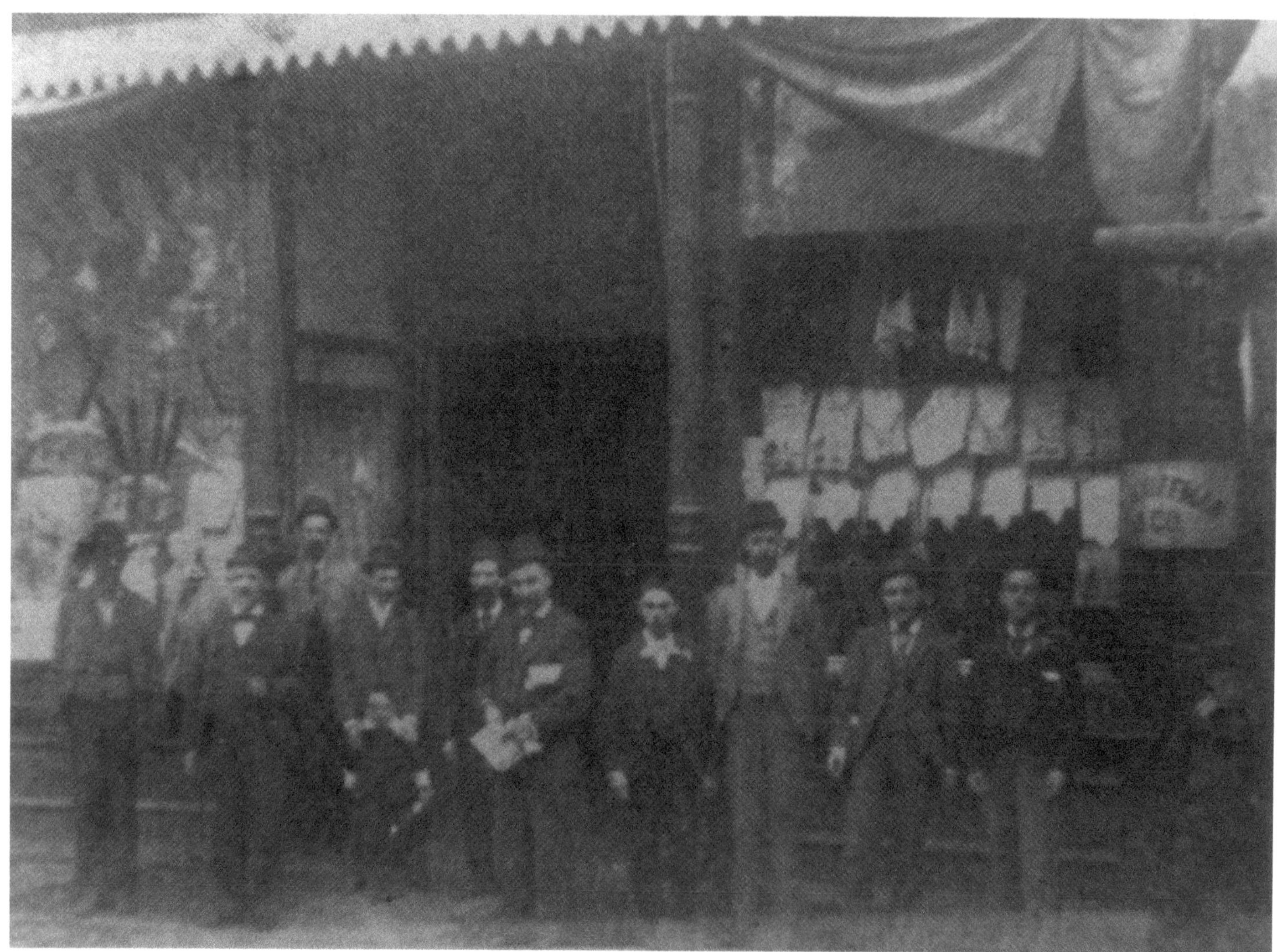

The I. Schiffman Store on the corner of Eustis Street and East Side Square was the 1902 birthplace of screen actress Tallulah Bankhead. It has changed little in appearance since the stone facade was added in 1895.

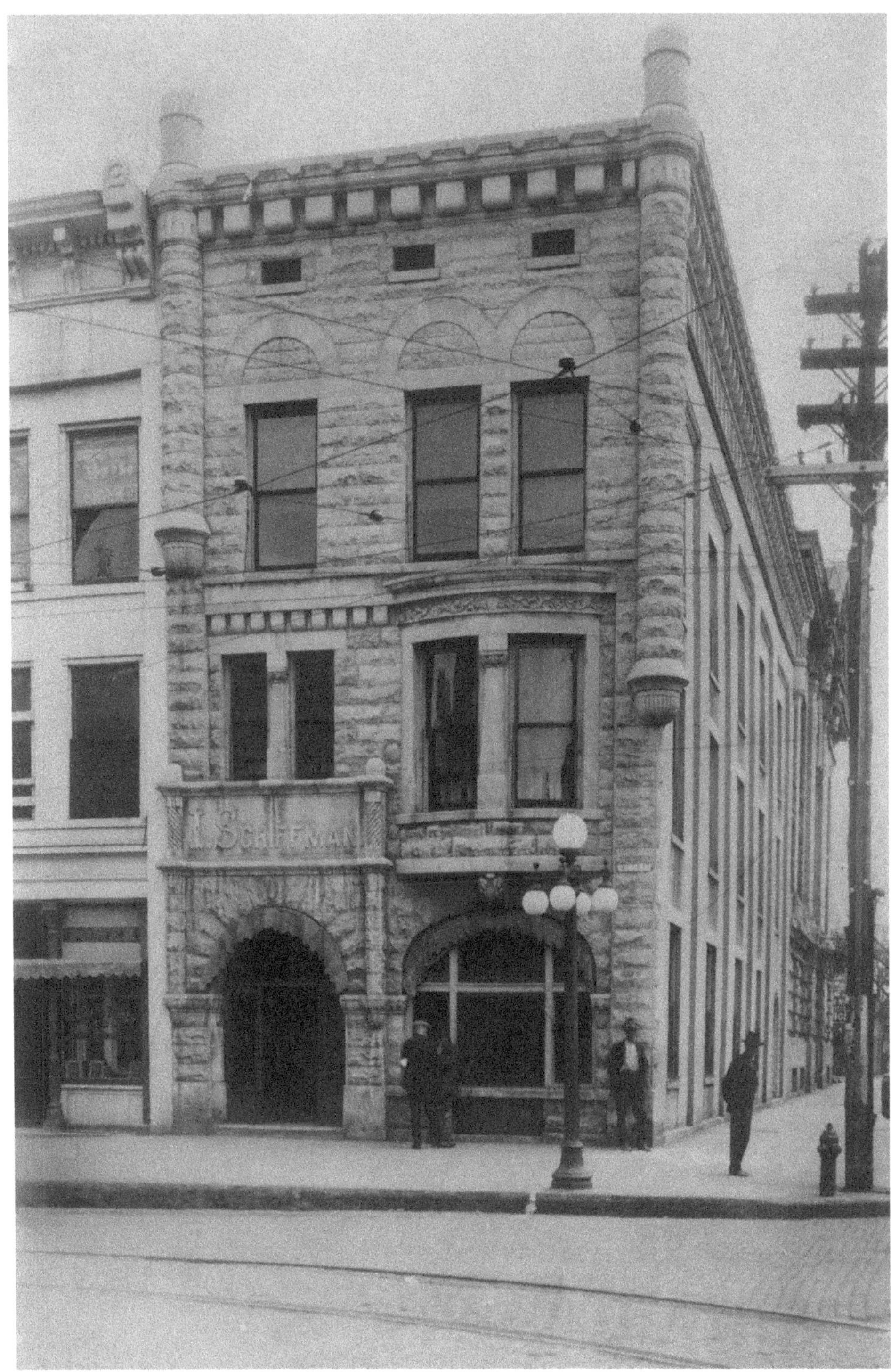

Southern Bell Telephone and Telegraph Company officially opened July 28, 1896, when Mayor W. T. Hutchens called the General Superintendent of Southern Bell in New York. The first long-distance words from Huntsville were, "The city of Huntsville, her people, send greetings to New York, hoping that the long distance telephone may be of both pleasure and profit to her people."

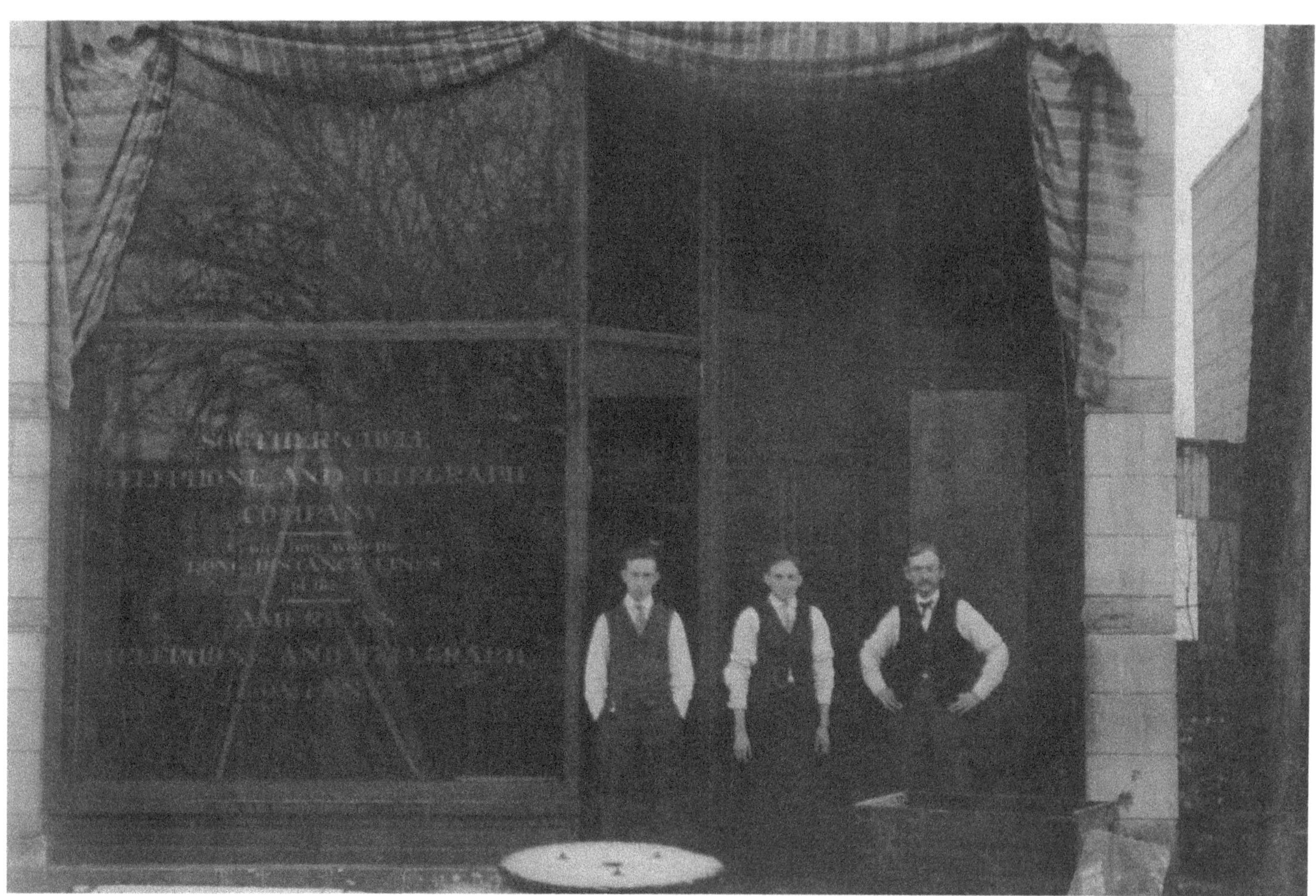

The new pump house at the Big Spring, completed in 1898.

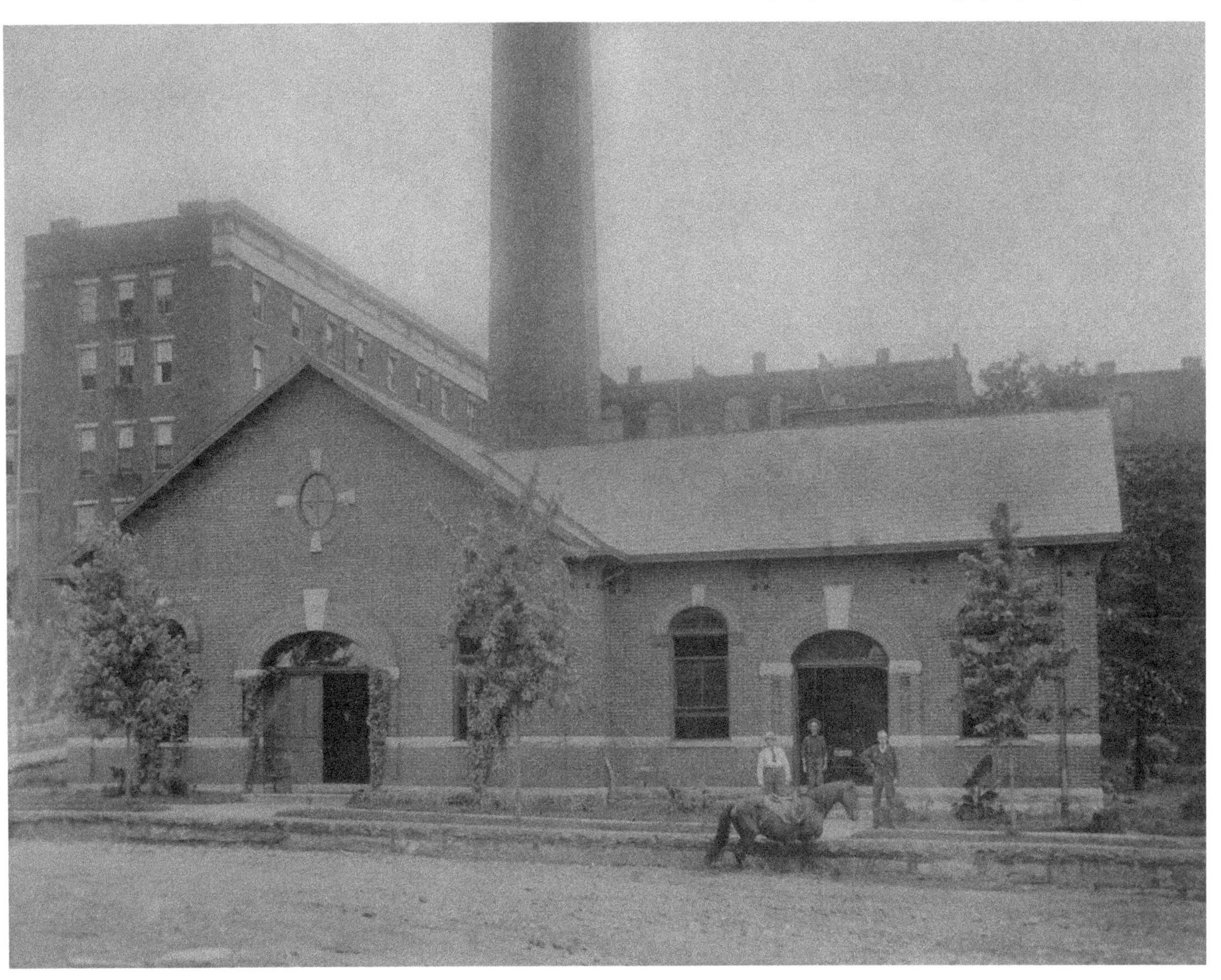

Thousands of spindles operated simultaneously in the spinning room at the Merrimack Mill.

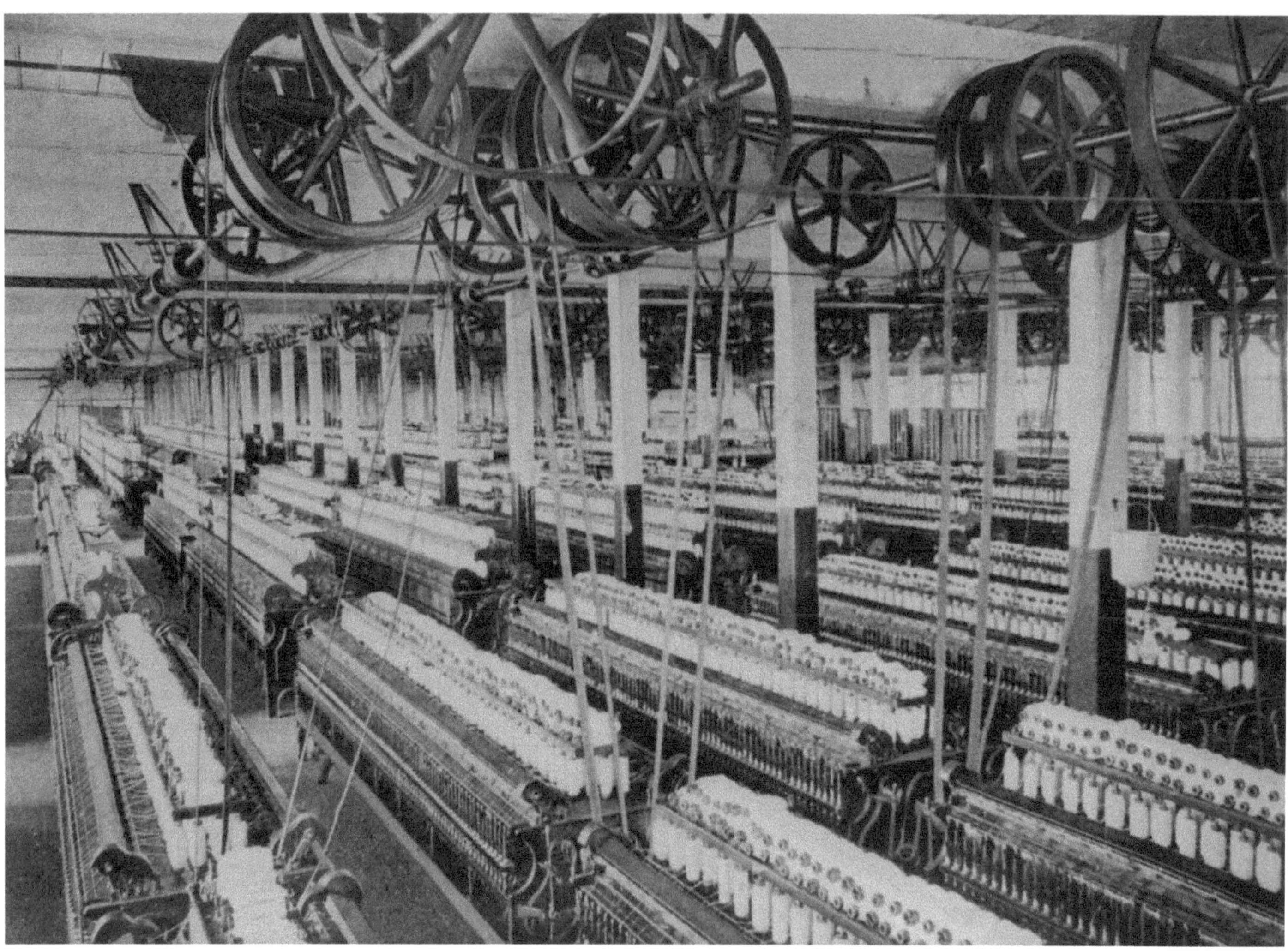

Employees at Merrimack Mill pause to pose for a photograph before returning to work.

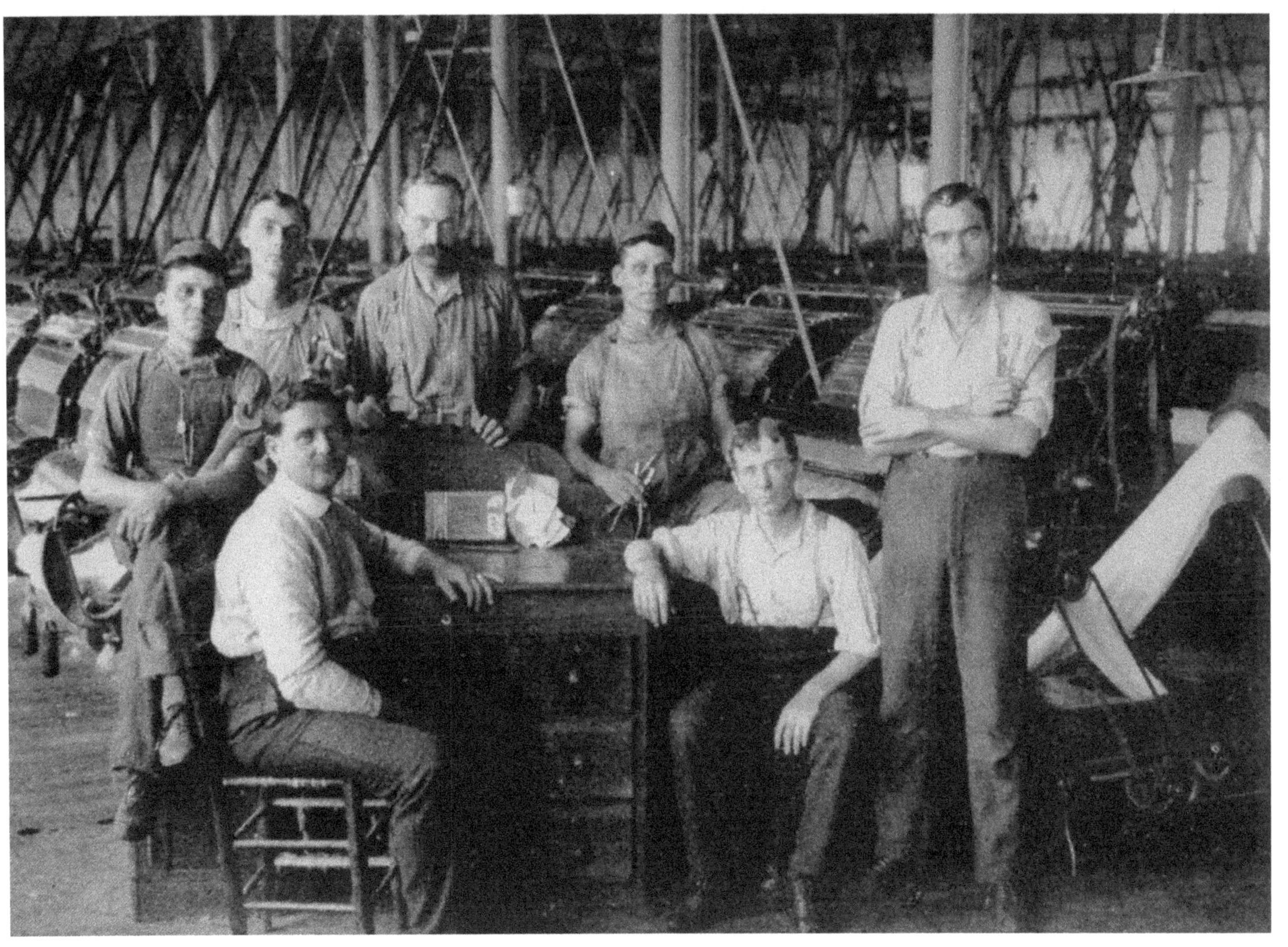

Patrons at Mauree's Sanitary Barber Shop on Walker Street in 1898 could get a trim, shoeshine, and beverage while being cooled by immense ceiling fans.

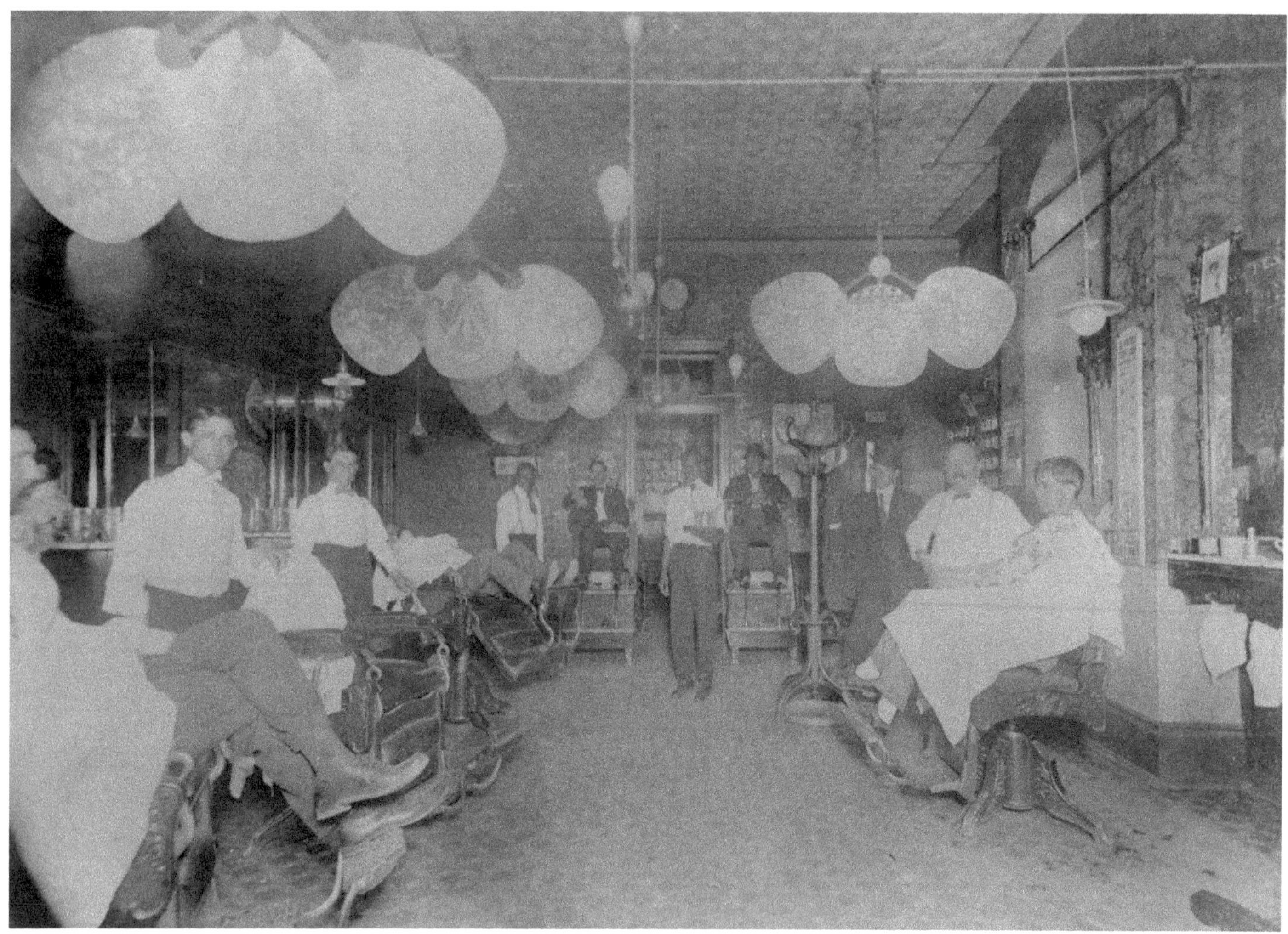

Barbers dressed in high style sport handlebar mustaches and cater to the needs of the uptown clientele. Note the stationary barber chairs.

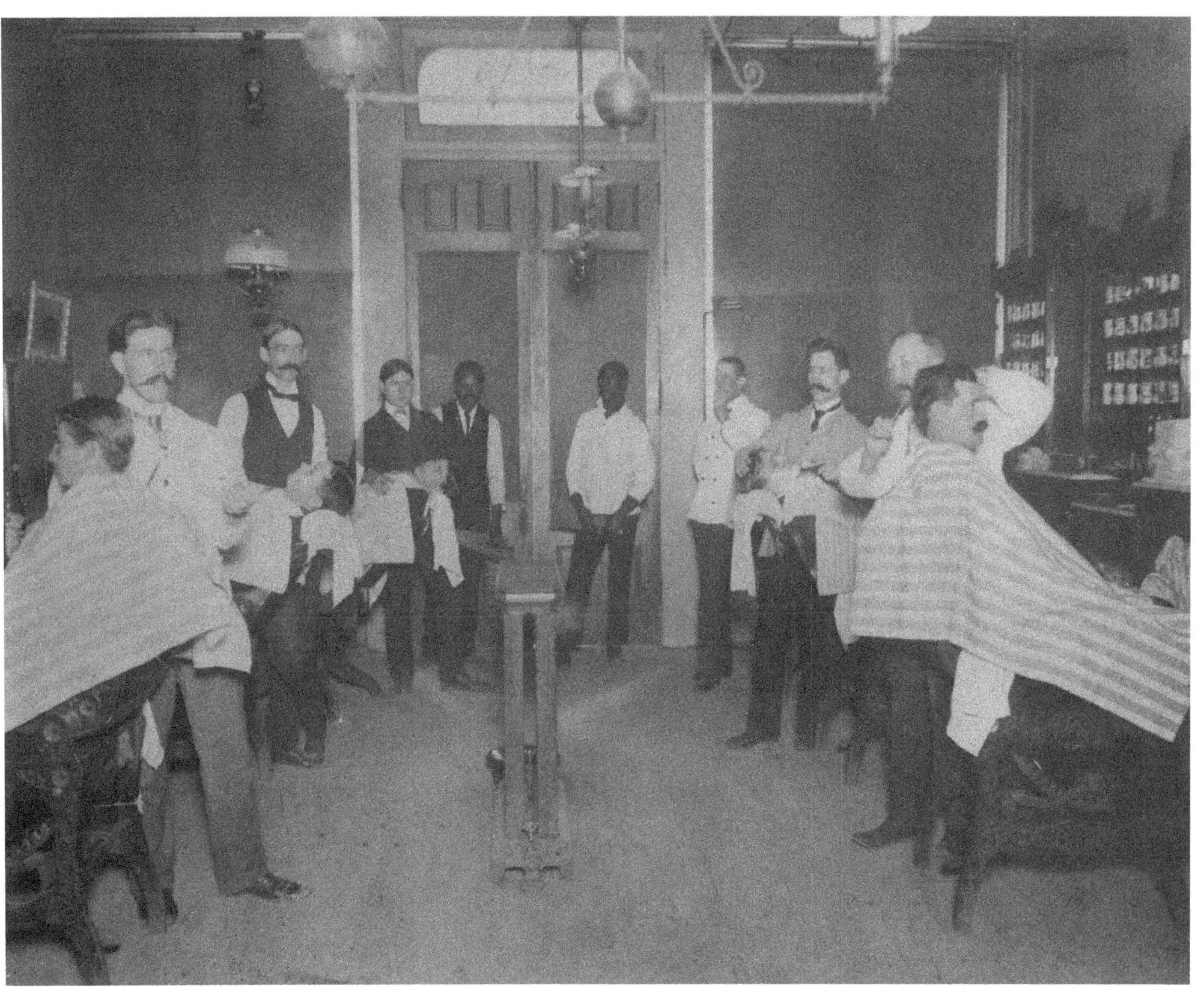

This photograph, taken March 1898, shows the overflow at the Big Spring after a particularly heavy rain. Water stood eight inches over the canal walk.

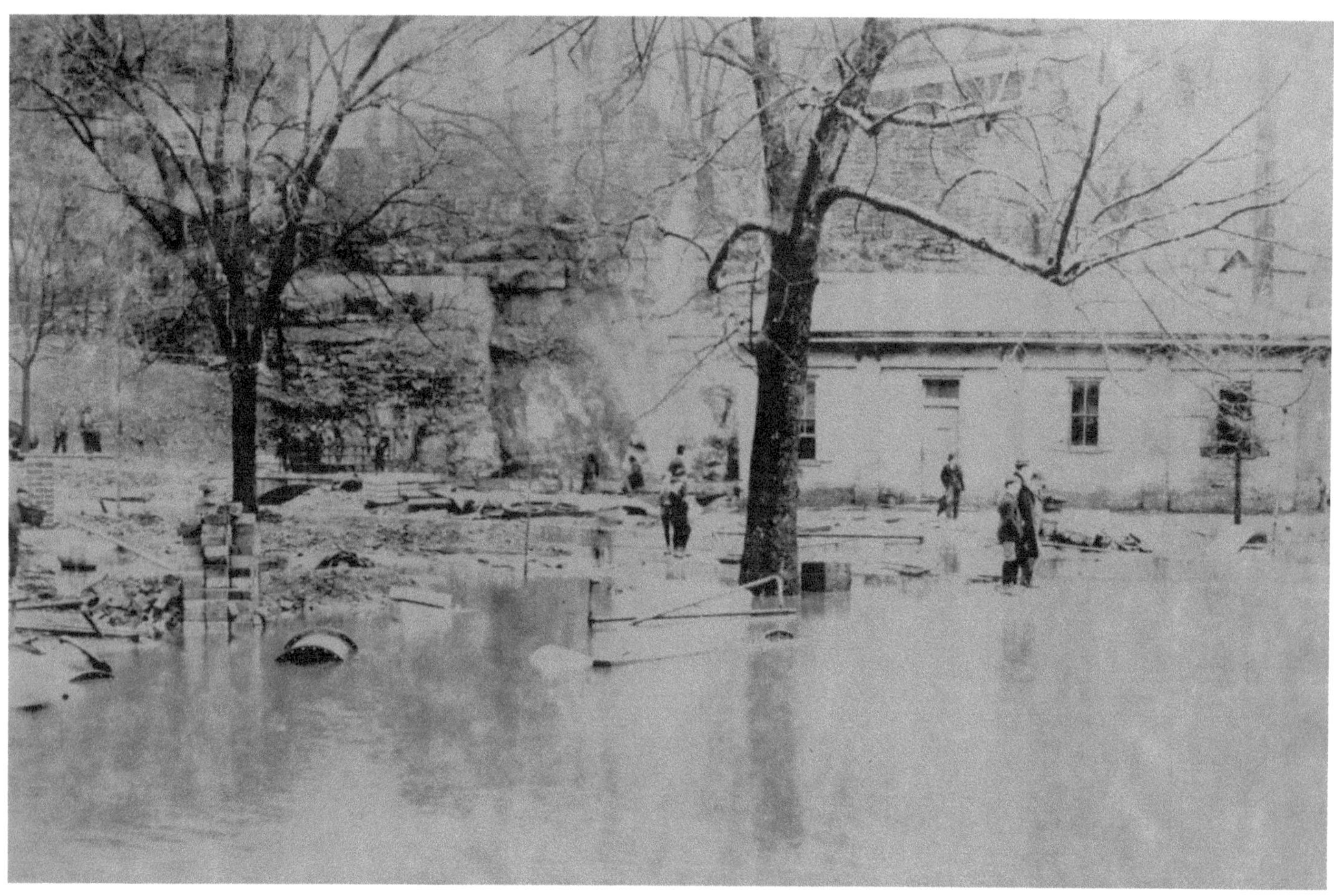

A severe winter cold snap, rare this far South, leaves icicles at the Big Spring in 1899.

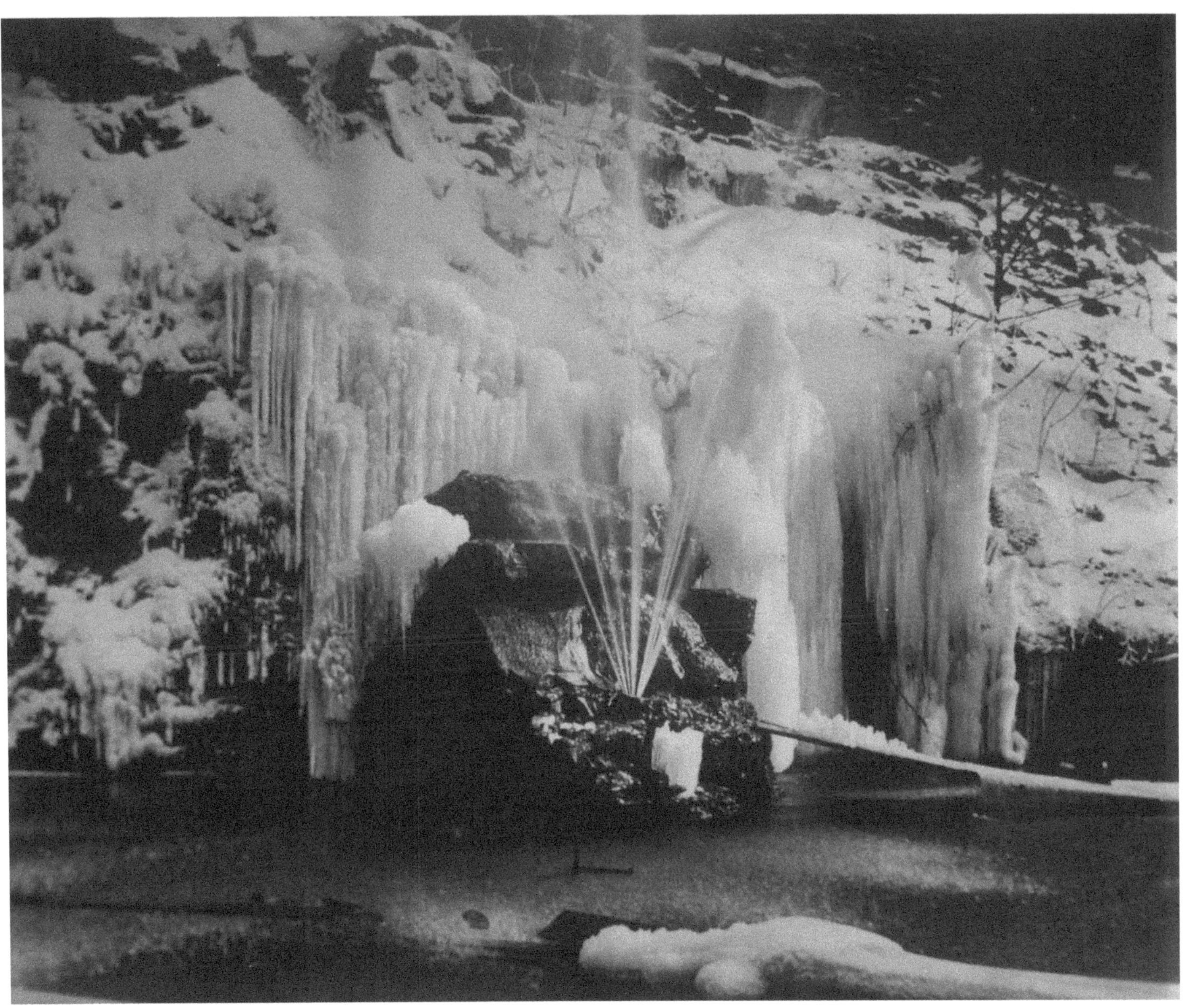

Laxson & Kelly was one of many general merchandise stores in Huntsville.

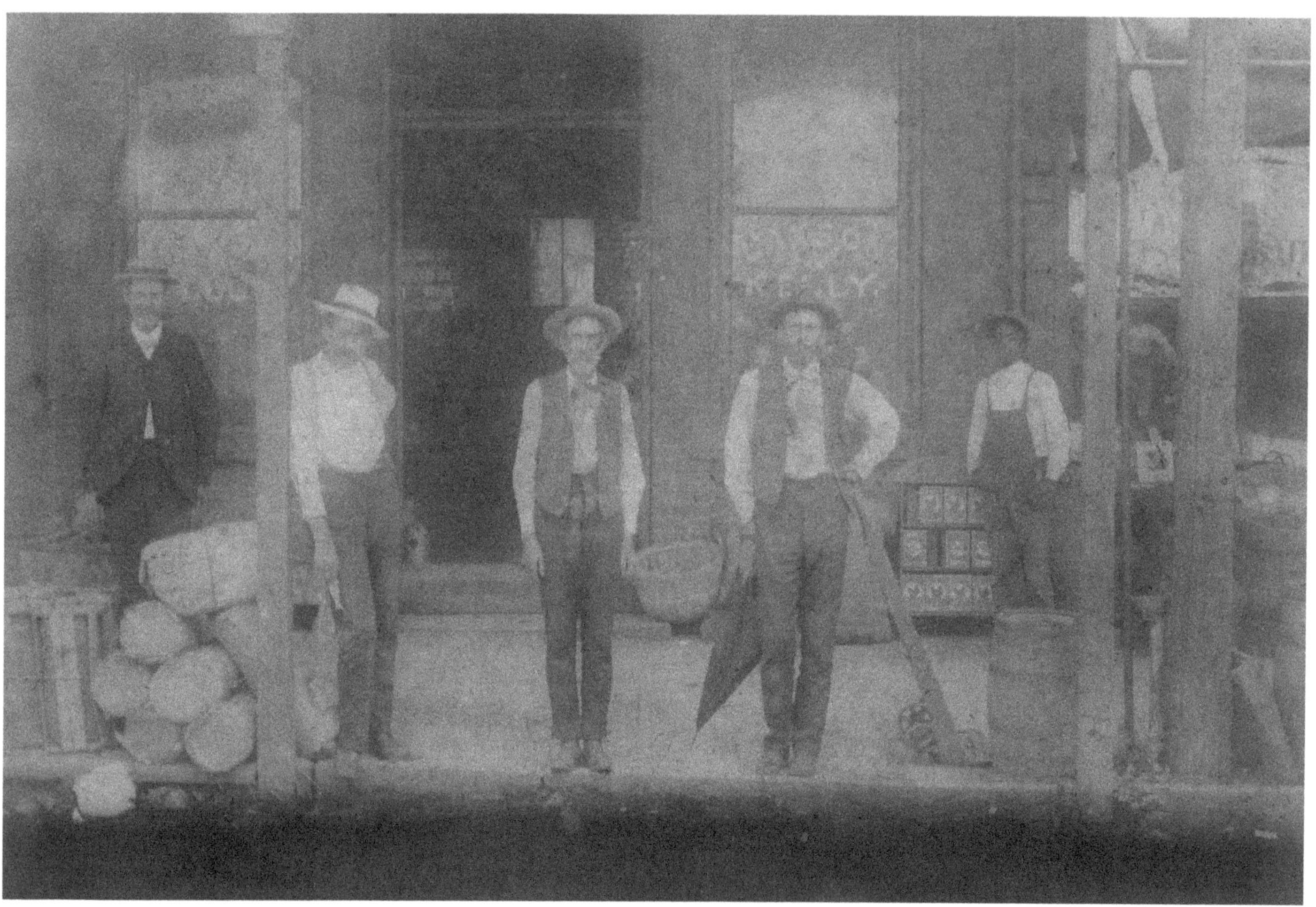

The fire station was attached to city hall, located on the corner of Washington Street and Clinton Avenue. Firemen and horses pose with their equipment in this photograph.

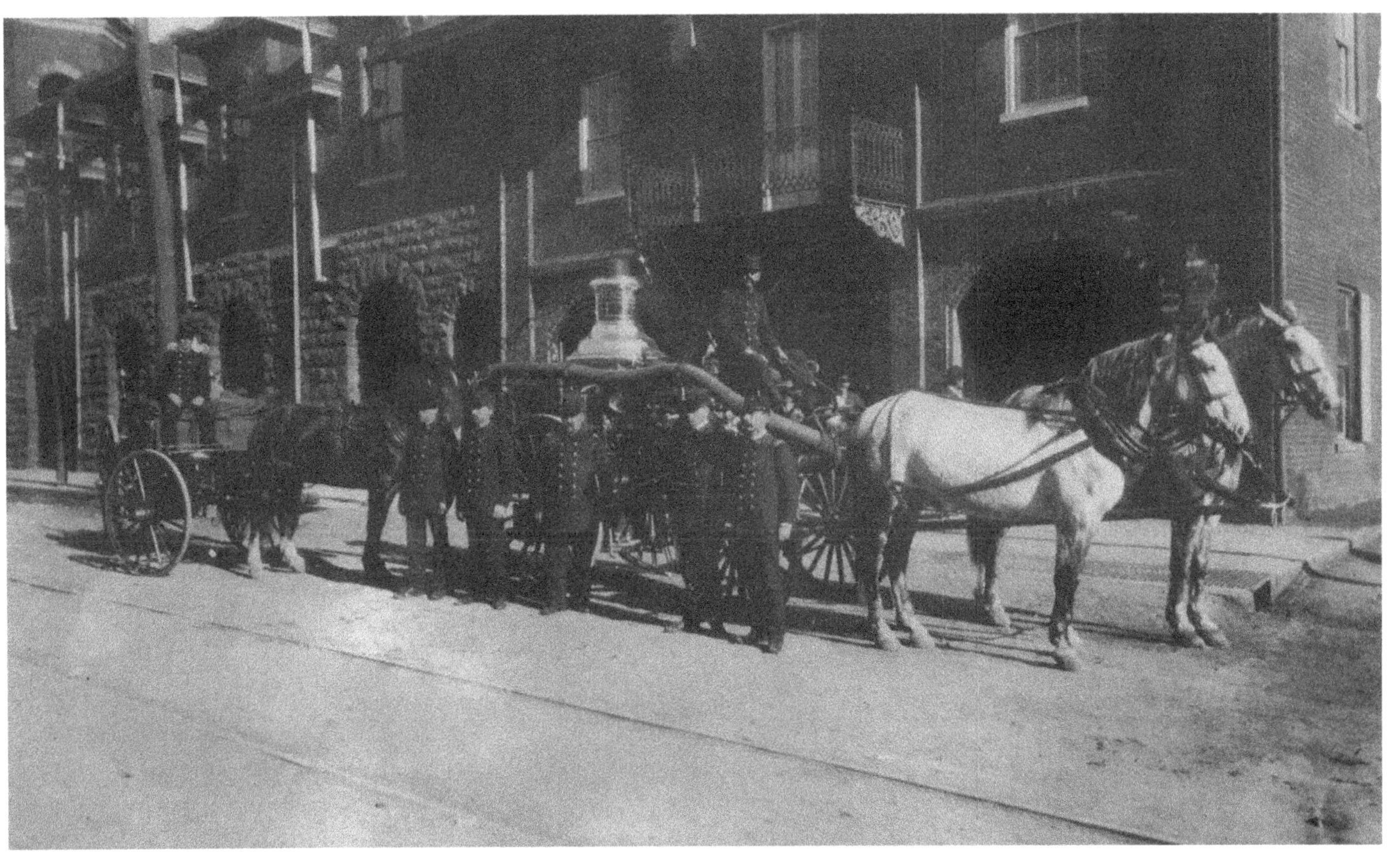

Dallas mill workers posed for this photograph. Note the boys, some as young as ten years old, who worked long hours for low pay. Child labor laws put children into schoolrooms instead of factories early in the twentieth century.

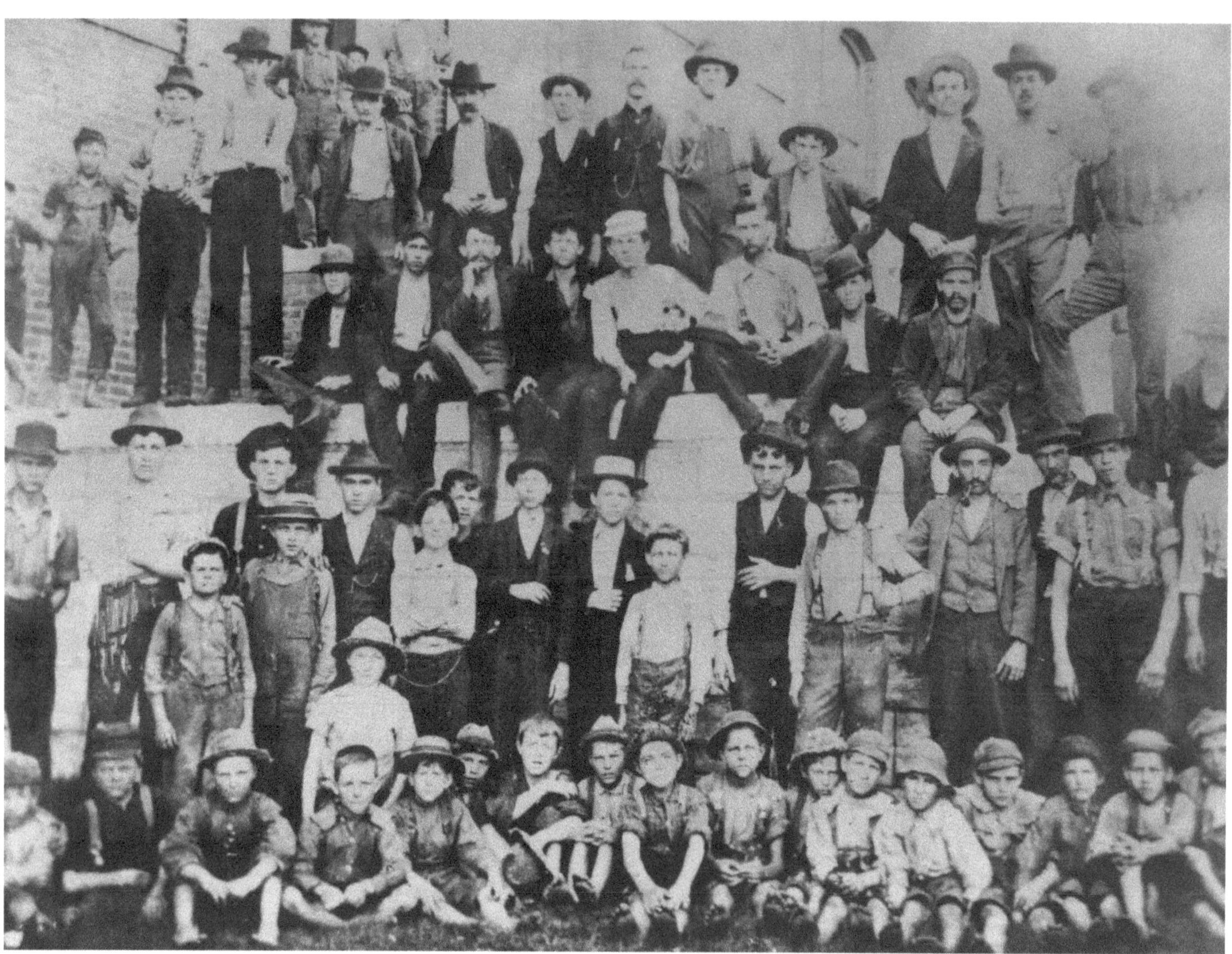

An Industrial Revolution

(1900–1919)

Local cotton mills expanded at an incredible rate, and with that growth came the need for more workers. Young children, forgoing an education to help put food on the family table, filled many of those back-breaking jobs, but on January 1, 1909, the child labor law went into effect and mill children were required to attend school for eight weeks of each year. Mill managers screamed that they would be forced to shut down, yet the mills continued to grow and prosper.

Huntsville was treated with a visit from President William McKinley in 1901, and in 1902, temperance reformer Carrie Nation created a stir when she approached a woman at the Huntsville Depot and dramatically shouted, "You ought to go home and tear off those plumes and gew-gaws and make corns on your knees praying for your lost soul!" Waving her trademark hatchet, she lectured on the sins of alcohol before leaving town.

In 1916, Huntsville made national headlines when the body of Judge William T. Lawler was found near a bridge on the Tennessee River. David Overton, who had run against Lawler in the recent election, was accused of the murder. After an extensive manhunt, he was captured in Tennessee and brought to Huntsville for a most sensational trial. In the meantime, two other men committed suicide during the investigation of a possible conspiracy. Overton was sentenced to hang, but in a dramatic turn of events, he escaped only to perish in a hail of bullets during a shoot-out with officers in Birmingham.

In 1917, another war took our young men away. World War I saw them fighting in France and Germany and, as in all wars, some did not return. In the meantime, an invisible but deadly enemy came to Huntsville—the Spanish Flu. Churches, schools, and theaters closed in an attempt to slow the spread of the disease. In 1918, during the month of October 294 deaths were reported. The final toll was nearly 400. In fact, more burials were conducted at Maple Hill Cemetery in 1918 than in any other year.

The contract to build the Lowe Cotton Mill was granted in 1900 to produce thread. Note the cotton patch in the common ground. The building on the right still stands in West Huntsville.

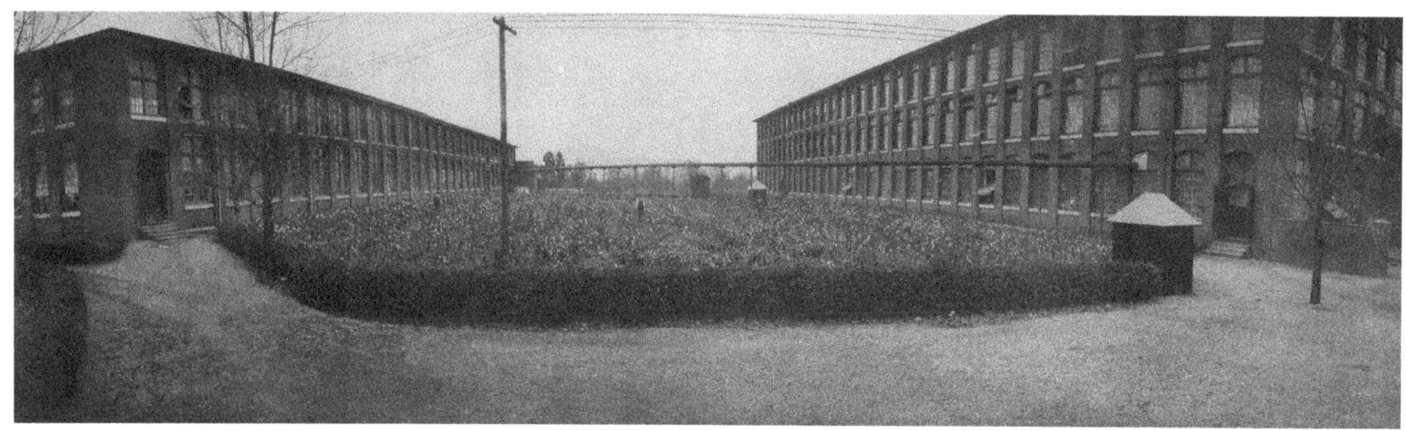

This photograph from around 1900 shows a stylishly-dressed woman identified as "Mrs. Monroe" riding her carriage past the Federal Courthouse located on Greene Street. This impressive building was a casualty of urban renewal.

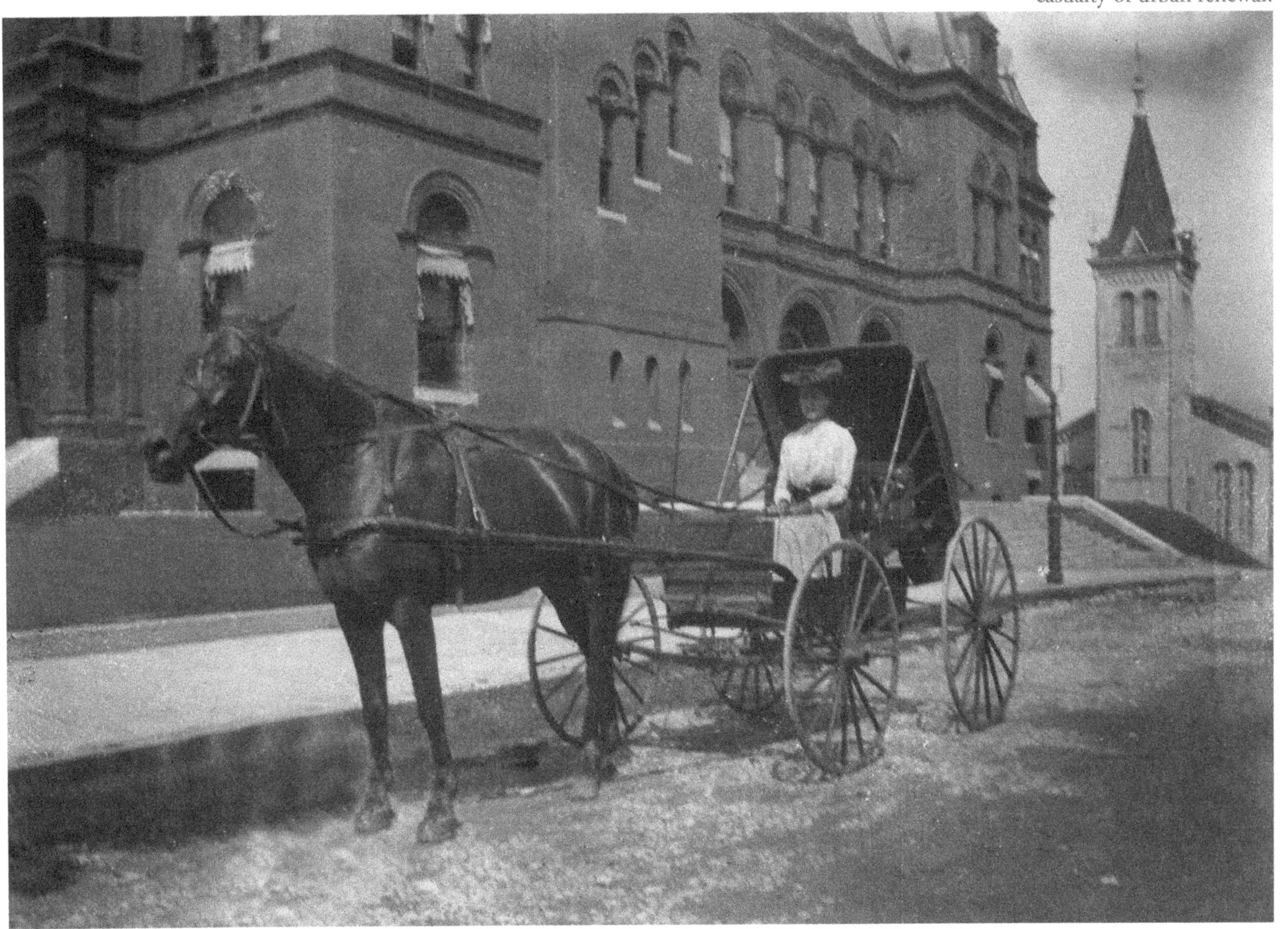

A crowd gathers in their Sunday best at the courthouse for a patriotic celebration.

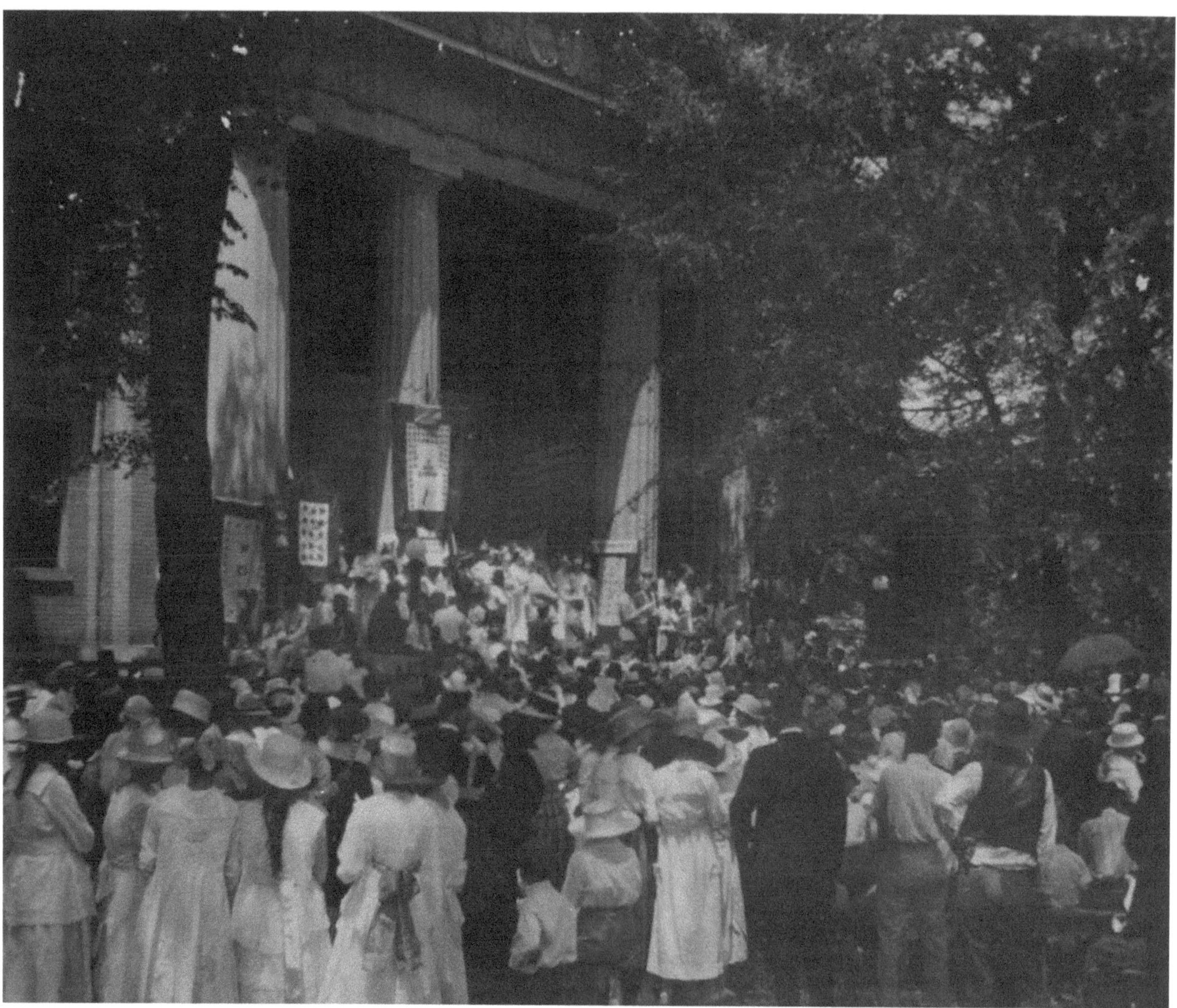

These people are enjoying an Elks picnic around 1901.

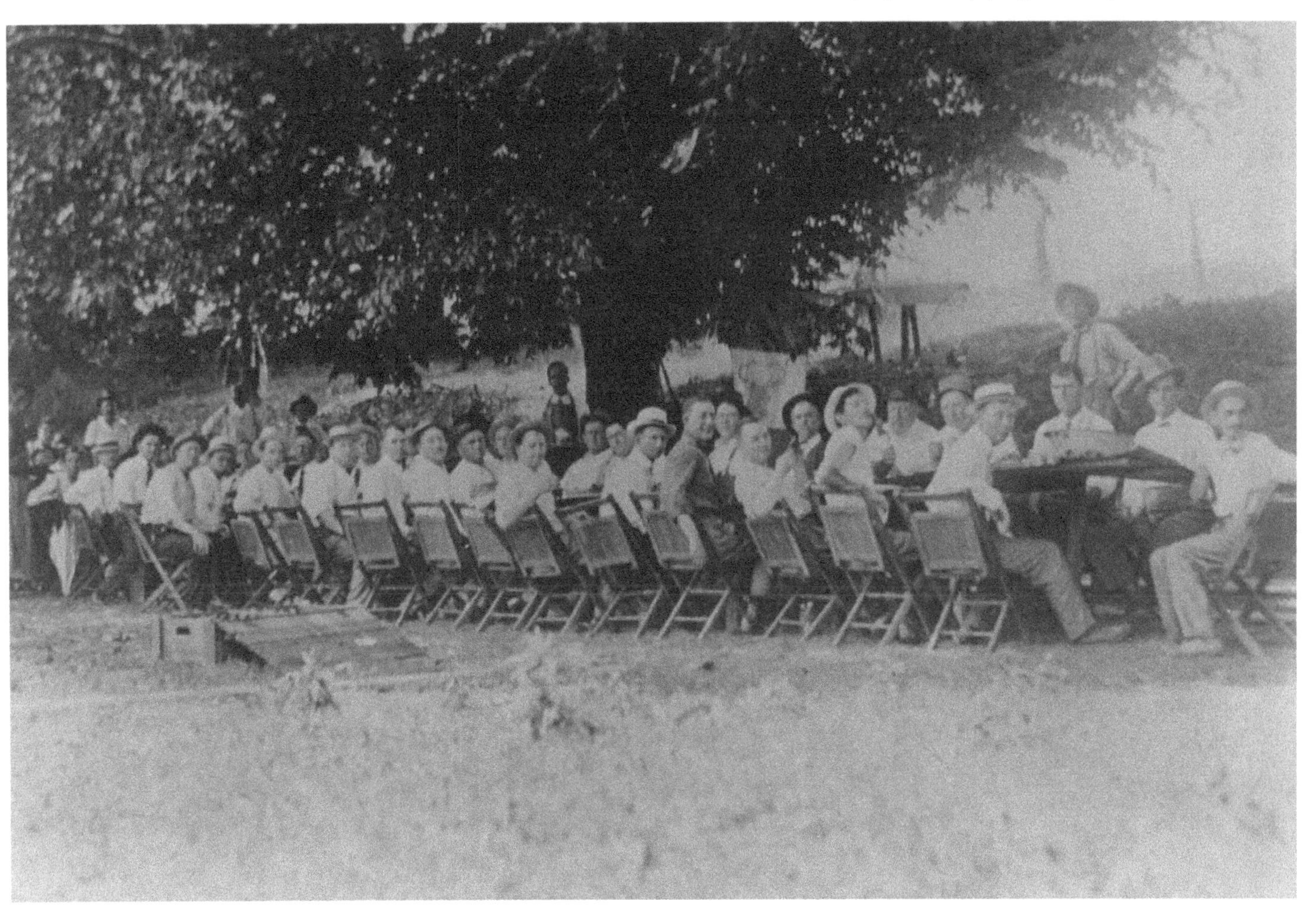

The Dallas Mill shows off an entry into the 1901 Cotton Festival Parade. A loom is sitting atop the float and in the store window behind is a flier advertising Buffalo Bill's Wild West Show.

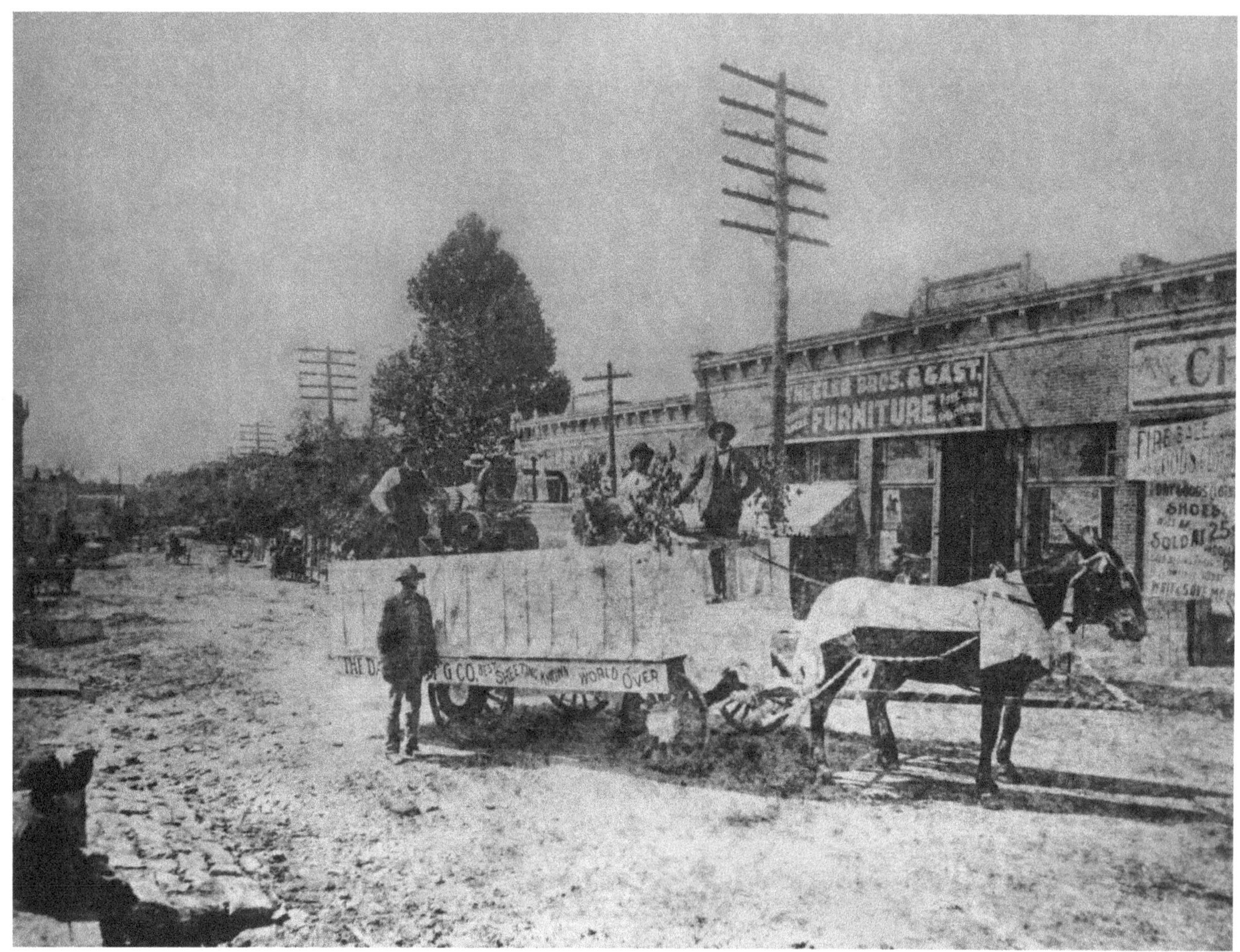

Two horses are gaudily dressed for the 1901 4th of July Parade. Inside the buggy are former Mayor Thomas Smith and Frank Murphy. Laughlin Funeral Home and Furniture Store stands behind them.

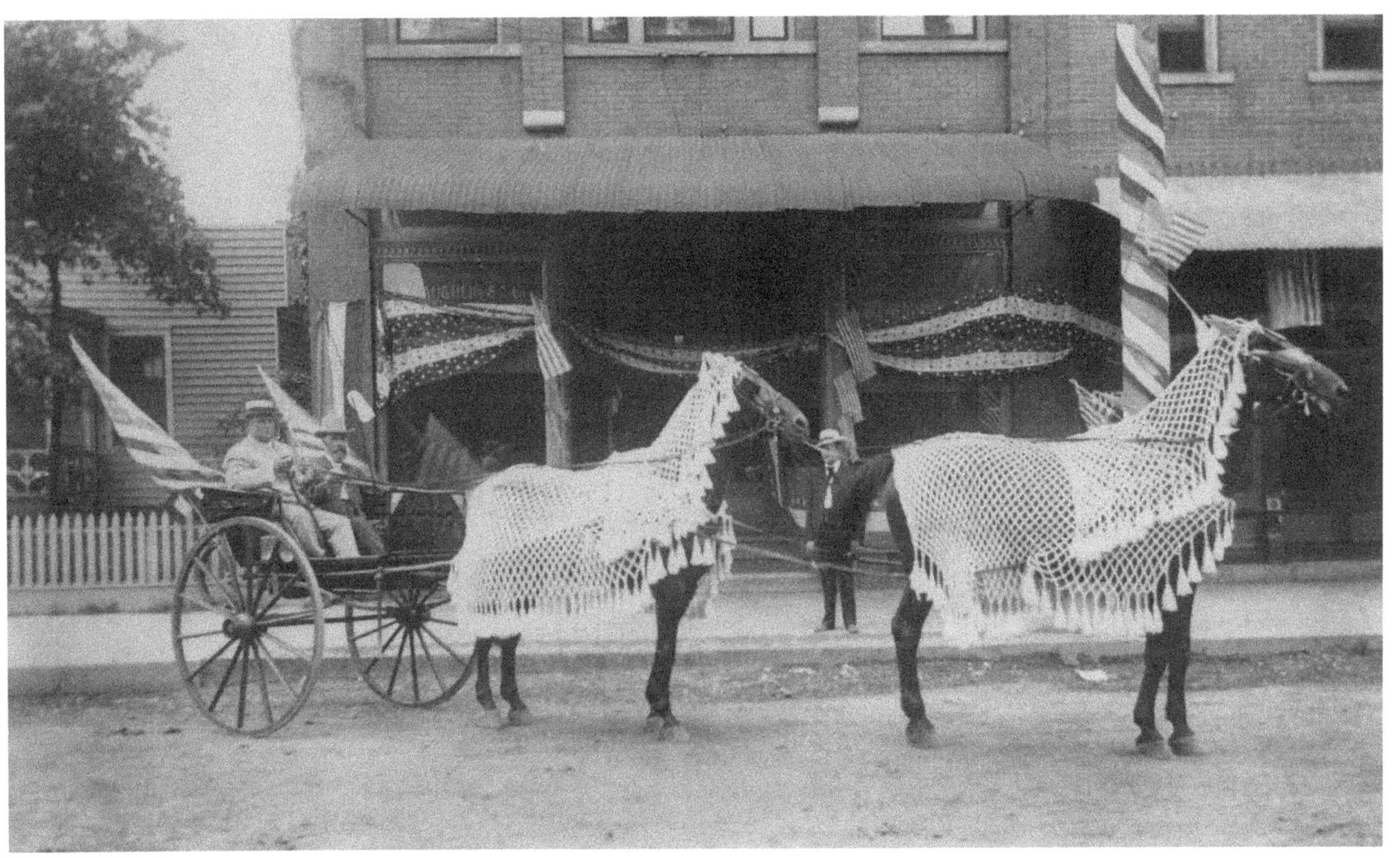

This jail, built with a stylish turret, was located on the corner of Greene Street and Clinton Avenue.

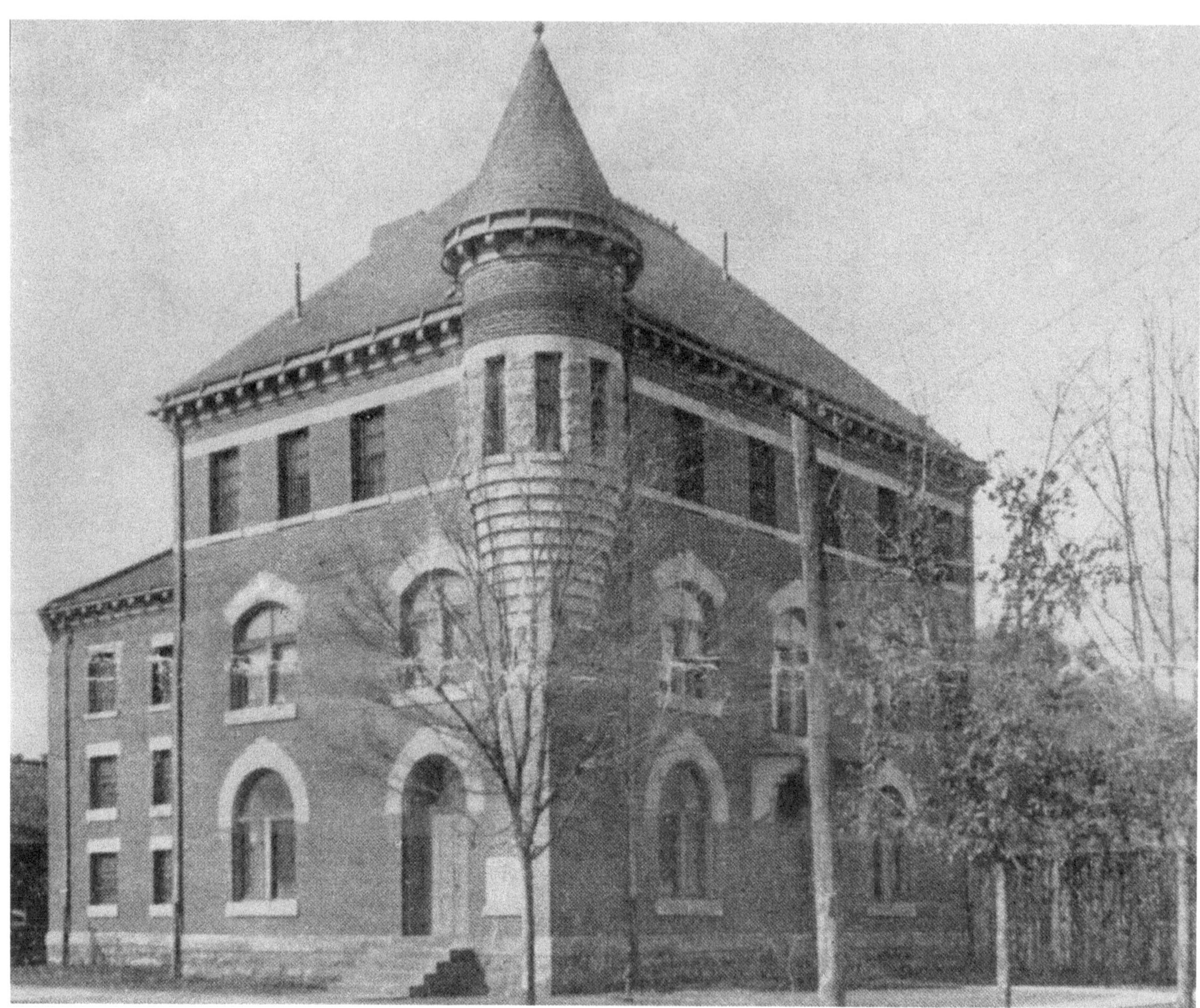

The sign at T. B. Overton's Washington Street establishment advertises horseshoeing as their speciality. In addition to fixing farm equipment, they also sold crop fertilizer.

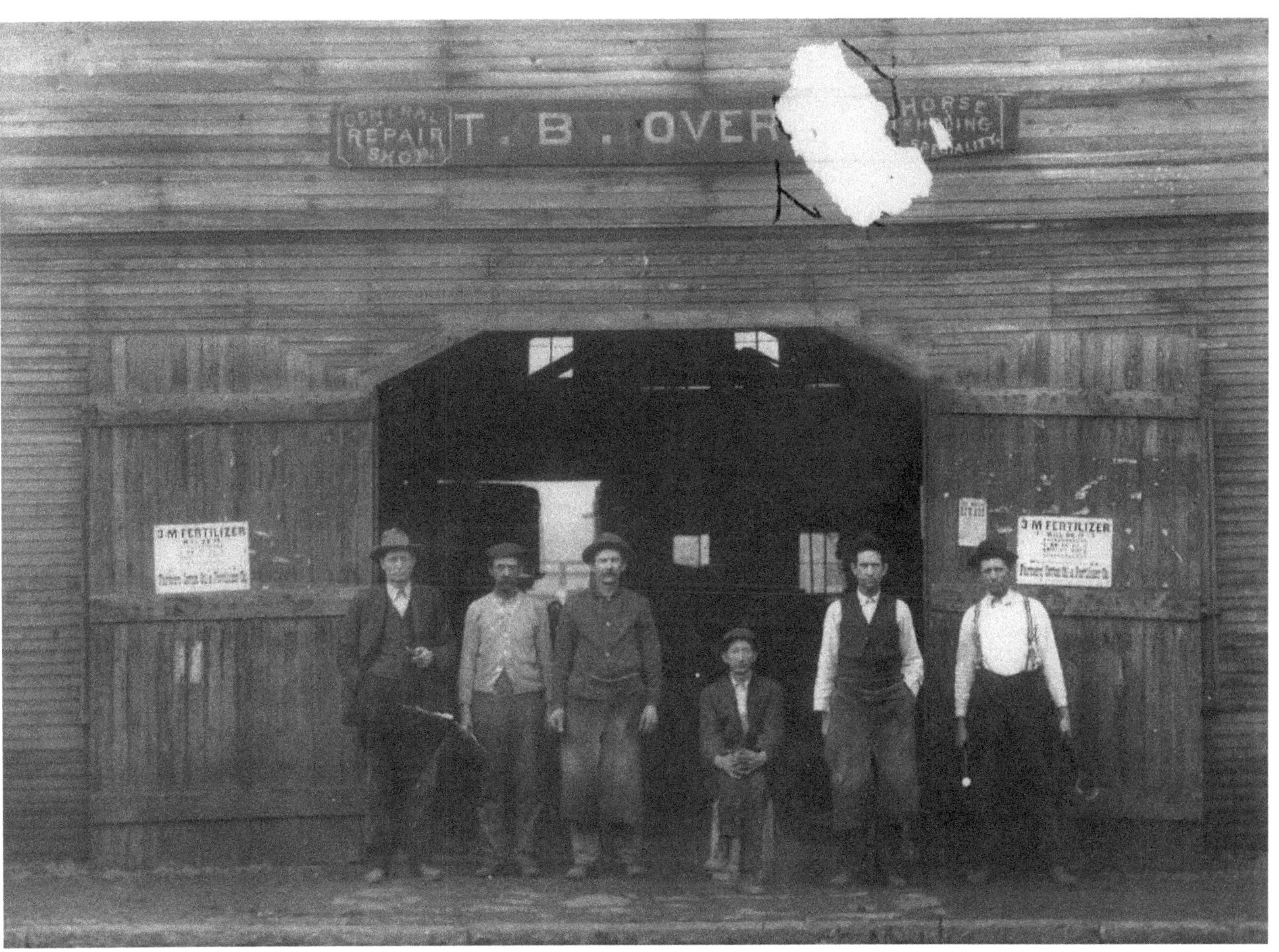

R. L. Sparkman, pictured on the right, carved many of the old headstones in local cemeteries. His business, Sparkman Marble & Granite, shared a building with the harness shop on East Side Square before it moved adjacent to Maple Hill Cemetery.

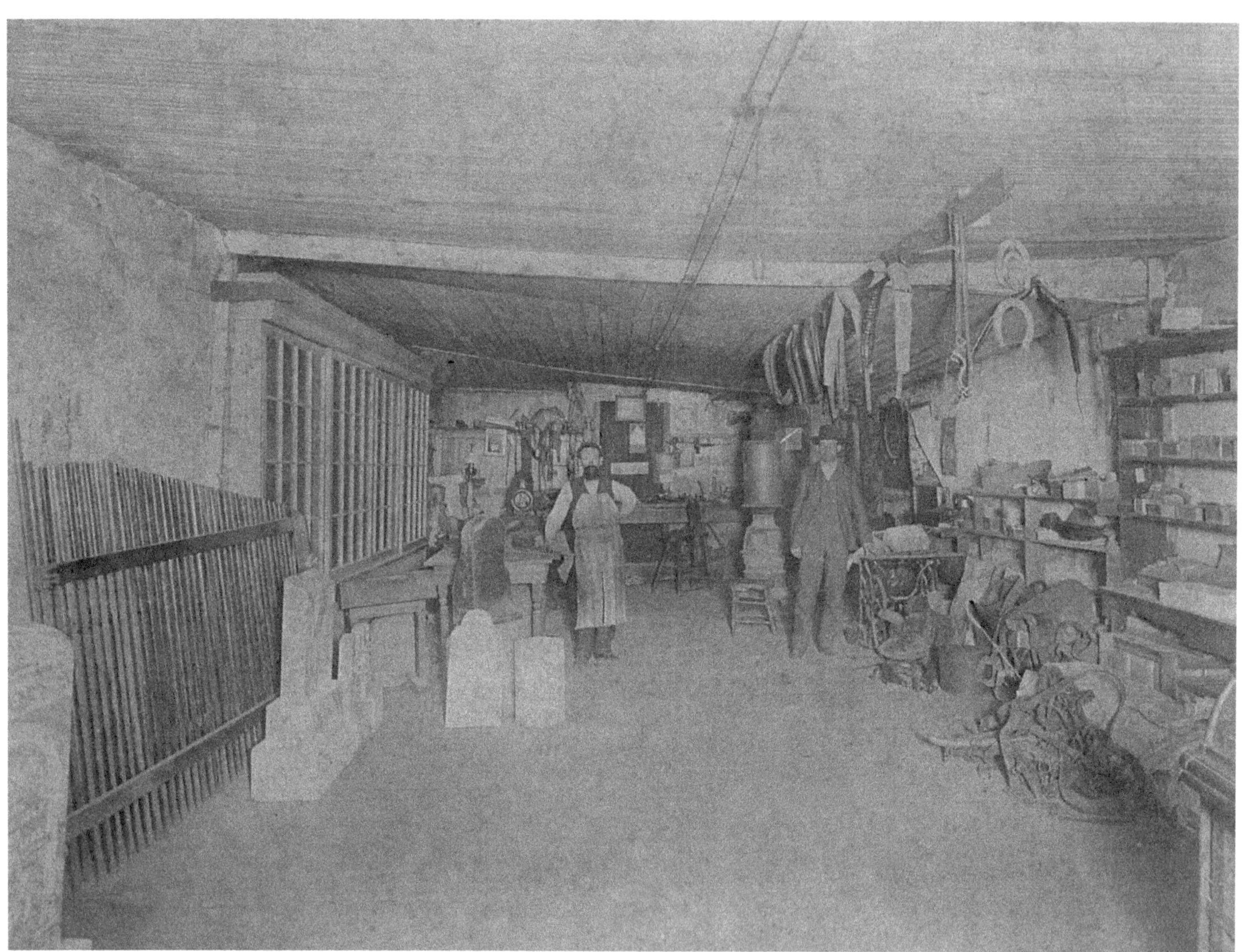

This photograph, taken in December 1904, shows one of Huntsville's smaller "flouring" mills, Spring City Mills, which was on West Clinton Street.

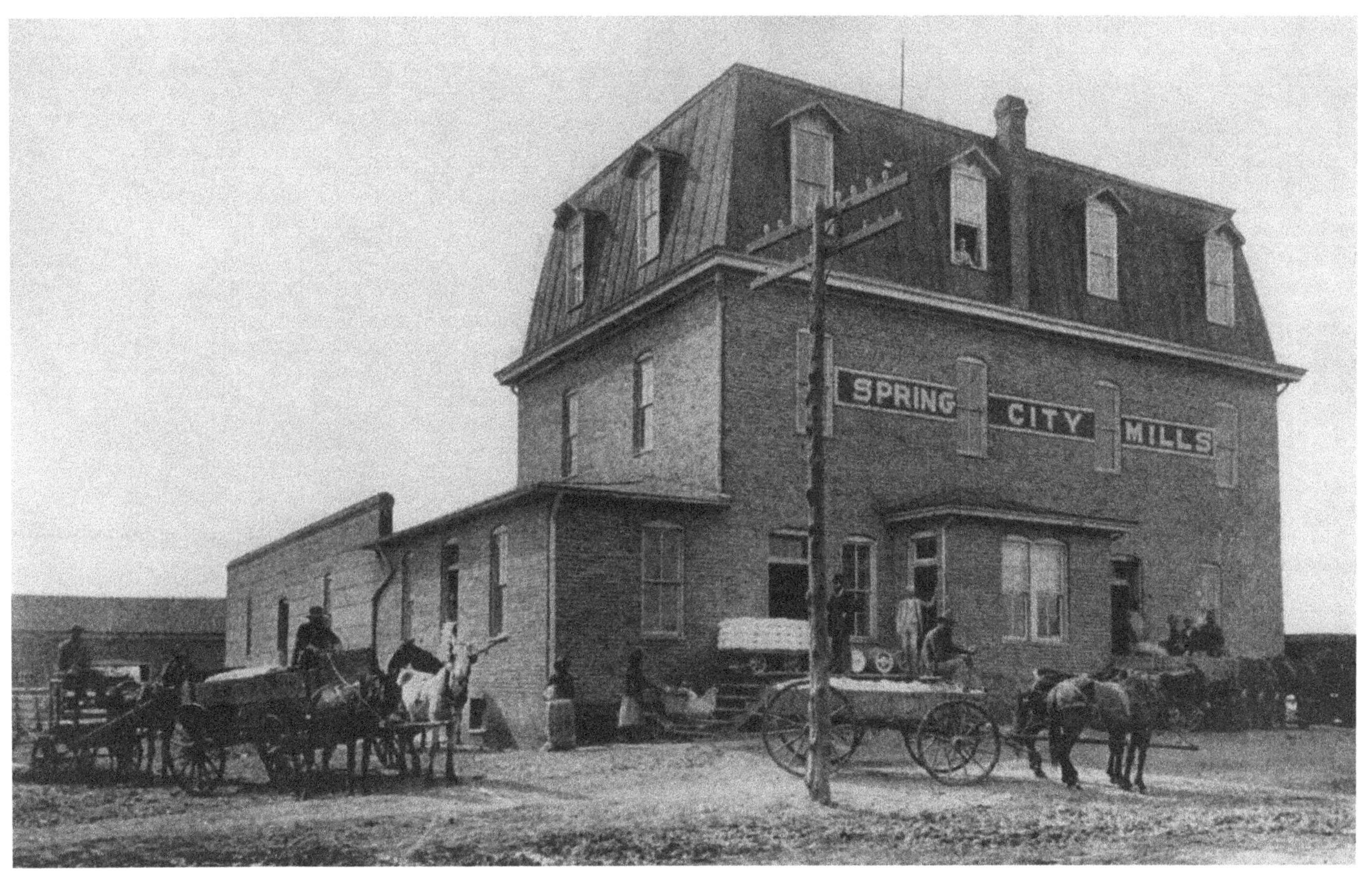

The Cumberland Presbyterian Church, first organized in the early 1800s, finally had a finished building in 1850. It was later torn down, a new building was erected over the same foundation, and it was dedicated at the time this photograph was taken. This building is now the Central Presbyterian Church.

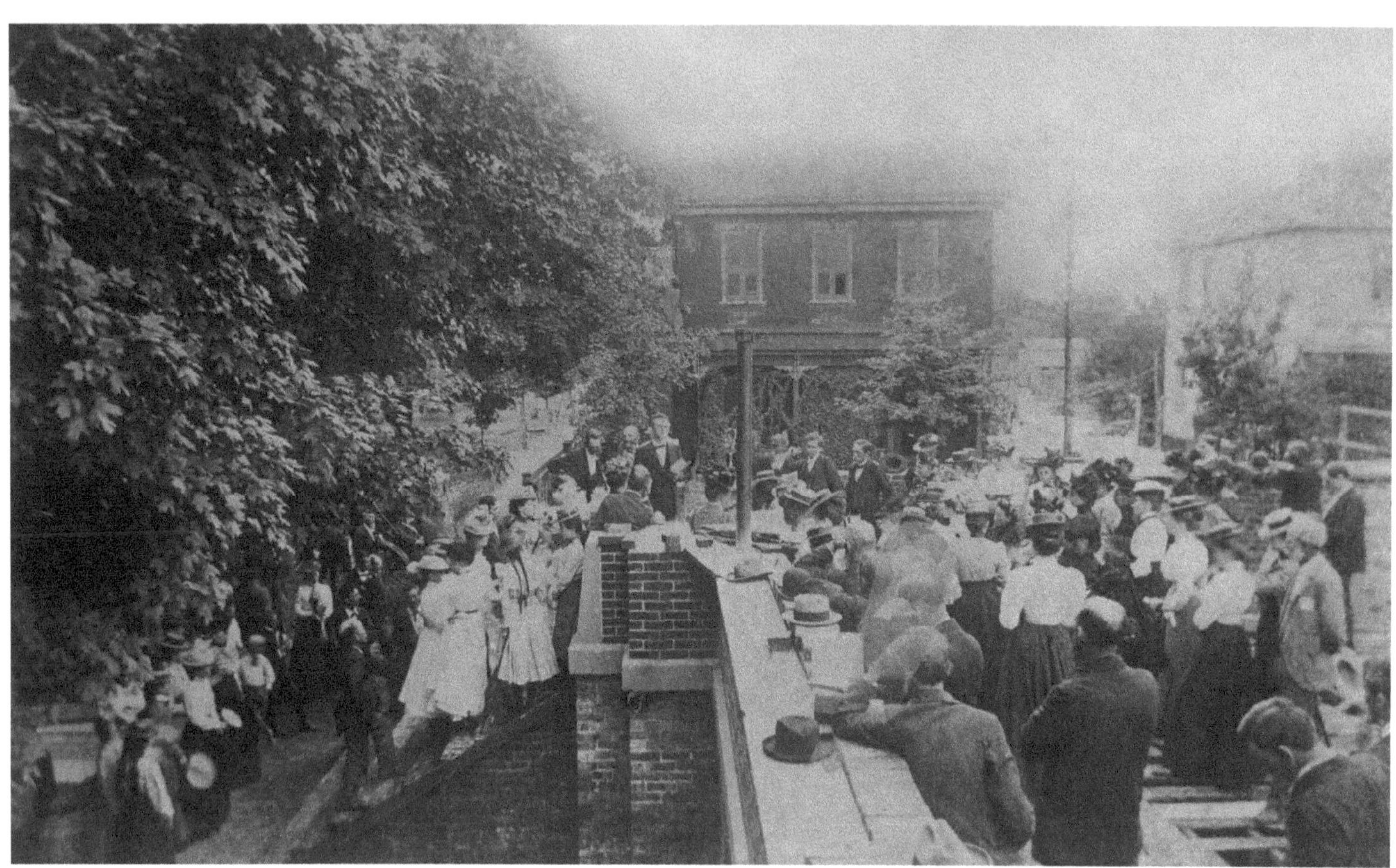

Many people will remember shopping at the dry goods store on the corner of Clinton Avenue and Washington Street. The business was known by several names before it became Dunnavant's. The building was gutted by fire in 1941 but was soon rebuilt.

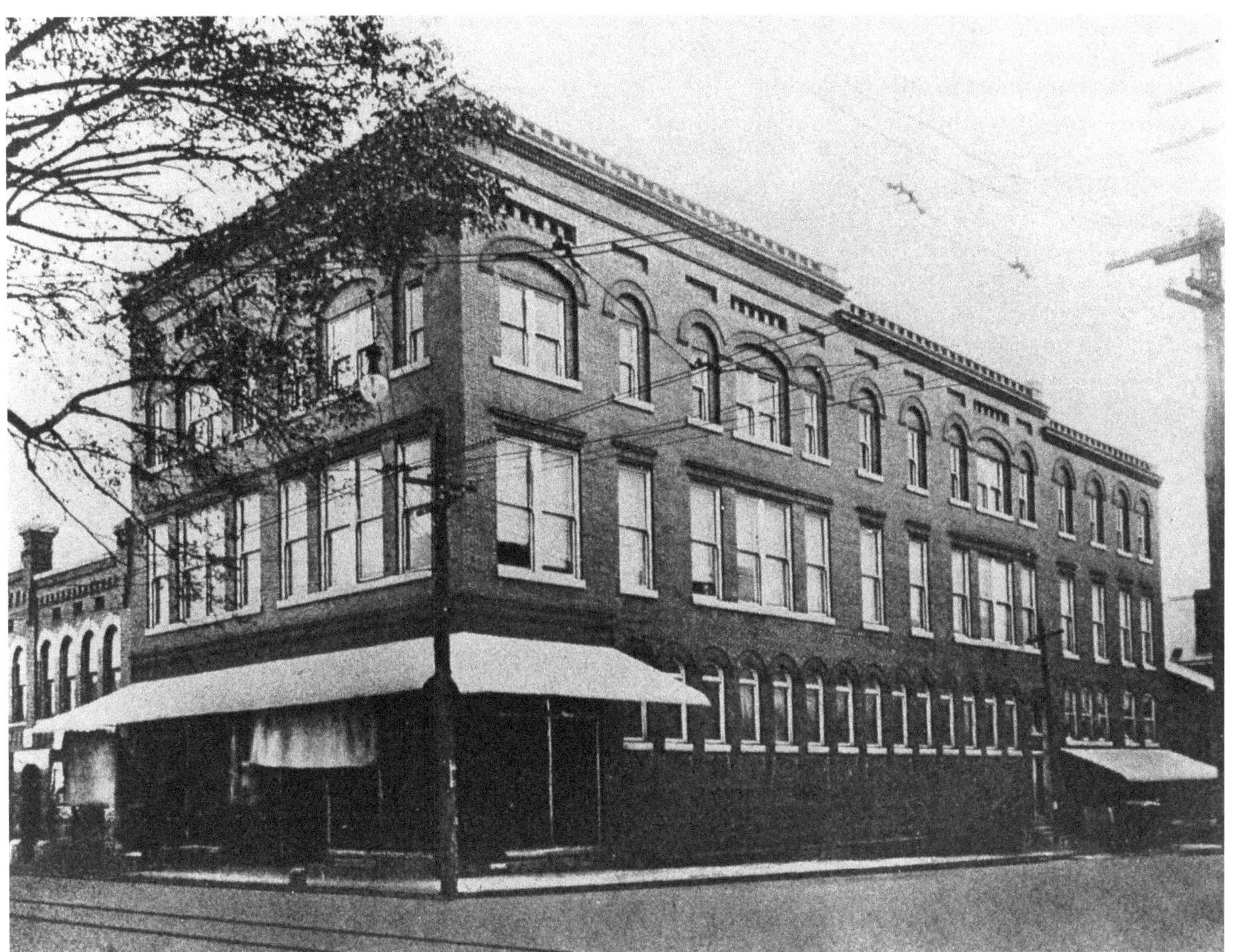

These distinguished gentlemen are members of the Oddfellows organization.

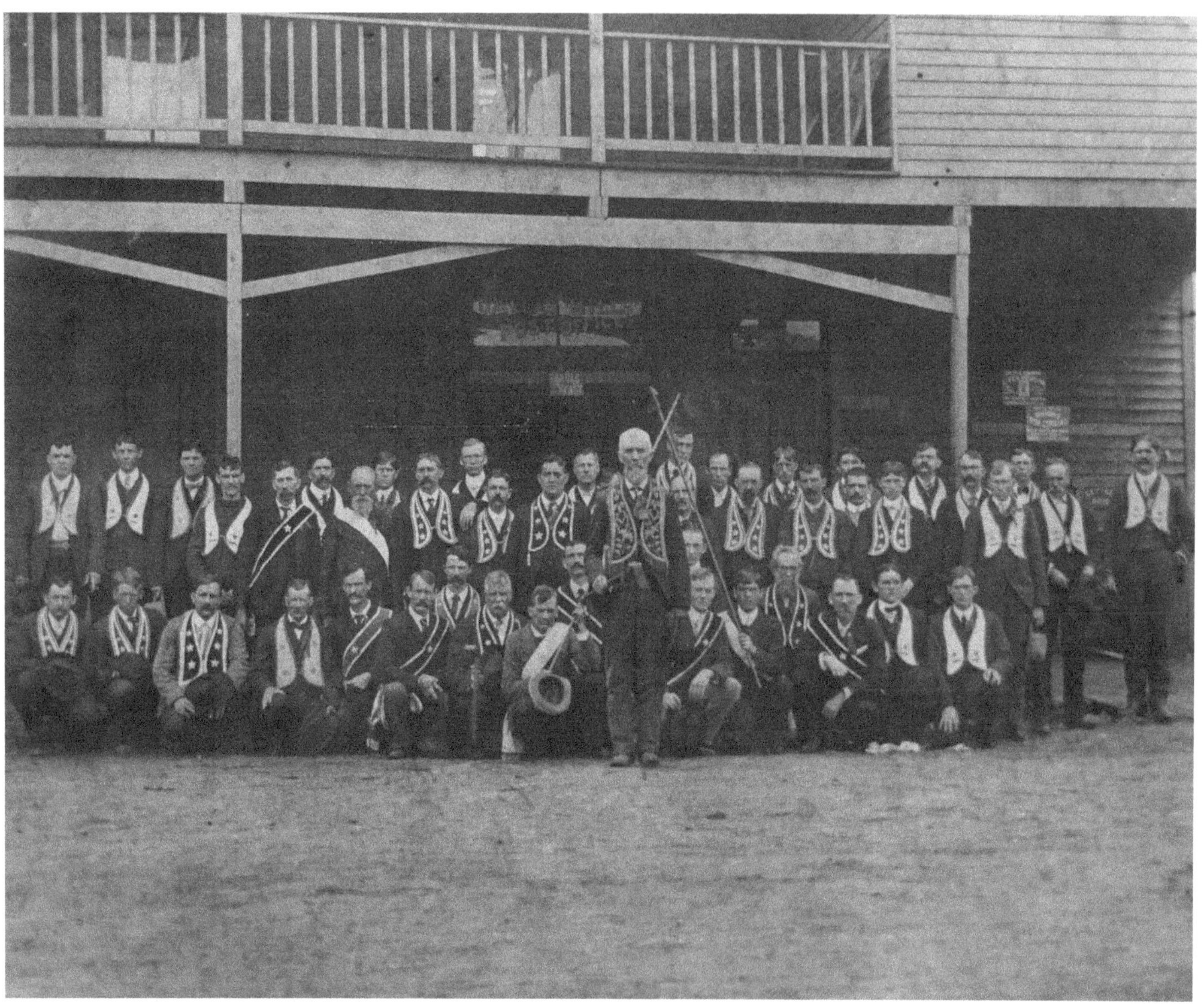

The dedication of a Confederate monument to honor the many young men from Huntsville who fought for the South during the Civil War was a well-attended event in November, 1905.

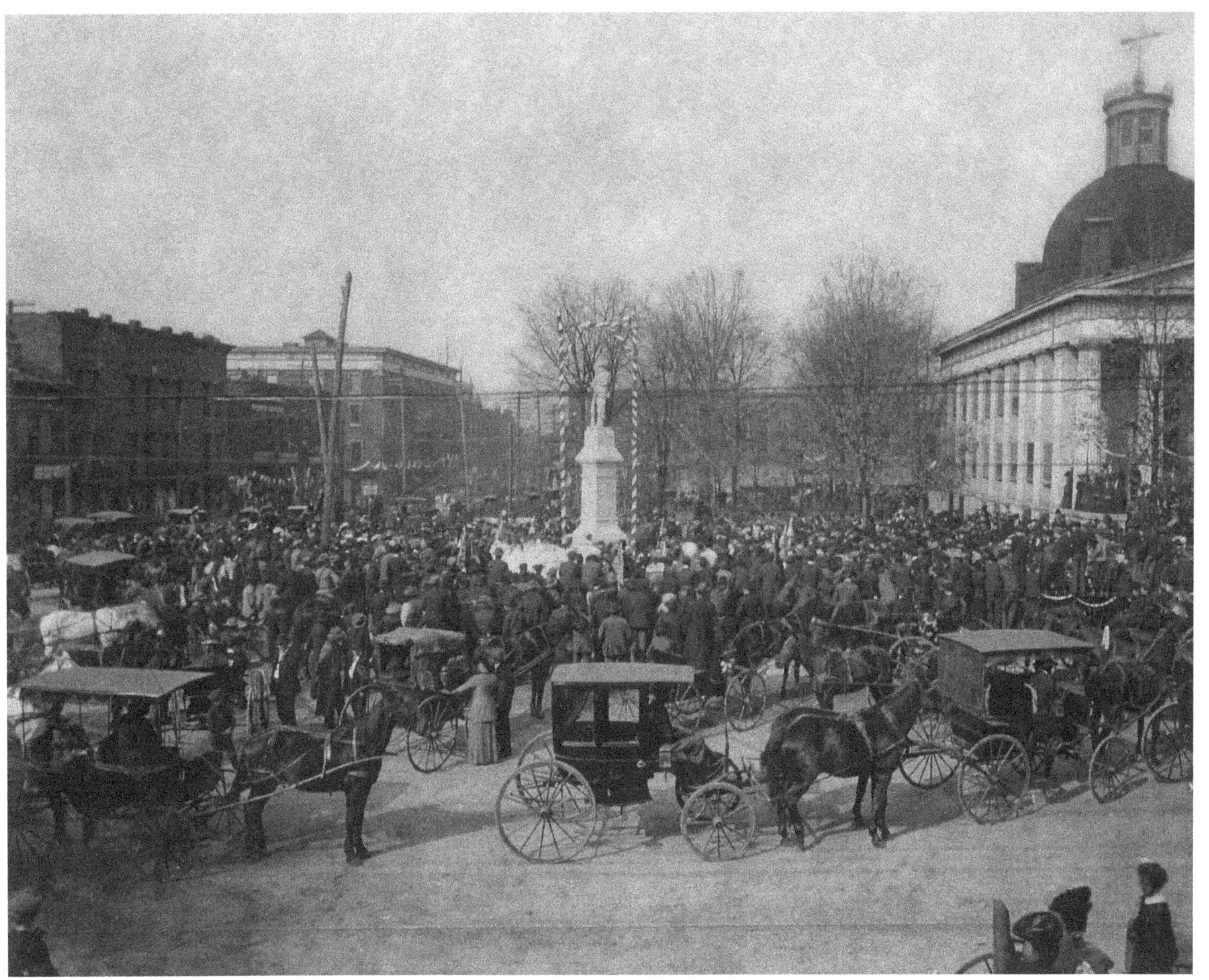

Deserted streets with South Side Square on the right and the third courthouse on the left. The Confederate monument stands high above the brick streets, crisscrossed with streetcar tracks.

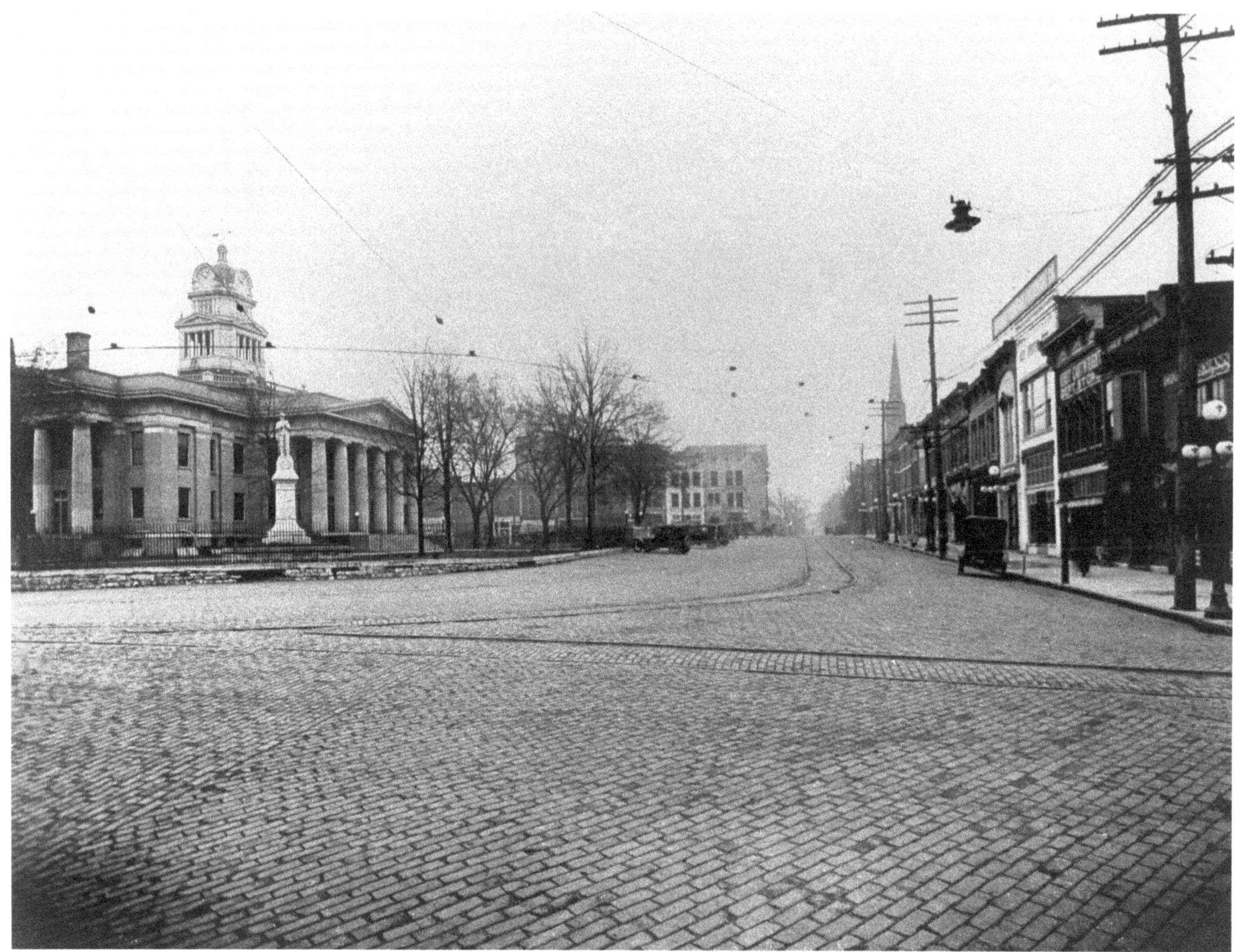

West Side Square, also known as Cotton Row, was busy during the cotton season. The bank known as "The Marble Palace" is seen at the far right and the monument to Confederate soldiers is at the left.

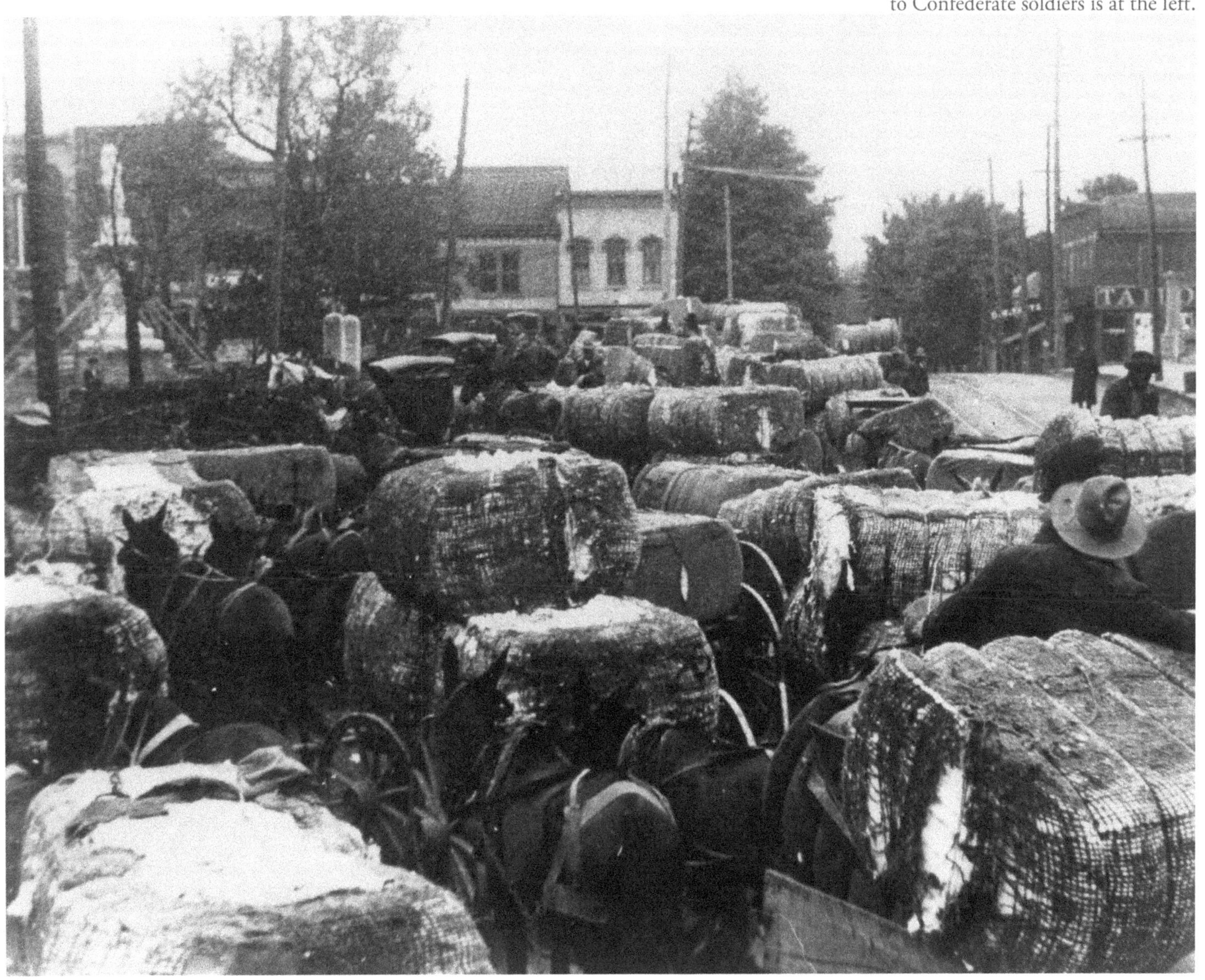

Merrimack Baseball Team
This photograph of the Merrimack Mills baseball team was taken about 1906. Joe Bradley, Sr., is standing at right and Superintendent Gordon Cobb stands to the left.

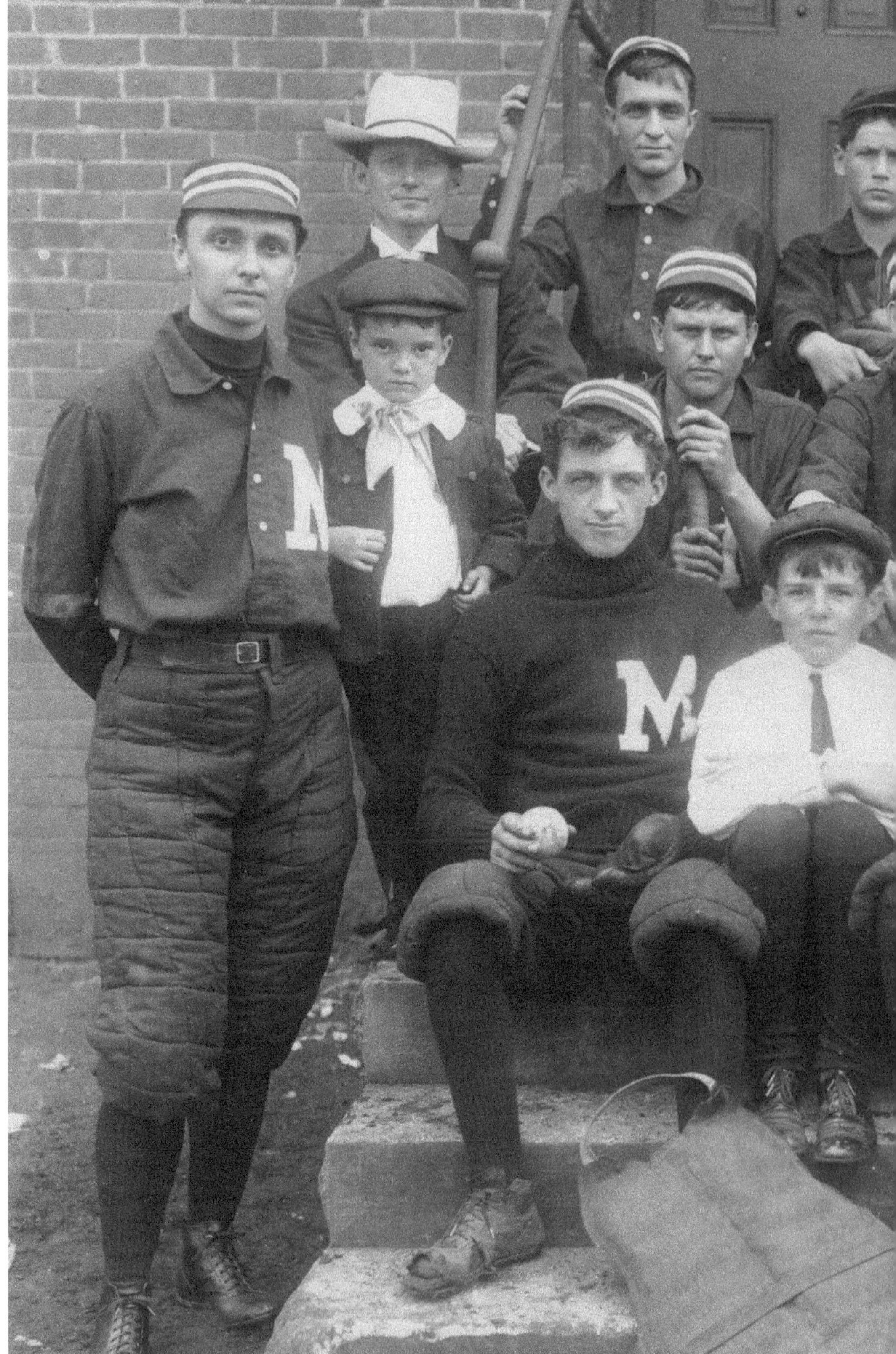

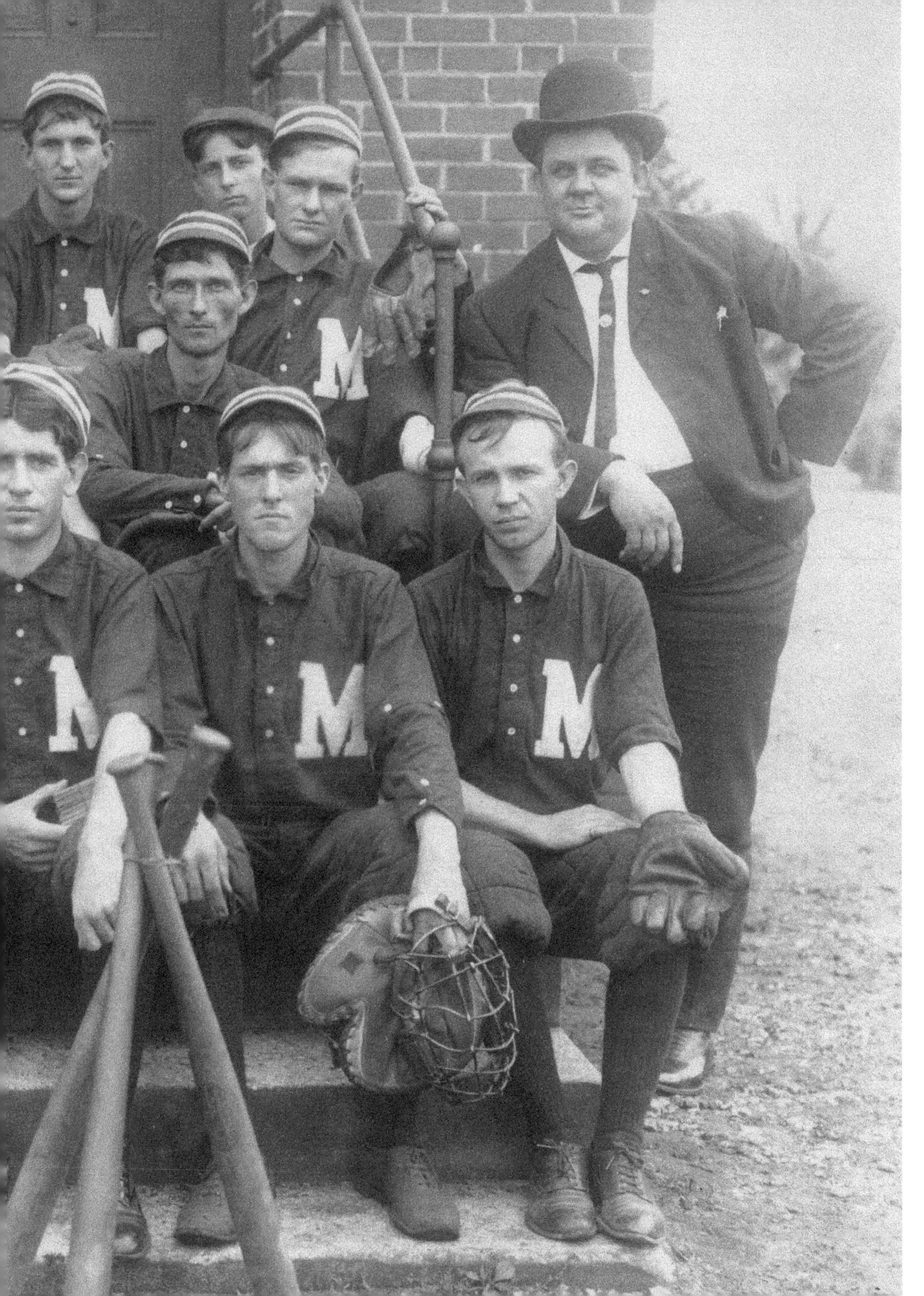
M
M
M
M
M

The Huntsville Hotel, built in 1858, burned to the ground in 1911 along with the annex, the opera house, and several businesses. This site, now occupied by a bank, is located on Jefferson Street near the Courthouse Square.

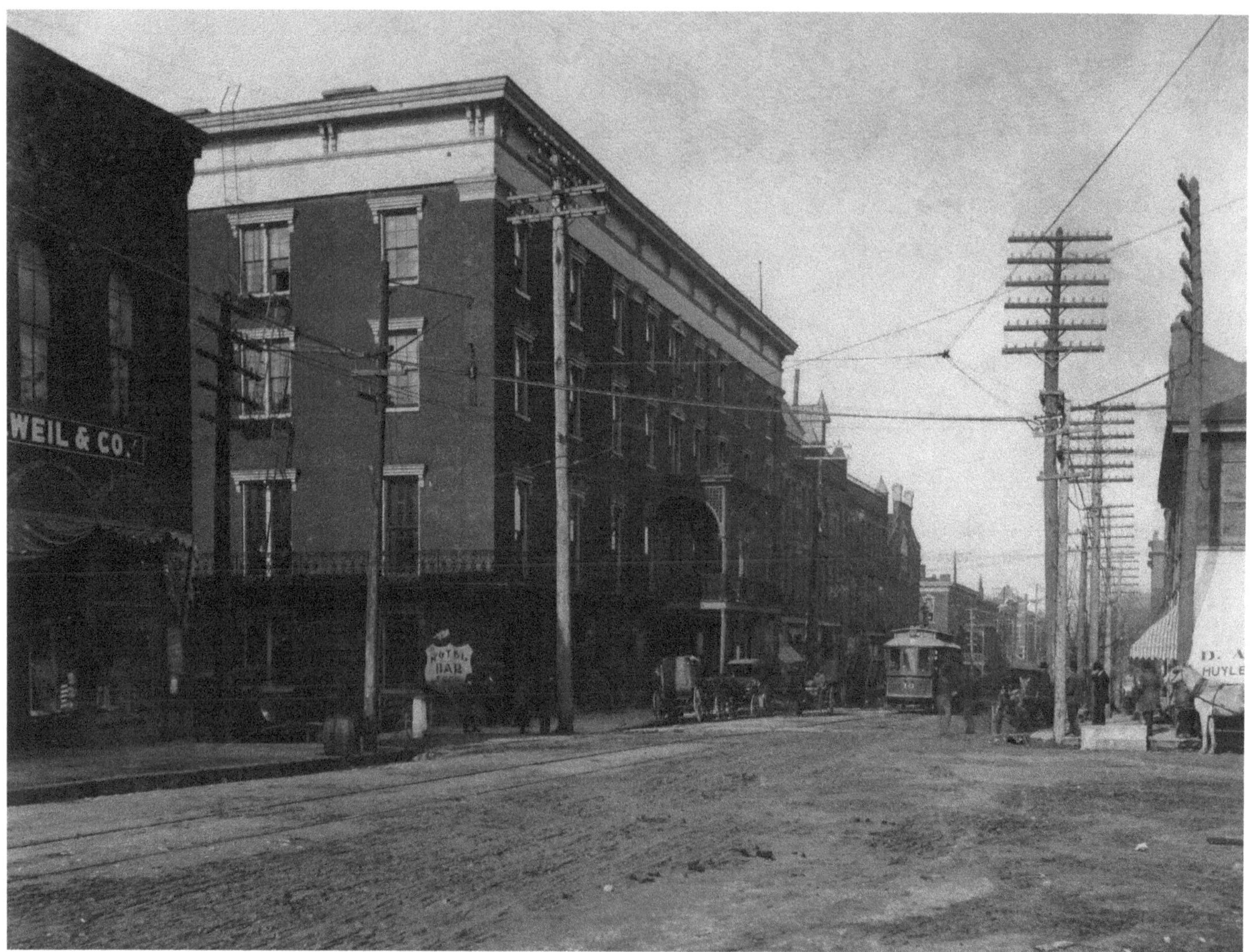

Several men, possibly employees, pose for a photograph inside London Plumbing Company at the corner of Clinton Avenue and Gallatin Street in 1907. Note the claw-foot bathtubs and ornate stove.

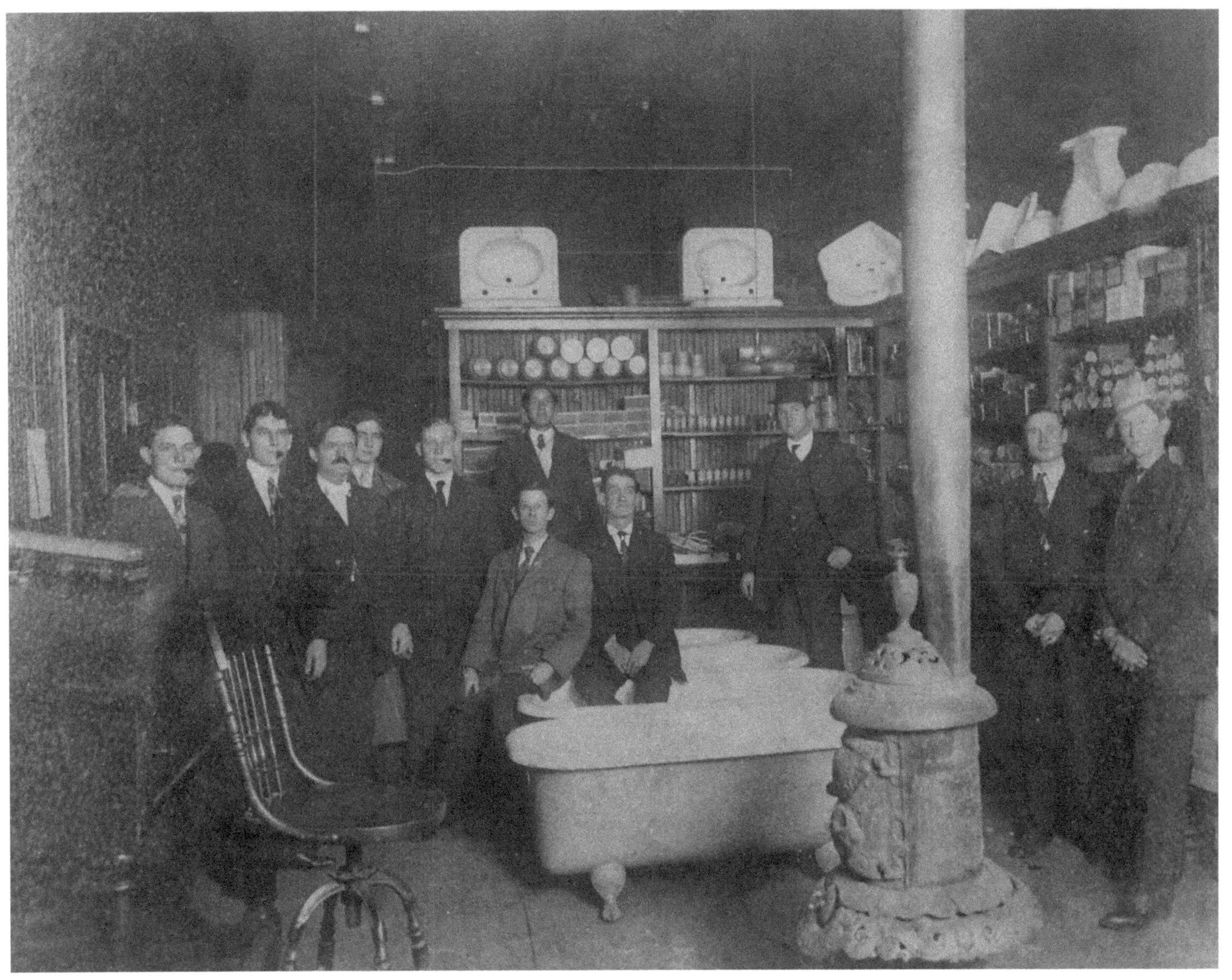

This photograph from around 1908 shows the aftermath of a fire that destroyed a theater on the corner of Clinton Avenue and Jefferson Street. The wrought-iron balcony in the upper-right corner belongs to the McGee Hotel.

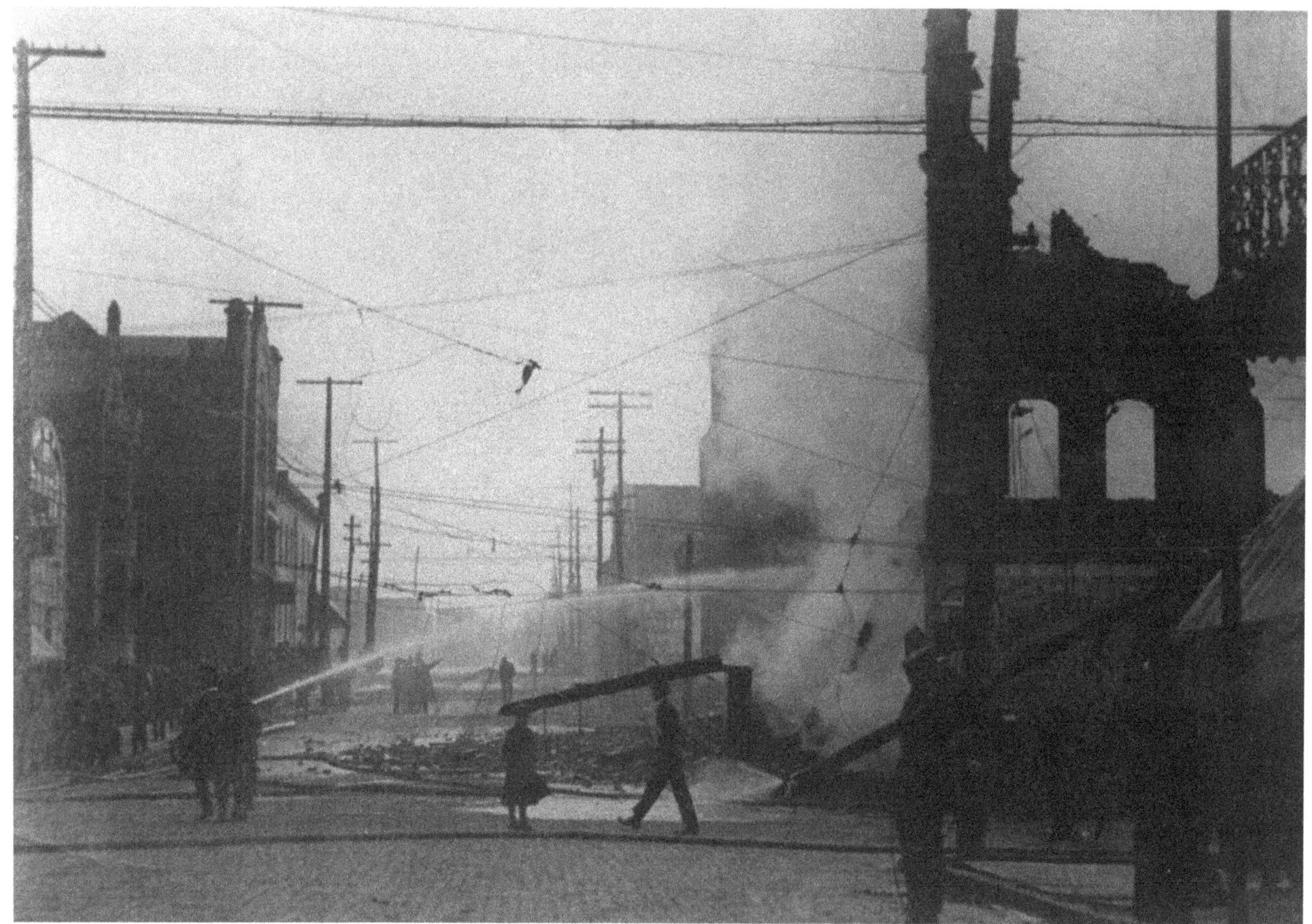

Members of a Baptist Church Sunday School posed for this picture about 1909. Billie Buckner, Merrimack Mill's first gatekeeper, is the man with the long beard at the right.

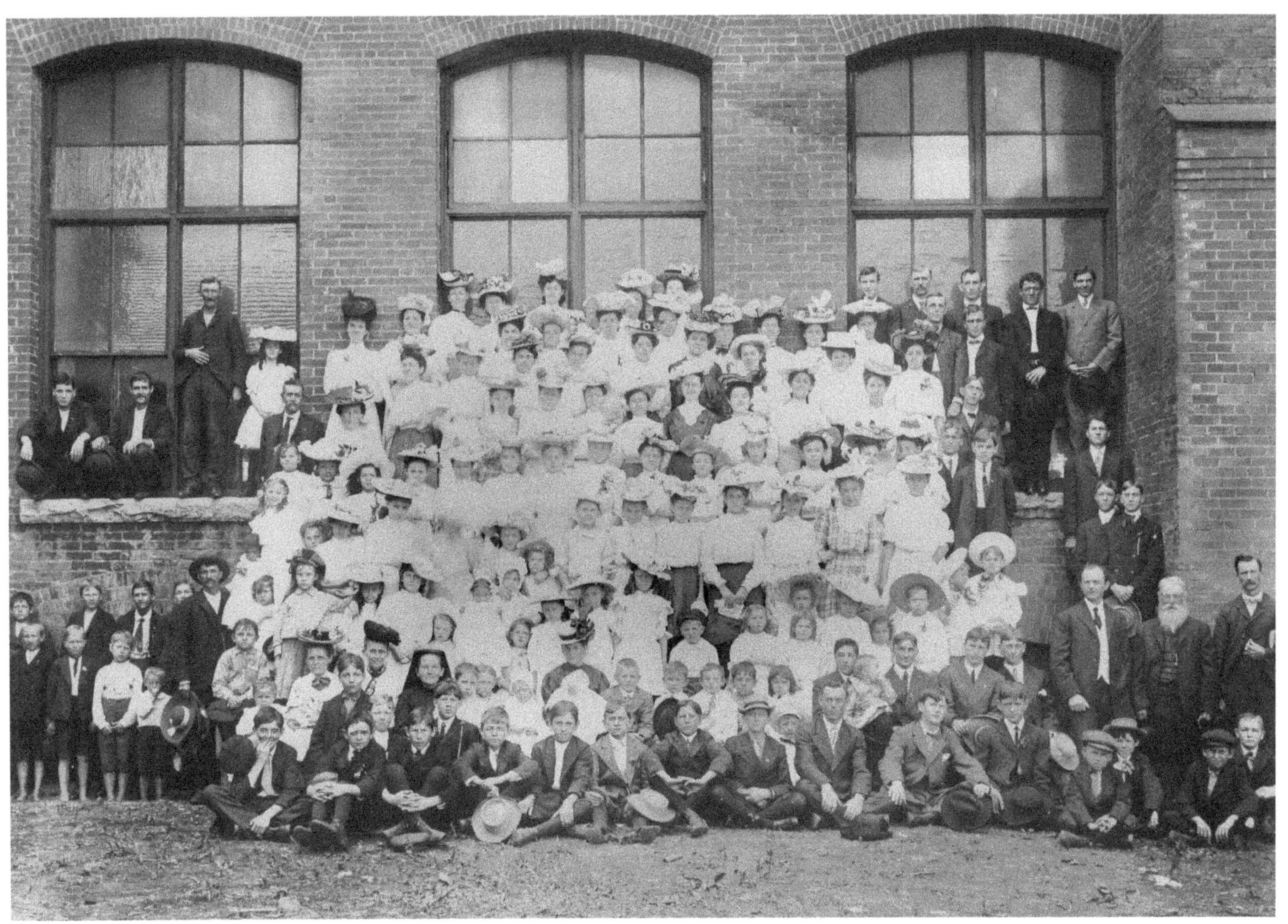

Two men pass the time in front of Porter's Grocery and Cabinet Shop in West Huntsville. Signs and a thermometer promote Royal Crown Cola.

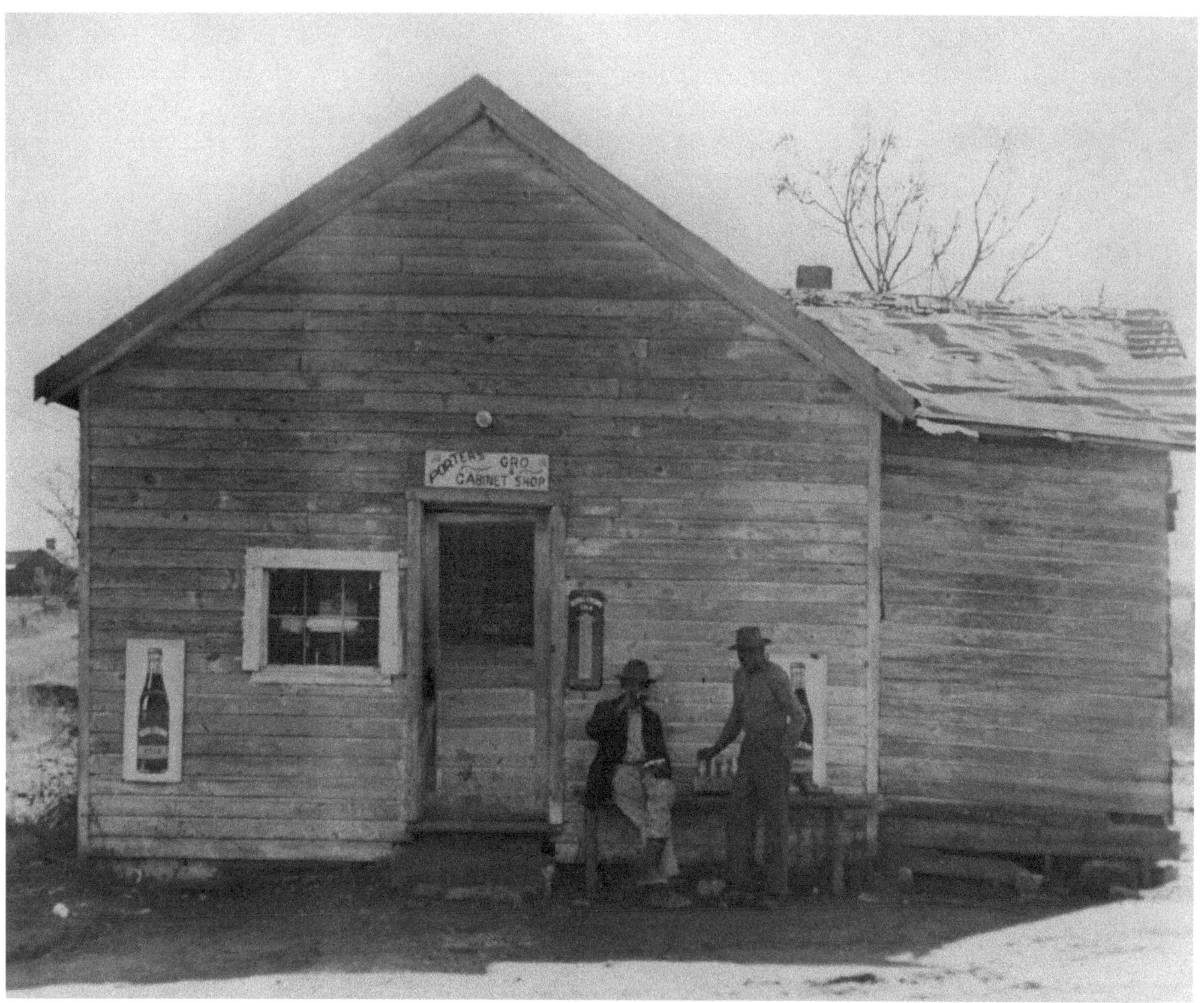

Three people dressed for an outing pose on their horses. Note the curious look on the horse at left.

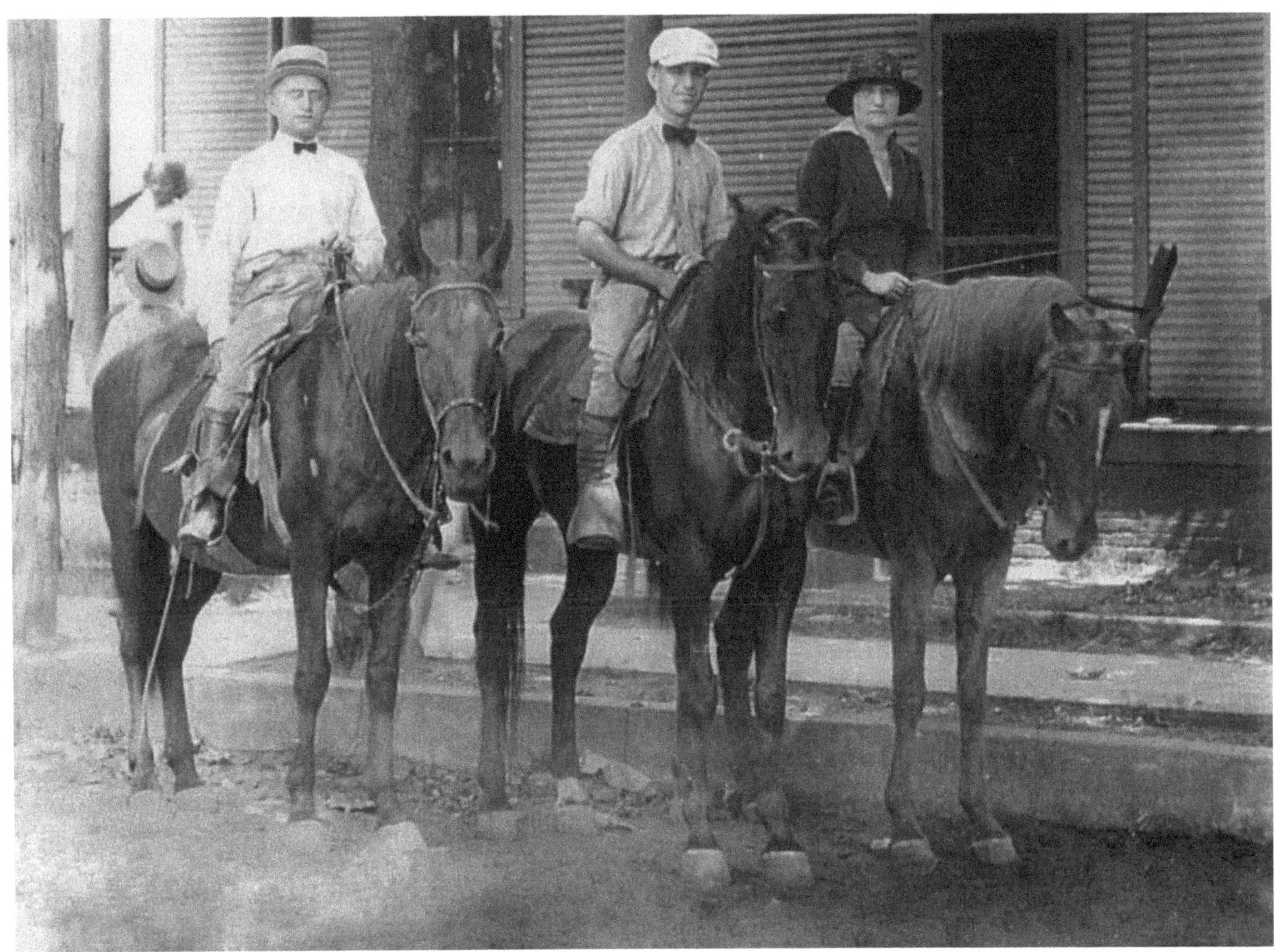

Mr. and Mrs. Wallace Oakes and their son Will stand in front of their grocery store, aptly called The Little Store, near the Big Spring. Wallace and Will are now buried in the Hough Cemetery in Lacey's Spring.

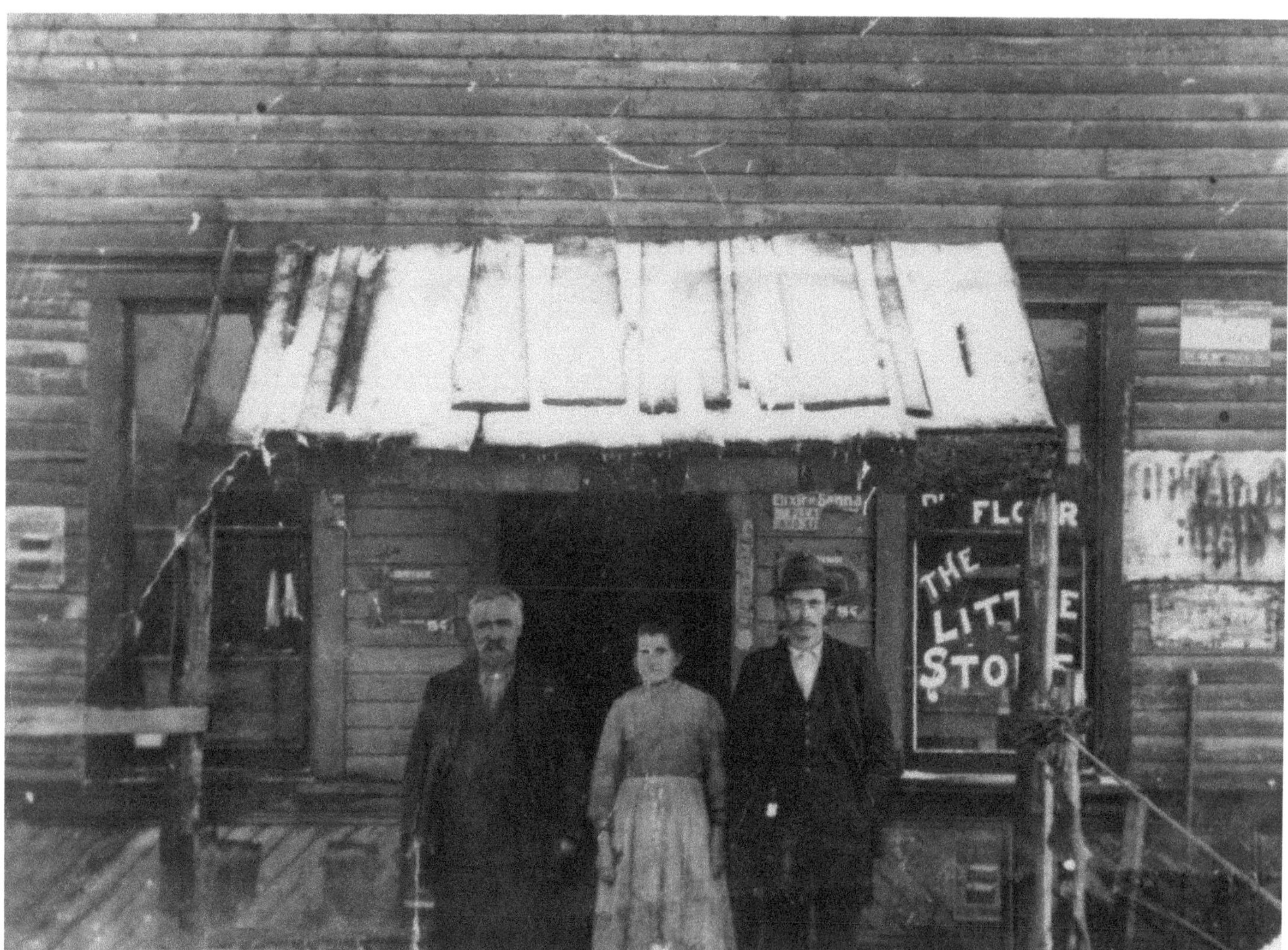

R. L. Sparkman, proprietor of Sparkman Marble and Granite, poses with his son Robert and wife Lillie. This new location, on Wells Street adjacent to Maple Hill Cemetery, was a wise move. Note the angel in the window; it now presides over a grave in the cemetery. Sparkman Marble is still in business today.

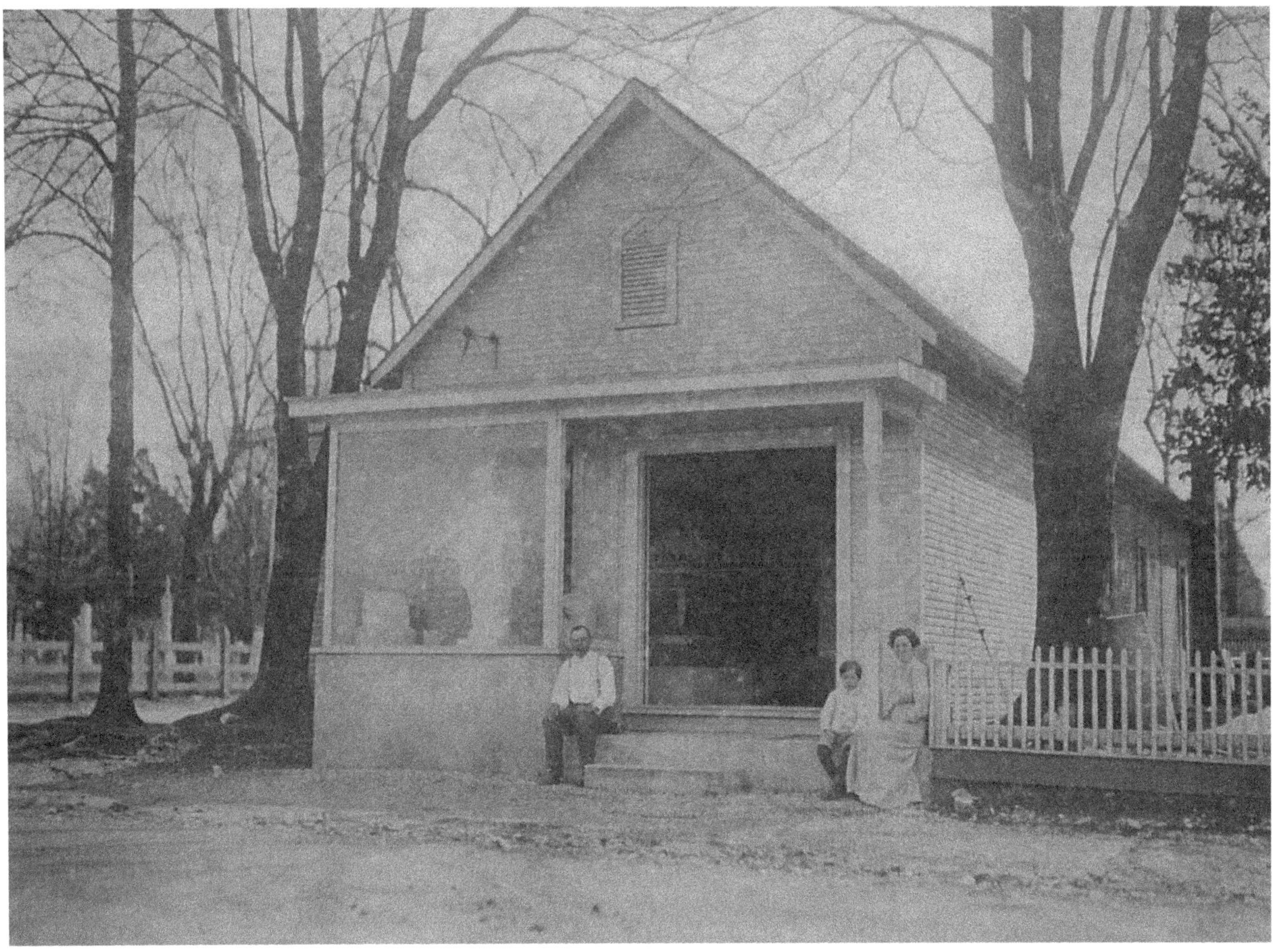

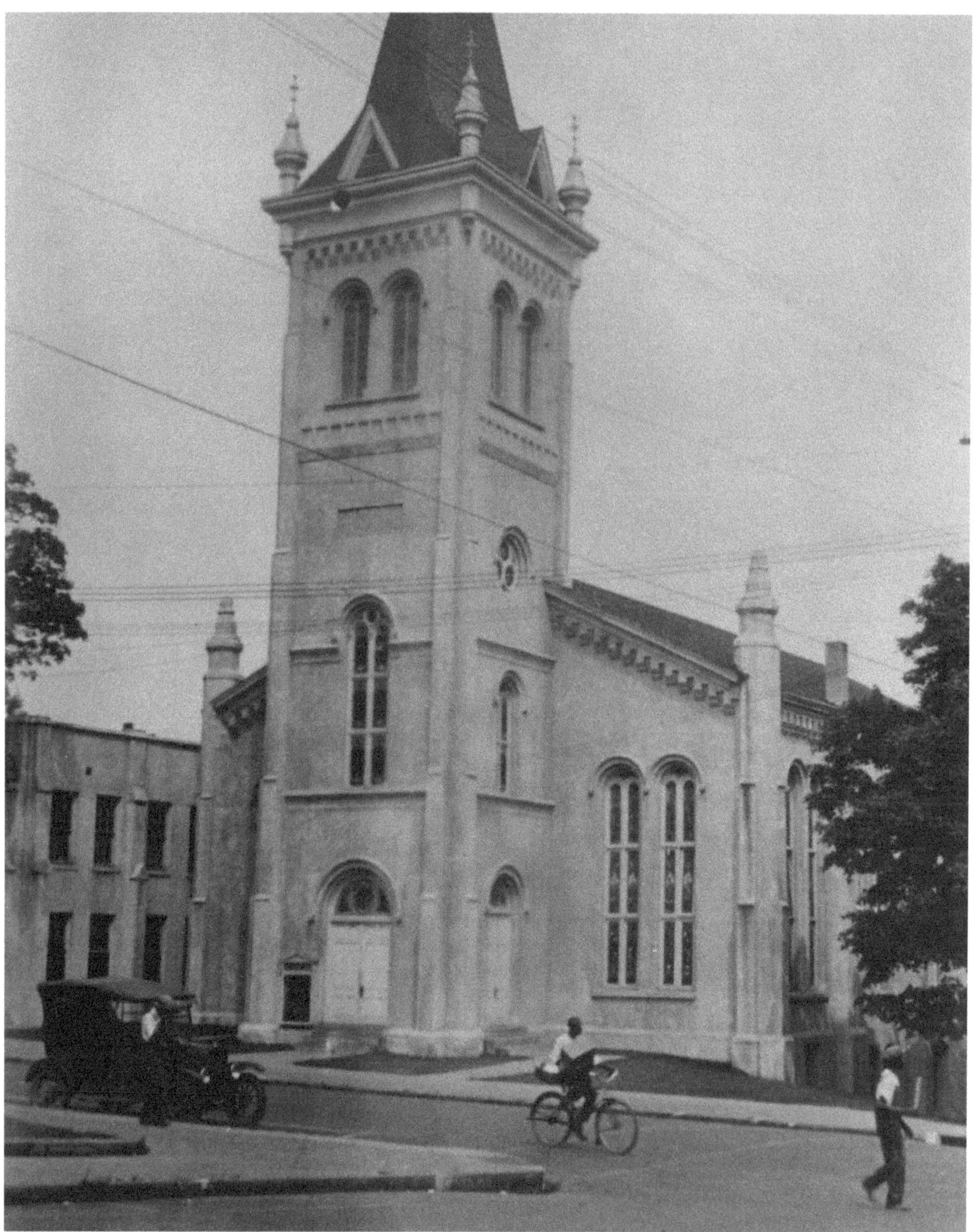

The First Methodist Church was the second building constructed on this site, after Union troops accidentally burned the first building in 1864. Located on Greene and Randolph streets and completed in 1874, it is quite beautiful inside.

Elephants parade around the square to announce the circus is in town. This picture was taken about 1913. The arrival of the circus was a much-anticipated event.

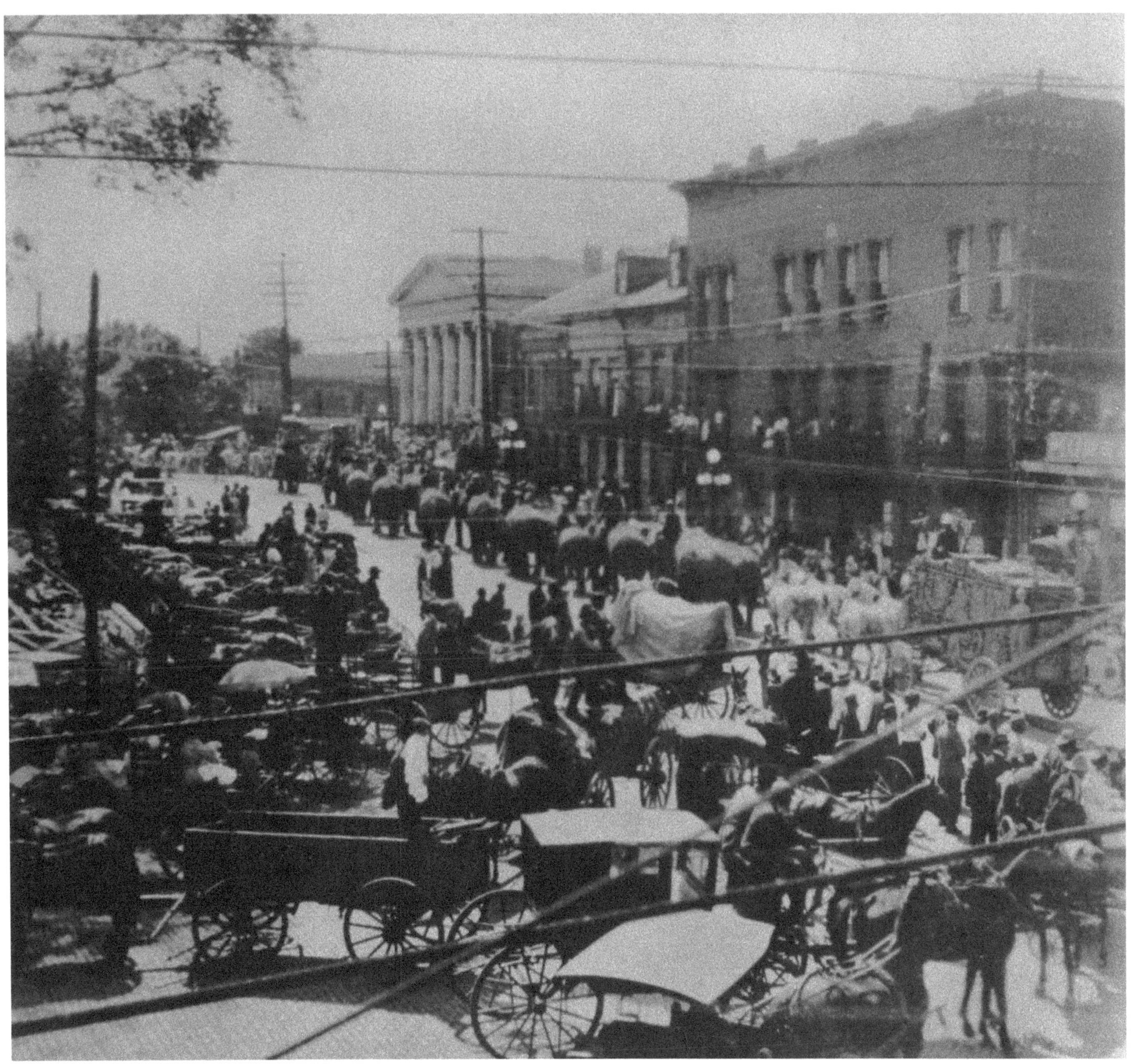

Crowds line the street to get a closer look at circus elephants as they parade through town.

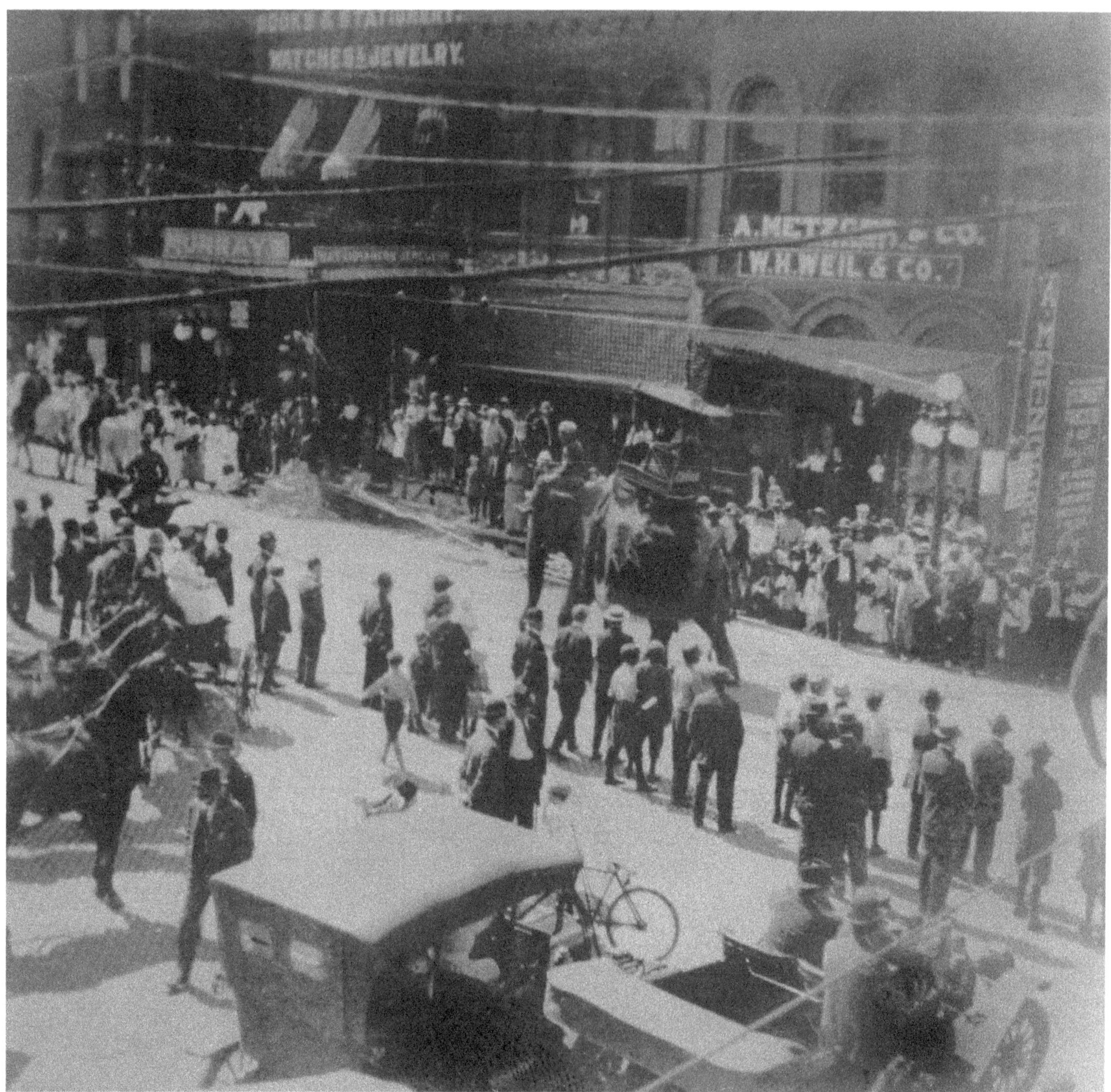

Members of the junior class at Huntsville High School dressed in their best clothes for this 1914 picture.

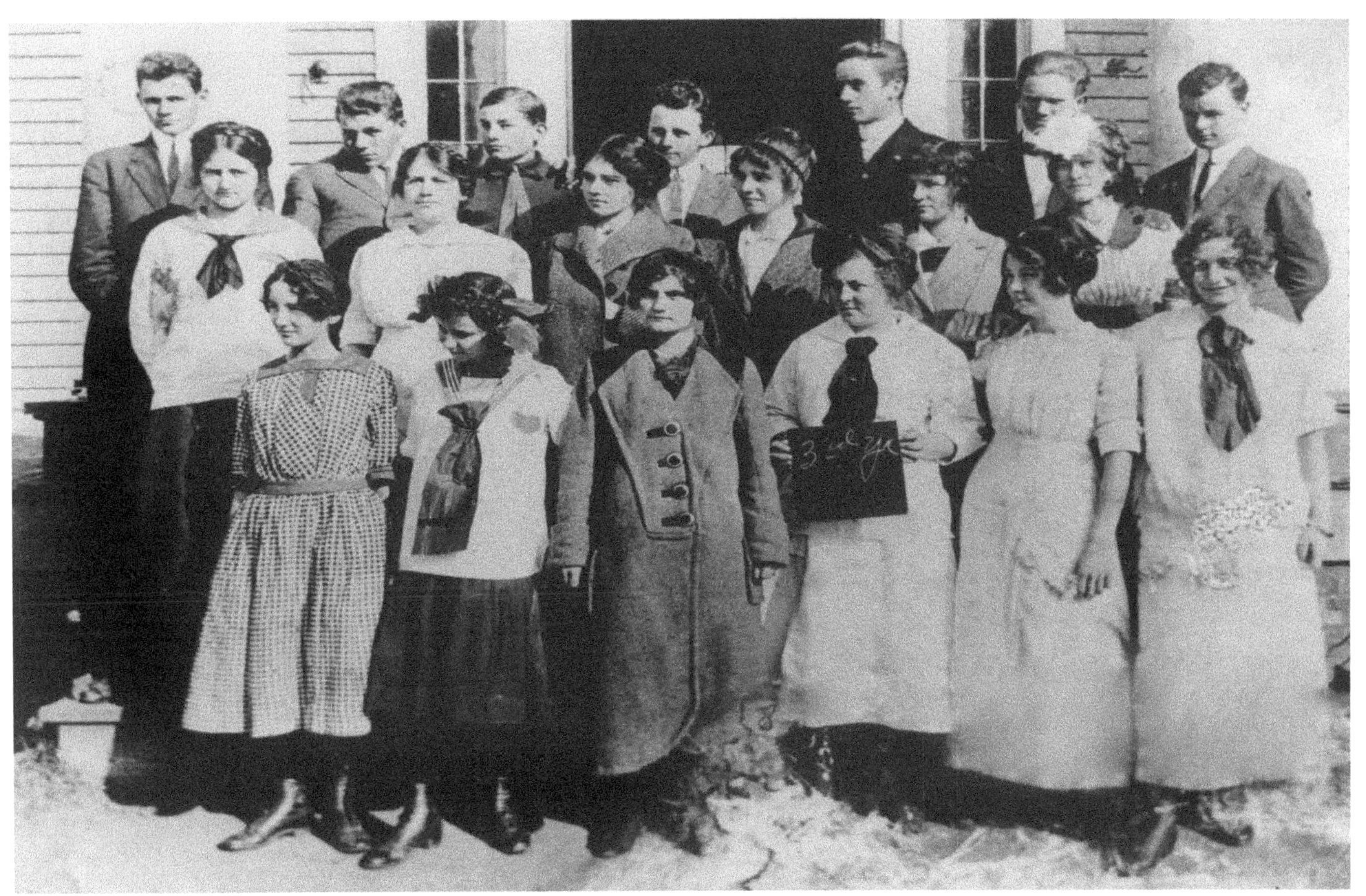

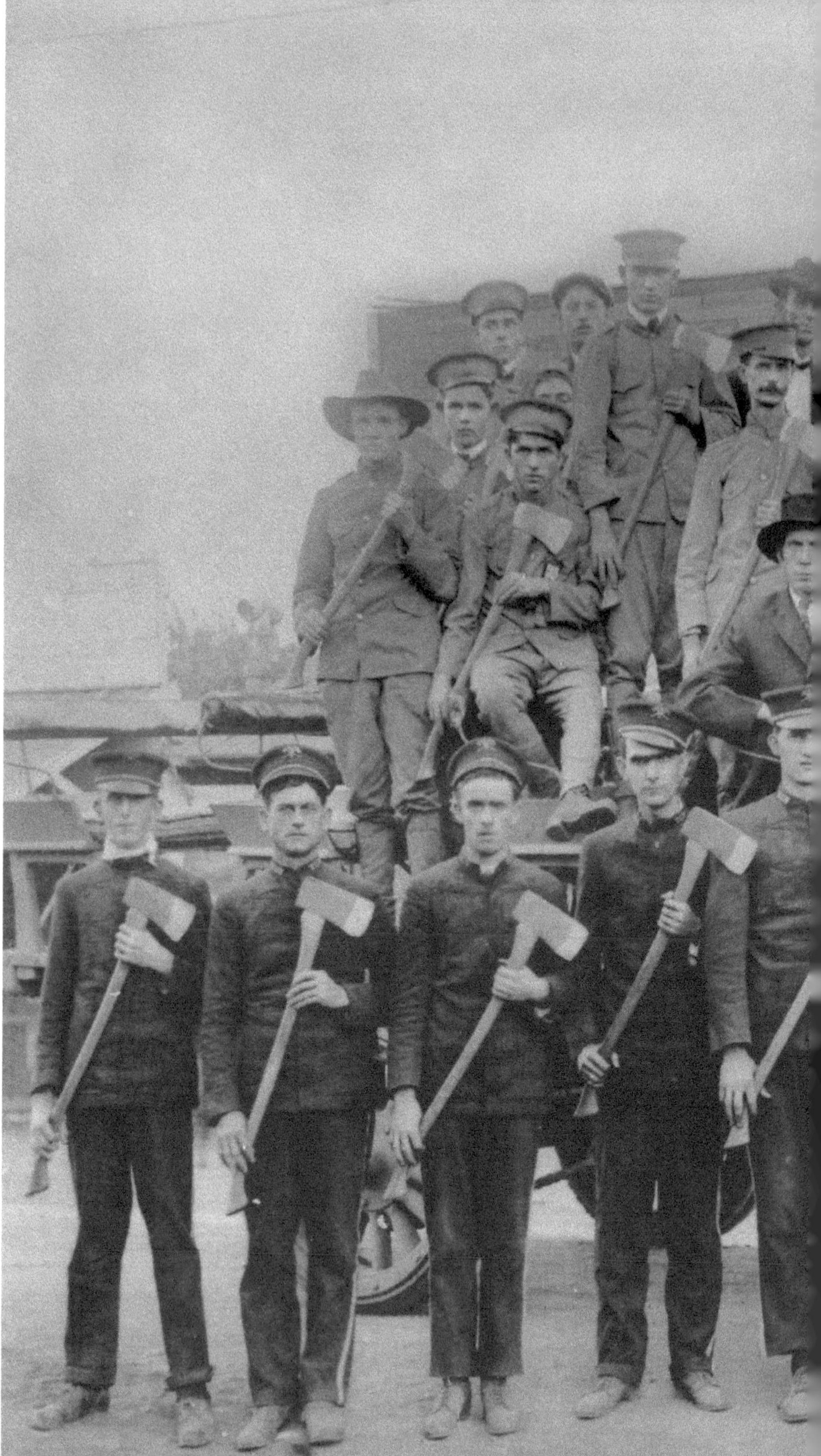

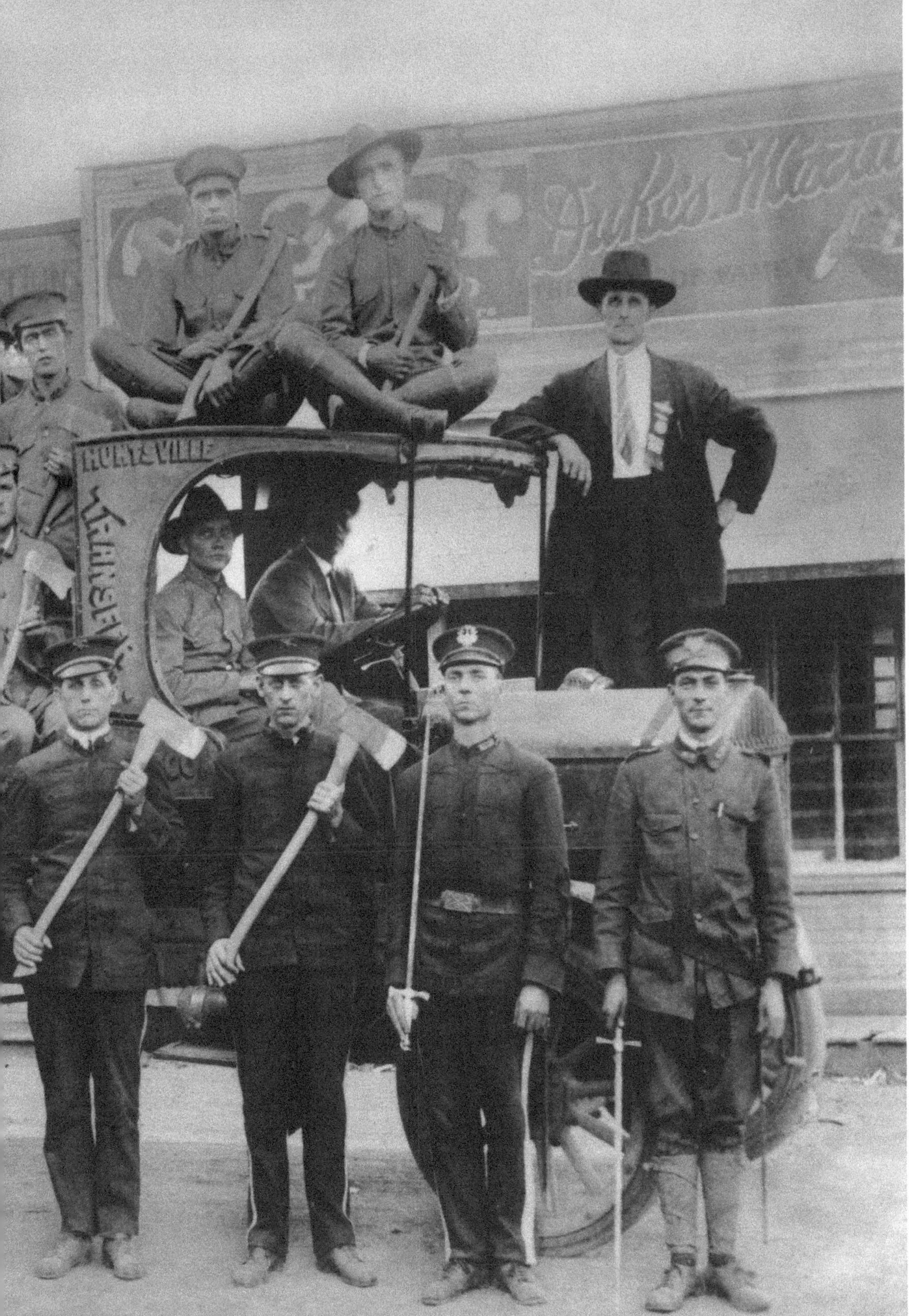

The axes and emblems suggest these men may have been members of Woodmen of the World, founded in 1890 as a benevolent fraternal organization.

Horses were watered at the Big Spring, a common sight at the time this was taken in about 1915.

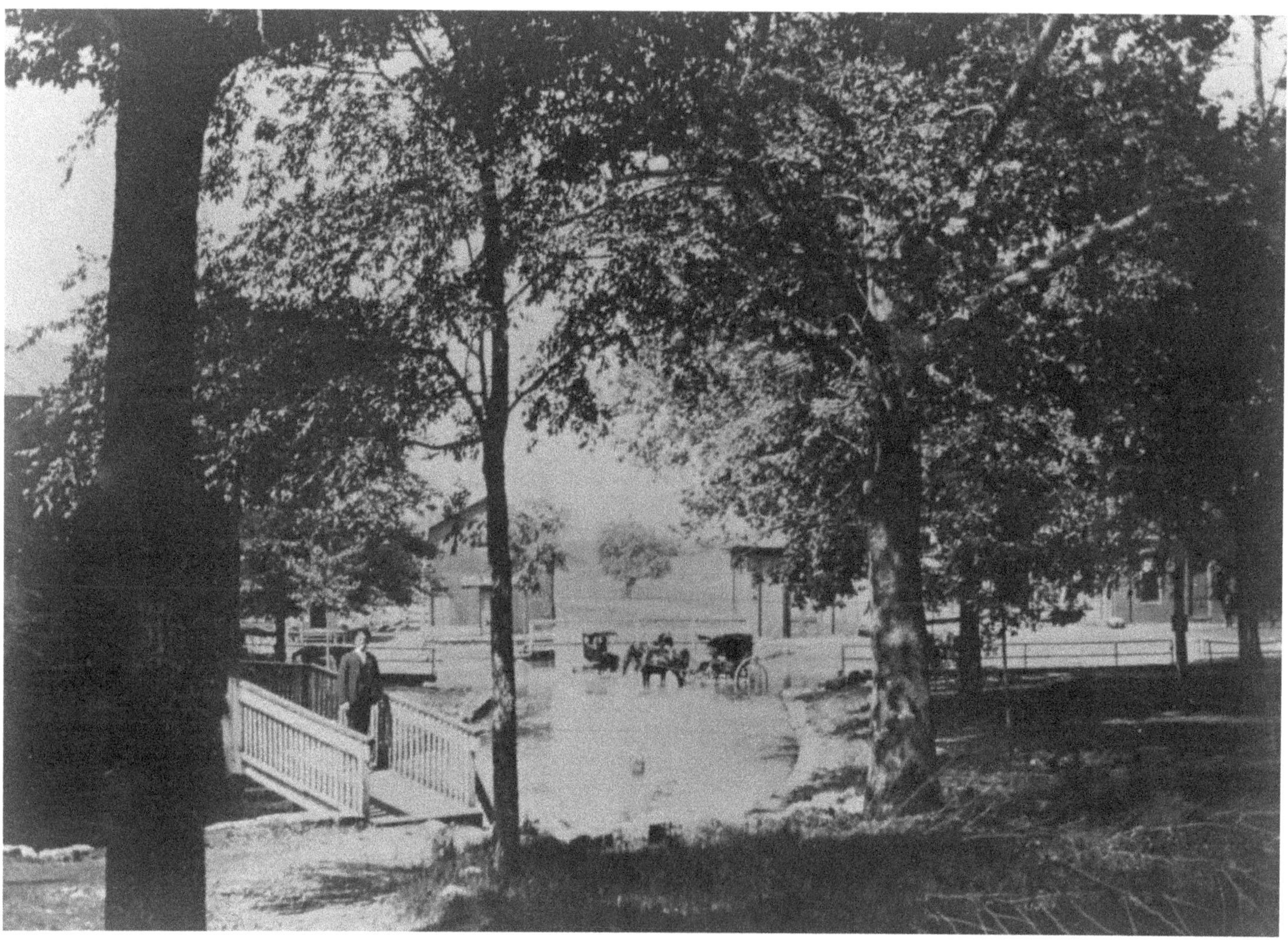

A streetcar ambles past a horse-drawn buggy on Clinton Avenue while Central Café prepares to feed hungry customers.

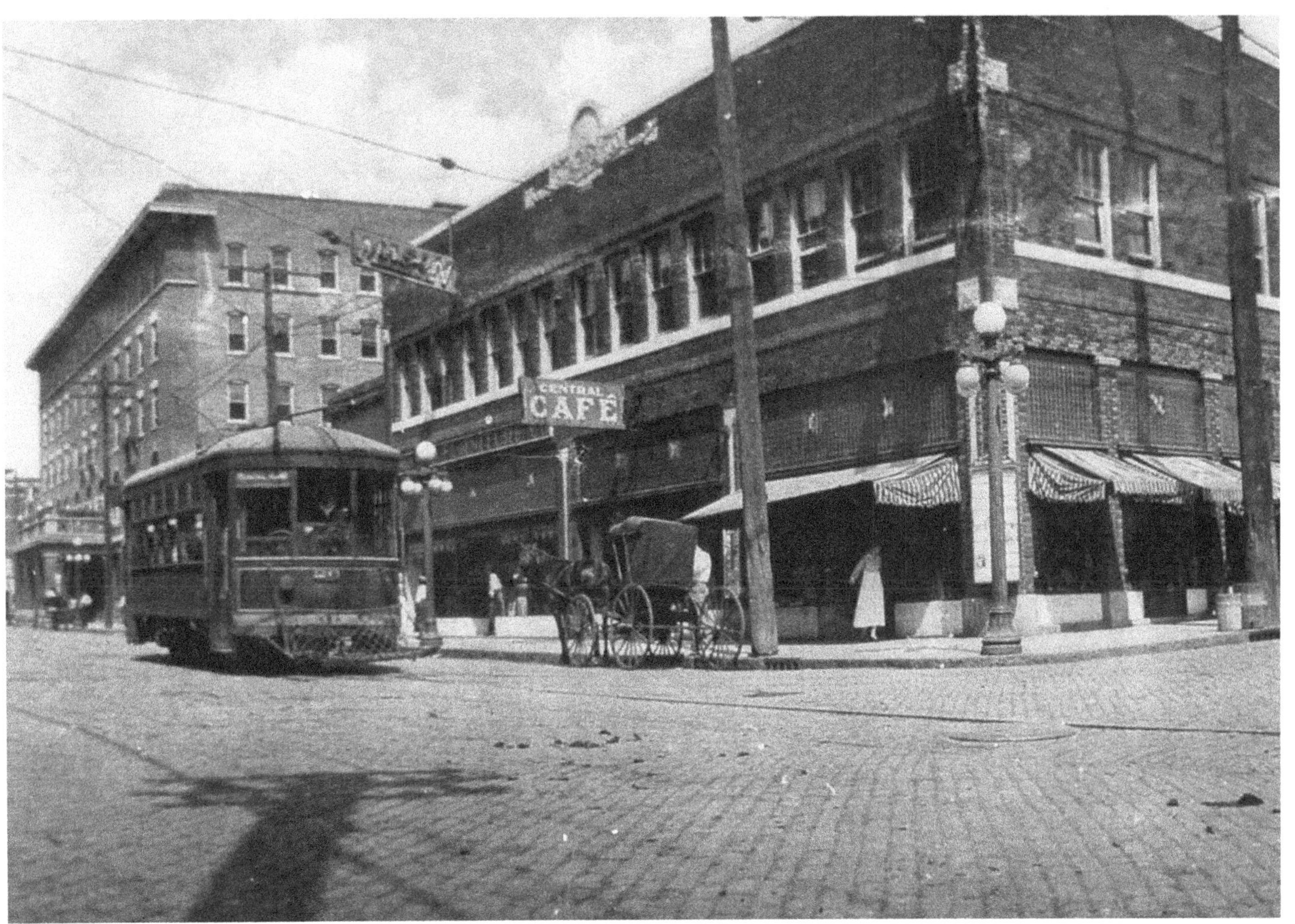

A crowd gathers to listen to a band concert.

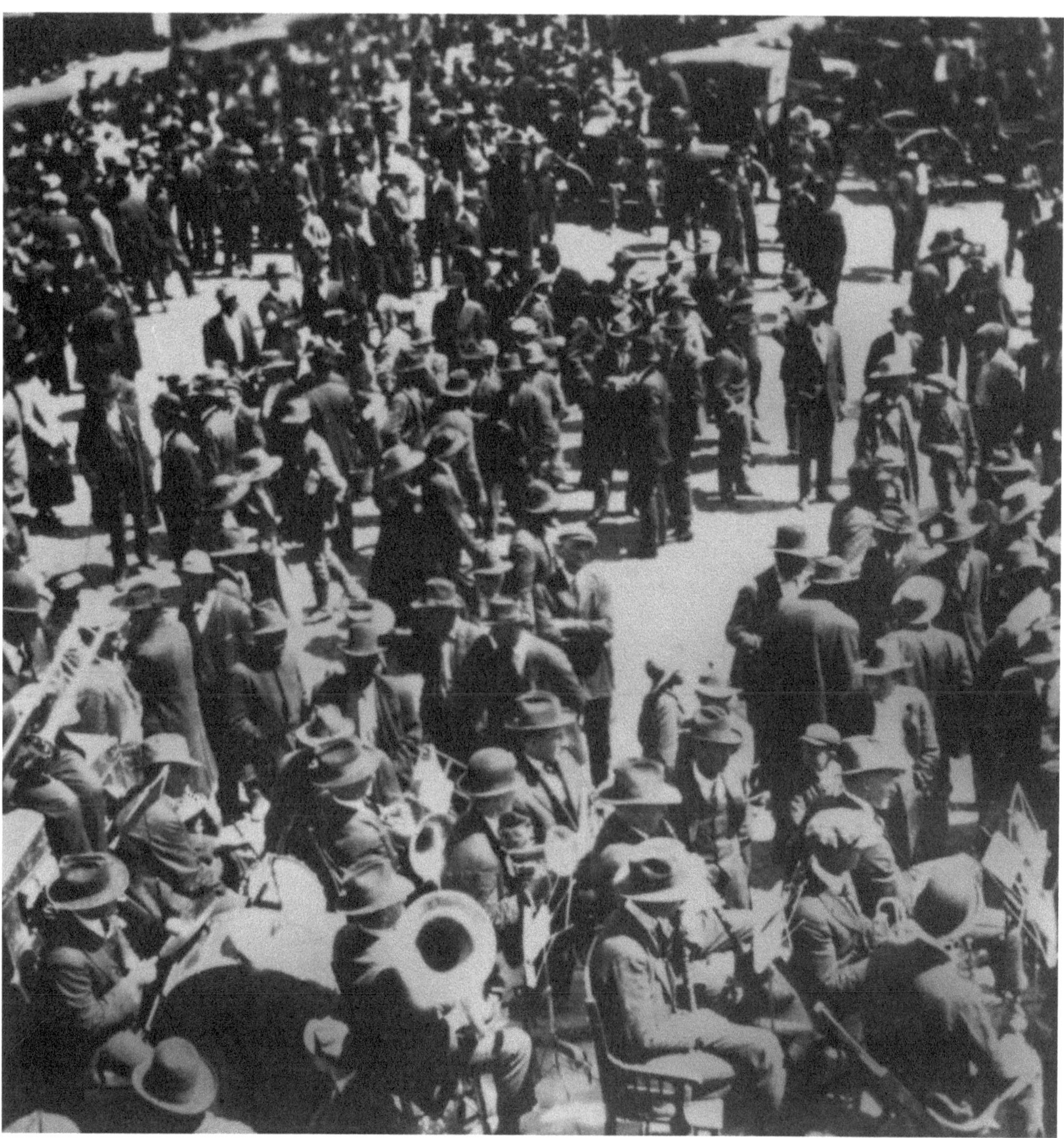

The Cumberland Presbyterian Church, organized and dedicated by pioneer minister Robert Donnell, became the Central Presbyterian Church after a national split in the early 1900s. A newer building now occupies this site.

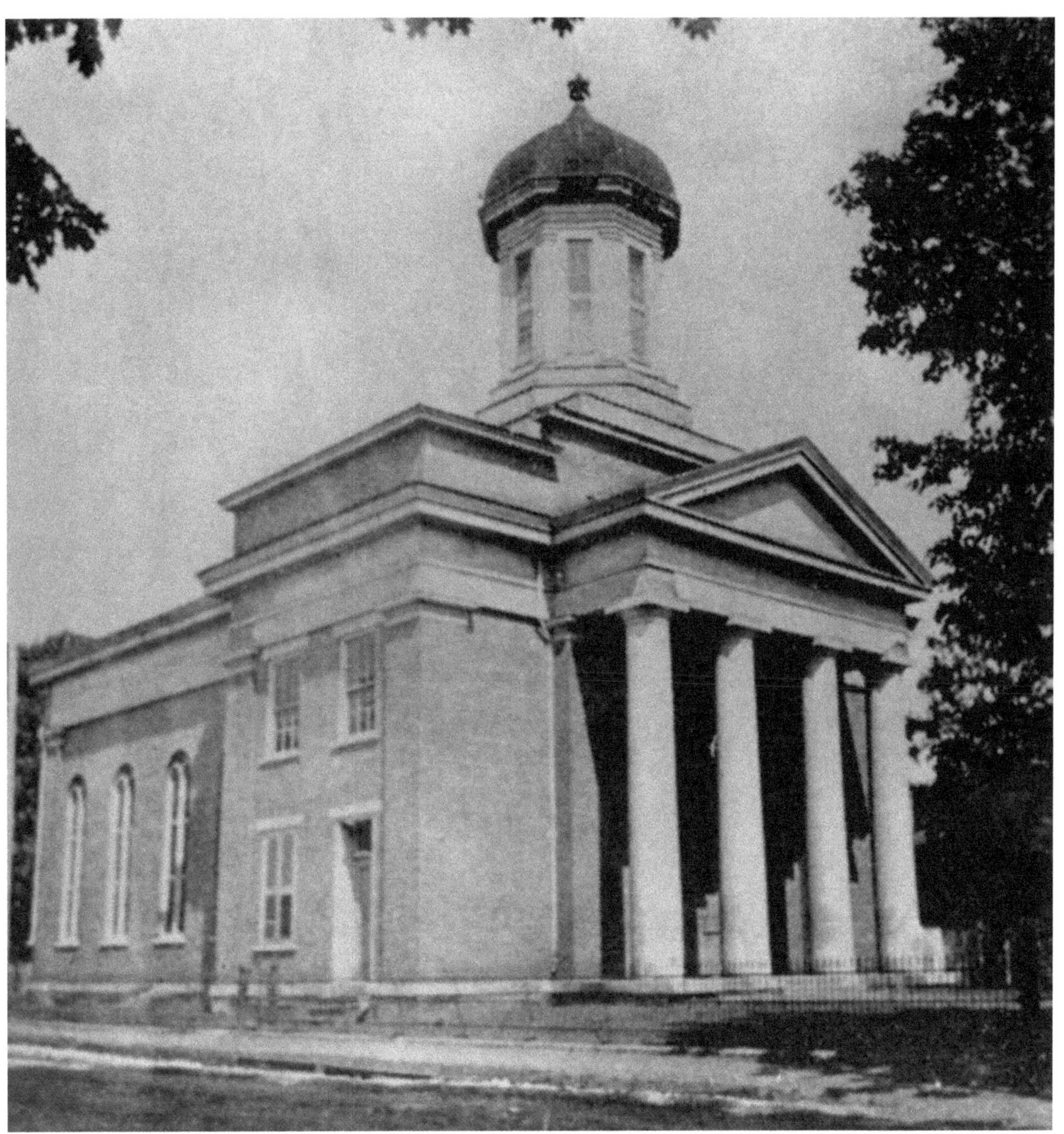

The Benevolent & Protective Order of Elks (BPOE) Lodge Number 698 entered this elaborately decorated car in a local parade. Note their "hood ornament."

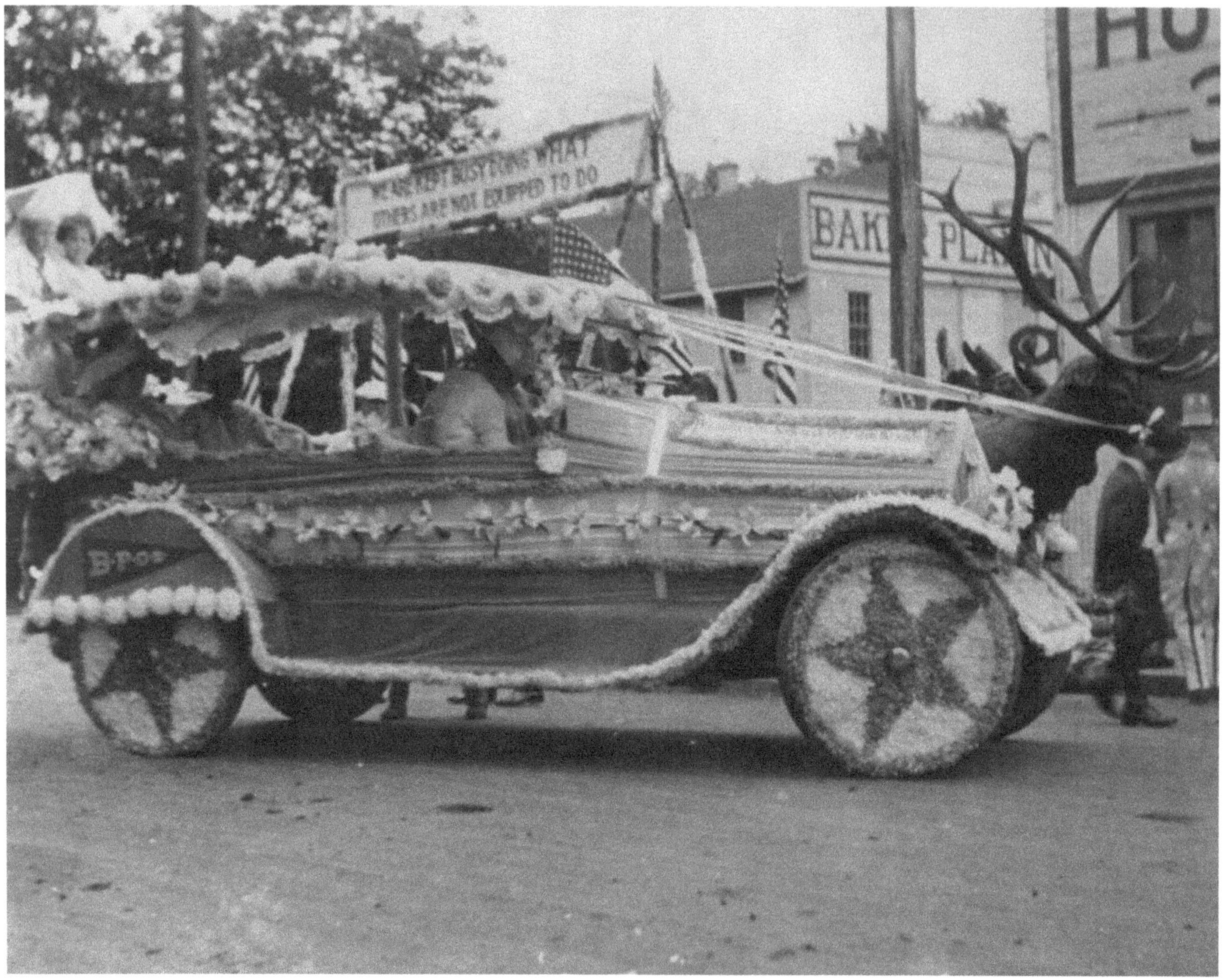

A horse-drawn wagon is up to its axles as it crosses the Big Spring. That all changed when a bridge was built on Gallatin Street.

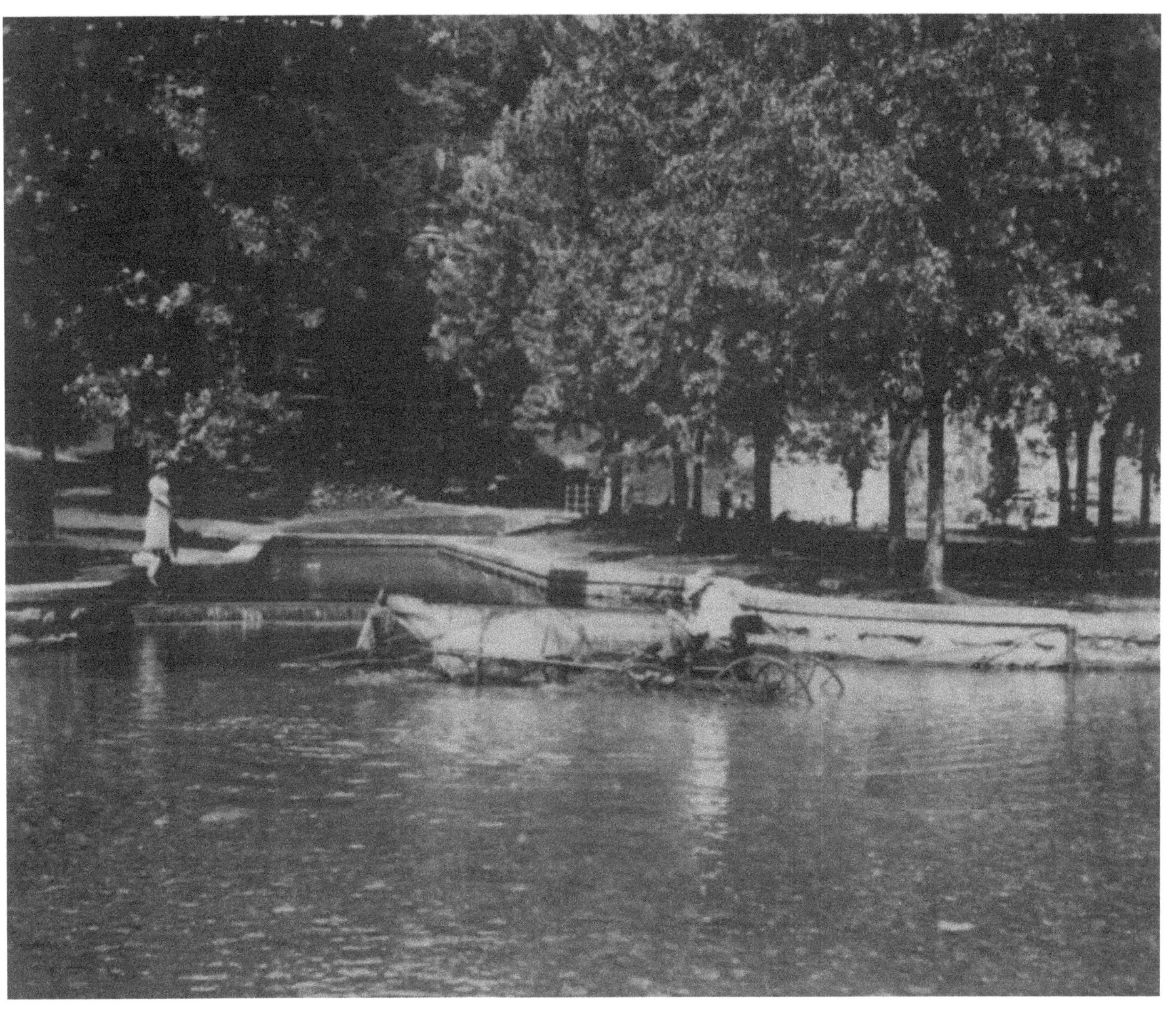

This photograph was taken in the Probate Office of the second Madison County Courthouse.

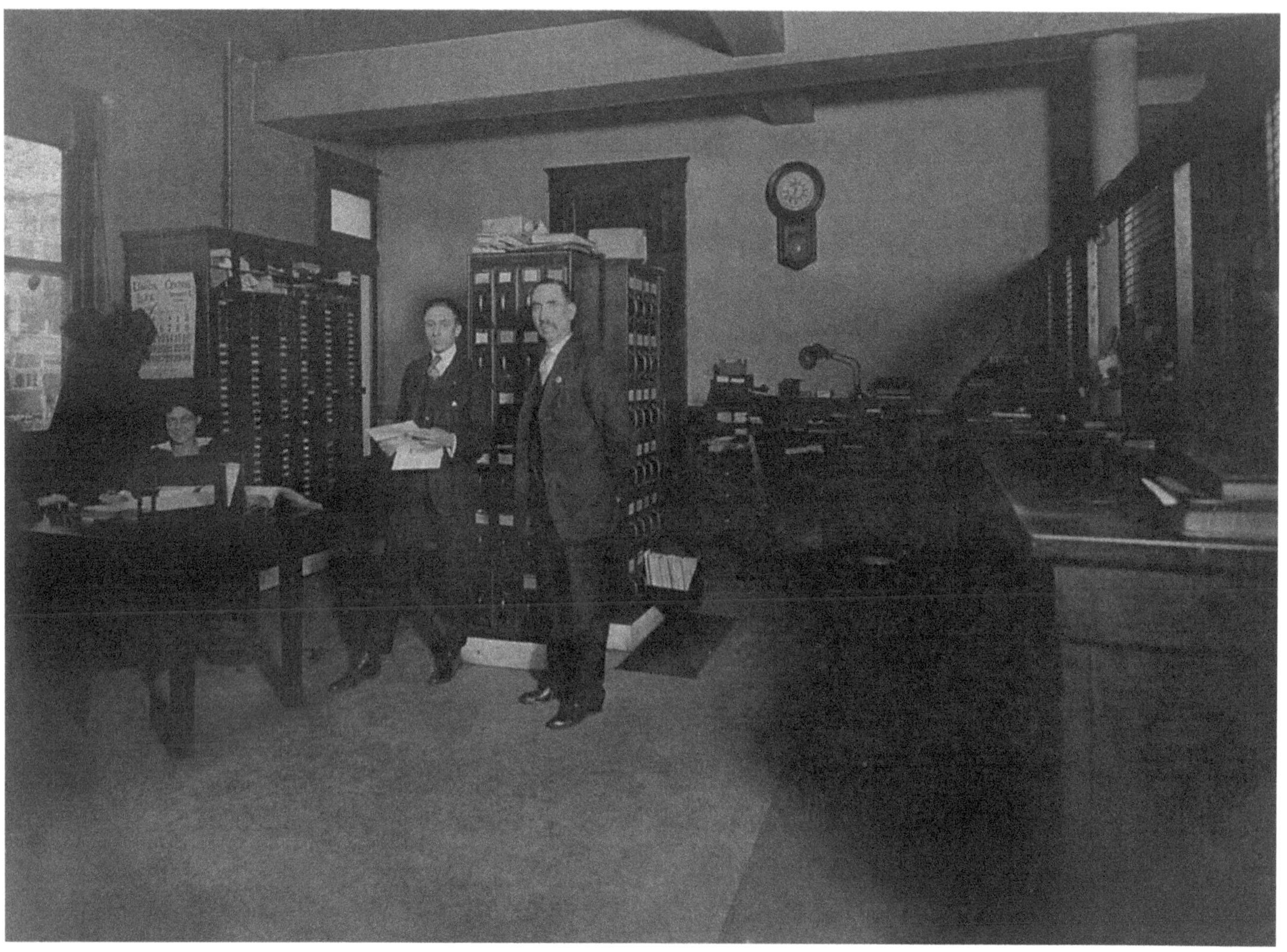

Members of the fire department pose in March 1919. It was a sad day for the fire house horses when they were put to pasture.

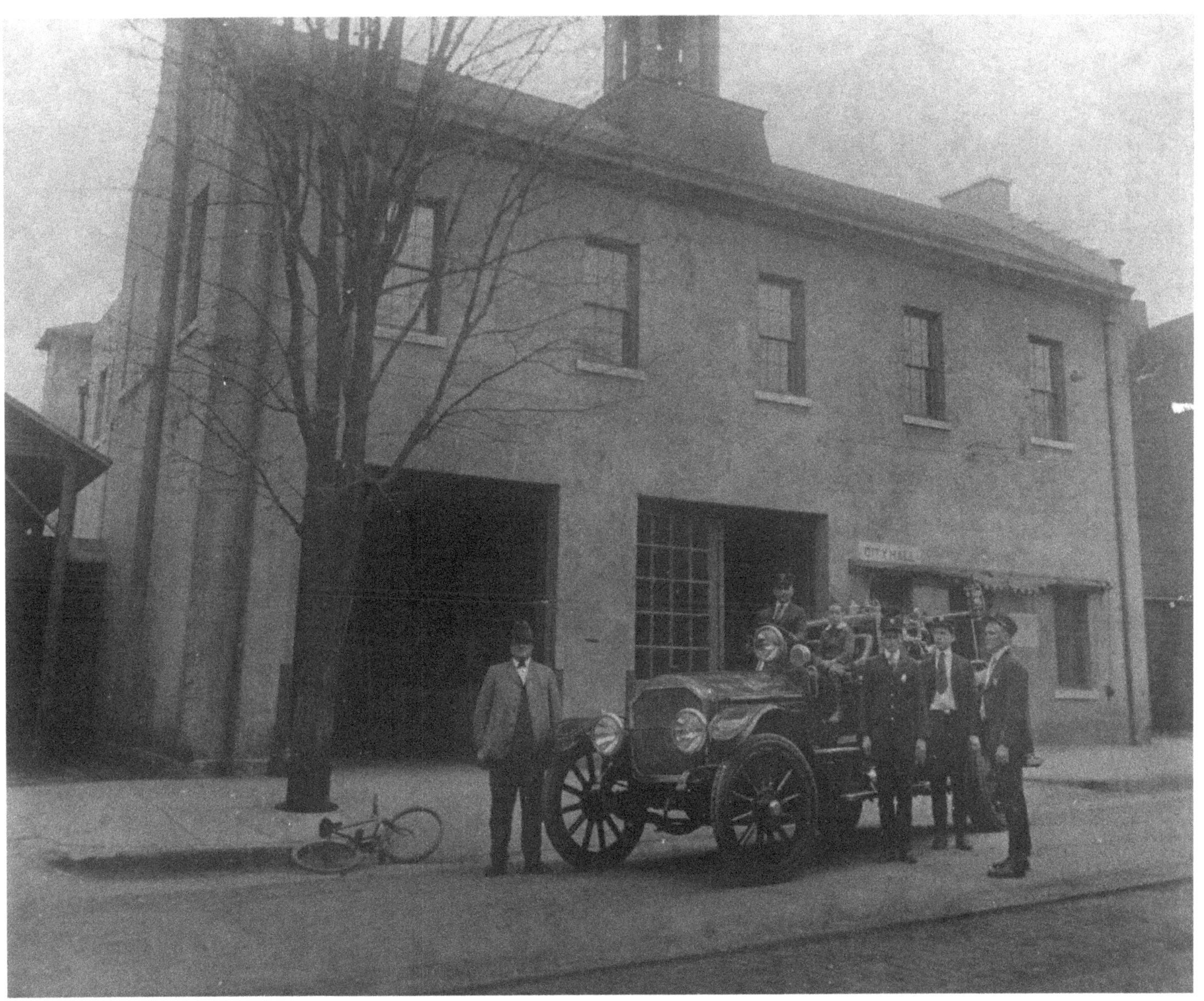

The third Madison County Courthouse, constructed in 1913, had an old-time clock tower. The building was replaced by the present modern high-rise in the 1960s.

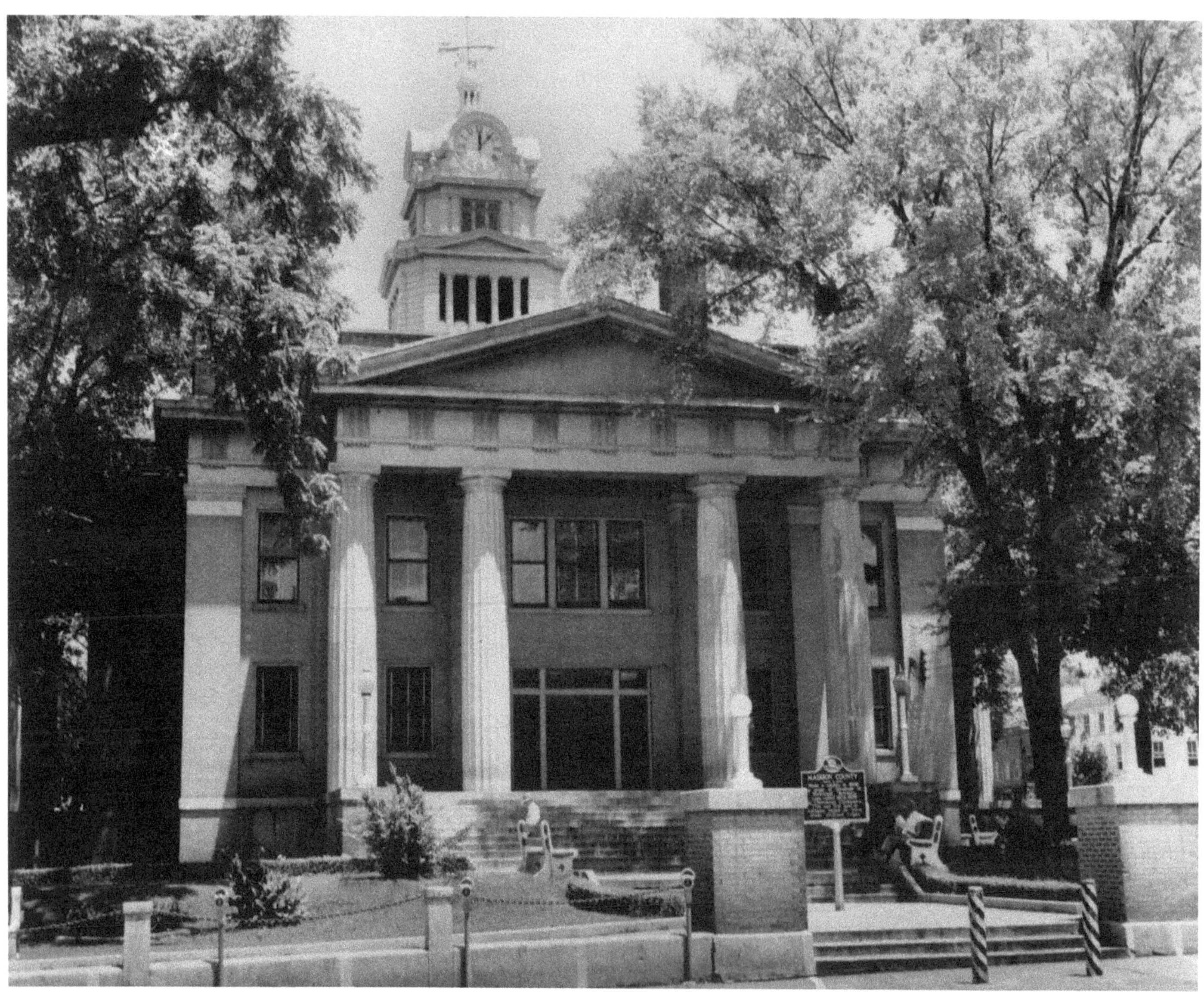

This postcard, looking south on Jefferson Street, captured Huntsville's bustling scene. Traffic lights had become a necessity. The Grand Theater is on the left.

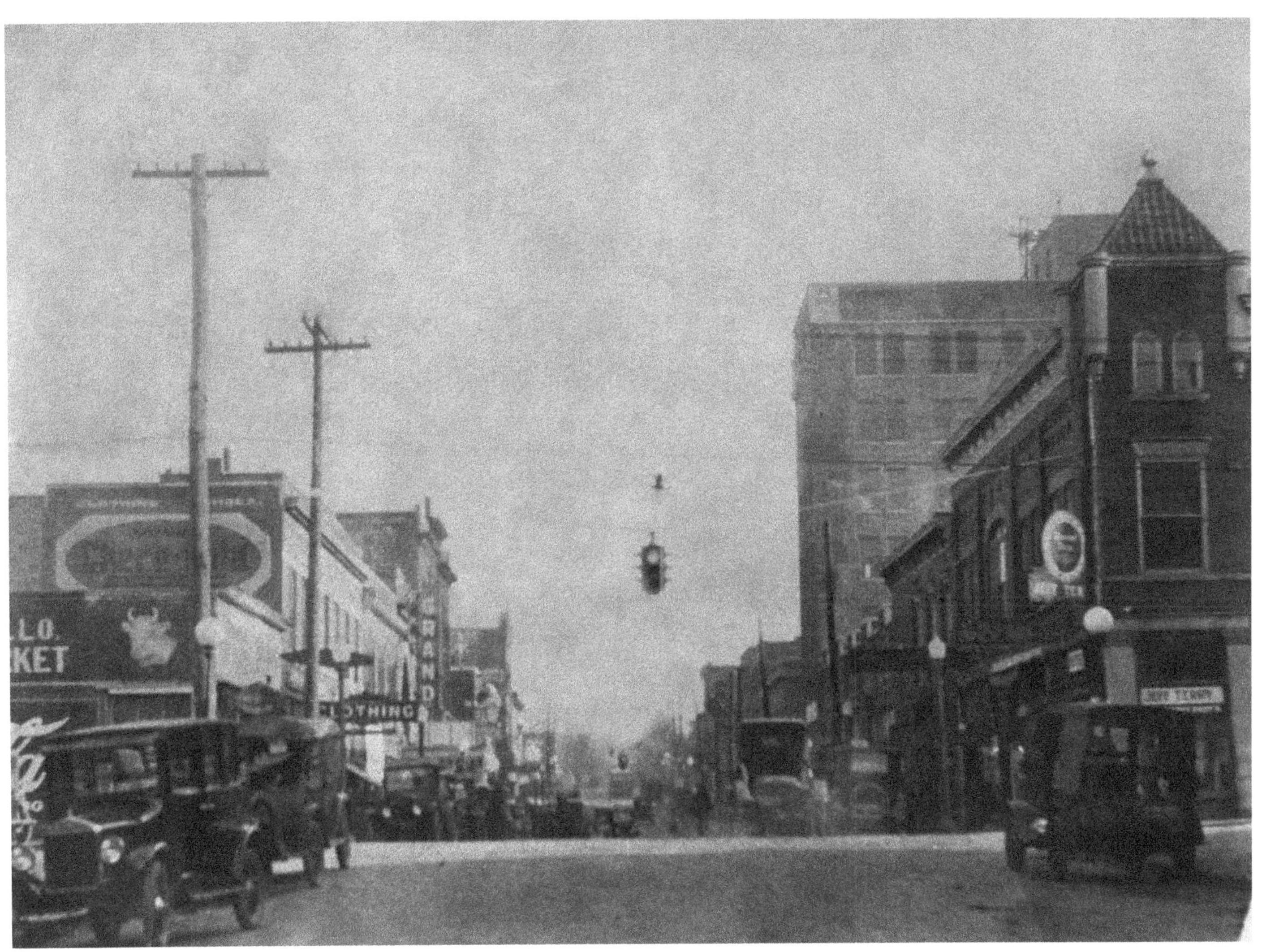

During the 1920s, the fire department and city hall were located on Madison Street. Brass was polished and cars shined for this photograph.

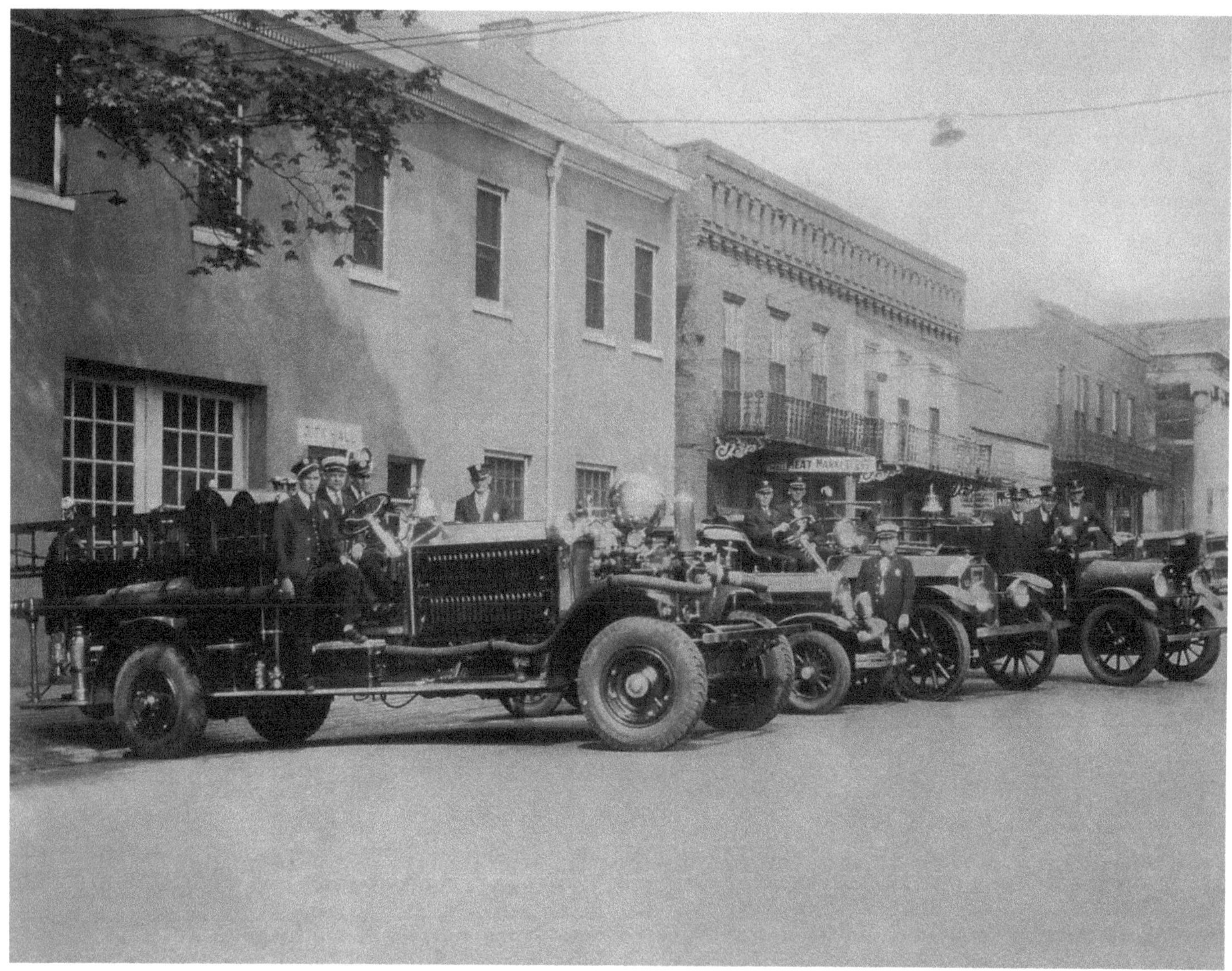

Prosperity to the Great Depression (1920–1939)

In 1920, Madison County's population was 51,268. Huntsville's alone stood at 8,018. The city was growing and progressing. New schools were constructed, cars were seen on the roads, and soon there was a need for traffic lights! The local mills remained the largest employers. A field was leveled for airplanes, and a bridge over the Tennessee River at Whitesburg replaced the ferry. Construction began on the Russel Erskine Hotel, a skyscraper in downtown Huntsville that would cater to upper-crust guests and host many high school proms in the years to come. In 1927, a resolution was passed requiring all citizens to work on the public roads five days per year to maintain and repair them. If that was not possible, they would have to pay $2.50 for each day of the five they did not work.

Despite the growth and progress, the citizens of Huntsville did not escape the devastating effects of "Black Thursday," October 24, 1929, when the stock market crashed. Even those who had no money invested in the stock market would soon suffer as jobs dried up and banks failed. Within months, businesses were folding, mills were filing for bankruptcy, and the price of cotton dropped. Crime soared. Moonshining became a problem. Labor unions demanded better working conditions, but many mills closed their doors for good.

With the election of President Franklin D. Roosevelt, help came in the way of labor camps, the Civilian Conservation Corps (CCC) and Works Progress Administration (WPA). As the economic crisis began to soften, the talk of war in Europe was beginning to heat up.

On March 15, 1938, eighteen Army planes on their way from Michigan to Florida on a training mission flew into a storm that spawned several tornadoes over Alabama. Caught somewhere near Montgomery with no place to land safely and dangerously low on fuel, they remembered an opening in the clouds over Huntsville. They turned around and circled low over the darkened city. Two astute policemen sent a plea over a local radio, asking people to drive to the local airport and line up their cars with headlights illuminating the runway, so the pilots in distress could land. The people of Huntsville met the challenge and the grateful pilots stayed the night at the Russel Erskine Hotel.

Traffic lights, like this one at the corner of Greene Street and Clinton Avenue, were once turned on with a key by local police officers. This picture was taken in 1924.

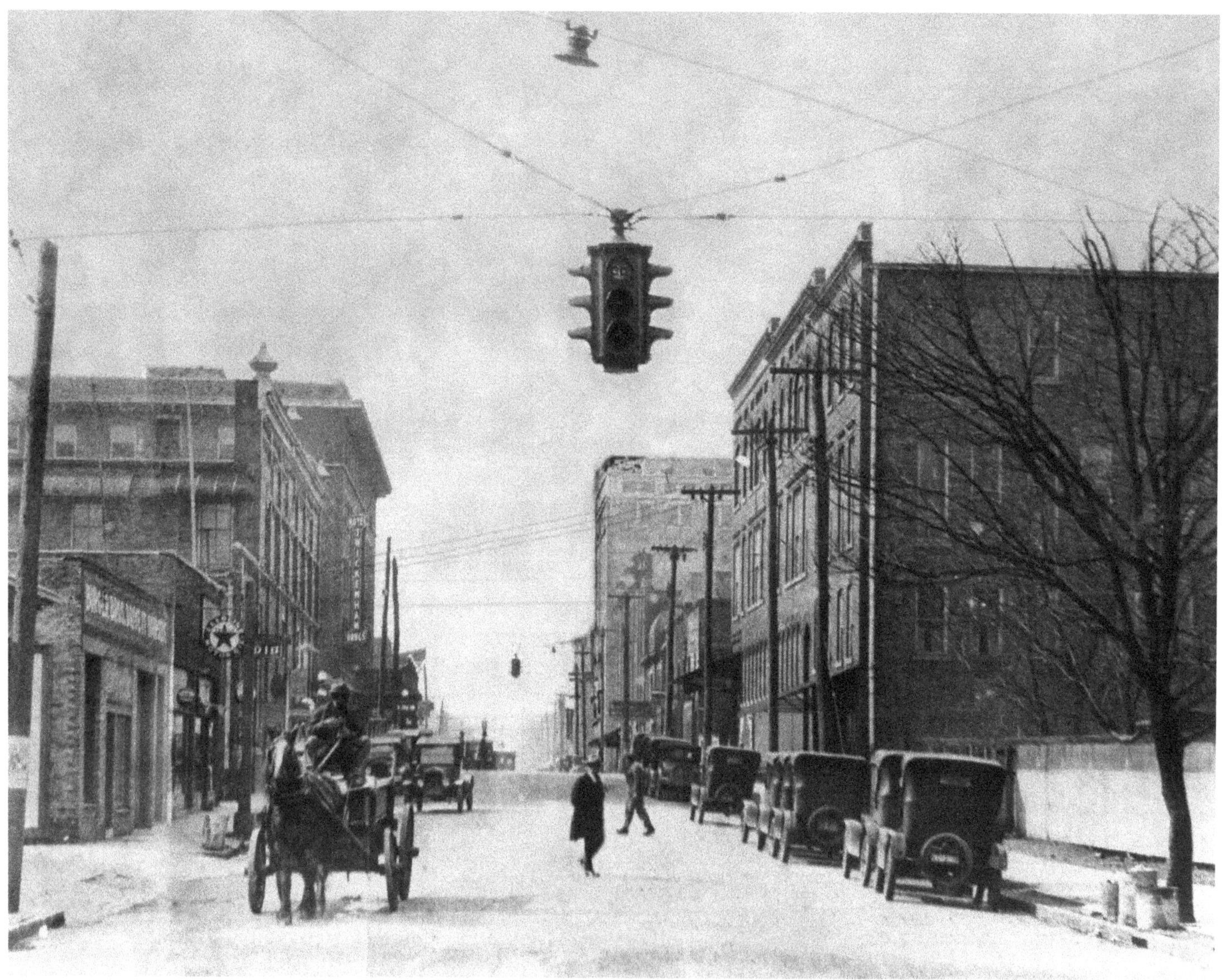

The 4th of July Parade brought everyone out to celebrate in style. This family sedan was transformed into an impressive float.

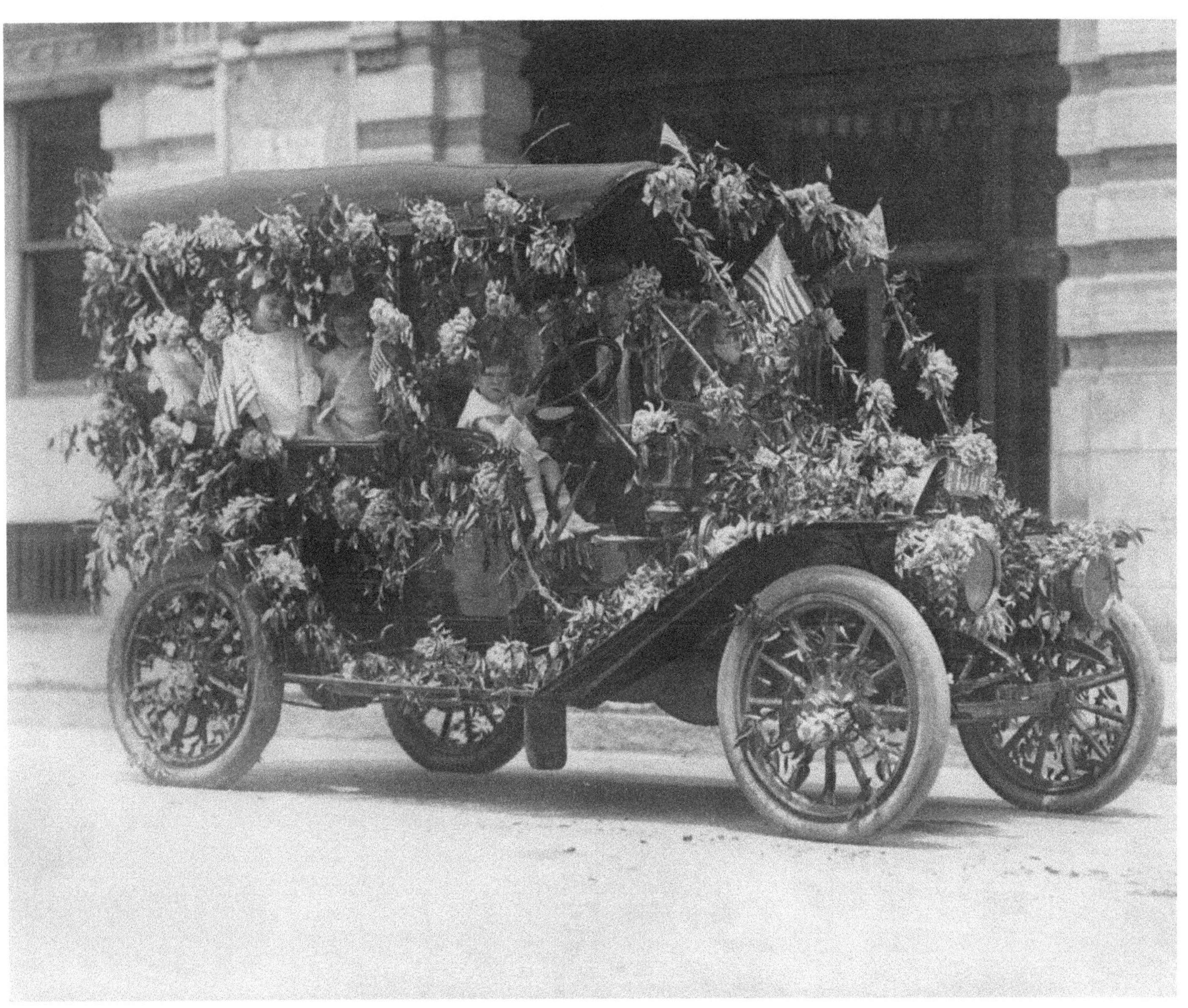

A local office supply company carried all the latest office needs.

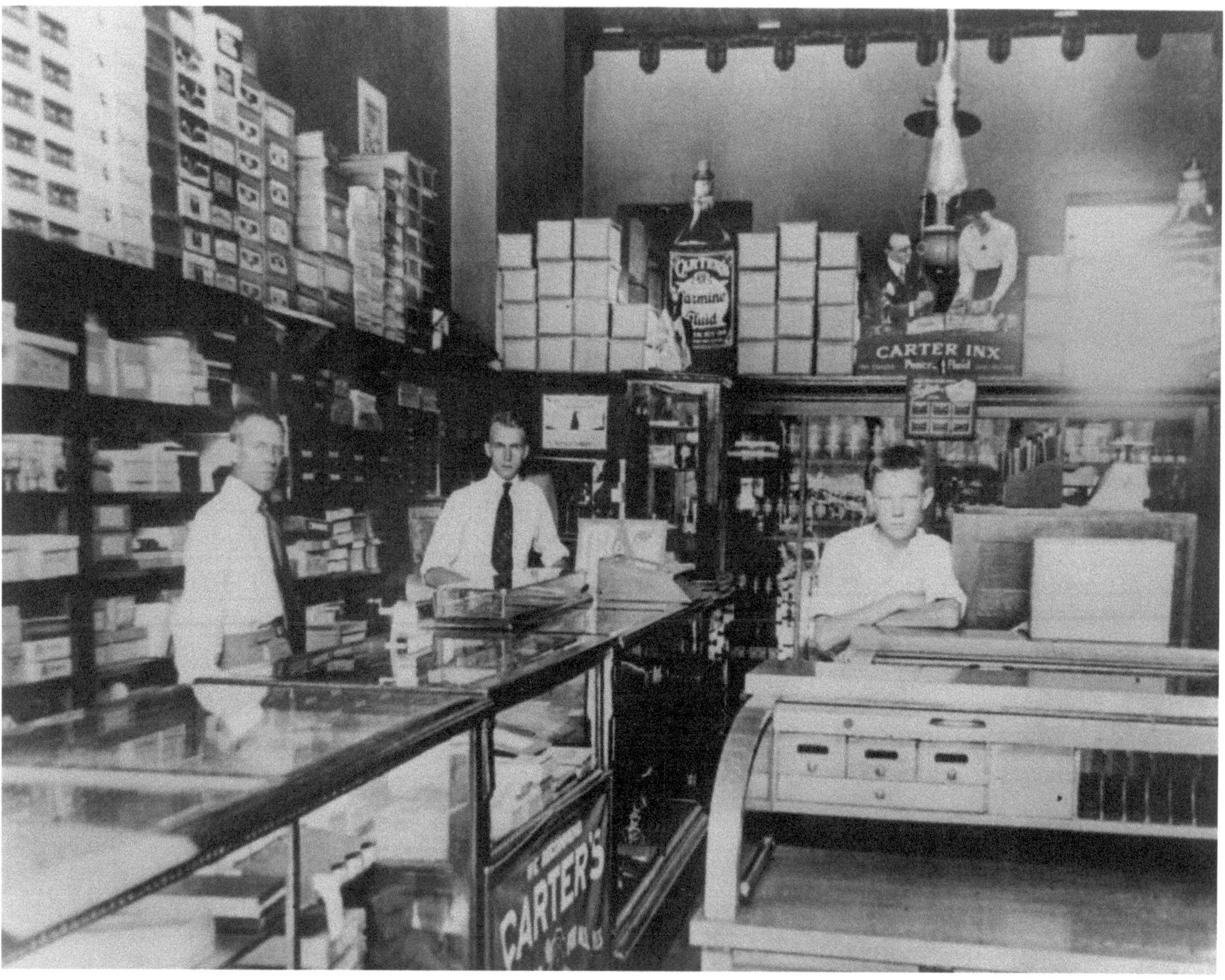

Crowds packed Huntsville's streets during special events. The store in back is bedecked with patriotic bunting.

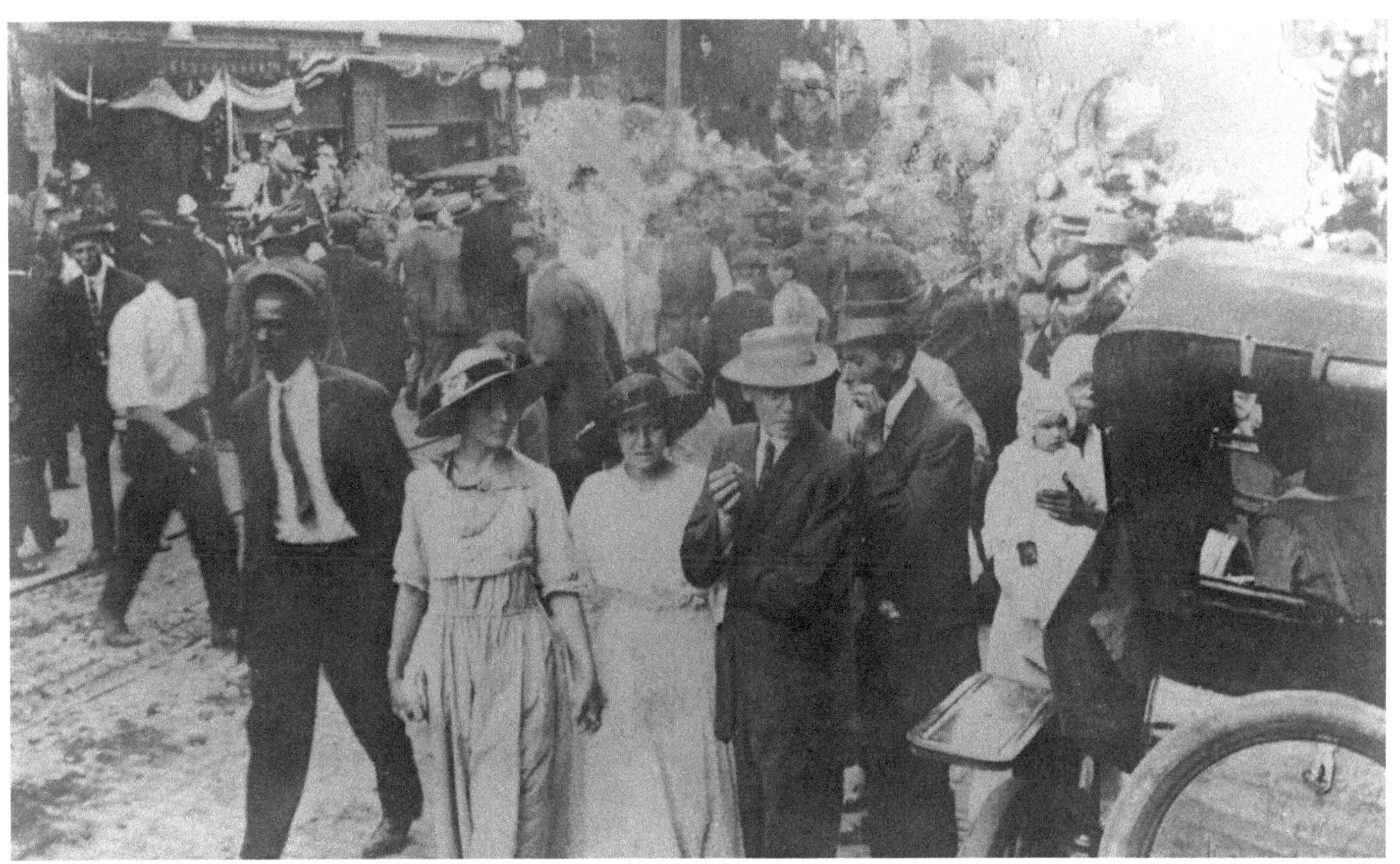

Saint Mary's Church of the Visitation was organized in 1861. The Civil War interrupted construction, which was not finished until 1872. Father Jeremiah Trecy was one of several local clergymen arrested by Federal troops during the war.

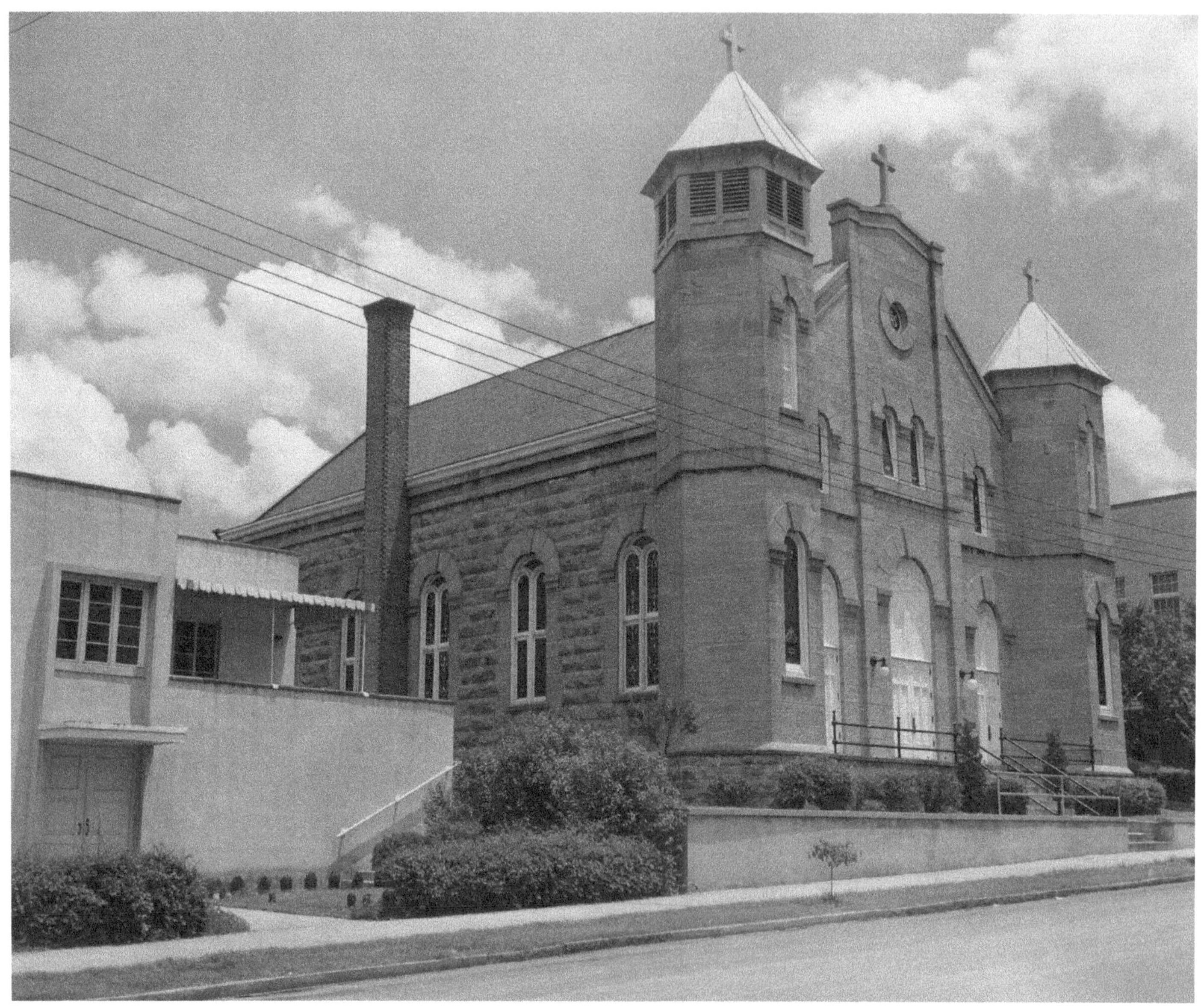

These happy people are teachers from Joe Bradley School, taking a picnic break in 1925.

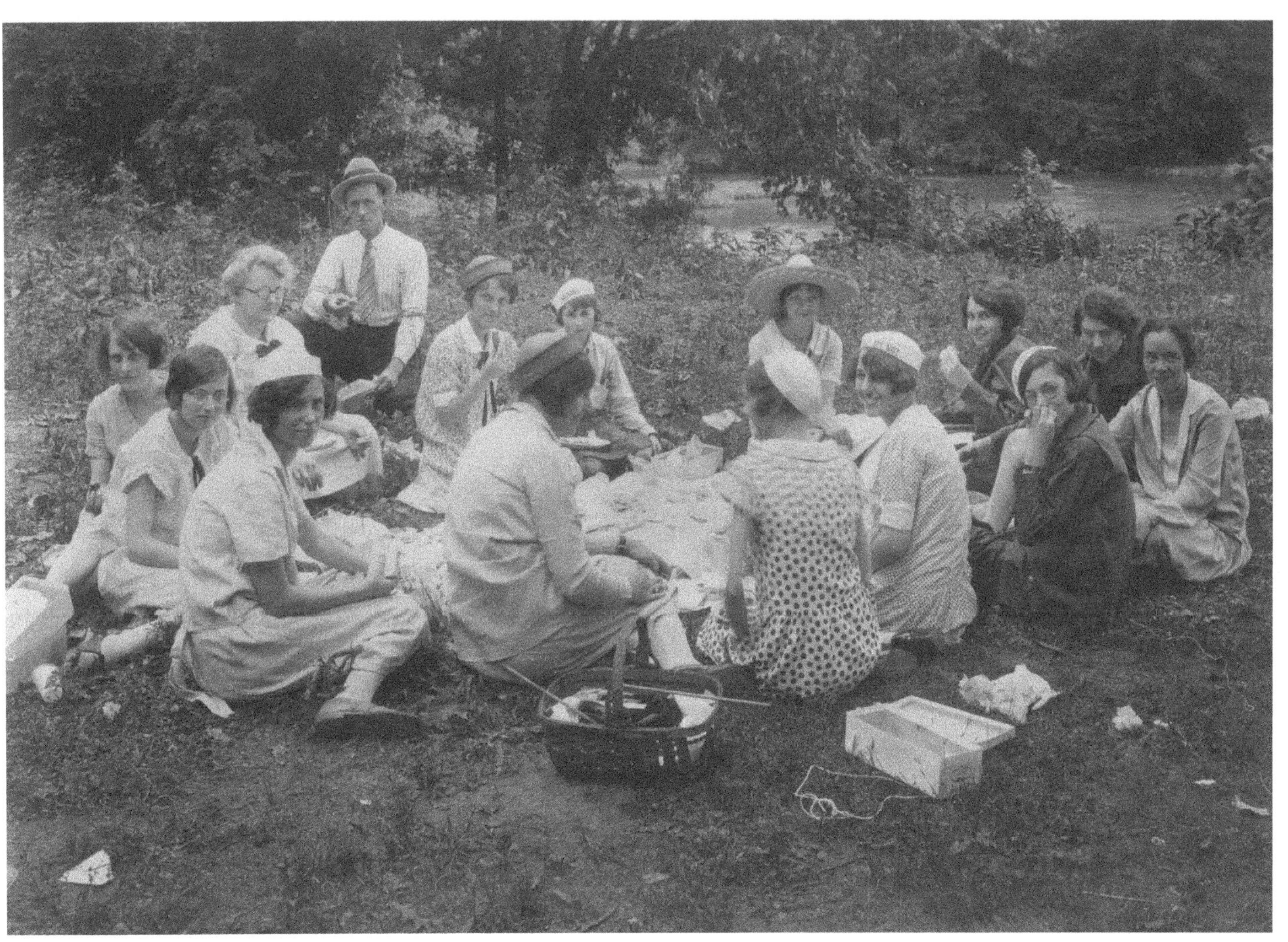

The dedication of Monte Sano Boulevard on July 4, 1927, was a joyous occasion. The new road improved access for visitors, who appreciated the beauty of the area and the healthy mountain air.

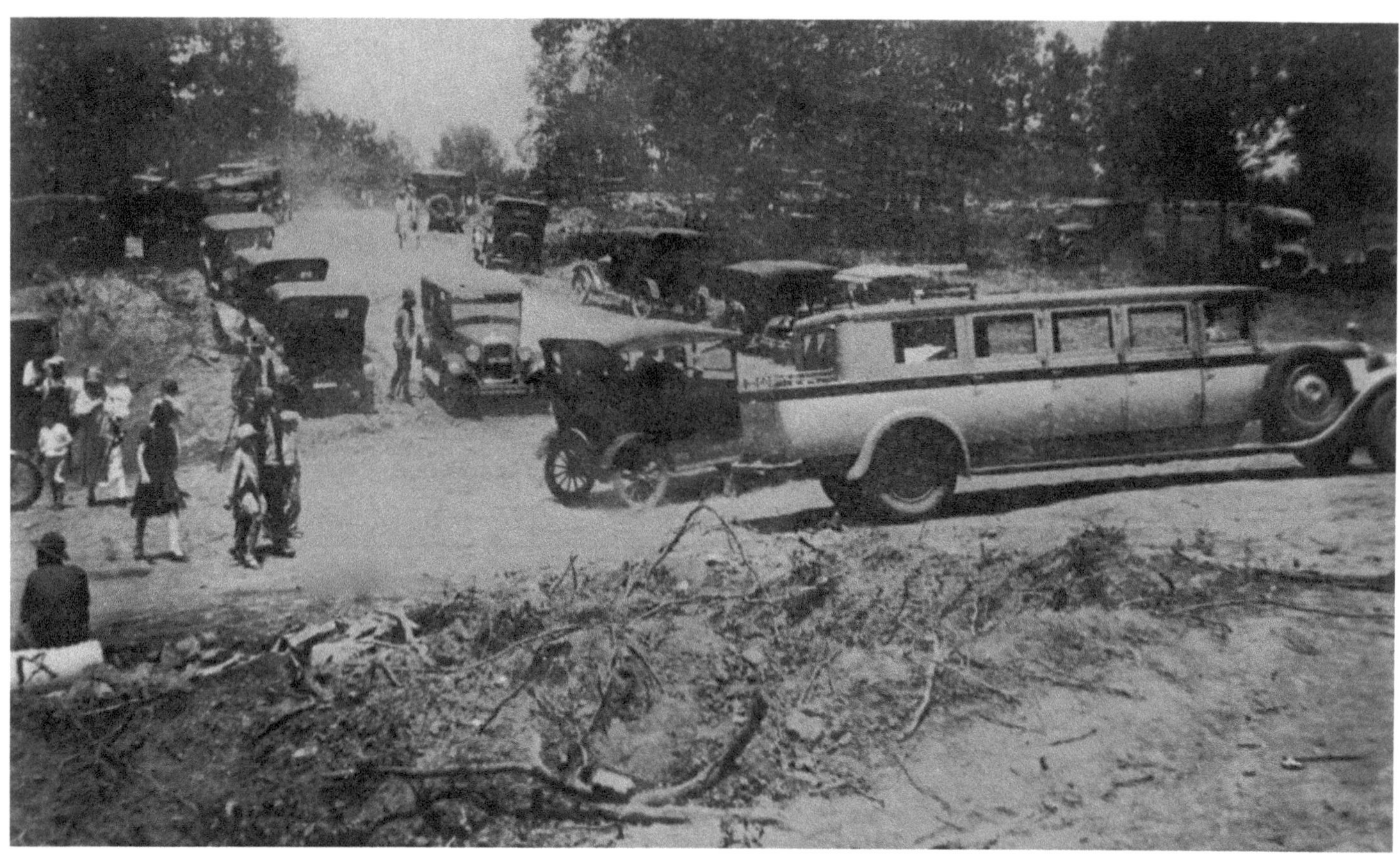

The American Legion held a convention in Huntsville in 1927. Local resident George Mahoney sits on the running board of a limousine.

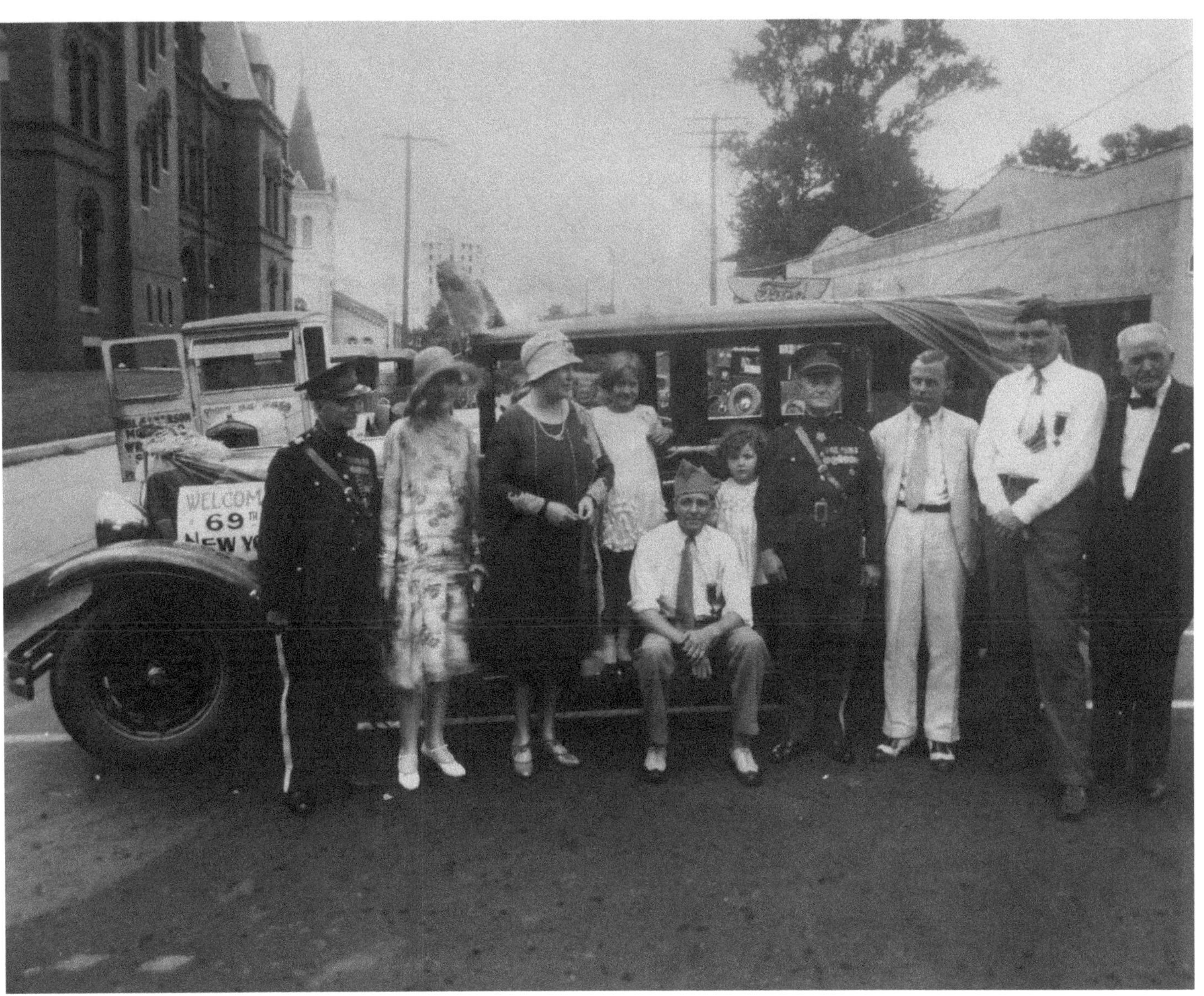

Weaving machines at Huntsville Manufacturing Company produced fabric made from local cotton.

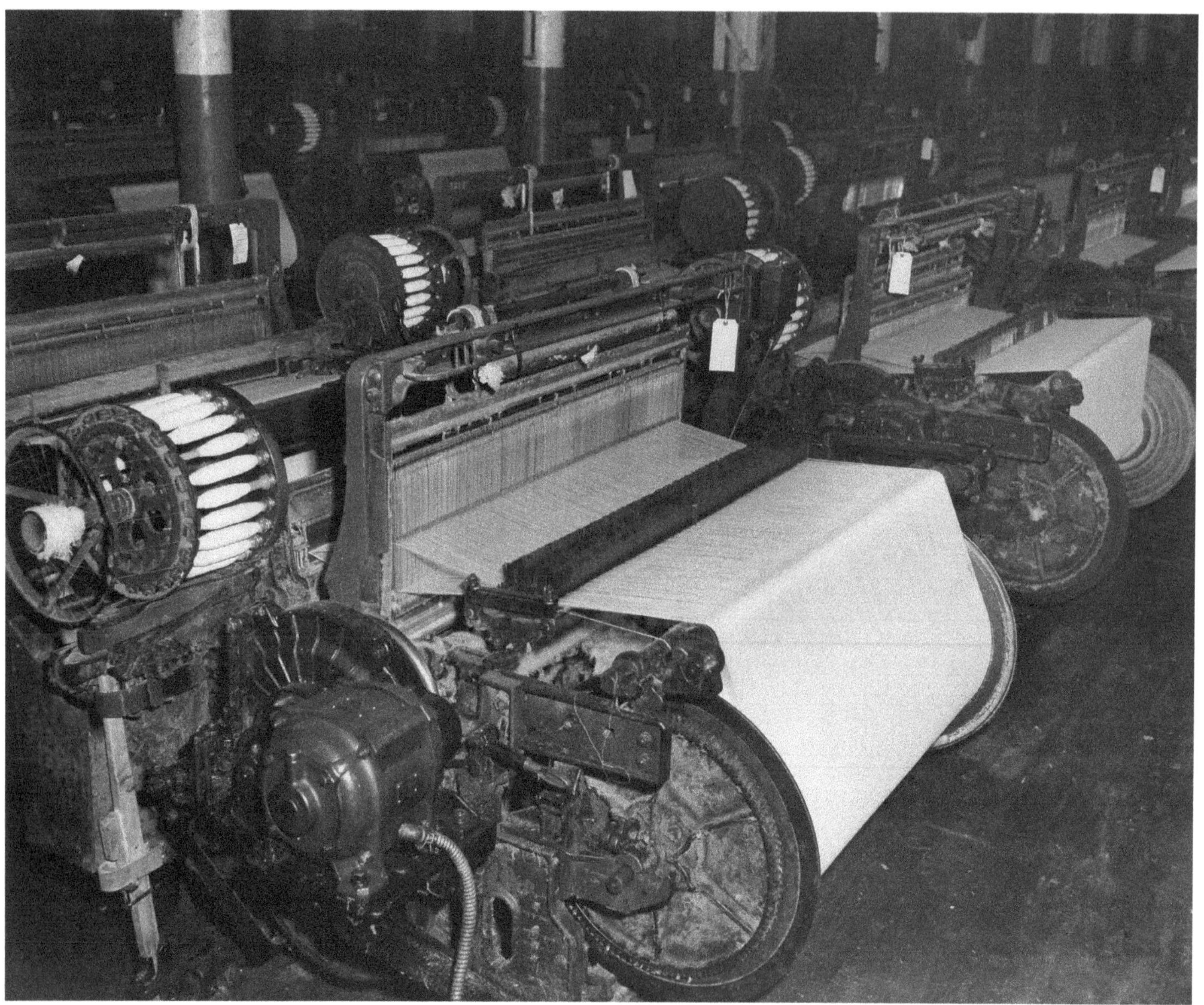

Clark Steadman's Bar B Q was a popular eatery, featuring the local favorite—barbecue. A pinball machine beckons a man with loose change on the left. Clark Steadman stands second from right.

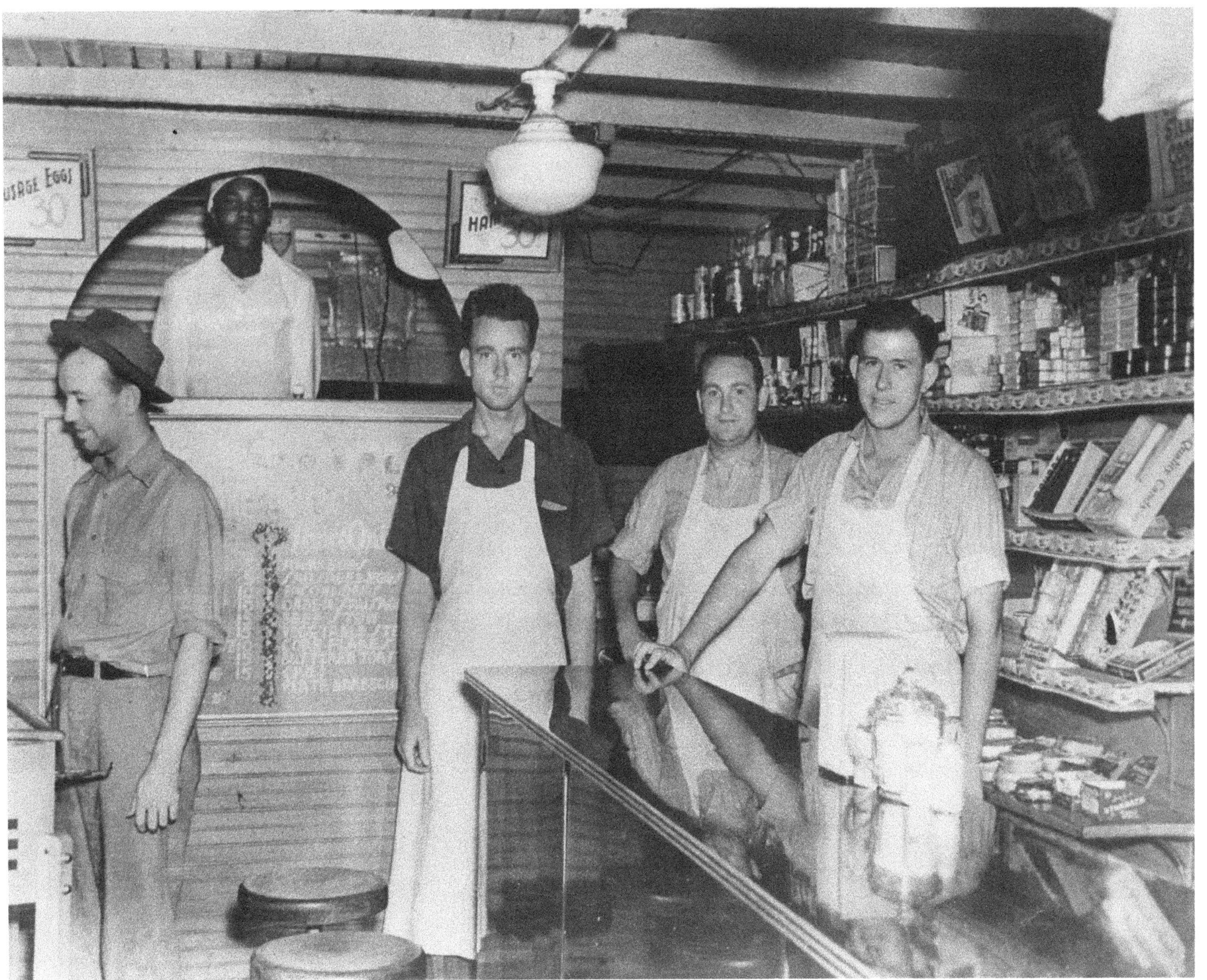

A vendor's stand sits on the Clinton Avenue side of the corner of Washington Street and Clinton Avenue. The building behind it has undergone renovation, but still resembles its 1930s appearance.

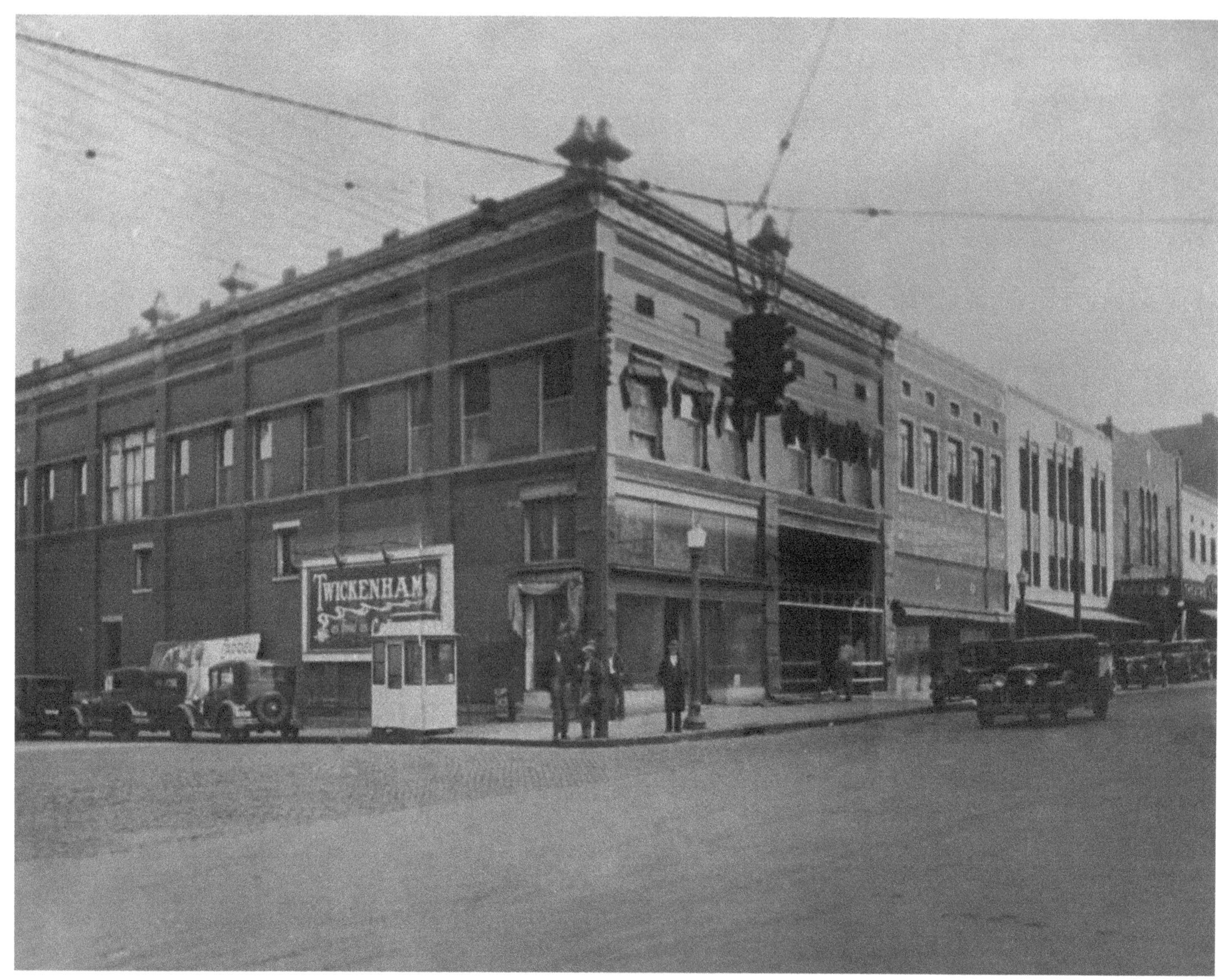

Members of Huntsville High School's football team pose in this 1930 photograph with their coach, Jesse Keene, who wears a Vanderbilt shirt in the third row.

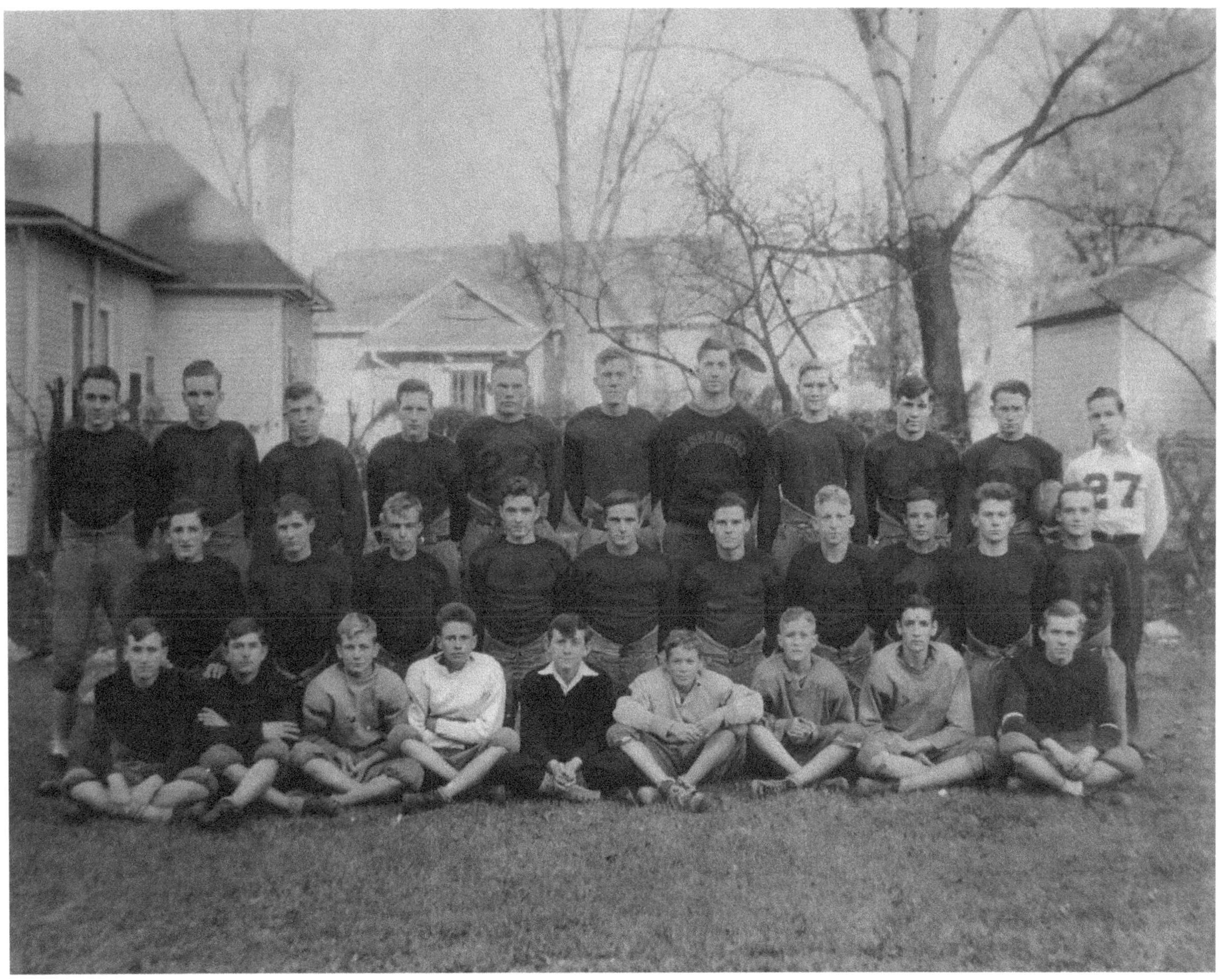

This 1932 Washington Street scene looking south shows thriving businesses despite the Great Depression sweeping the nation.

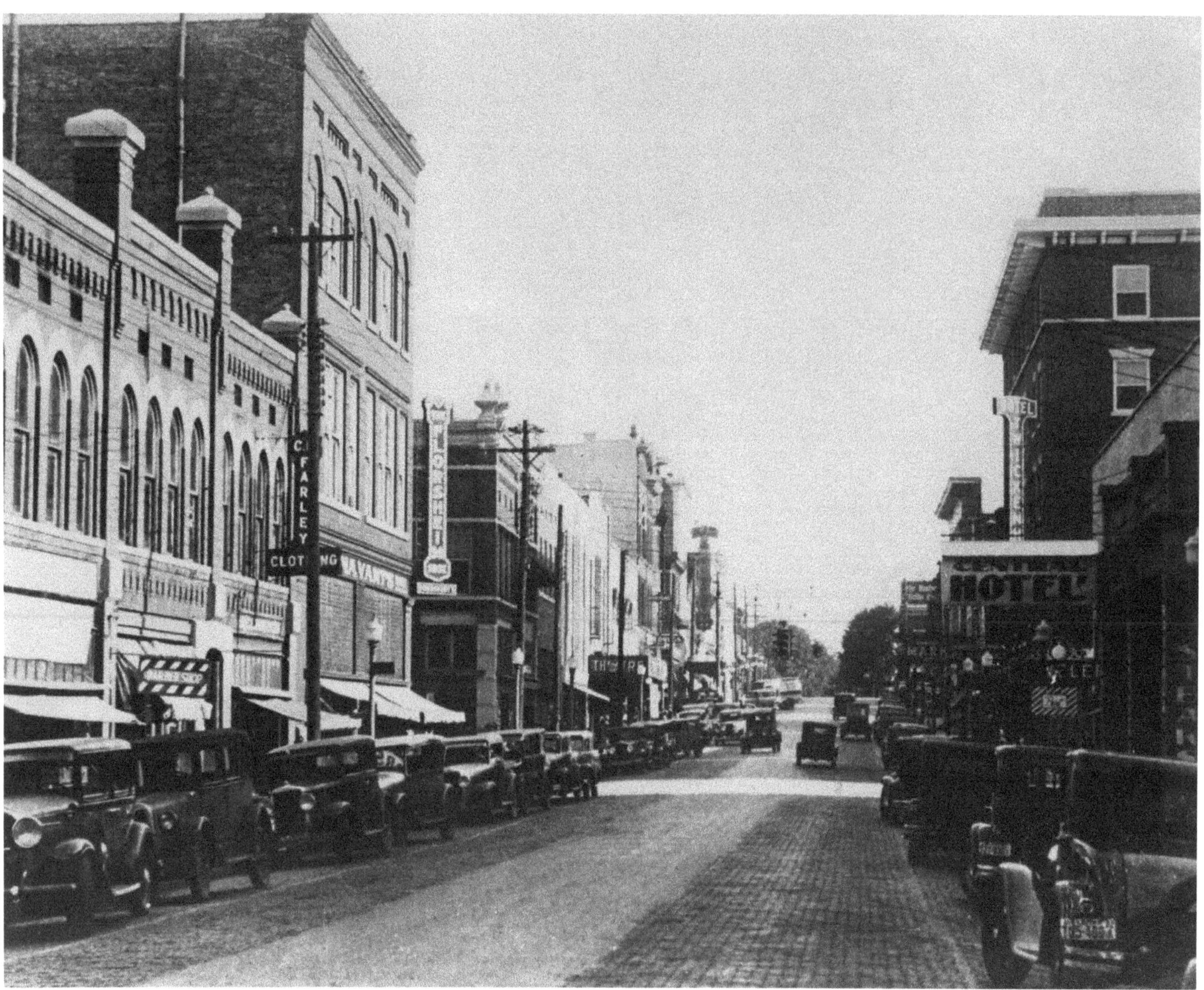

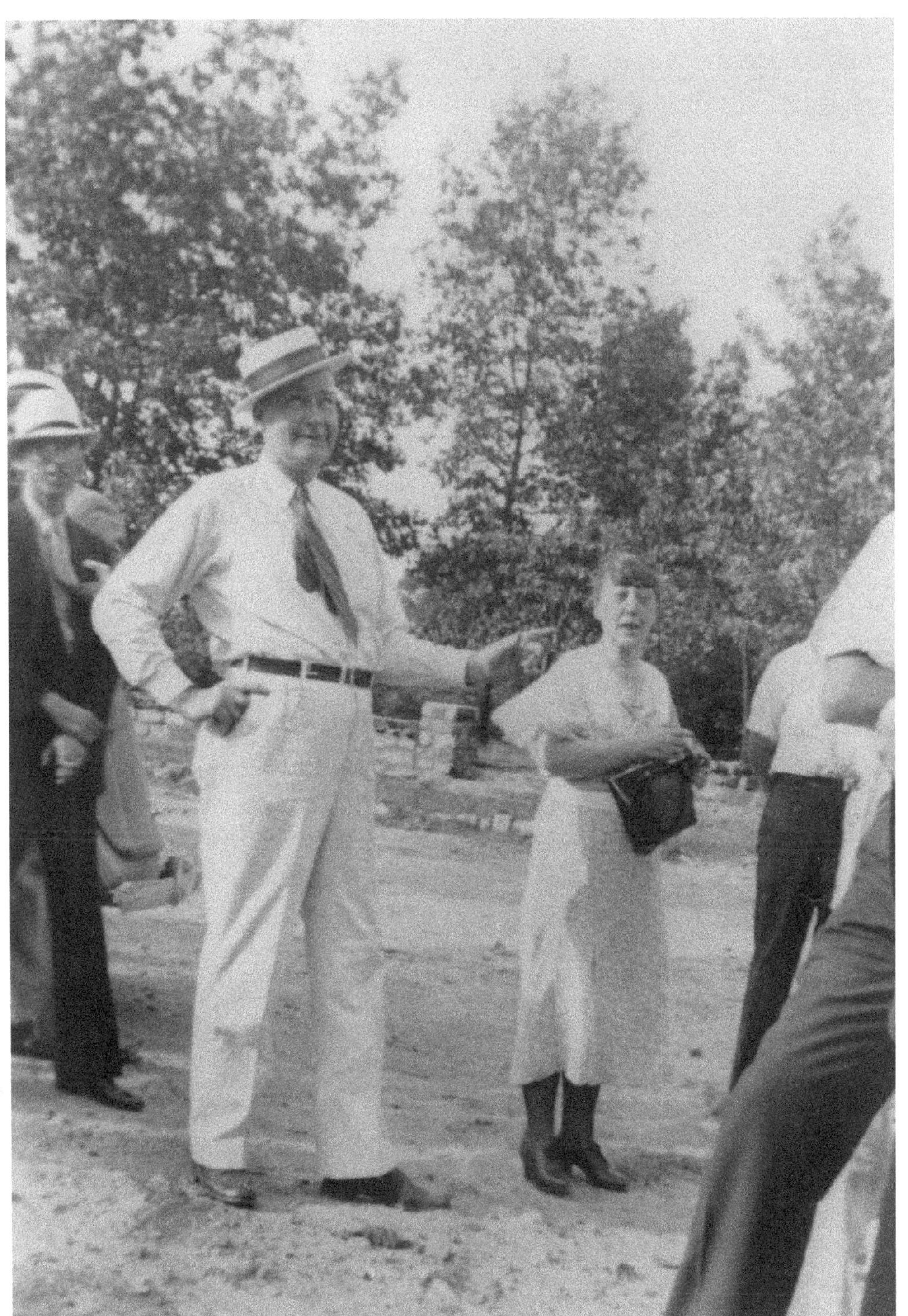

Bill Adcock and Mollie Dowd, representatives of the United Textiles of America, make a 1934 visit to do some union business. A series of strikes in 1933-34 affected mills and increased the depression's strain on the local economy.

Members of the Madison County Sheriff's office stand in front of the city jail built on Washington Street in 1930. Sheriff Frank G. Hereford, who served from 1911-1915 and again from 1935-1937, is standing fourth from the left.

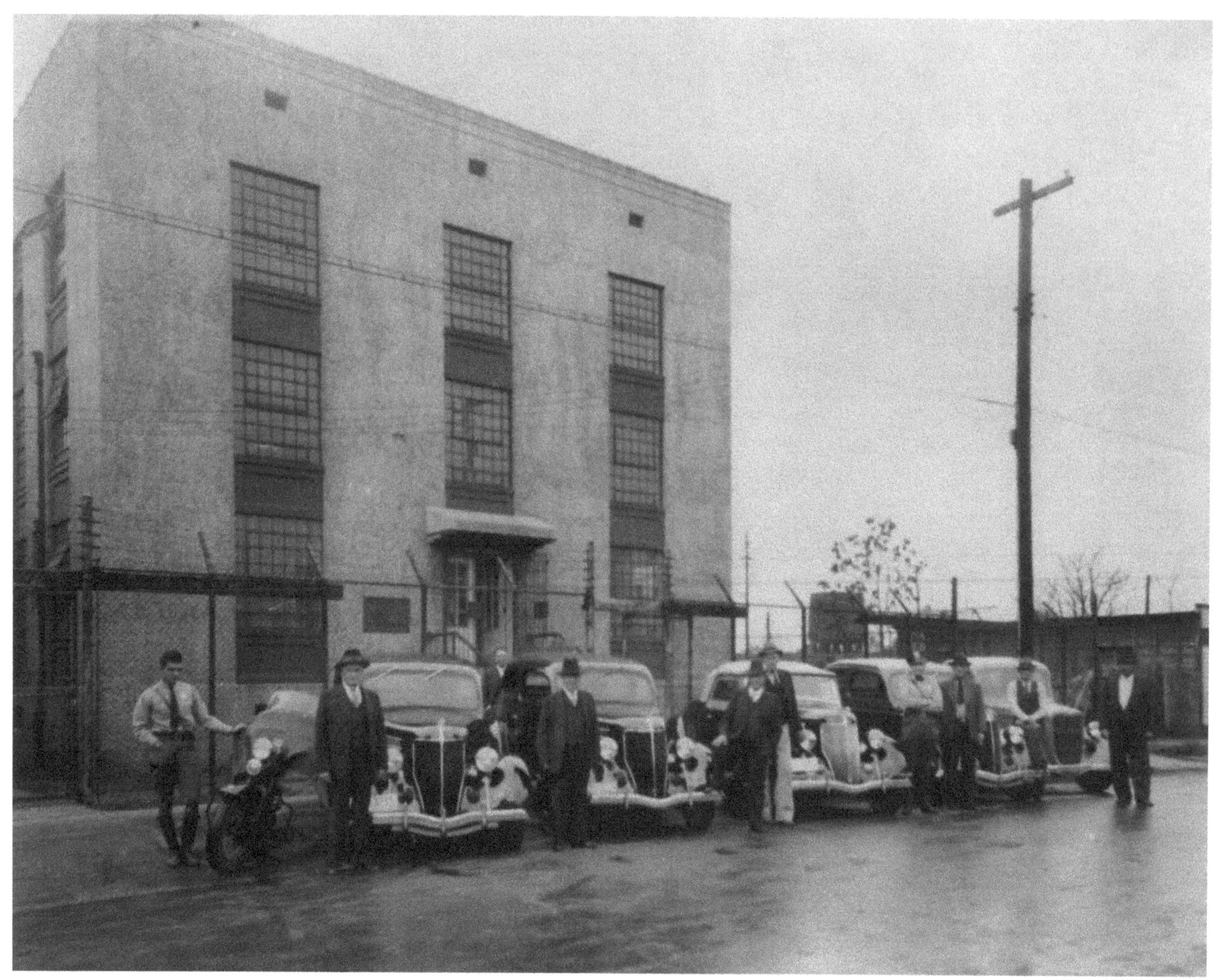

Young's Style Shop on Washington Street displays the latest footwear for fall of 1936. This sale advertises "Williams Smart Shoes" from $1.99 to $2.49 and Tweedie's for $5.00 and $6.00.

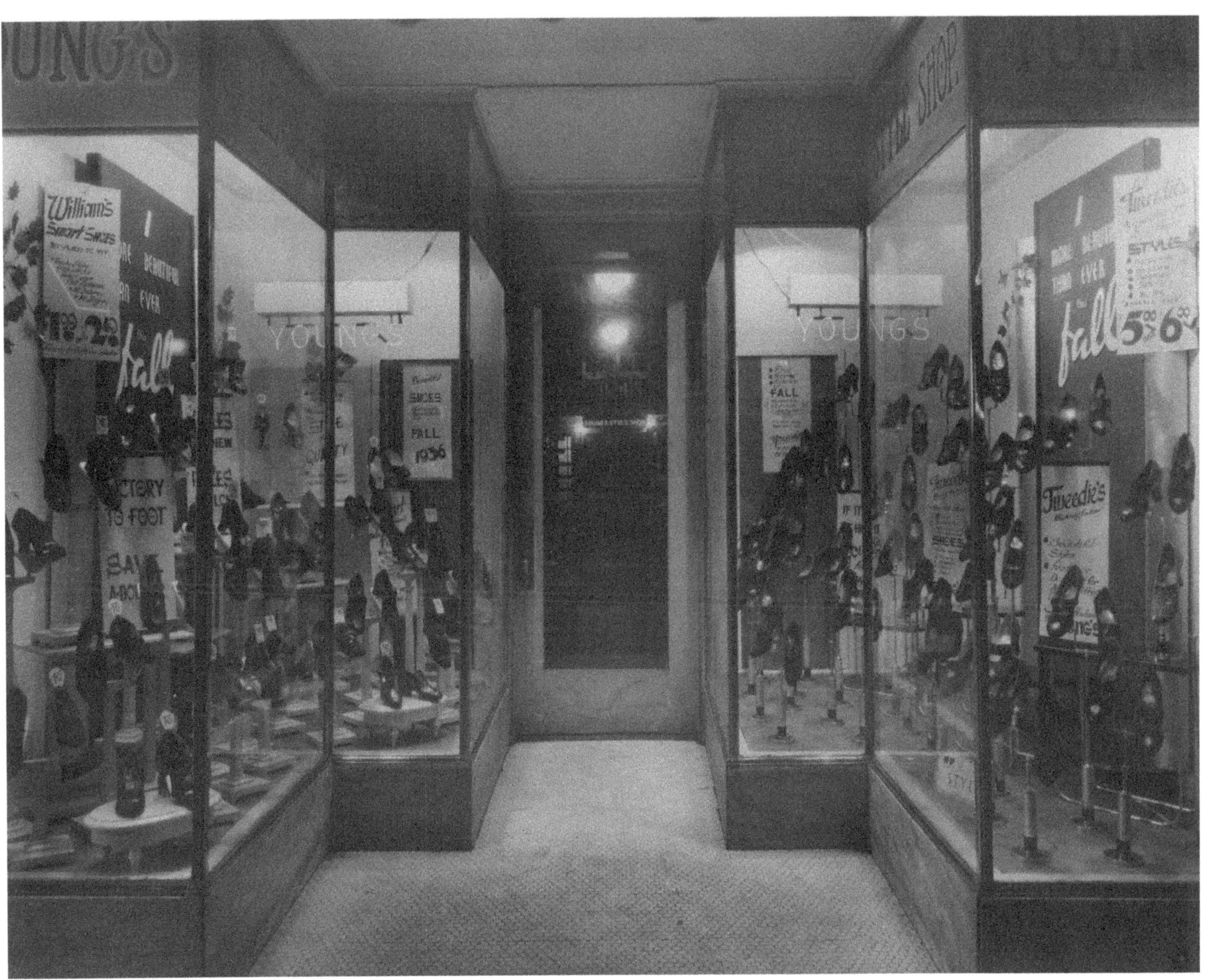

The congregation of this church formed in 1929 and built their church on East Clinton Street. Their first service here was held in 1937. Although the original building still stands, the size of the church has expanded considerably.

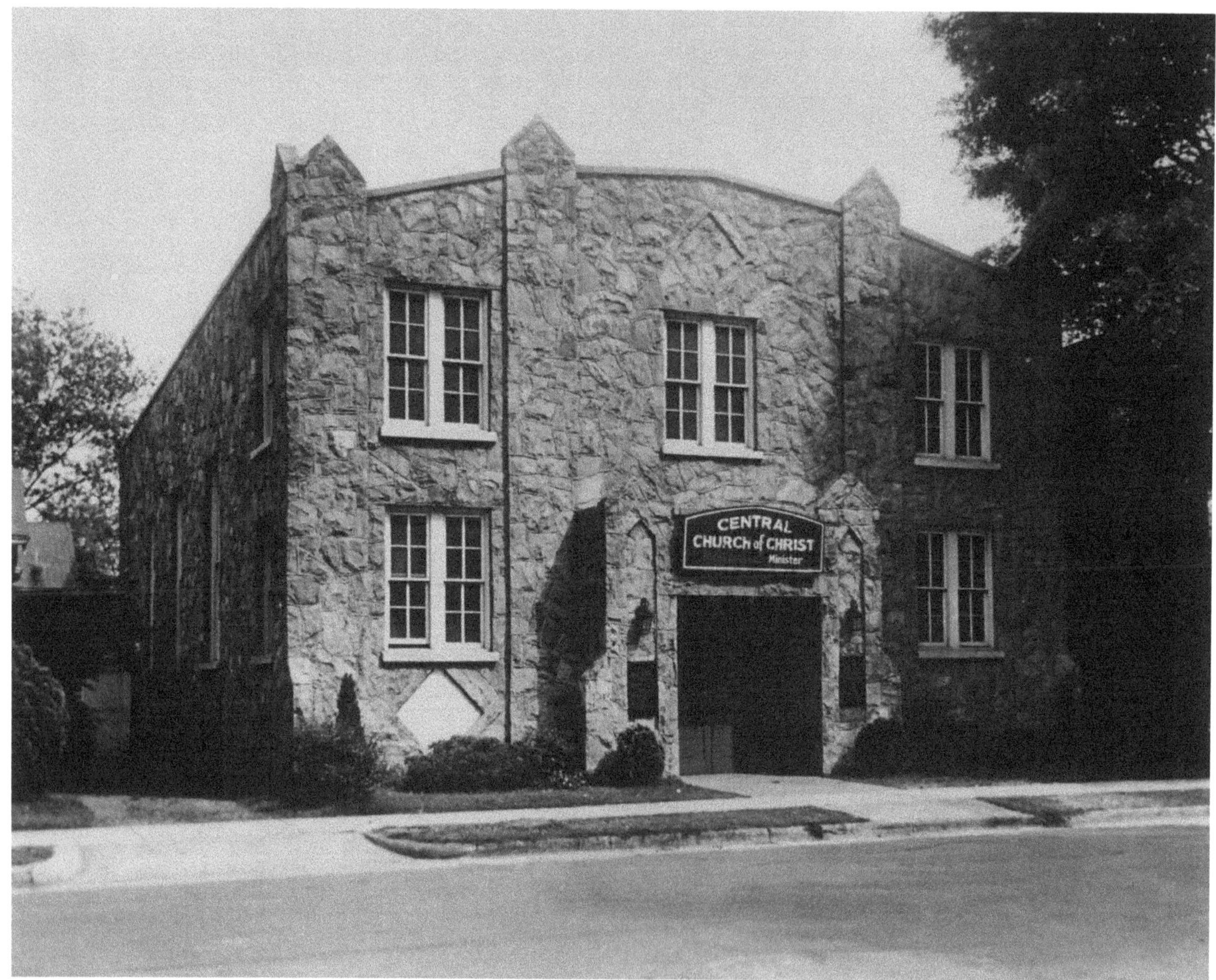

Jefferson Street was the location for the Double Cola plant, the Grand Theater, and Sterchi Brothers Furniture. An "A" and "N" hang at odd angles on the Sportland billiard hall sign at right.

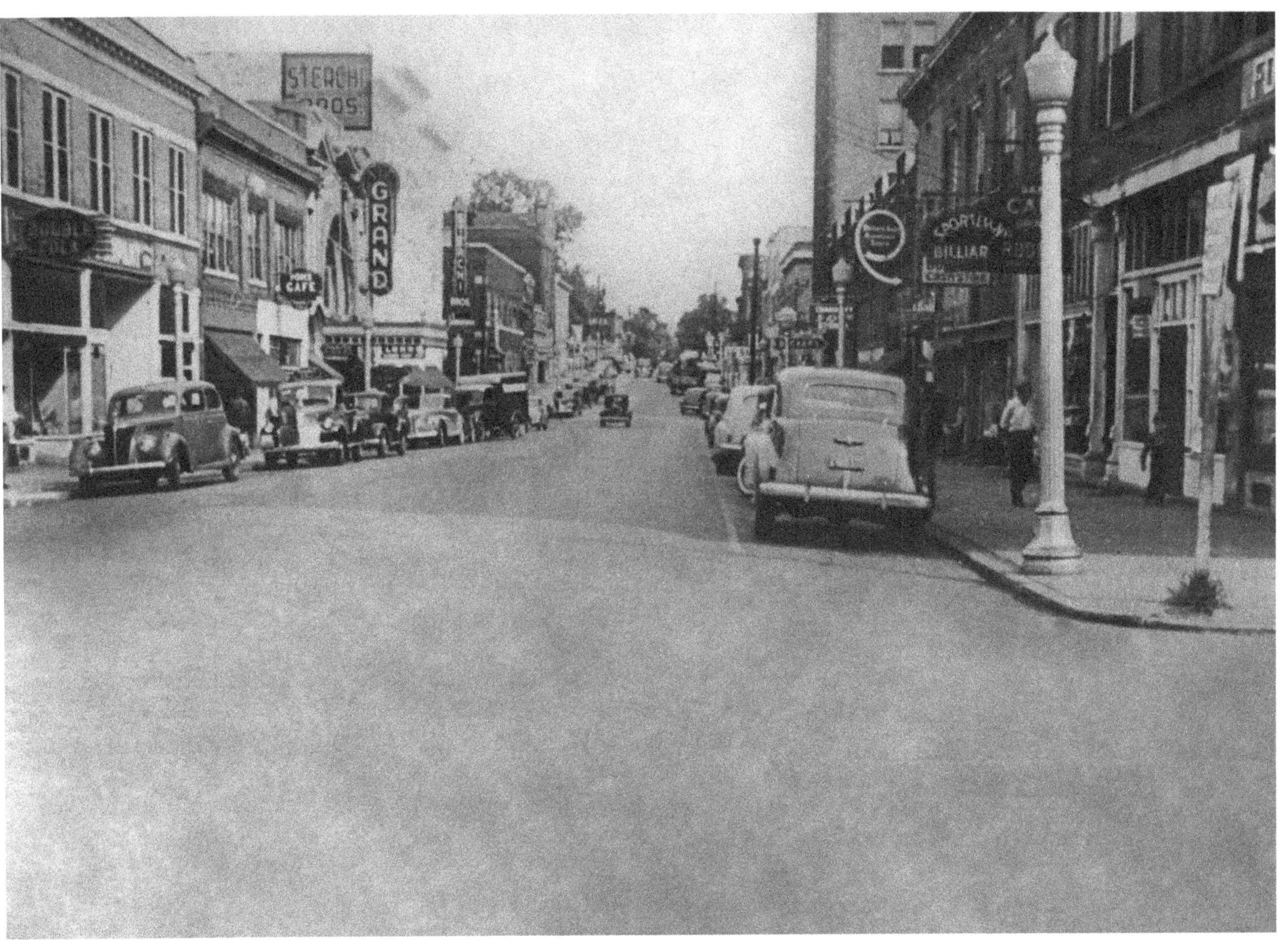

Shoppers walk along Washington Street in this photograph facing south.

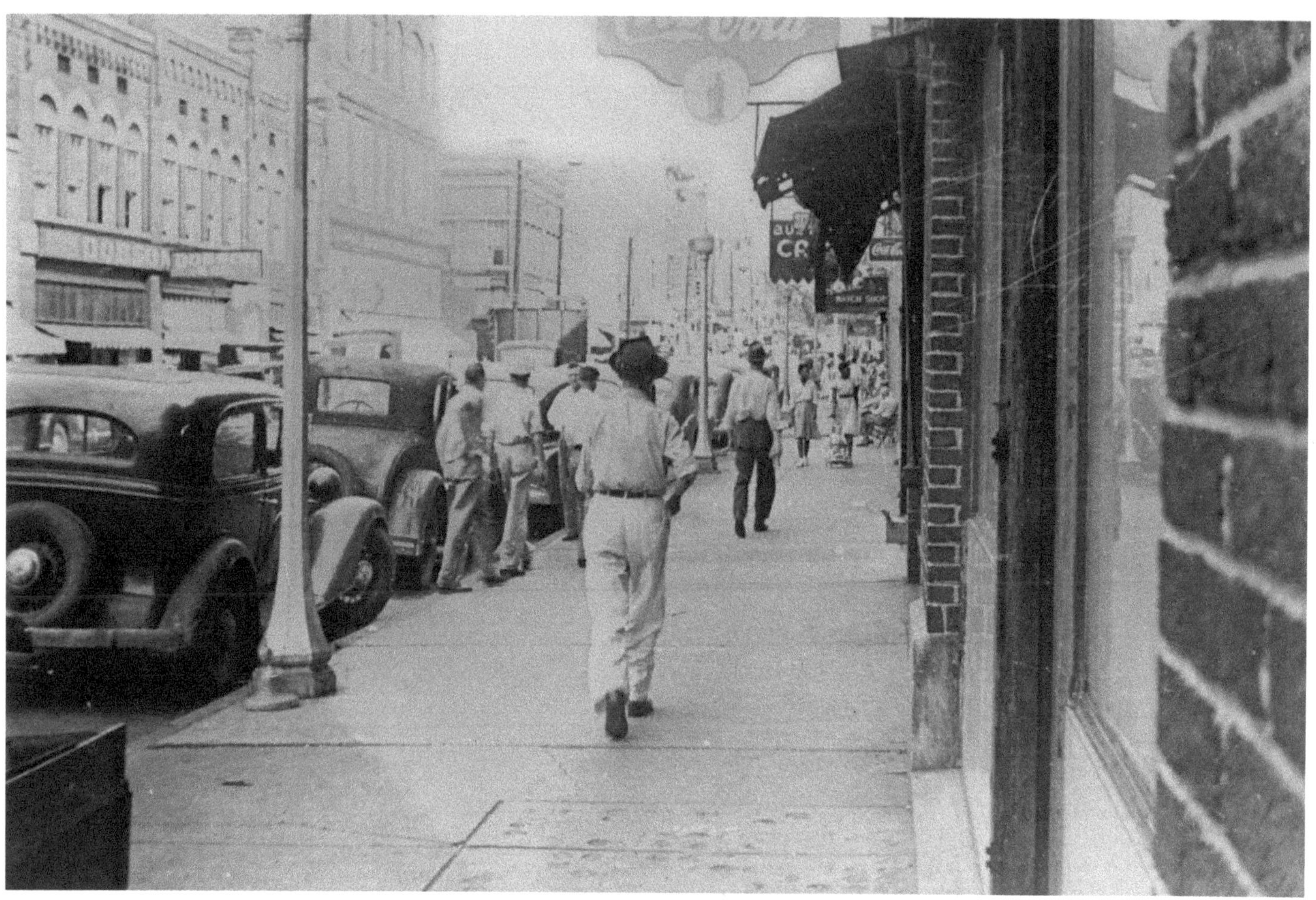

Civil War veterans and two former slaves who went with their masters into war pose in 1938 in front of the marker dedicated by the Twickenham Chapter Daughters of the American Revolution. It was at this spot, on the corner of Gates and Franklin Streets, where forty-four delegates met in 1819 to draft Alabama's constitution. This block is now Alabama's Constitution Village, a museum complex which recreates the buildings that stood here in 1819.

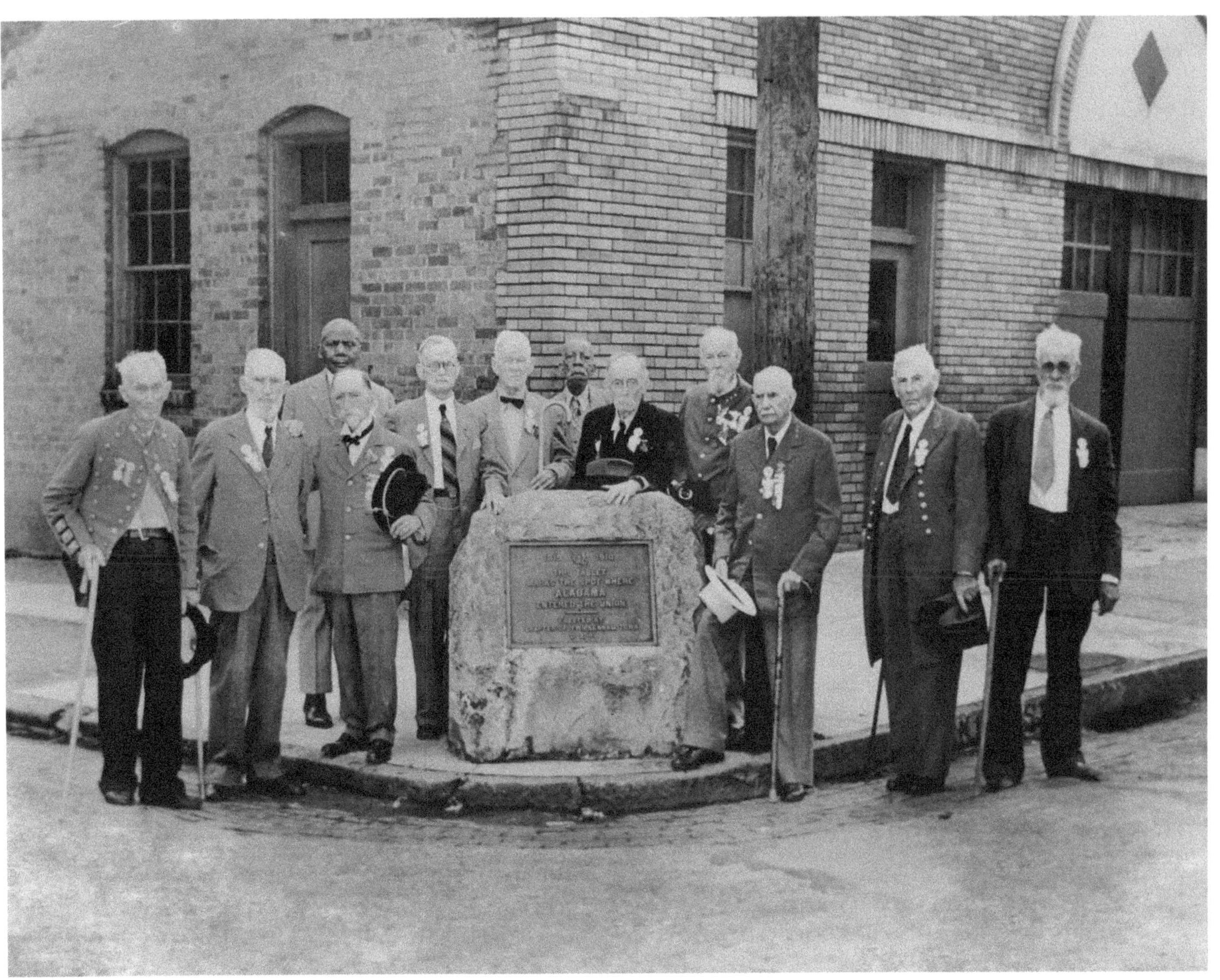

The Temple B'nai Sholom was founded in 1876. This Romanesque-Renaissance Revival building was dedicated in 1899. It remains the oldest synagogue in continuous use in the State of Alabama.

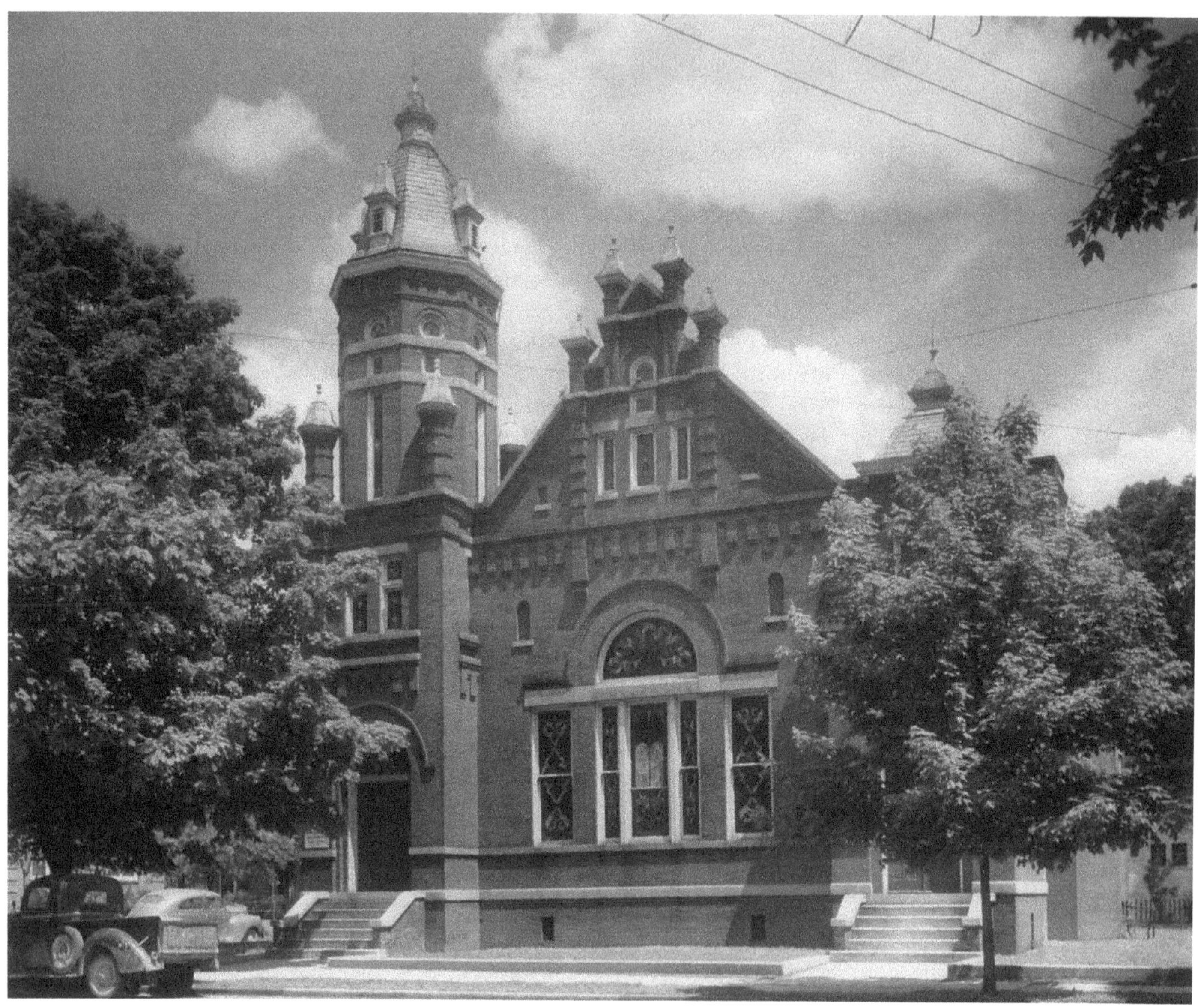

Monte Sano Park was dedicated on August 25, 1938. Dignitaries included Senator John Sparkman and Congressman William Bankhead, father of actress Talullah Bankhead. Bankhead National Forest in Northwest Alabama was named in his honor.

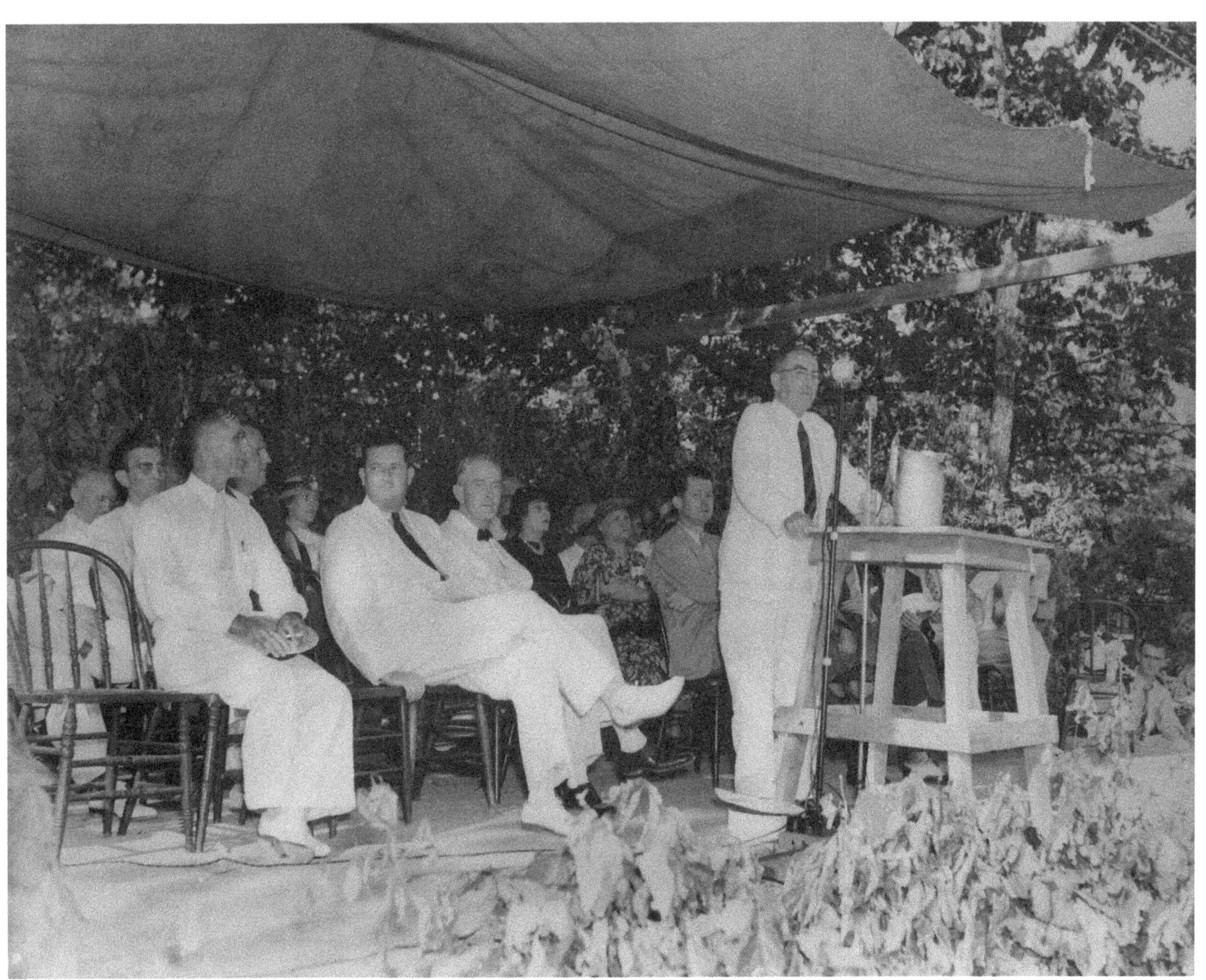

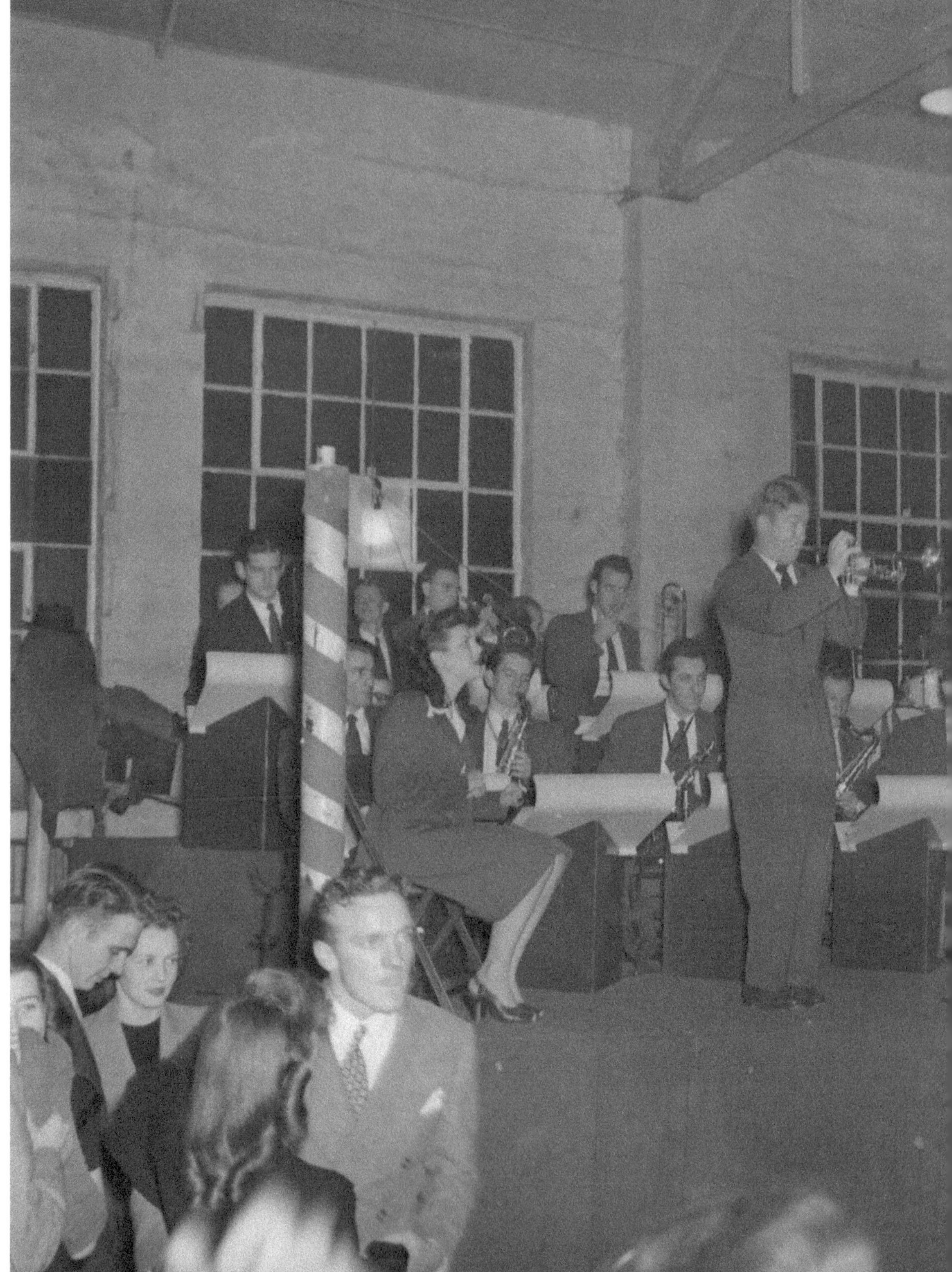

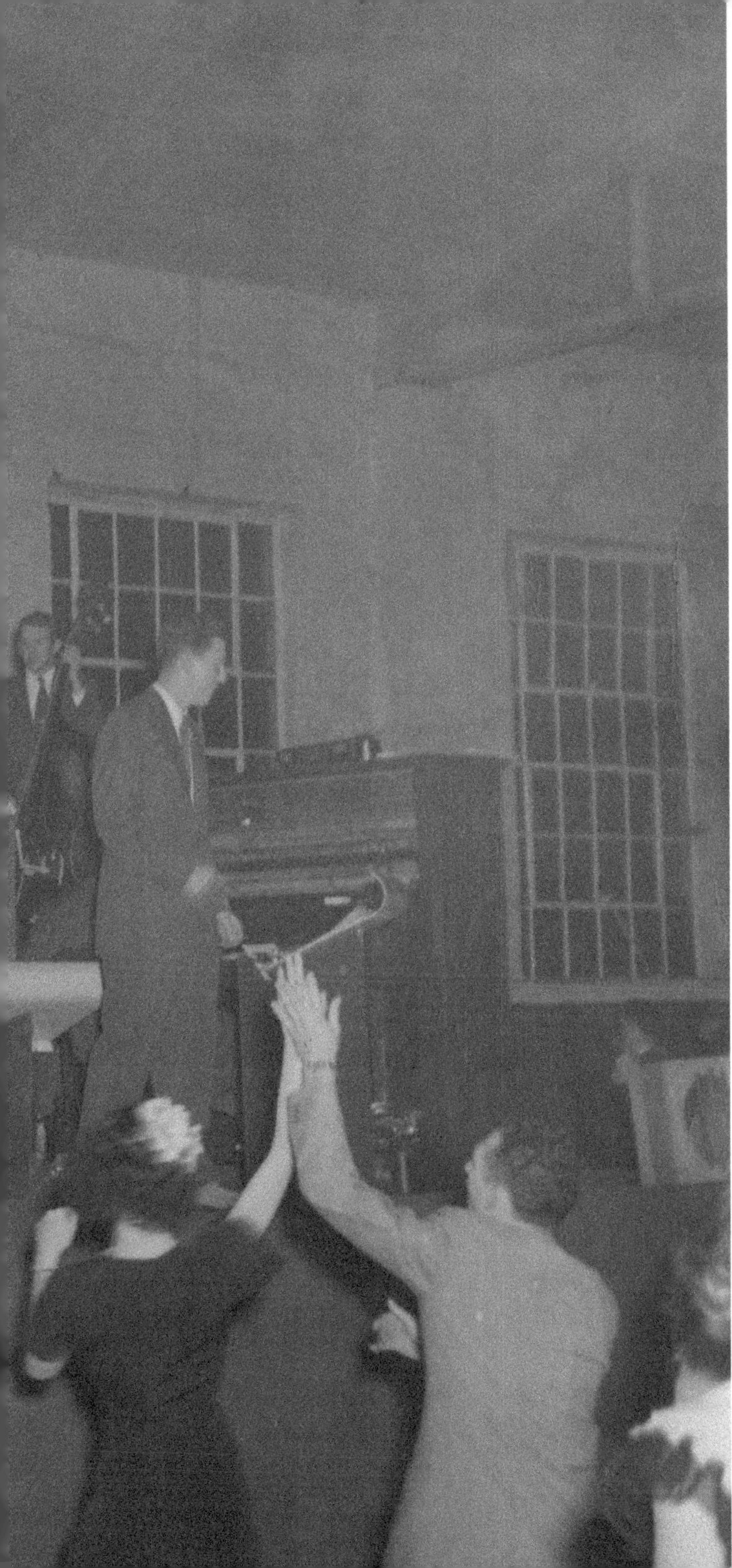

Dancers cut a rug to Big Band music at Dallas Street Armory.

Charming ladies sit on floats rounding the corner at Courthouse Square during a 1939 parade.

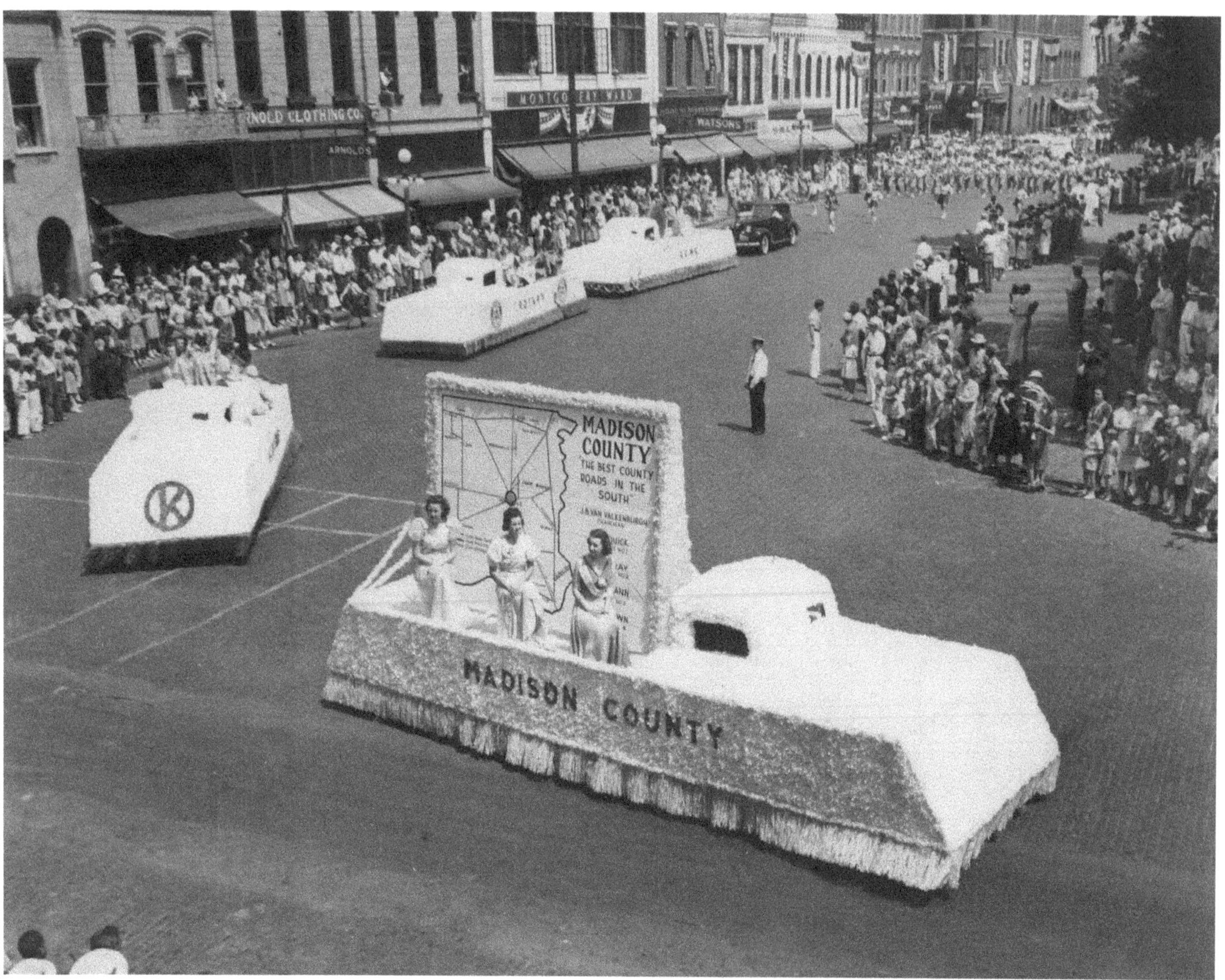

From Cotton Fields to Rocket Ships

(1940–1970s)

This period marked the biggest change in Huntsville's history. Military factories churned out weapons for World War II. As men went off to fight, housewives folded their aprons and went to work on assembly lines. Whites worked alongside black laborers in the factories; there was no time to worry about segregation.

Celebrations marked the end of the war. Arsenals and factories fell silent, but in 1950, Wernher von Braun and his German rocket team were about to transform the town forever. Redstone Arsenal was secured, thanks to Brigadier General Holger Toftoy, to develop rockets and missiles that would eventually take Americans to the moon. Scientists and support staff poured into town with their families and the area happily struggled to accommodate the population boom.

The Civil Rights Movement made headlines all over the South during this period. While neighboring cities struggled with bloodshed and demonstrations, Huntsville was relatively untouched. Huntsville City Schools were the first in the state to integrate and signs of segregation, such as separate drinking fountains, were removed with hardly a mention.

In the race to space, each milestone was celebrated with parades and speeches, and in the sultry summer of 1969, Huntsville erupted with excitement when American astronauts walked on the moon. Much of their training, as well as the design and development of the space capsule, happened on Alabama soil, but then Dr. von Braun was transferred to Washington, D.C. Much of the leadership in America's rocketry was farmed out to Houston, and Huntsville suffered a recession. Local entrepreneurs helped turn things around, and after a few bumps in the local economy, the job market began to level out, then expand. Huntsville remains one of the highest repositories of PhDs in America, and many research and development companies call it home, putting us in the same league as California's Silicon Valley.

The landscape of Huntsville has been transformed in the past few decades, but amid the factories and bedroom communities, one can still see patches of the fluffy, white cotton that brought our ancestors to the Tennessee Valley more than two hundred years ago. We won't forget our past, those fields seem to say, and we have the photographs to prove it.

Building 7101 served as the first headquarters for Redstone Arsenal. It was built in 1941. A Hermes Missile is on display at the right.

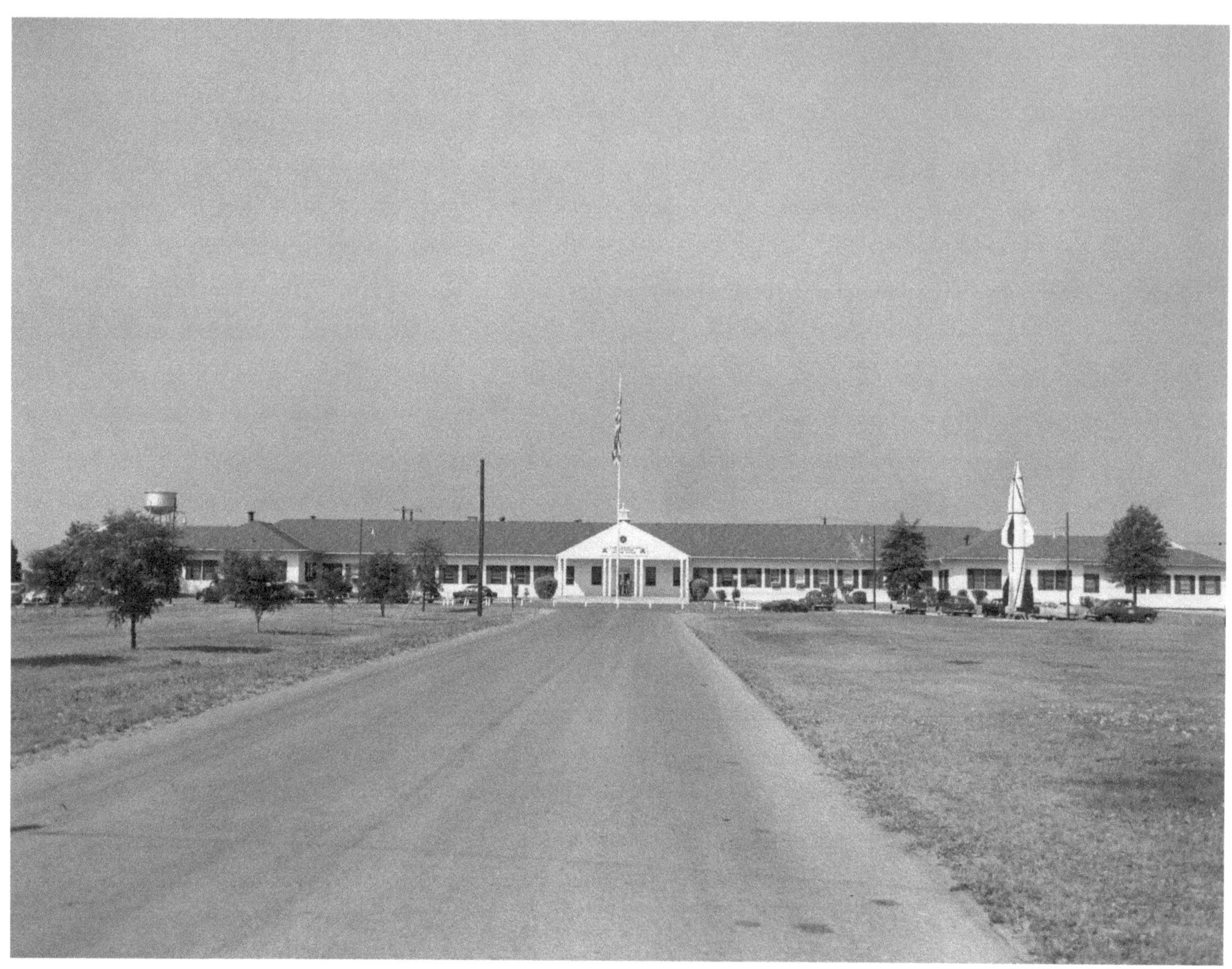

Mill workers at Huntsville Manufacturing Company check spools to keep them humming.

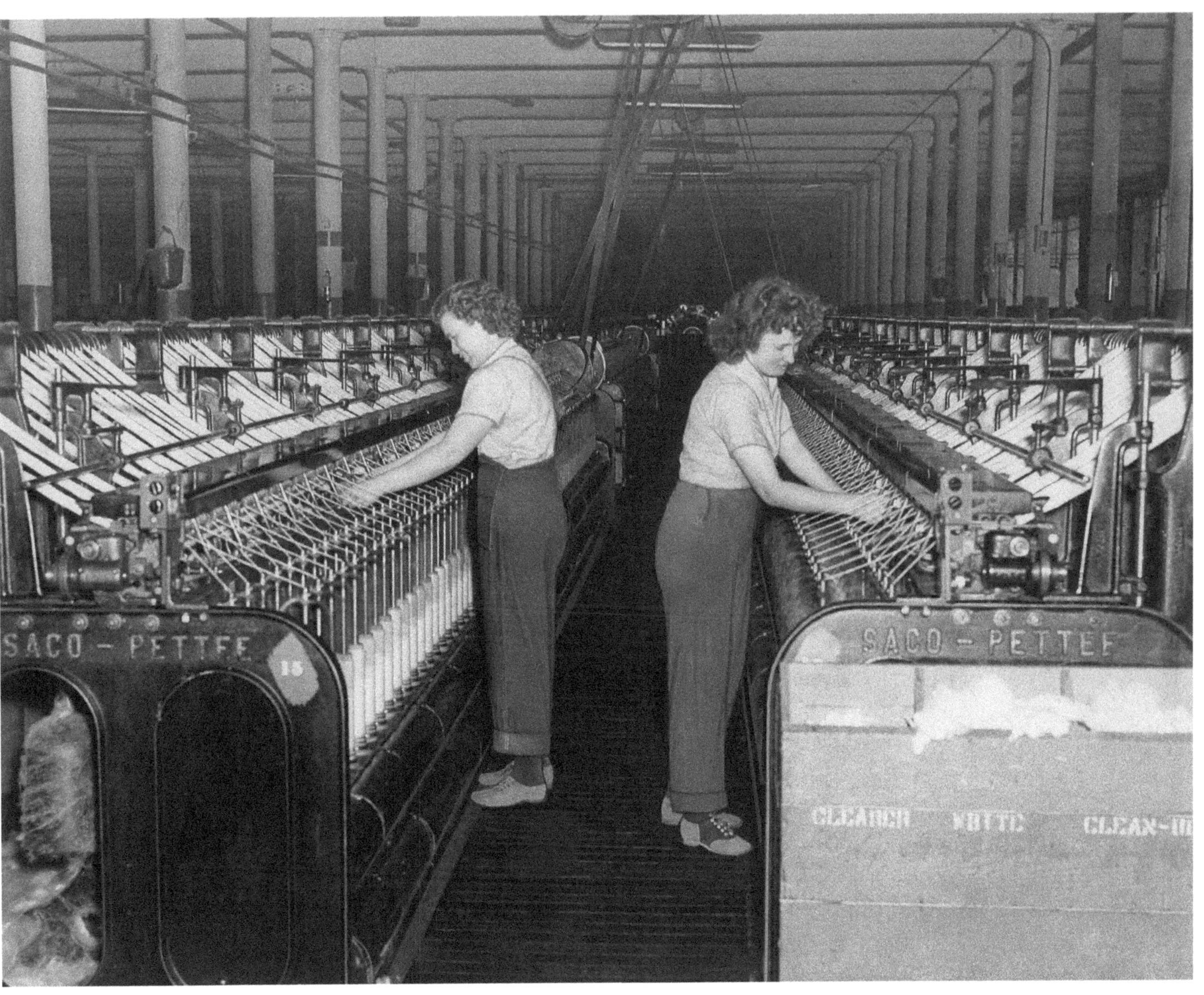

A parade was held to celebrate Army Day on April 6, 1942. The Redstone Ordnance Plant sent several vehicles to participate. The Ordnance Plant was renamed Redstone Arsenal on February 26, 1943.

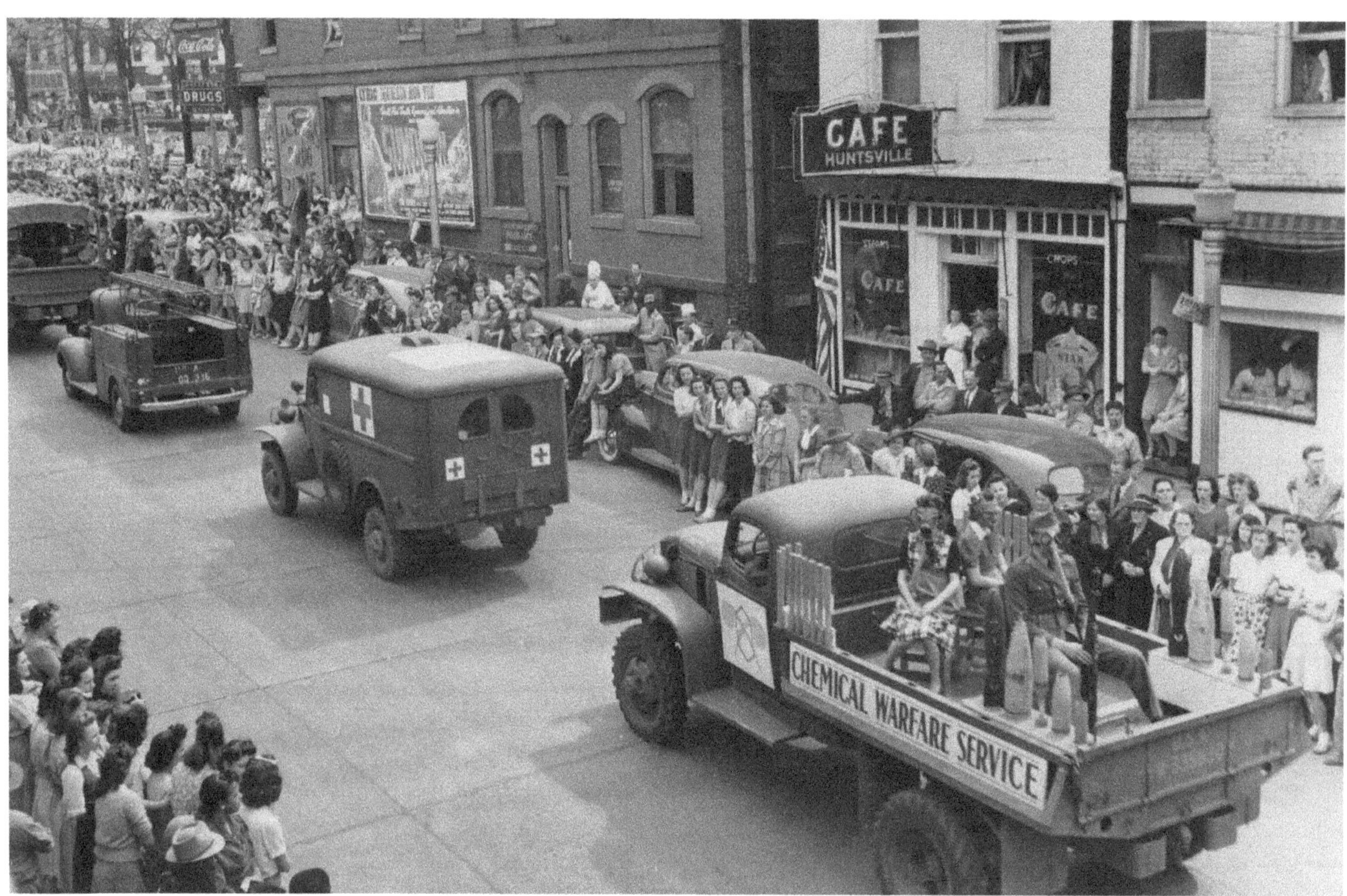

Backwoods trails all across Monte Sano Mountain made it a great place for horseback riding.

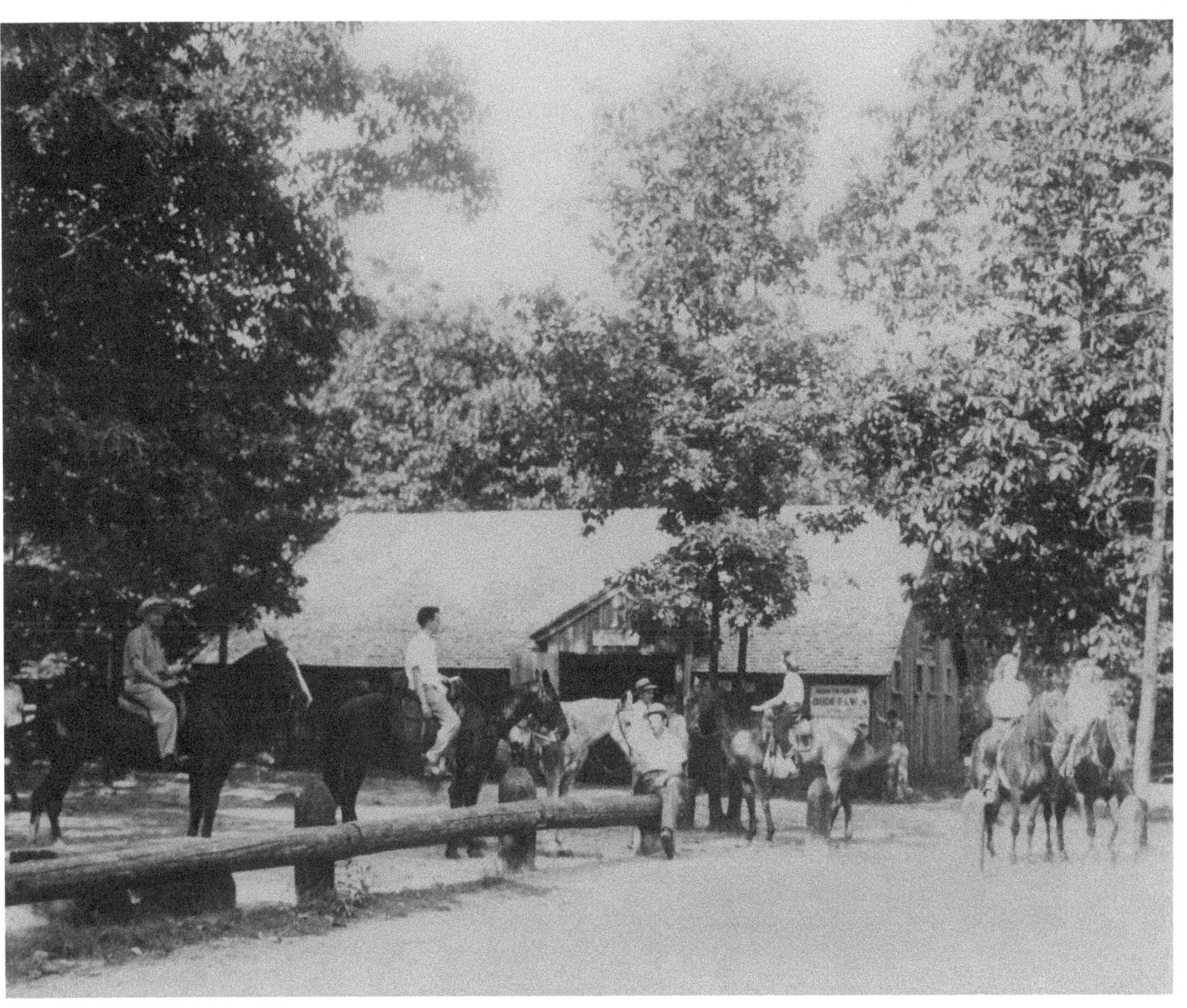

A group of ladies saddle up at a dude ranch on Monte Sano Mountain.

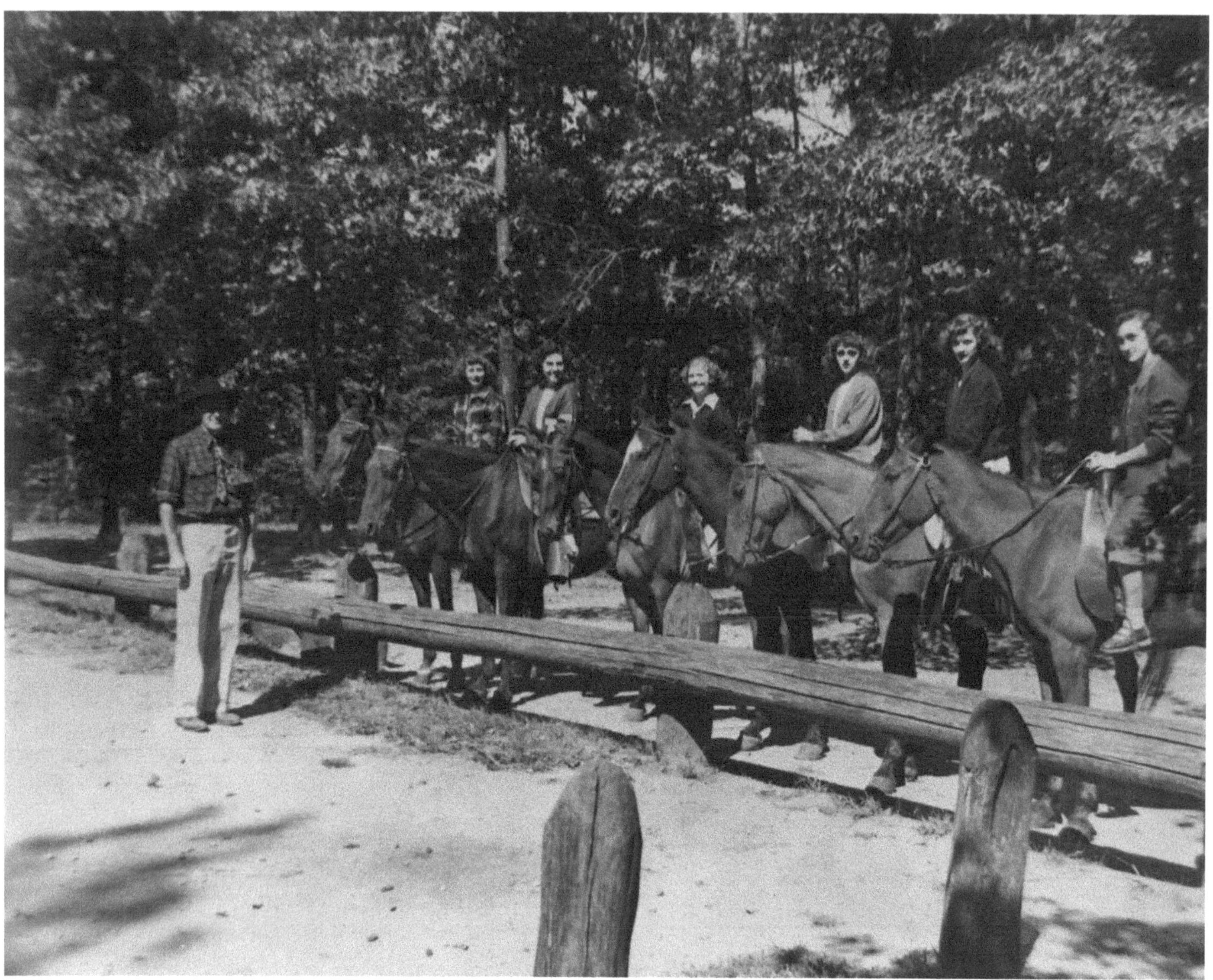

The Randolph Street Church of Christ was built in 1887 and remained much the same in appearance over the last 120 years.

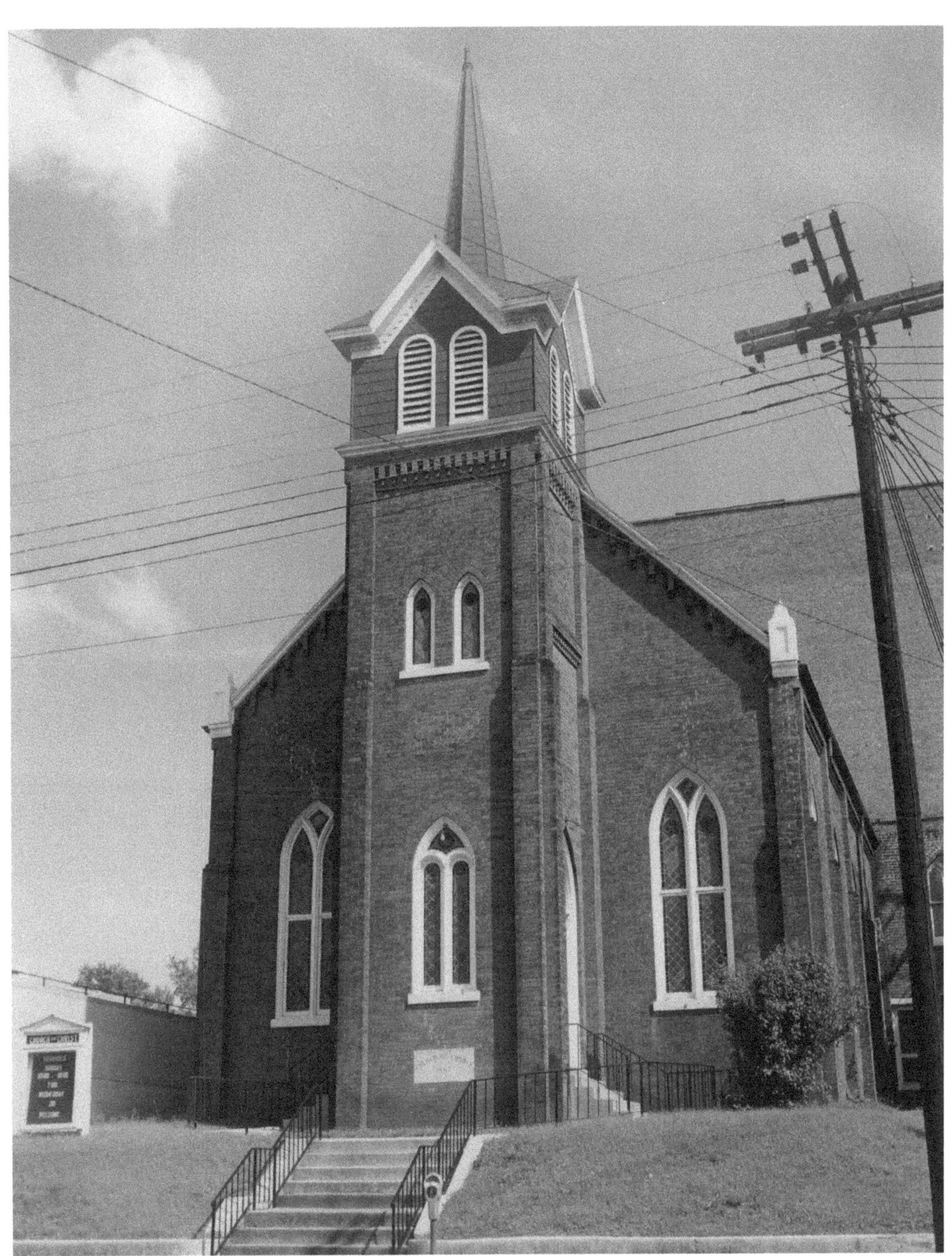

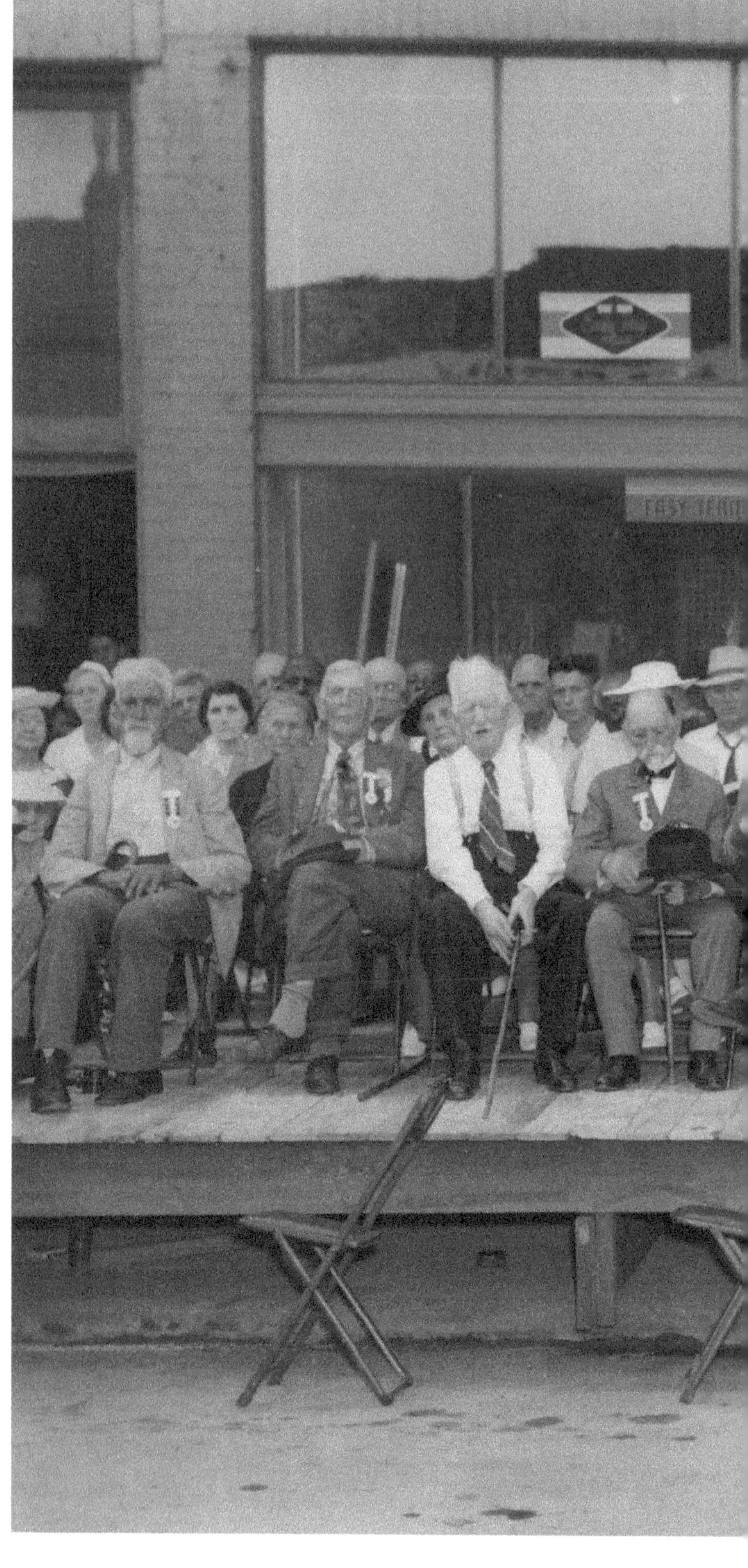

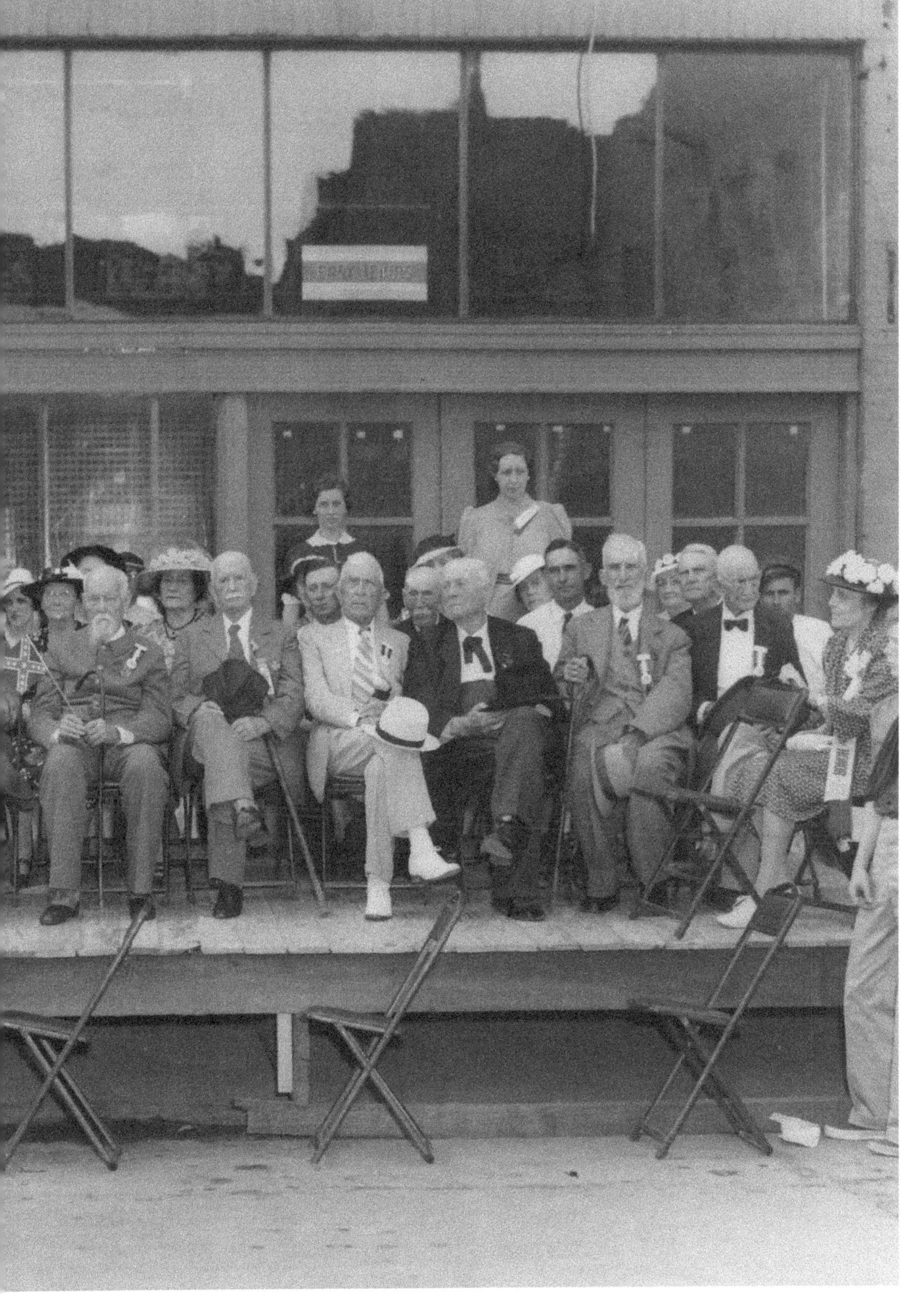

Confederate veterans gather for a reunion. J. A. Steger, the bespectacled man sitting just to the left of the man holding the Confederate flag, died at age 102 in 1948. He was the last living Civil War veteran from Madison County.

The eloquent Henderson National Bank, located to the right and on the corner of Randolph and Washington Streets, burned in 1946.

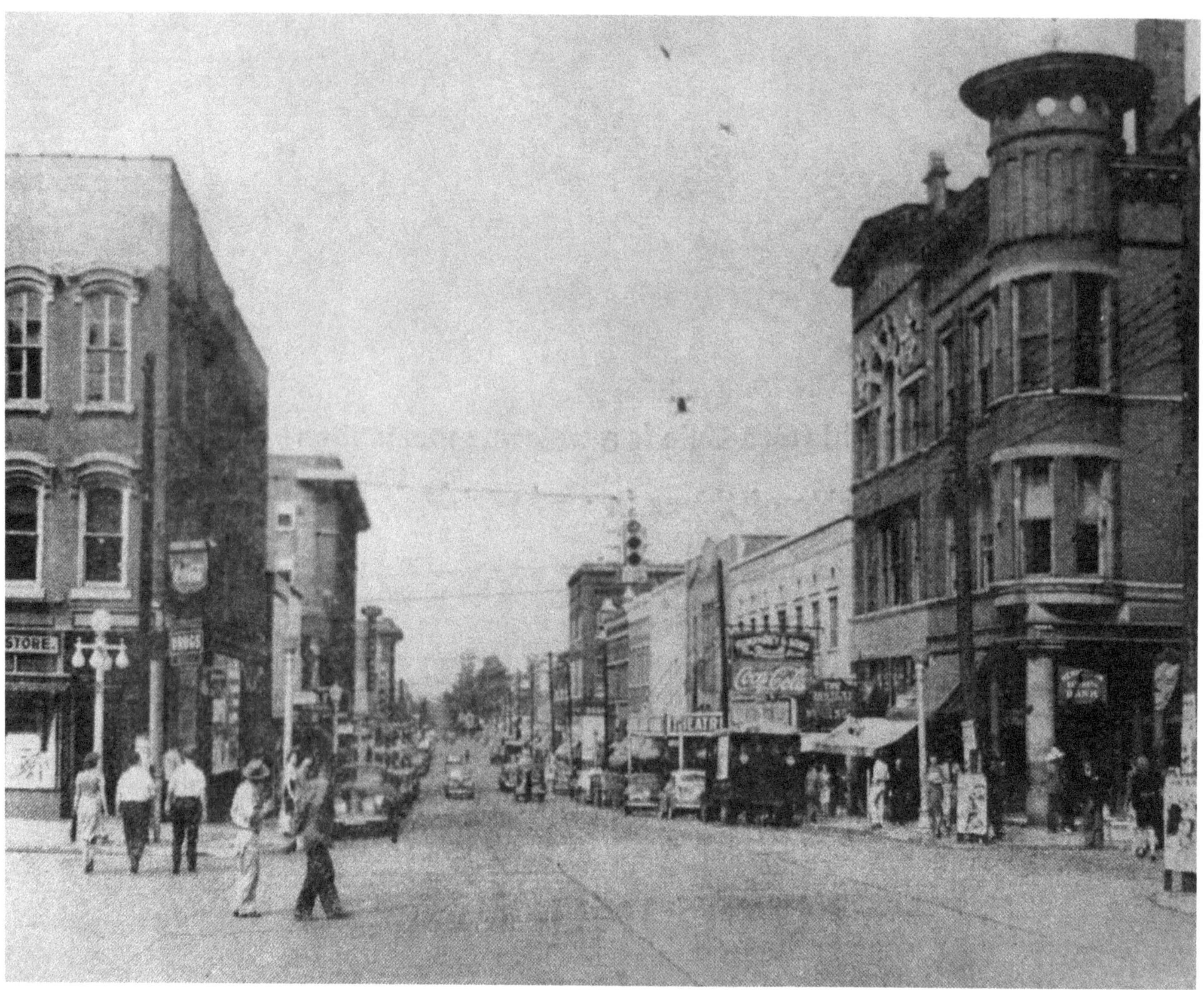

These people lined up around the block may have been waiting to apply for jobs or sign up for unemployment benefits. A Chapman Dairy truck sits on the right side of the street.

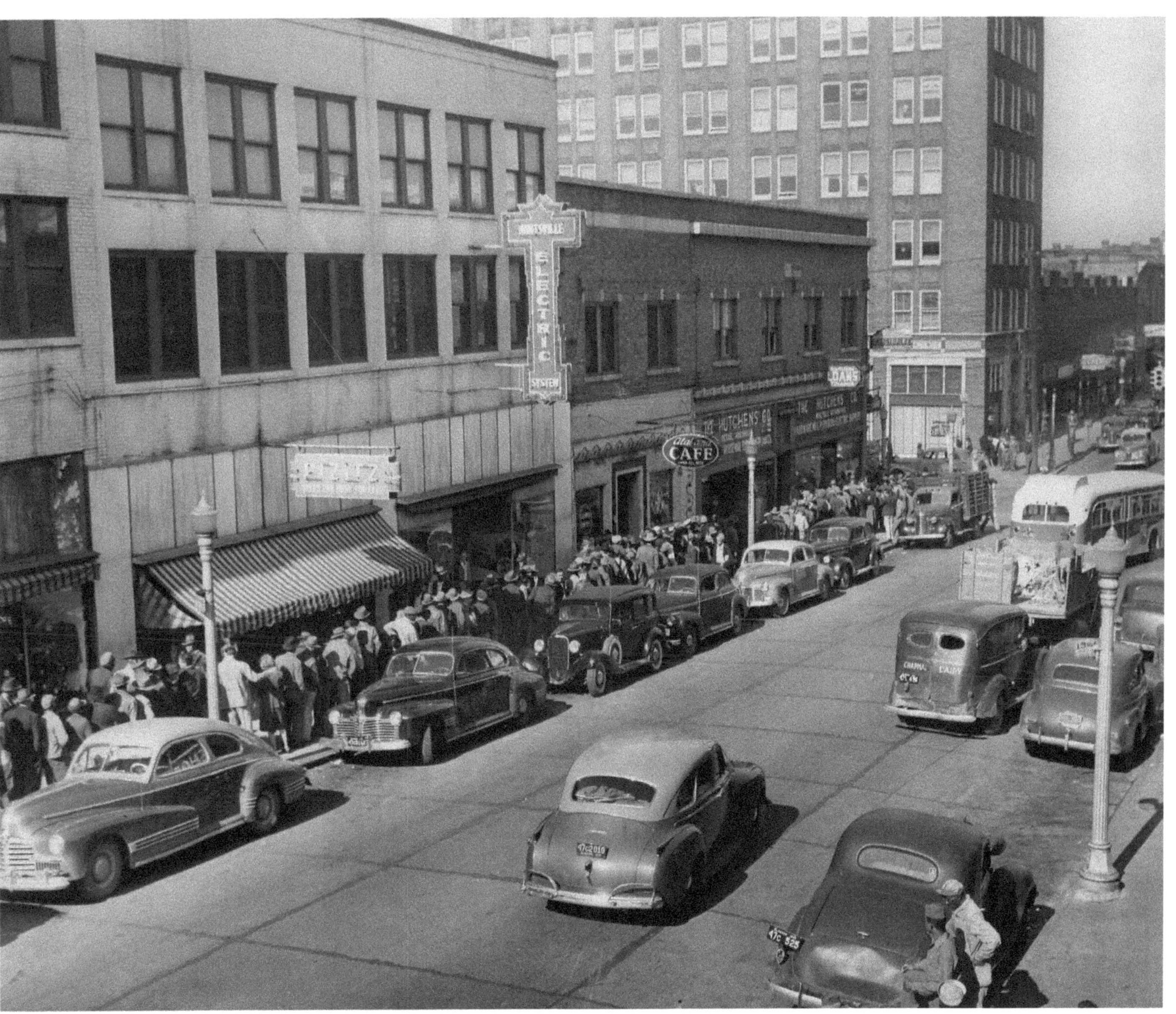

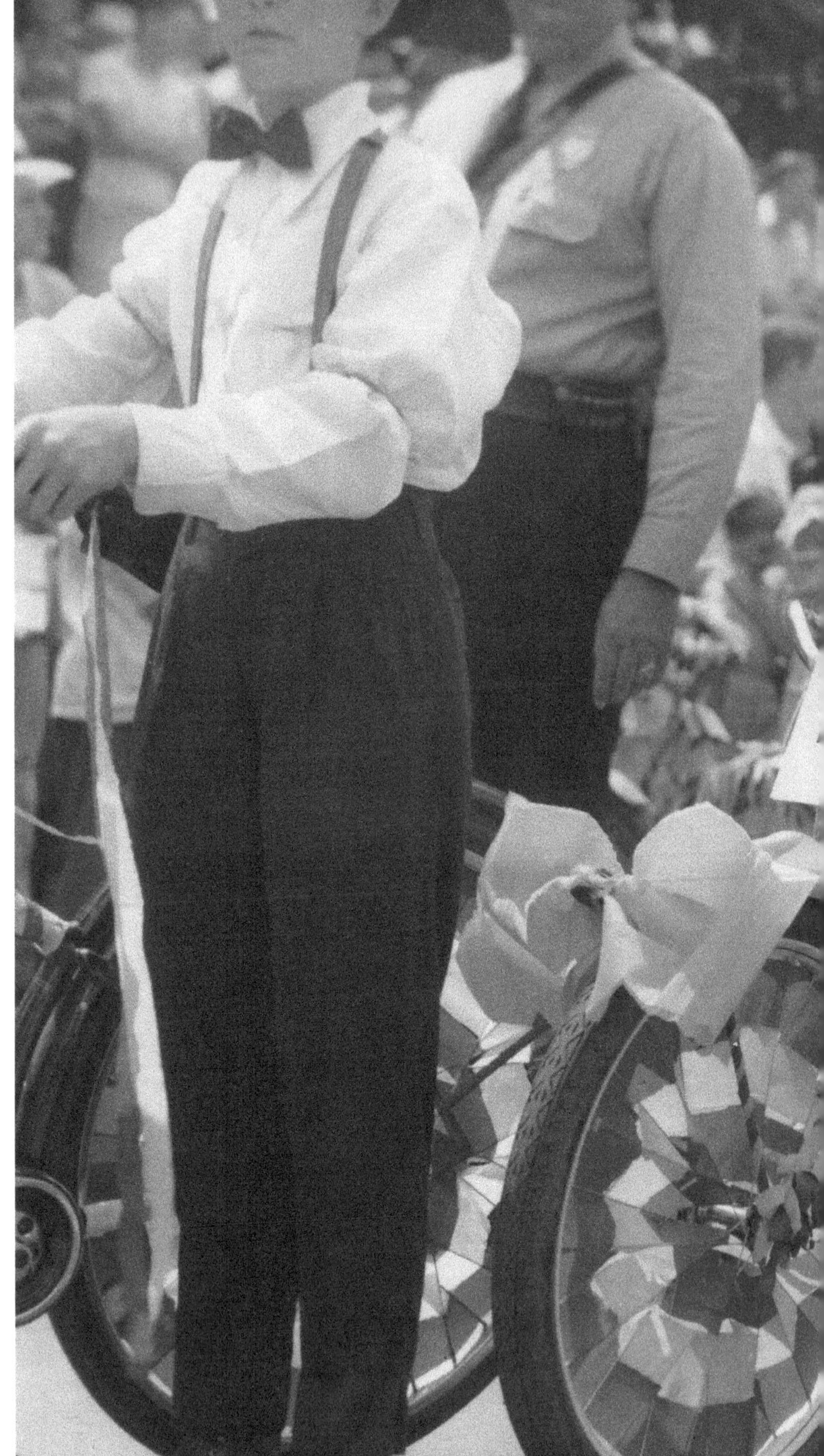

Even the children display their patriotism during a World War II-era parade.

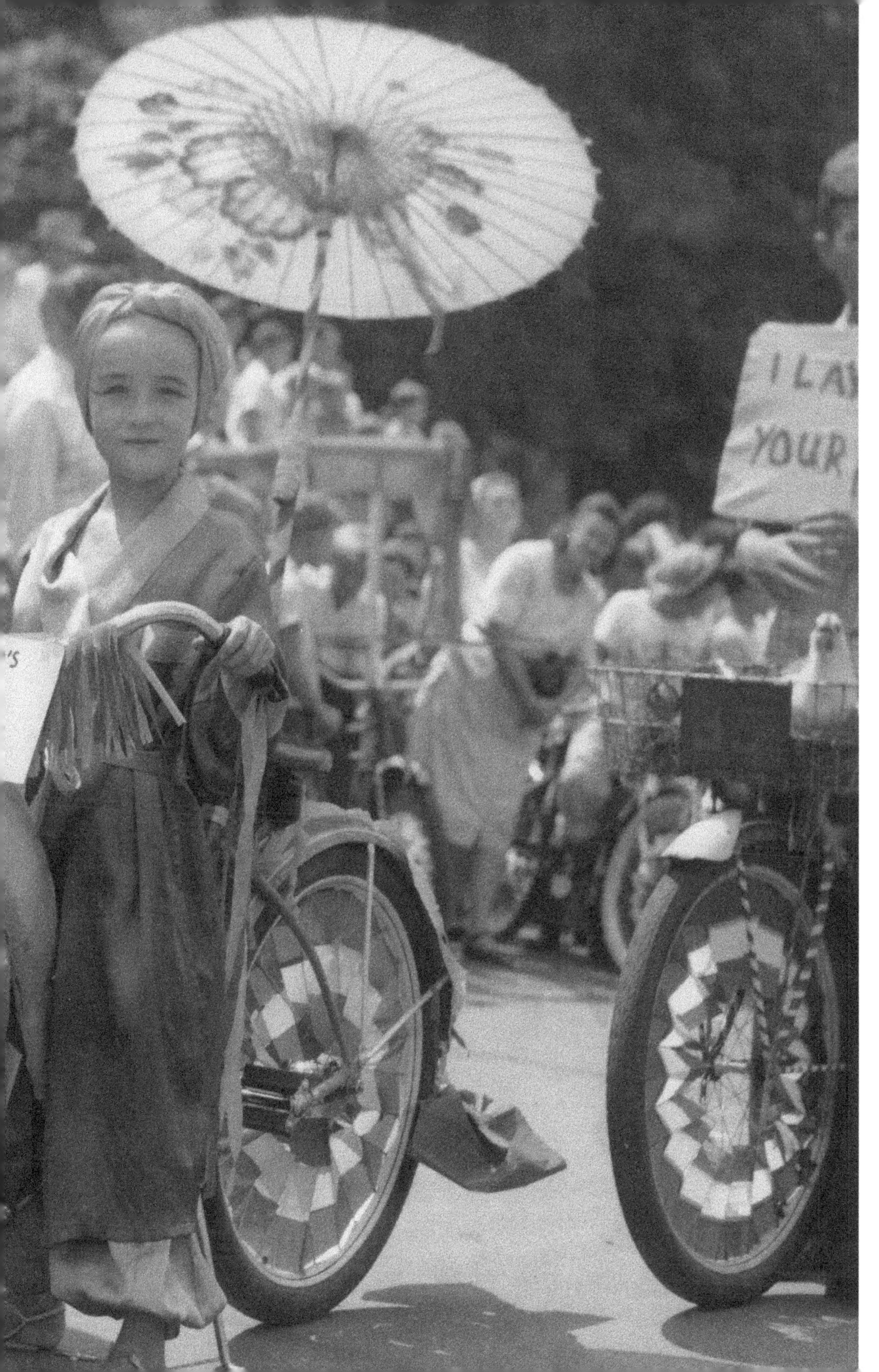

The annual Cotton Ball was a big celebration, even if you didn't know the difference between a cotton boll or a boll weevil!

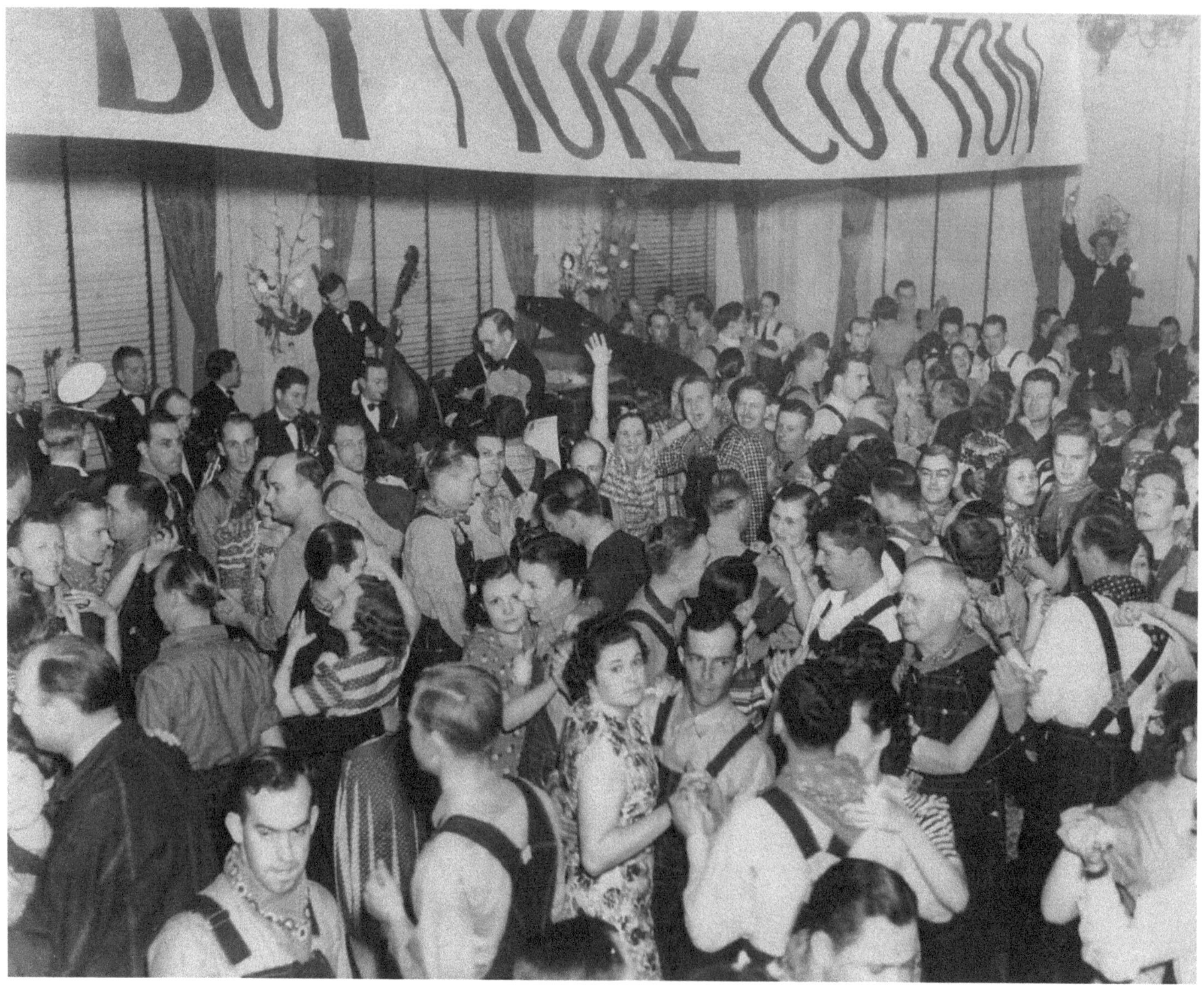

Huntsville celebrated V-J Day (Victory over Japan) on August 15th, 1945, while listening to Monroe's Band at the Madison County Courthouse. Huntsville's fighting boys would be coming home!

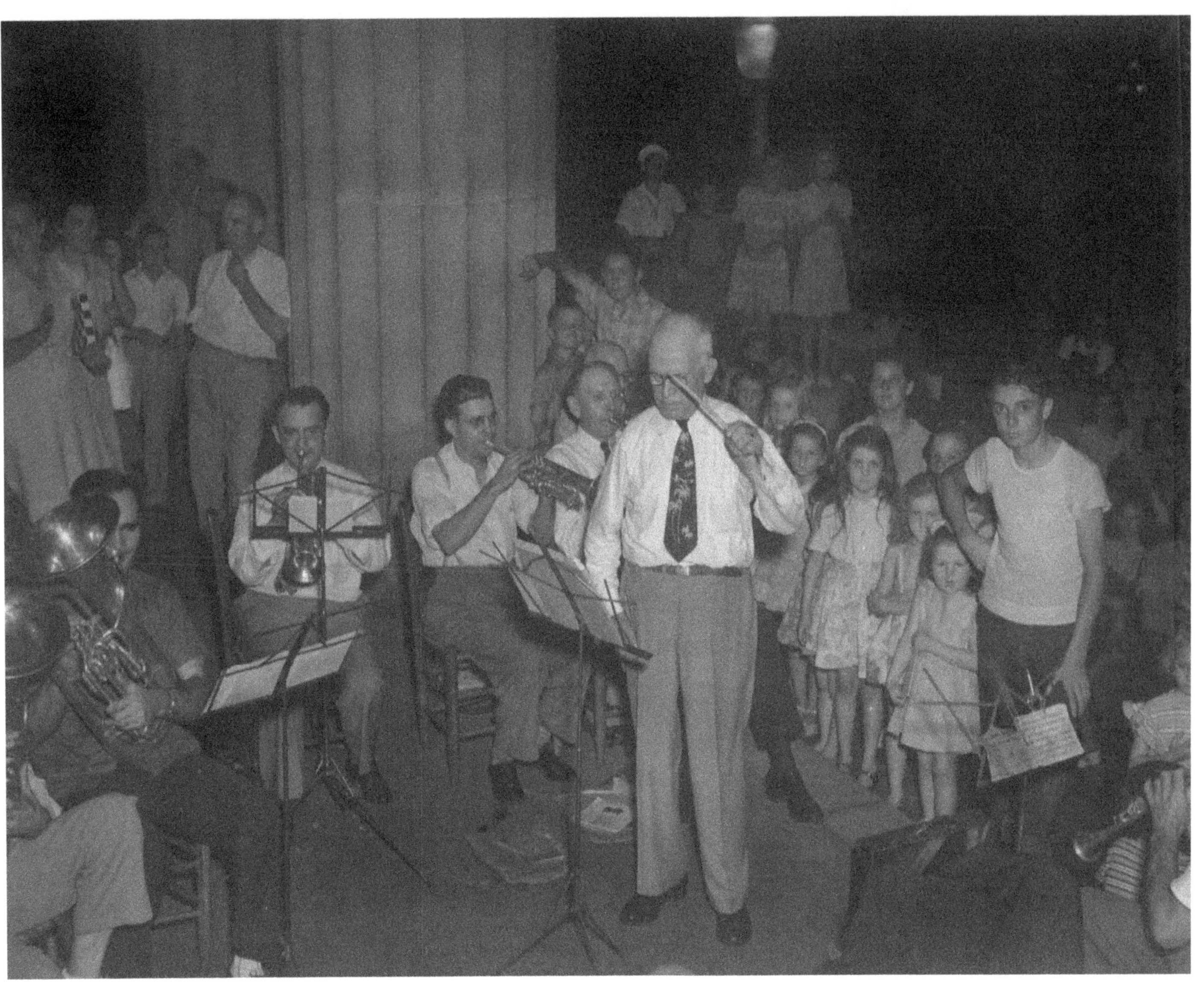

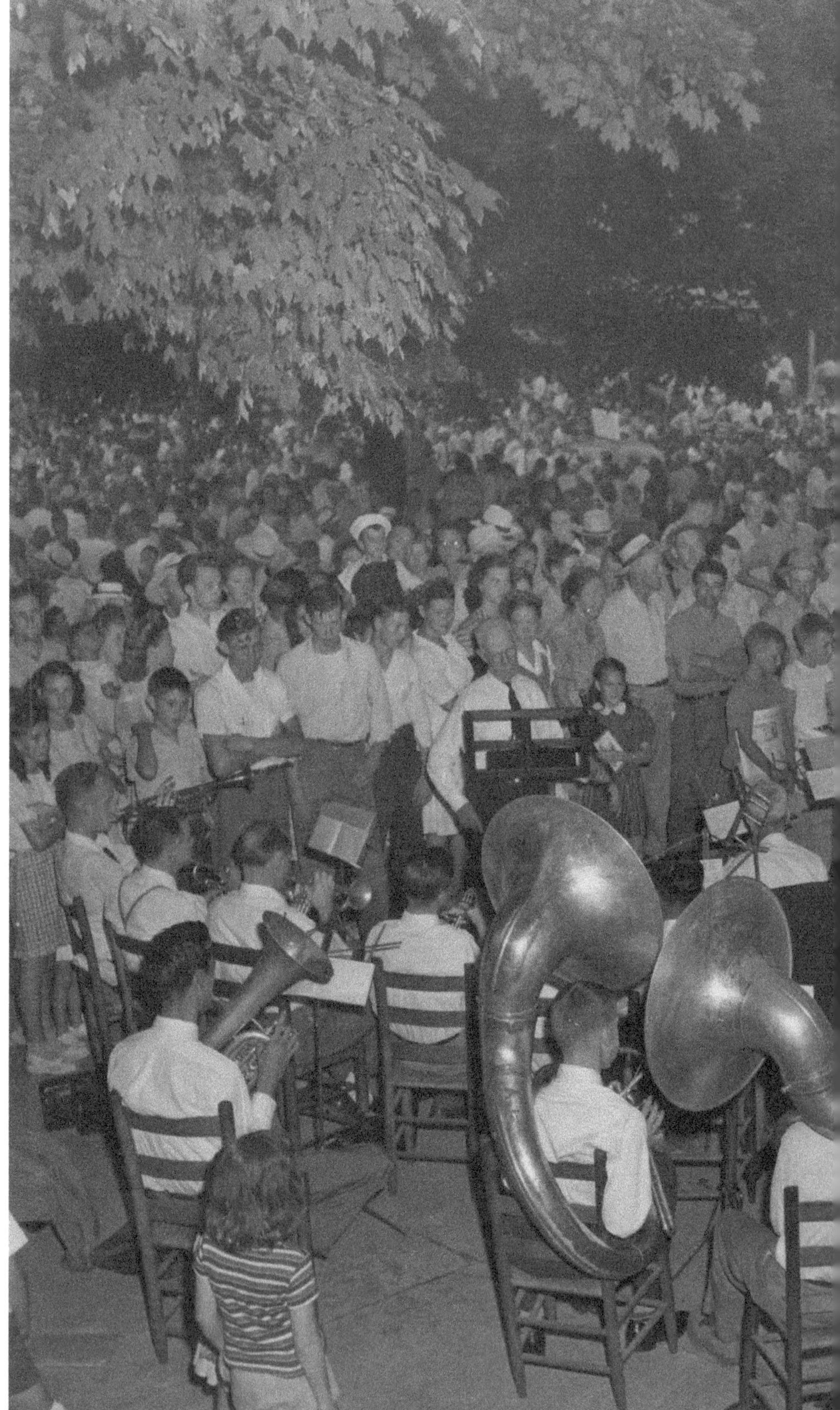

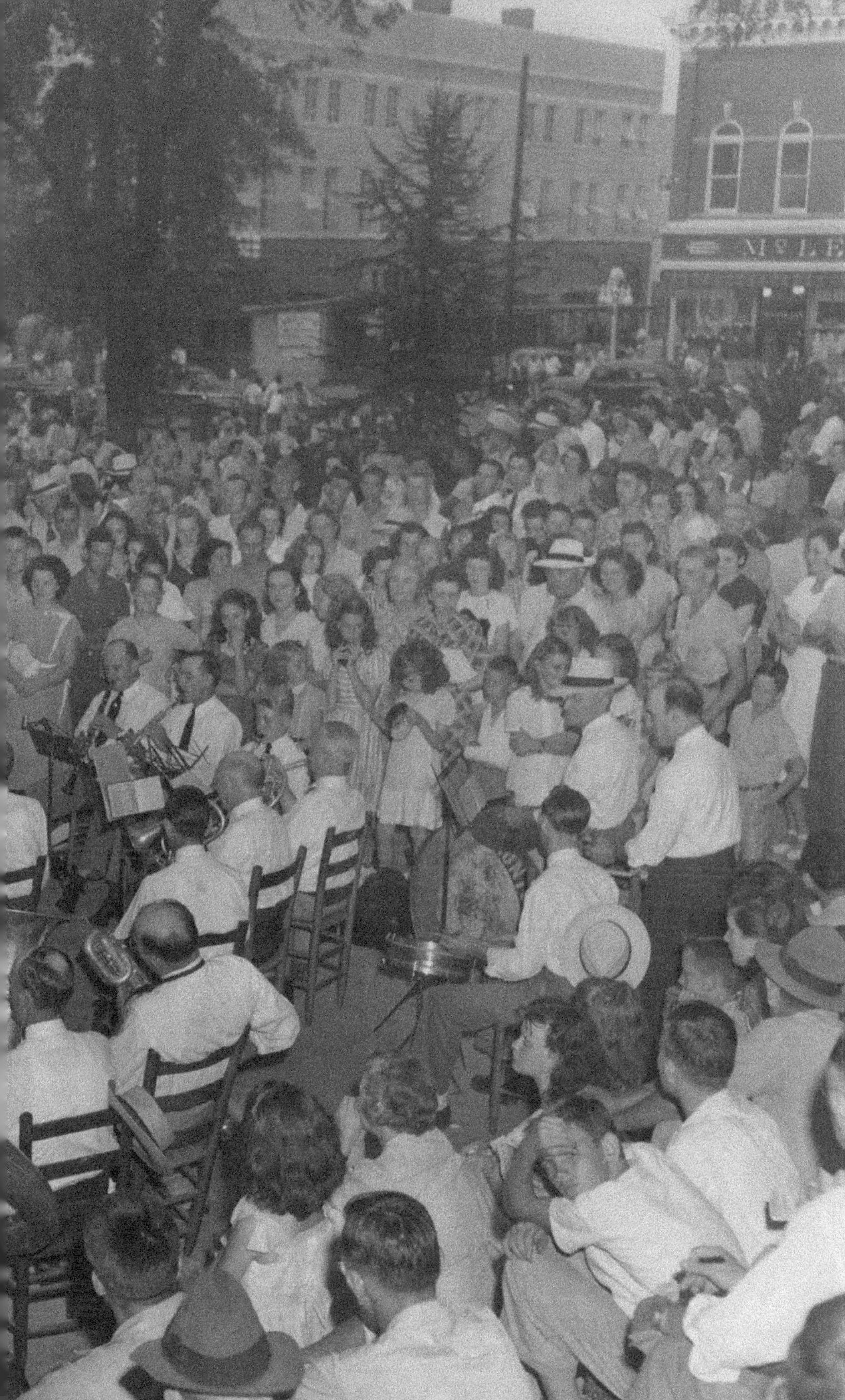

A celebration to mark the end of World War II was called for! In this picture, Monroe's Band entertains an enormous crowd at the Courthouse Square.

The Russel Erskine Hotel towers in the background at the left. It was named for Huntsville native Albert Russel Erskine, who became the millionaire president of Studebaker Automobile in South Bend, Indiana. He took his own life after the company went into receivorship in 1933.

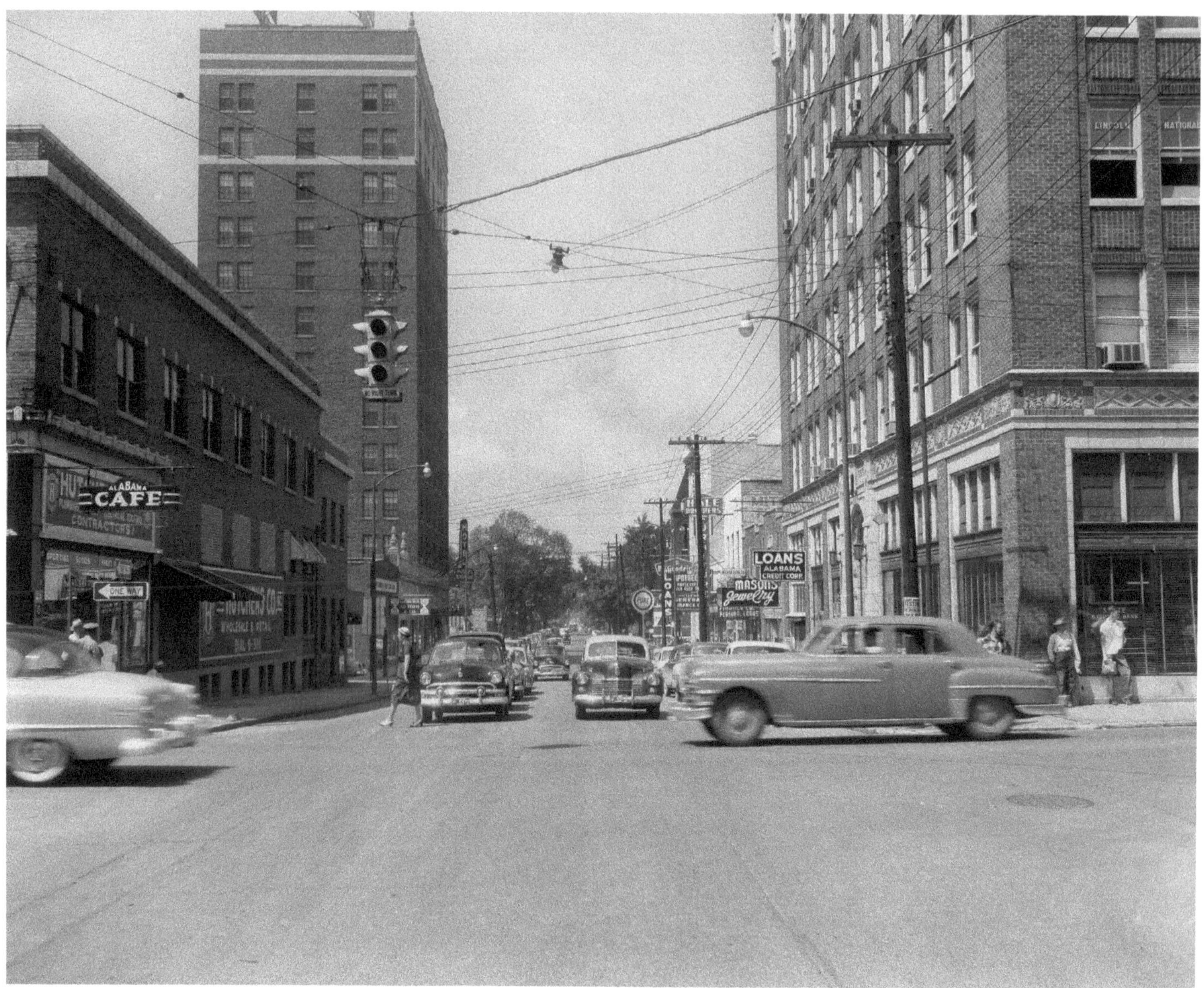

F. W. Woolworth Company on Washington Street was the original "5 and Dime" store. The sign to the far right at Kress' Store reveals inflation: "5-10-25."

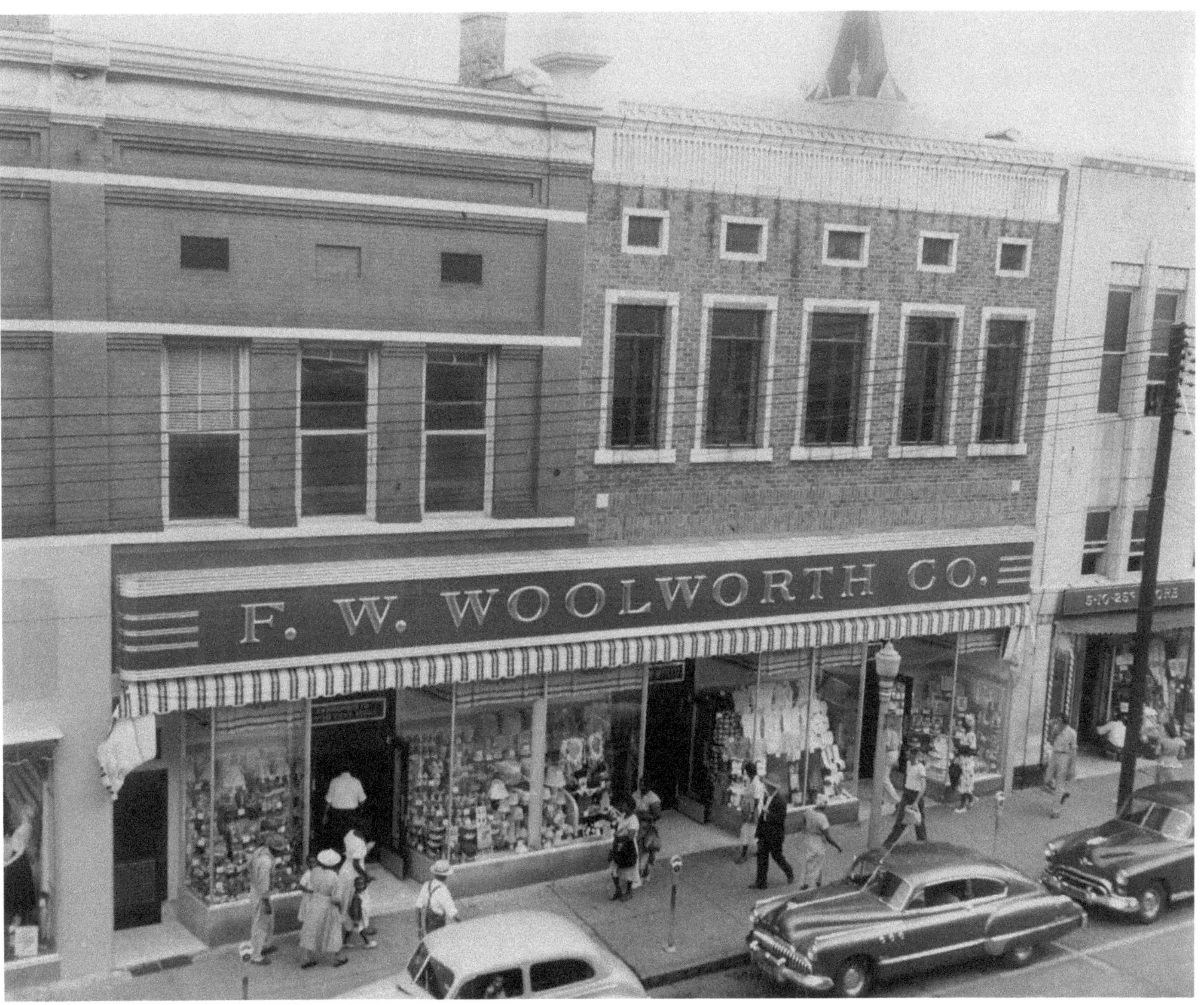

Members of Lakeside Methodist Church hold a somber celebration to mark the 80th anniversary of the end of slavery. This picture was taken in 1946. The church burned in 1969.

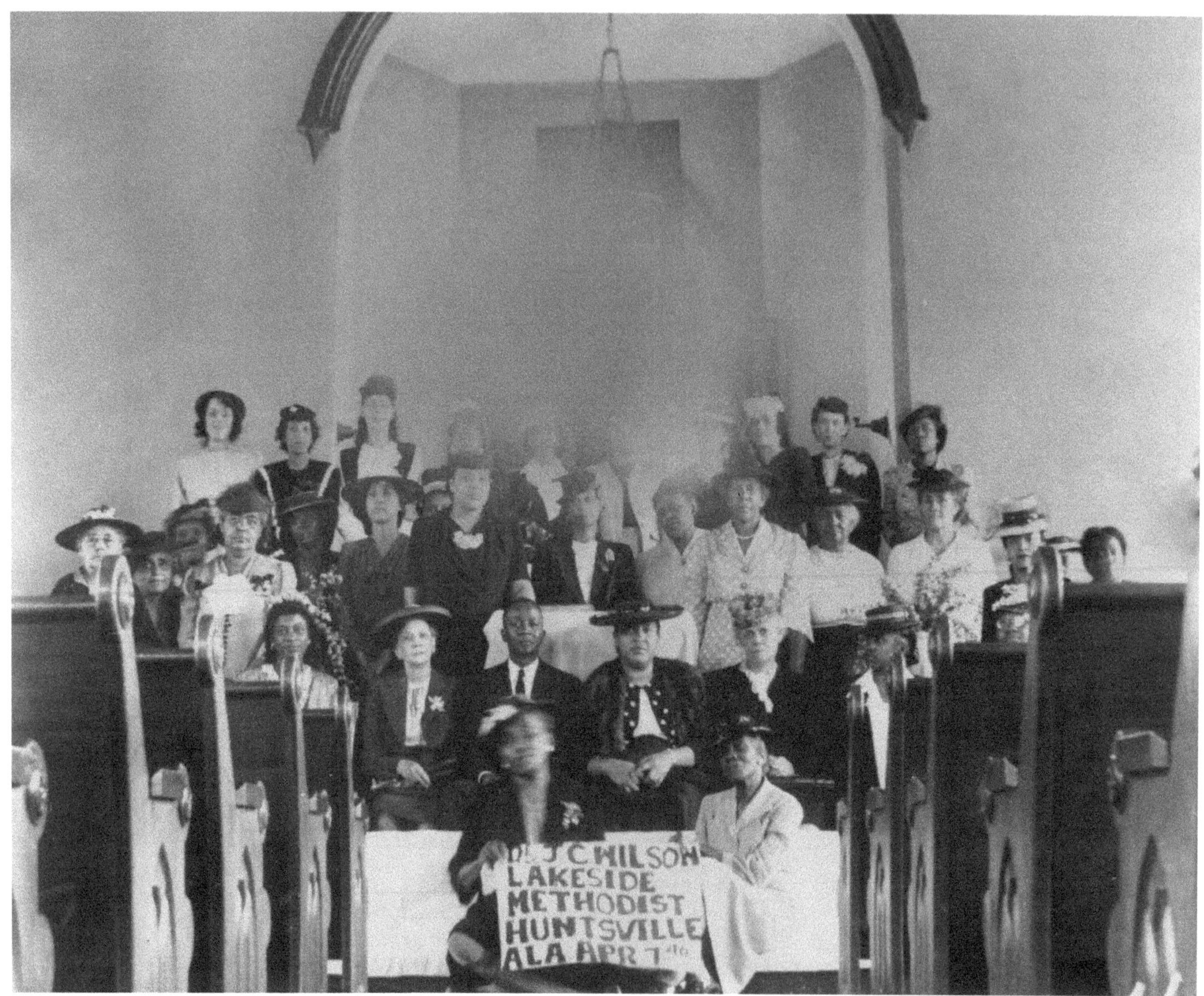

Southern Furniture Store opened in 1946. Ten years later, local disc jockey Grady Reeves sat in the display window to promote the Trade-O-Rama. Anyone who caught him sleeping during the 67-hour marathon would win a new range or refrigerator.

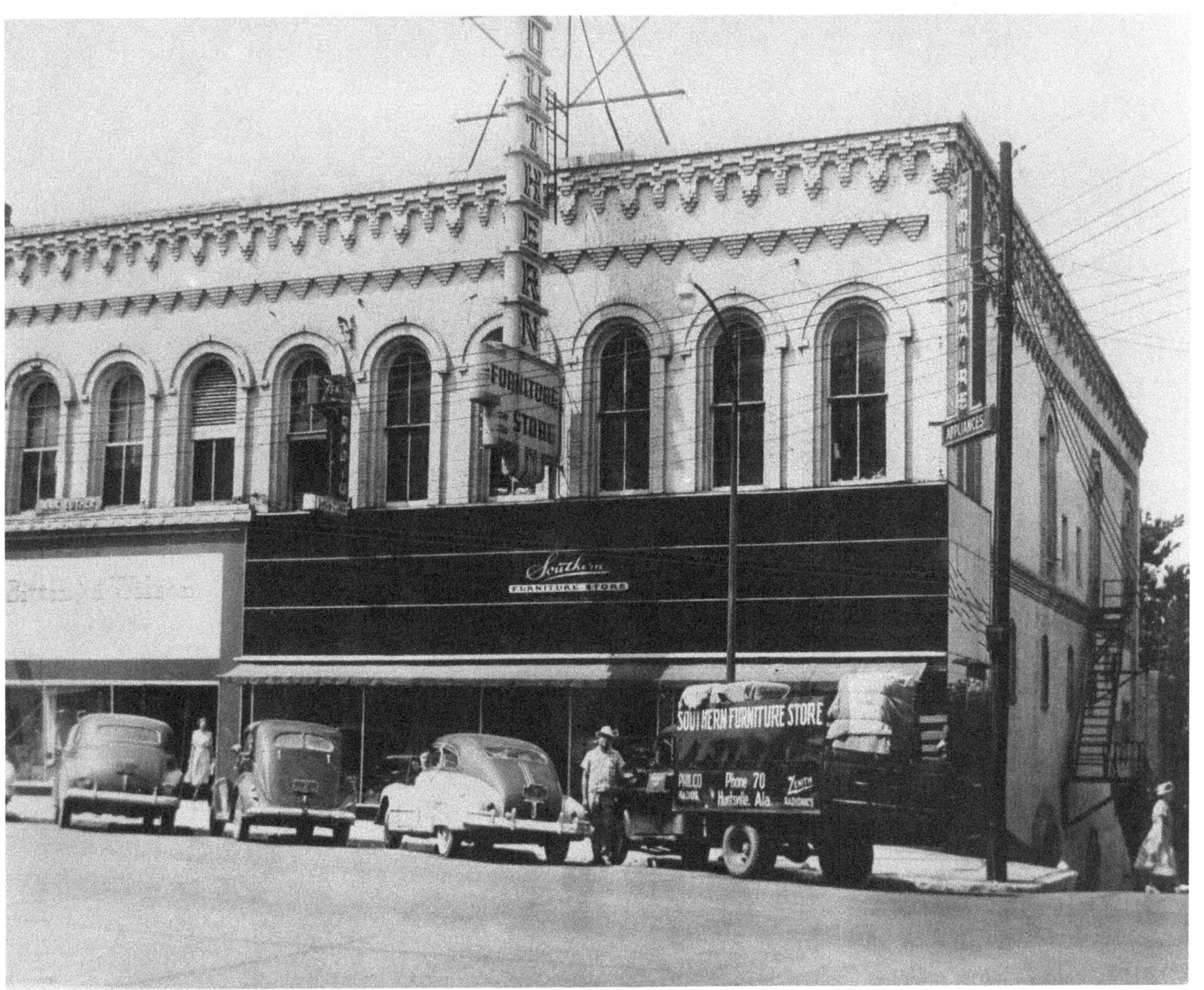

This photograph of the office at Dallas Manufacturing Company was taken in March 1948.

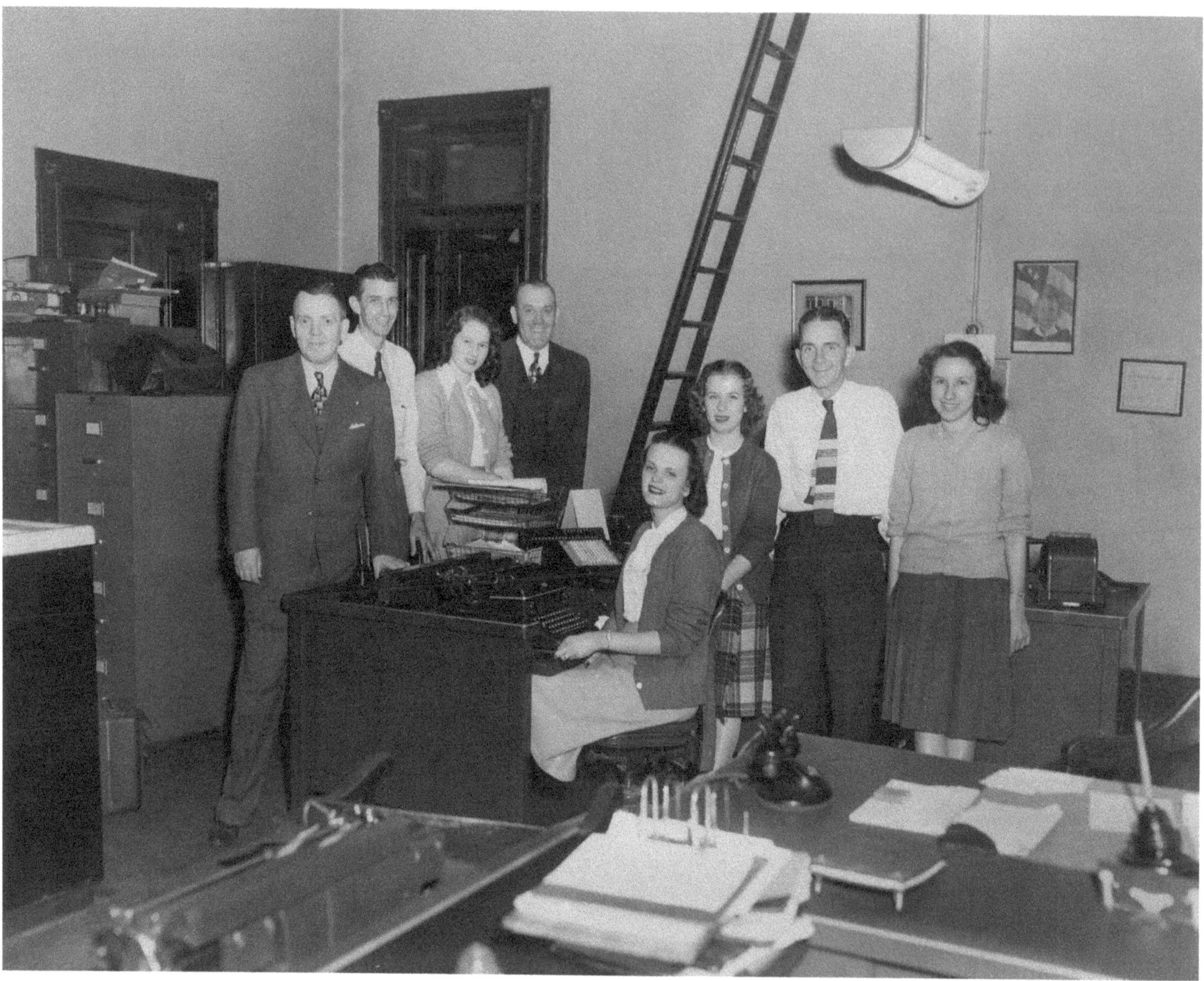

"Bumper Lite" tape was placed on this city sedan as part of a Junior Chamber (J. C.) campaign to promote automobile safety in 1953.

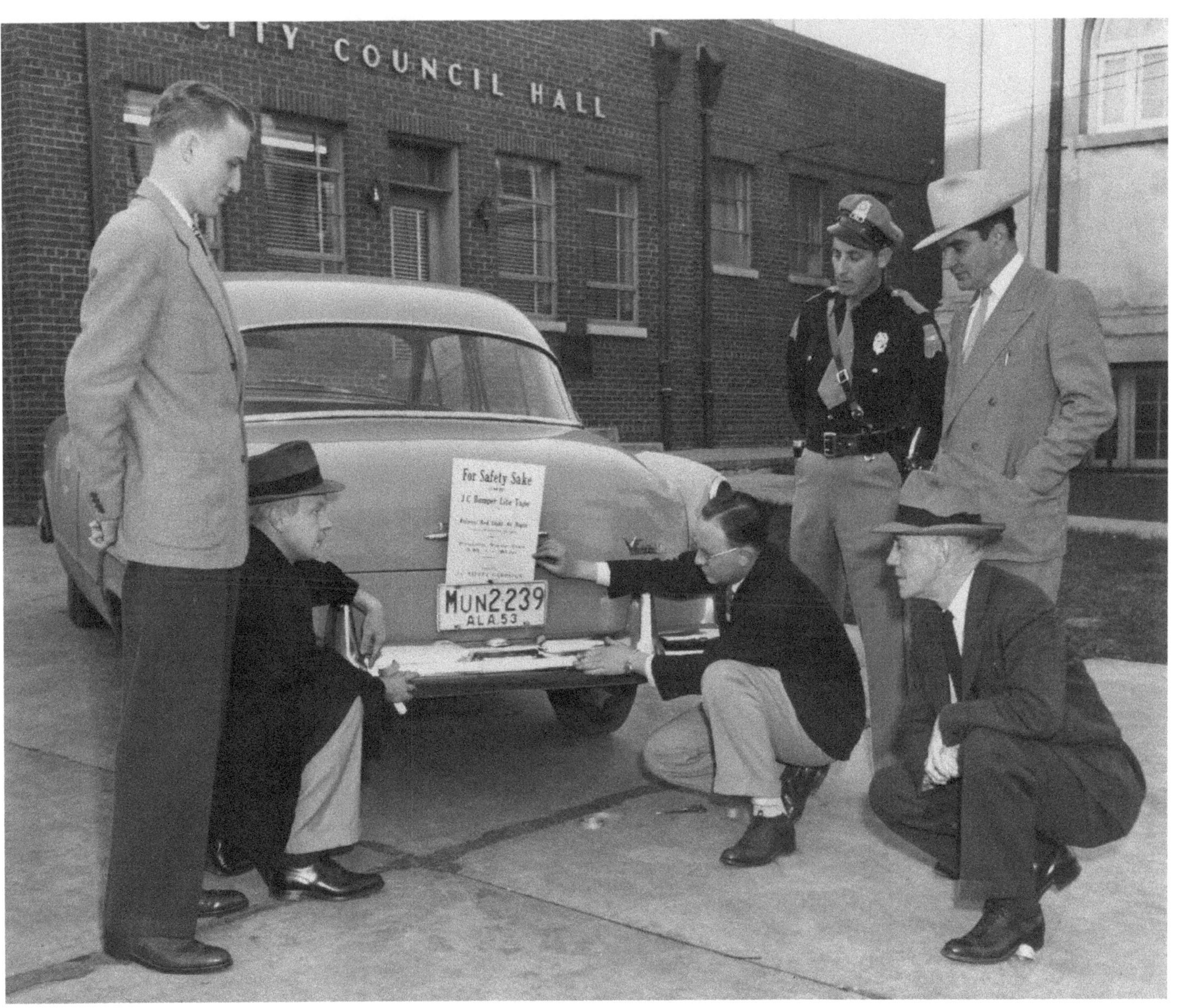

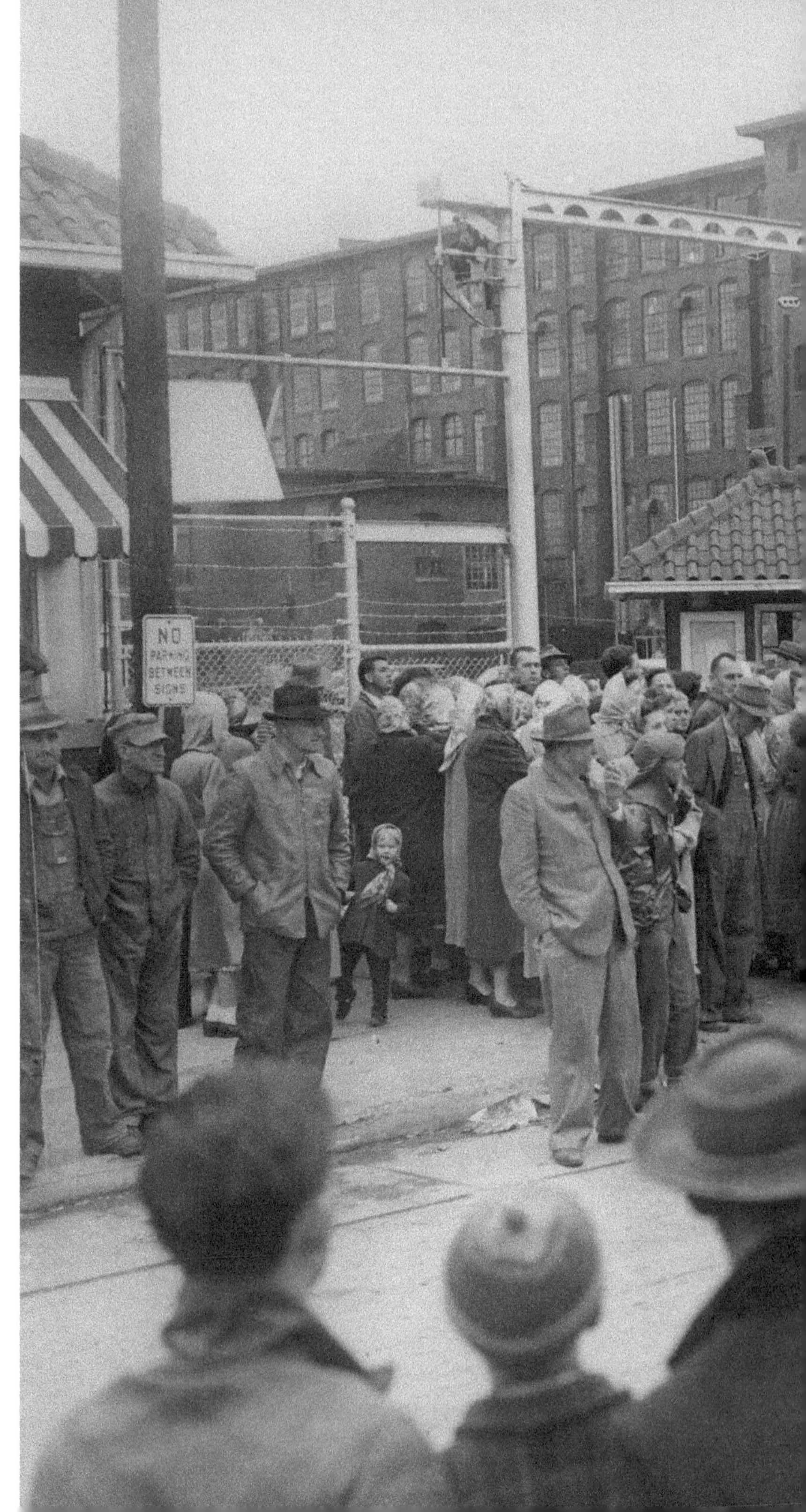
NO
PARKING
BETWEEN
SIGNS

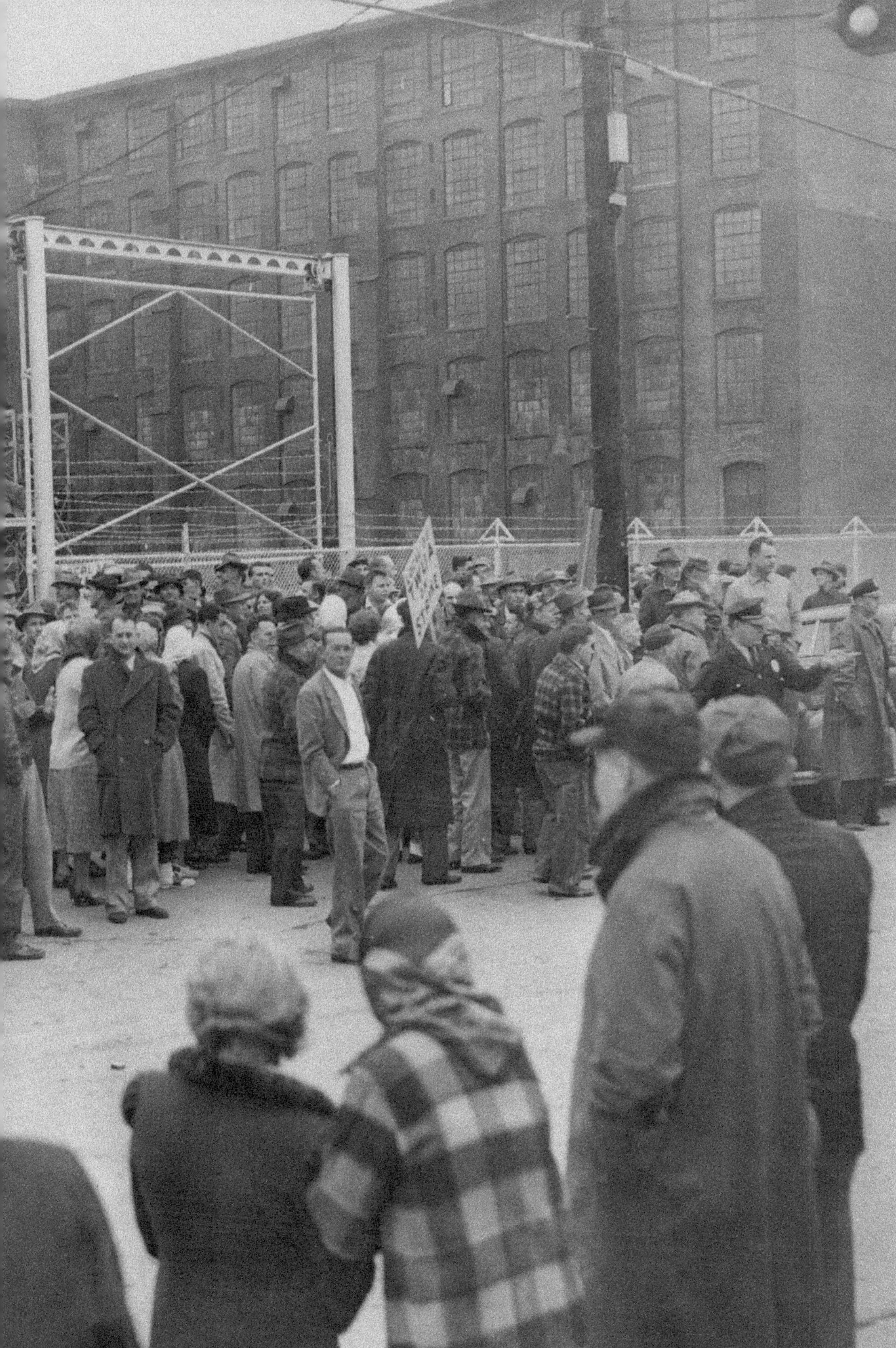

Workers at Huntsville Manufacturing strike for higher wages in 1951, a common scene at many local mills and businesses.

Huntsville Manufacturing Company proudly touted their new equipment and colorful products in this exhibit around 1953.

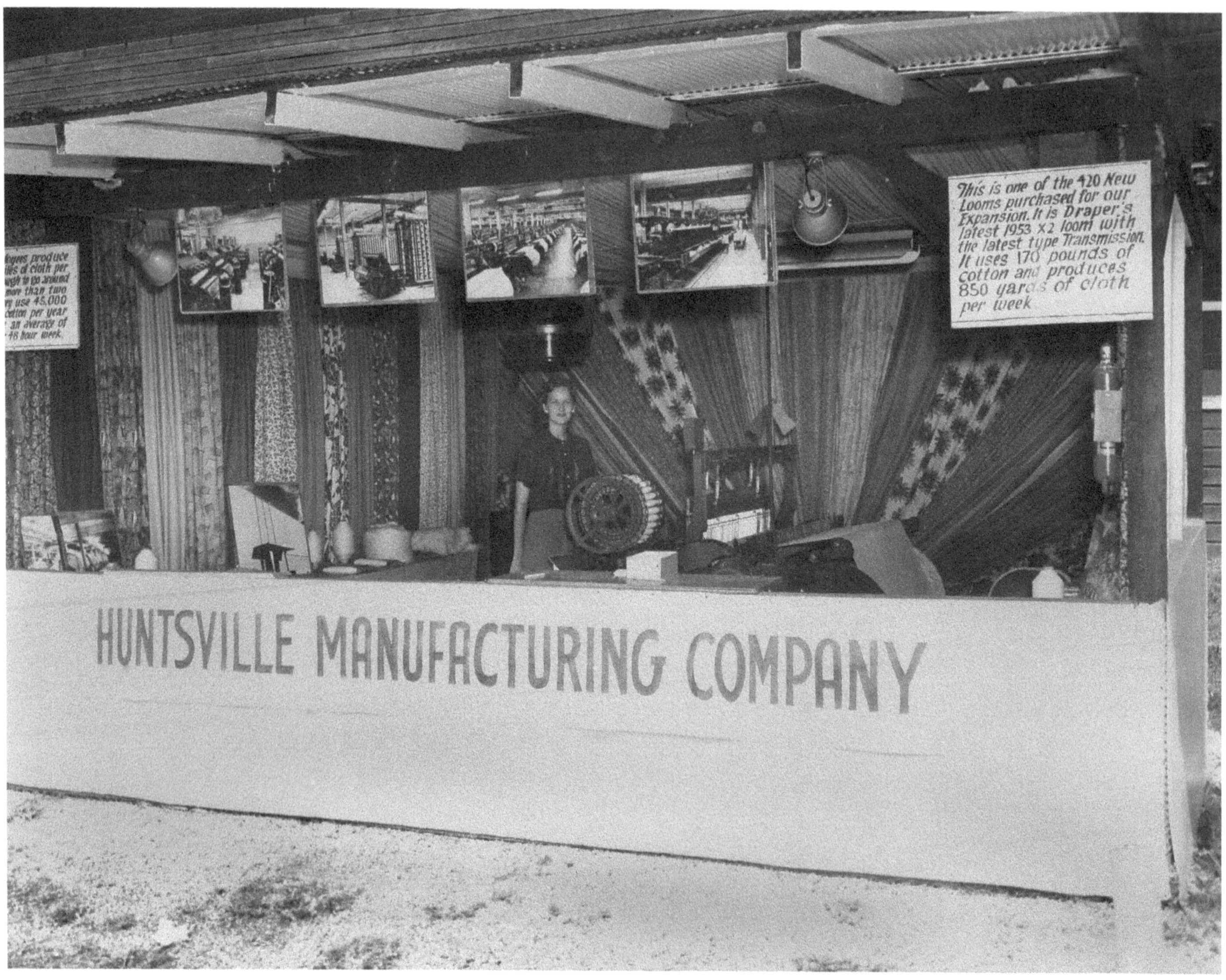

J. C. Penney Company promised stylish clothing at reasonable prices. A 1953 Studebaker Loewy Coup is parked in front. Like most retail stores, J. C. Penney moved to the mall in 1966. This building, on East Side Square, is now a law library.

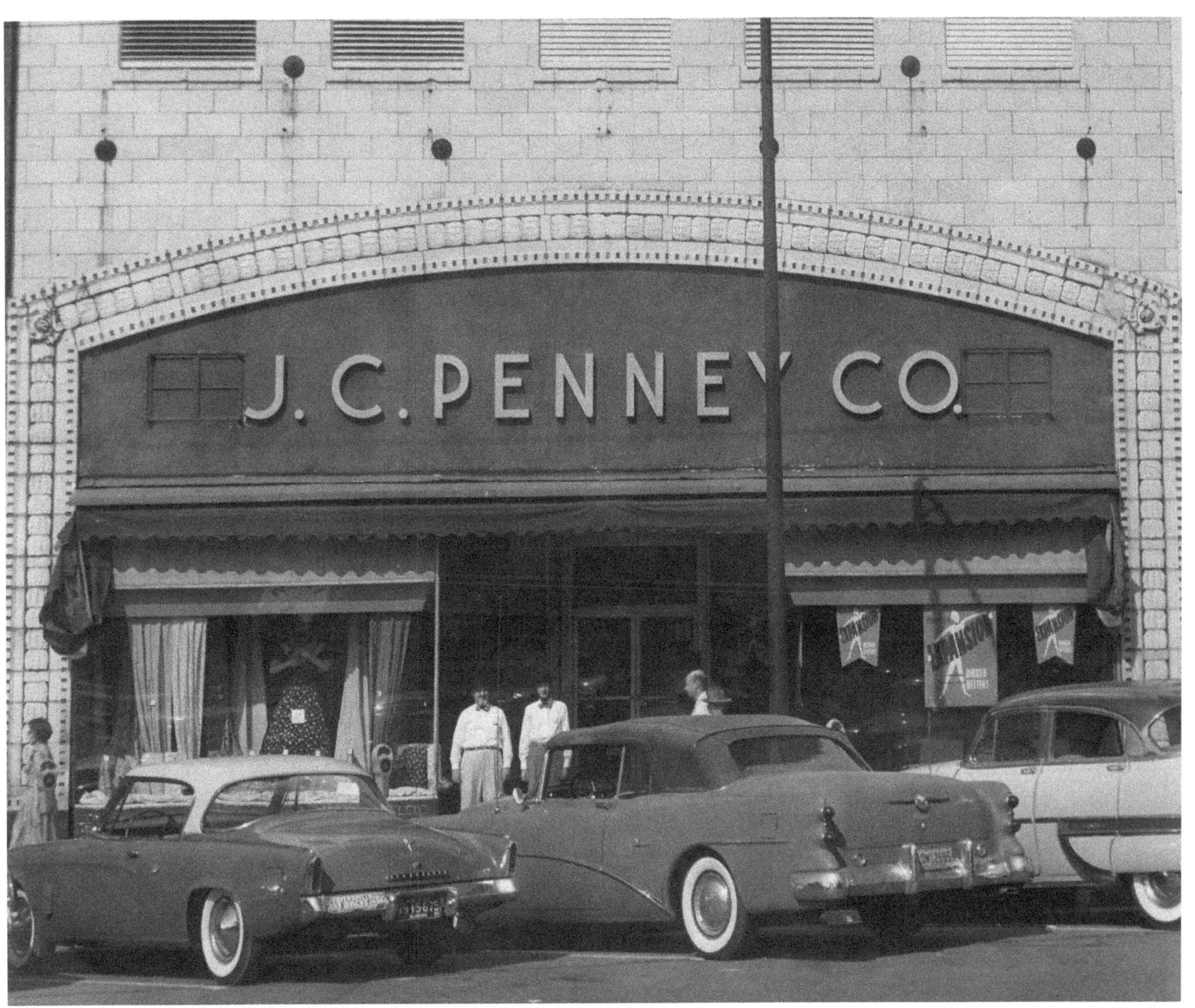

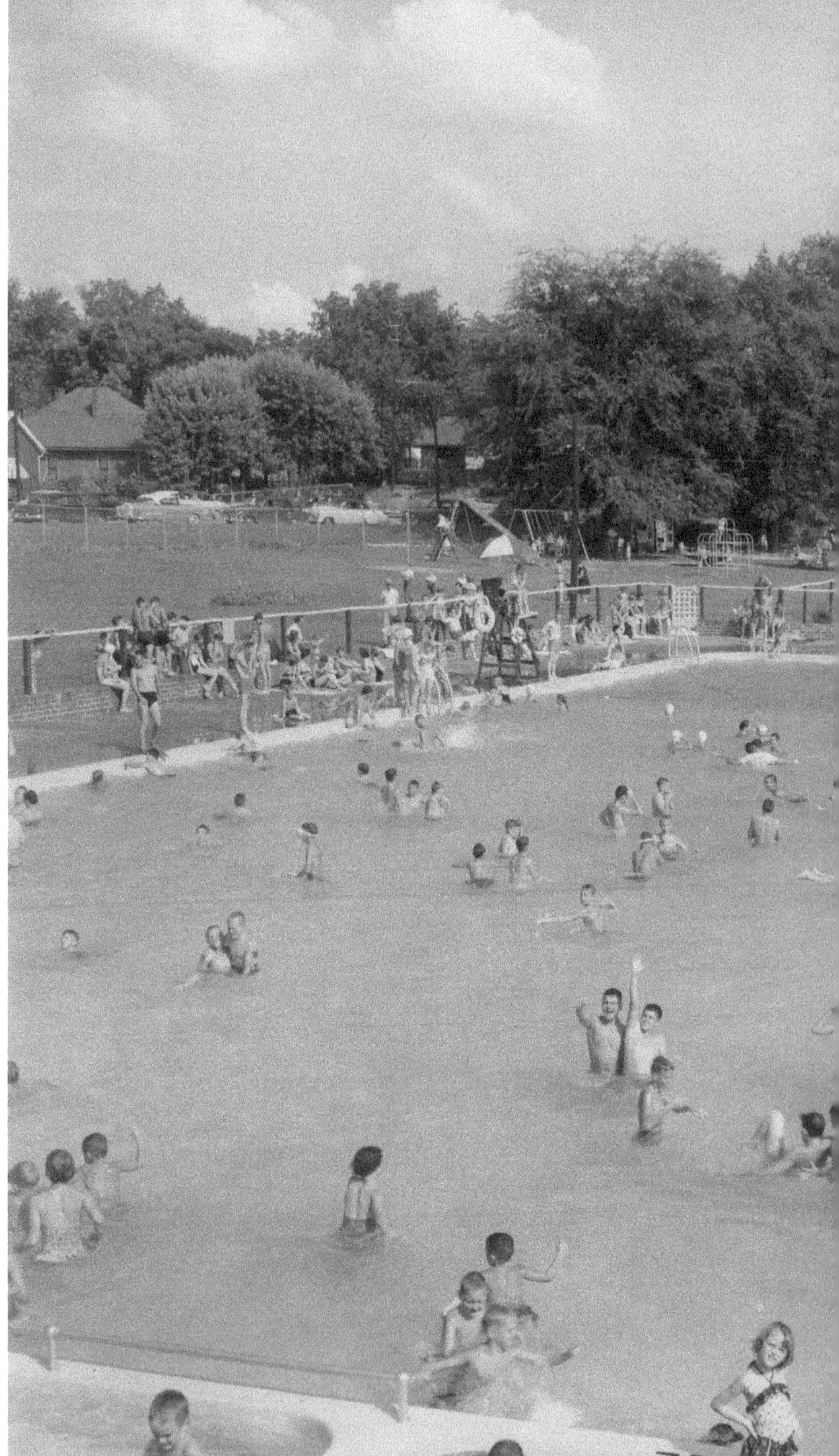

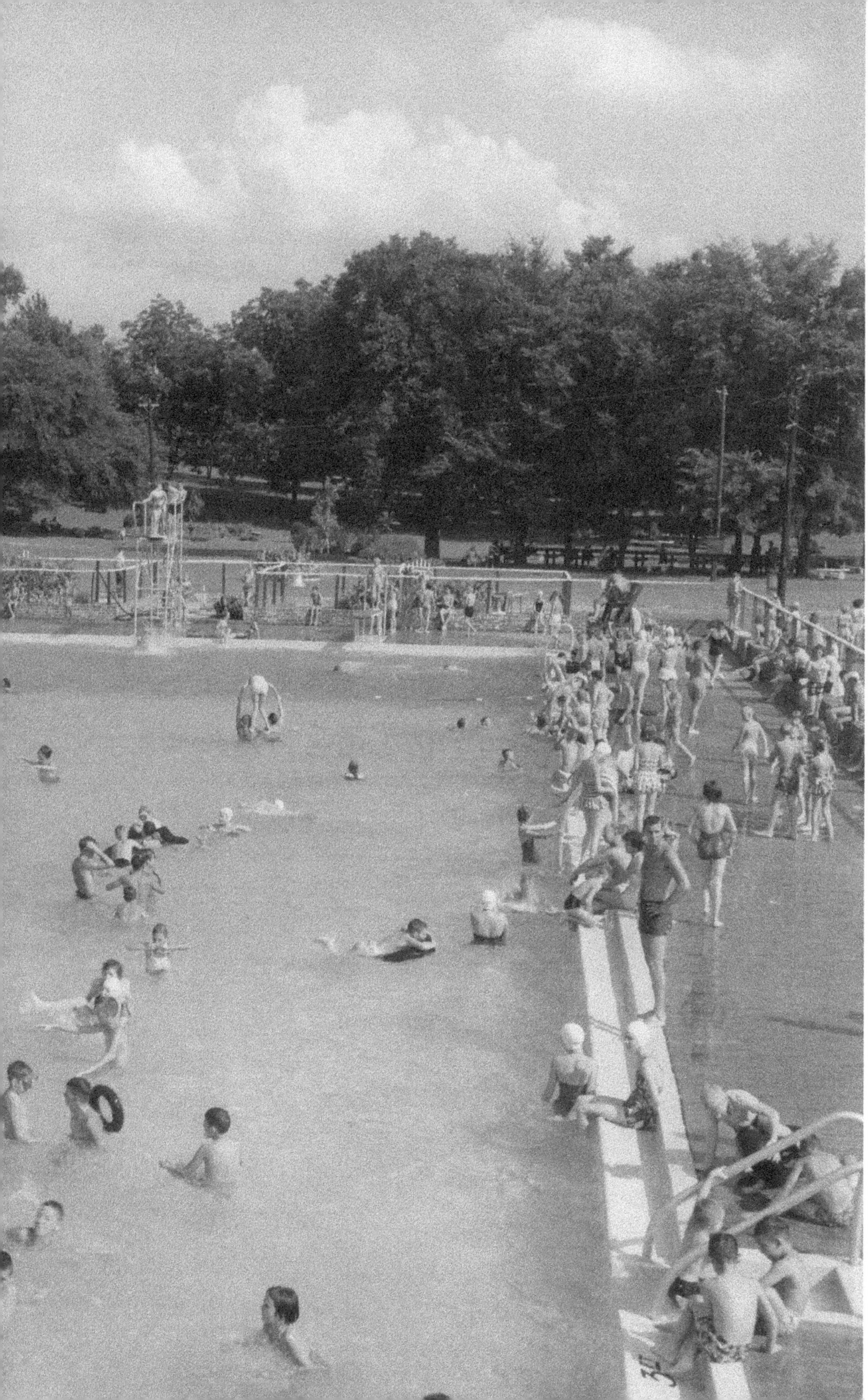

The Big Spring Pool was a popular place for kids and adults to escape the summer heat, but like many facilities of the time, it was only open to whites. Note the boys in the water making faces and waving to the photographer.

This chain link fence was placed around the Big Spring to deter anyone from sabotaging the water supply during World War II but remained in place for several years after the war.

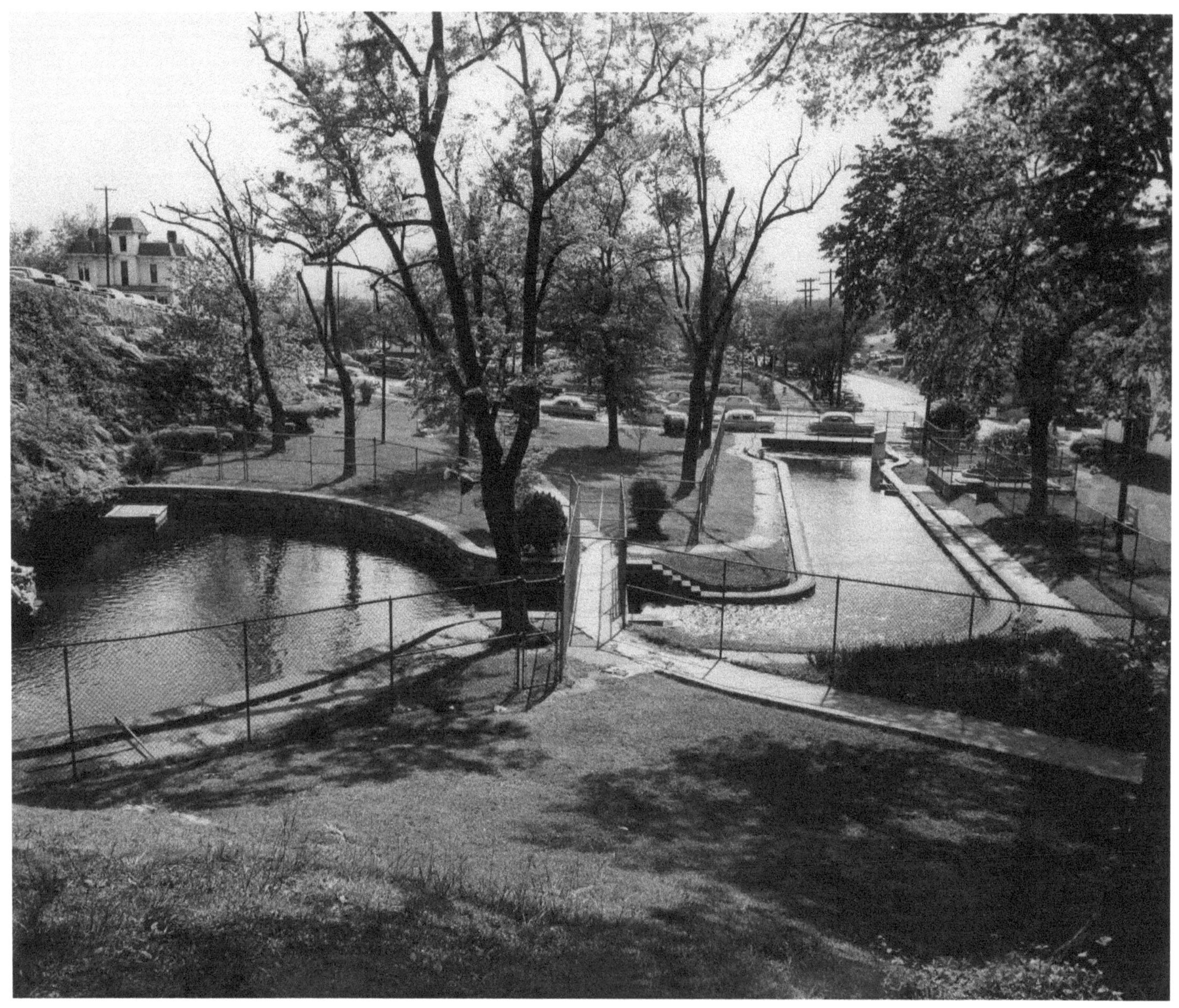

This photograph of the office of Standard Loan Company, located at 112 ½ North Washington Street, was taken on December 20, 1954. Employees were working late that night, according to the wall clock.

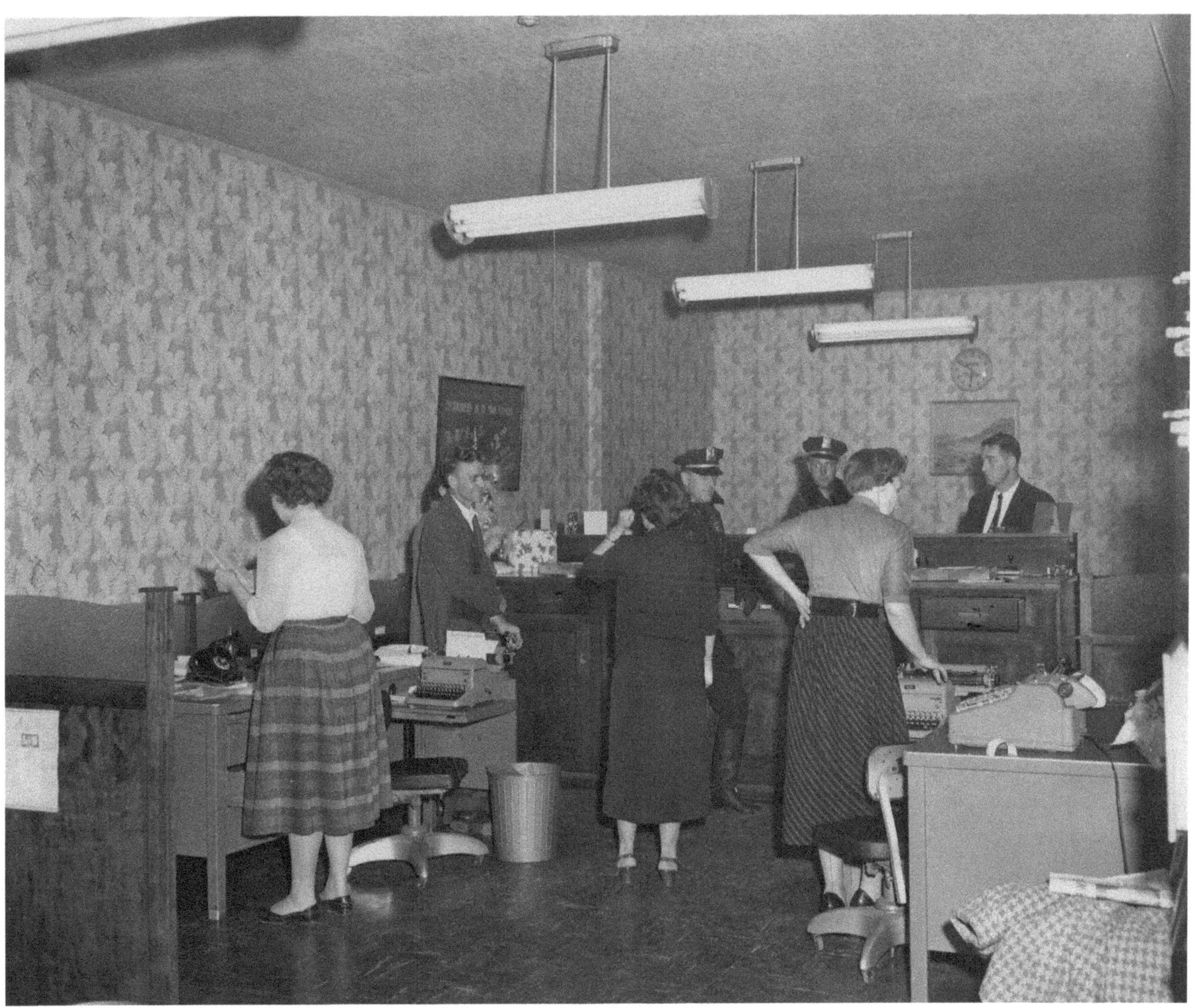

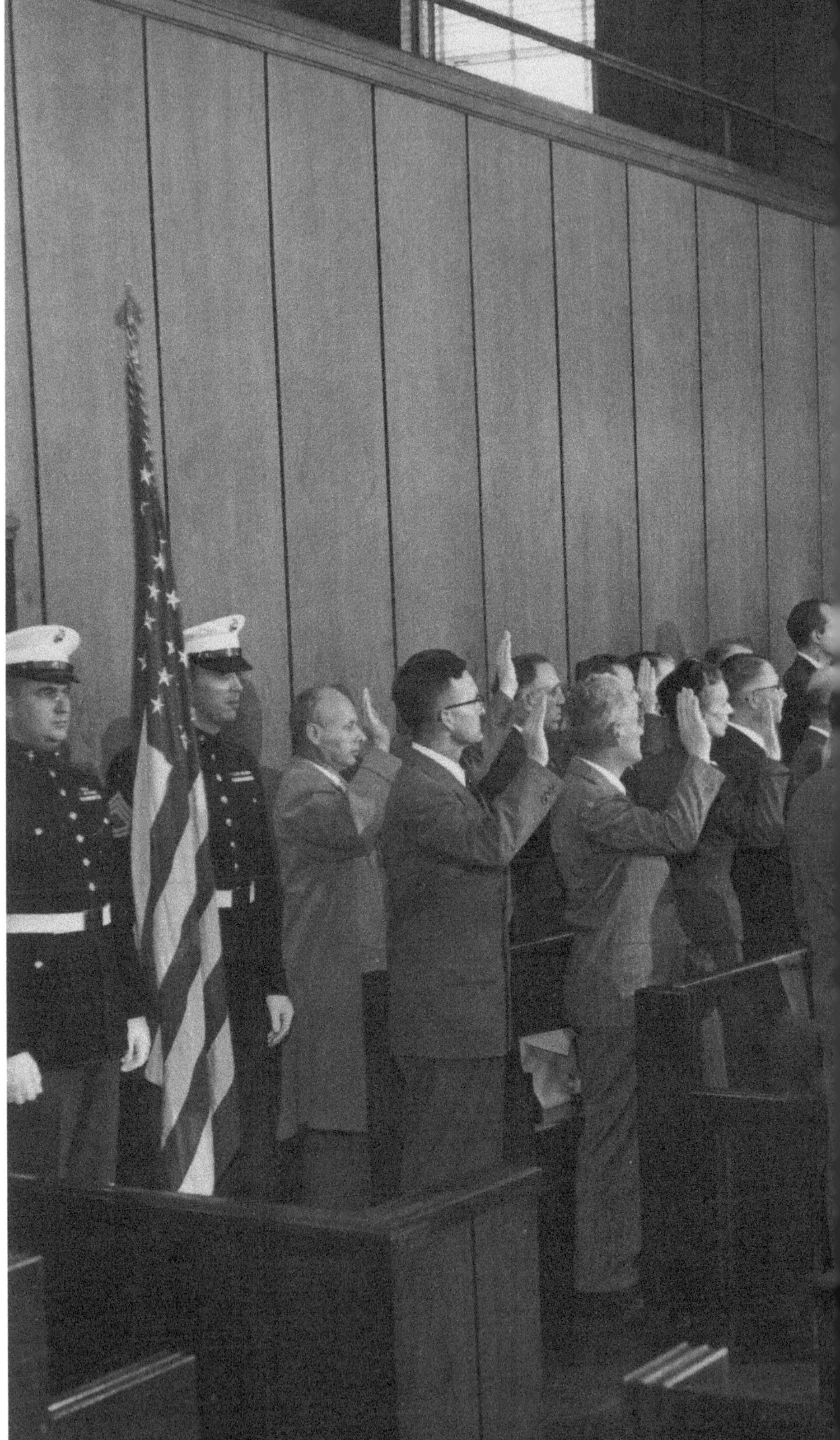

This historic photograph is of the German "Paper Clip" Scientists and their wives taking the oath to become American Citizens in 1954. Recruited from postwar Europe under Operation Paperclip, a Cold War program to obtain German rocket scientists for the U.S. and deny them to the Soviet Union, many chose to turn their initial six-month stay into a lifetime in their new country.

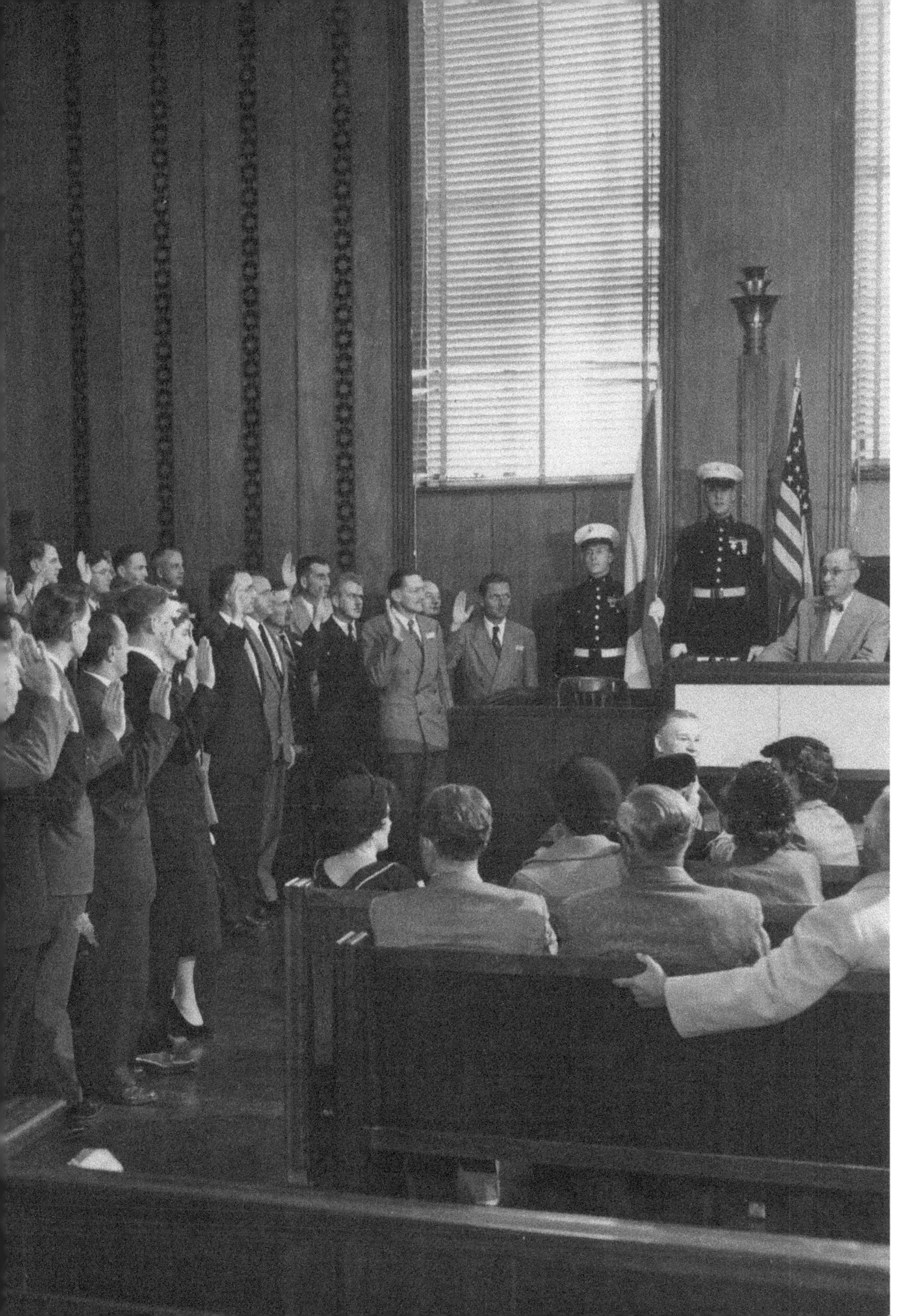

A Christmas float sponsored by the *Huntsville Times* features "elves" who seem a little apprehensive in this parade around 1955. Santa sits in his sleigh and tosses candy to the children in the crowd. In the background is Hill's, which burned in 1962, and two cafes that were torn down in the 1970s.

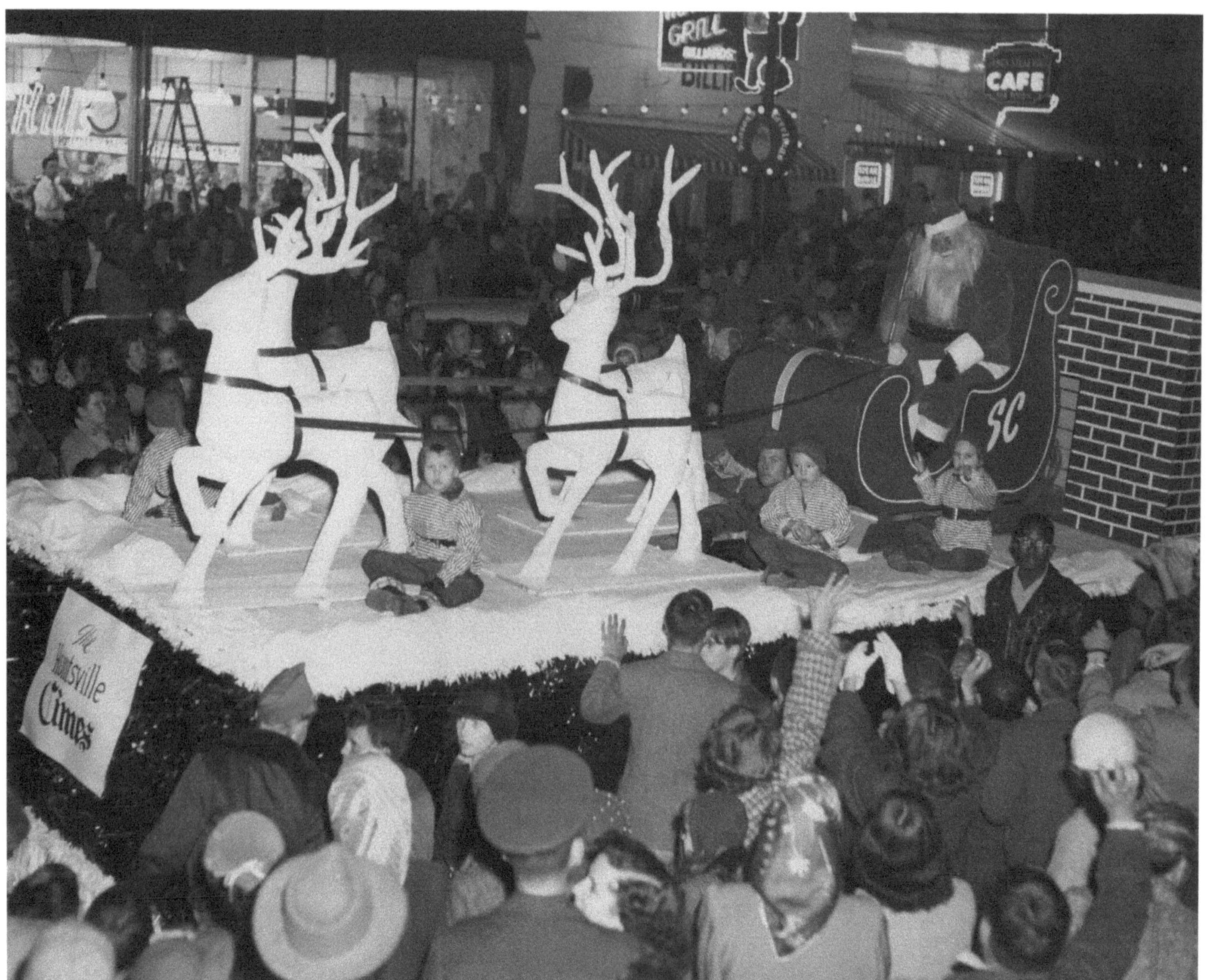

An event at the Courthouse Square shows a number of booths set up all around the park. Sailors pose with pretty young ladies, near the U.S. Naval Reserve booth to the right. This photo was taken on May 21, 1955, by a U.S. Navy photographer.

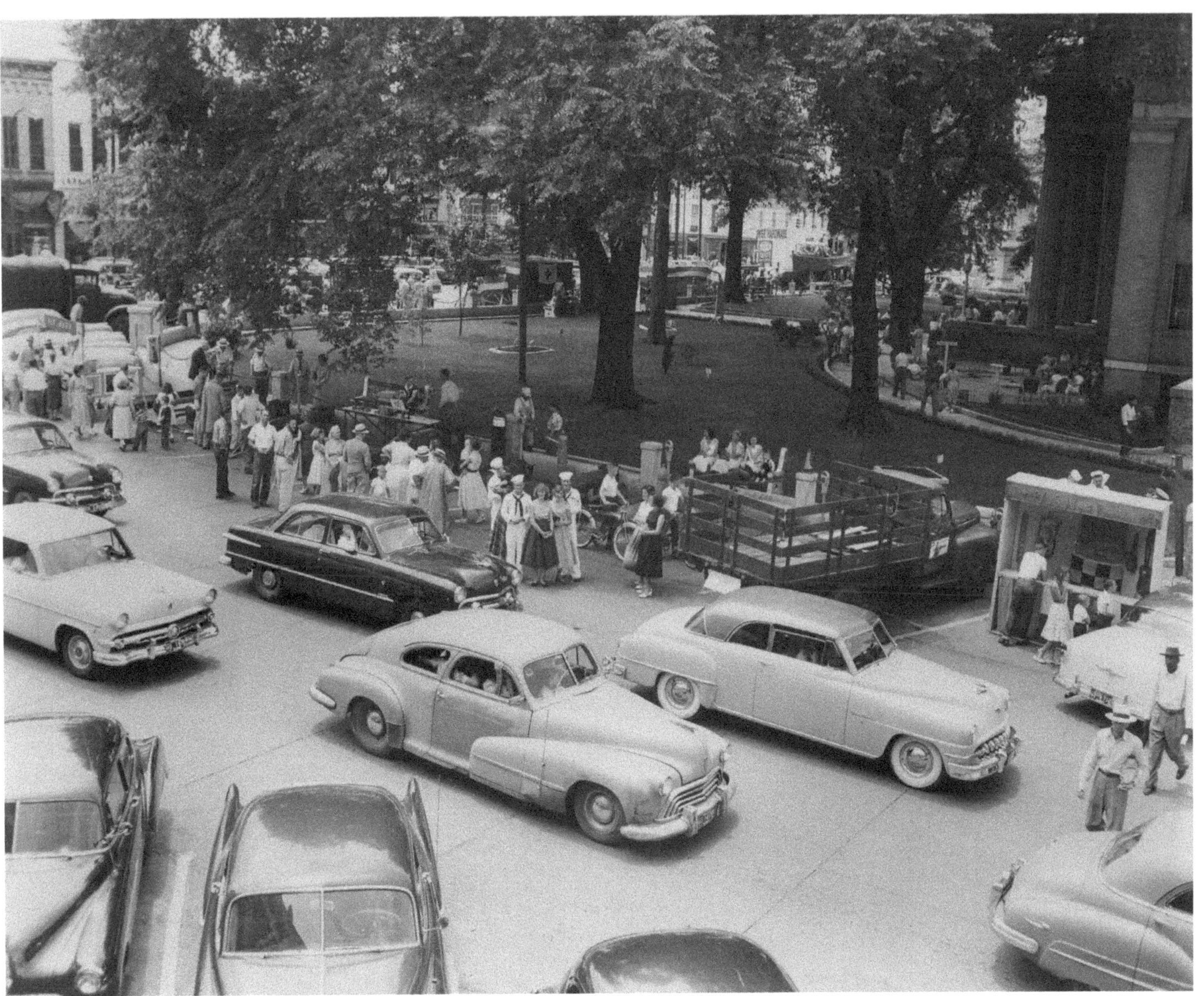

Good weather invited people outside to mingle at the Courthouse Square. Before television drew people inside, downtown Huntsville was rarely deserted. Members of the U.S. Naval Reserve have a booth to show off their work and maybe even recruit a few new members.

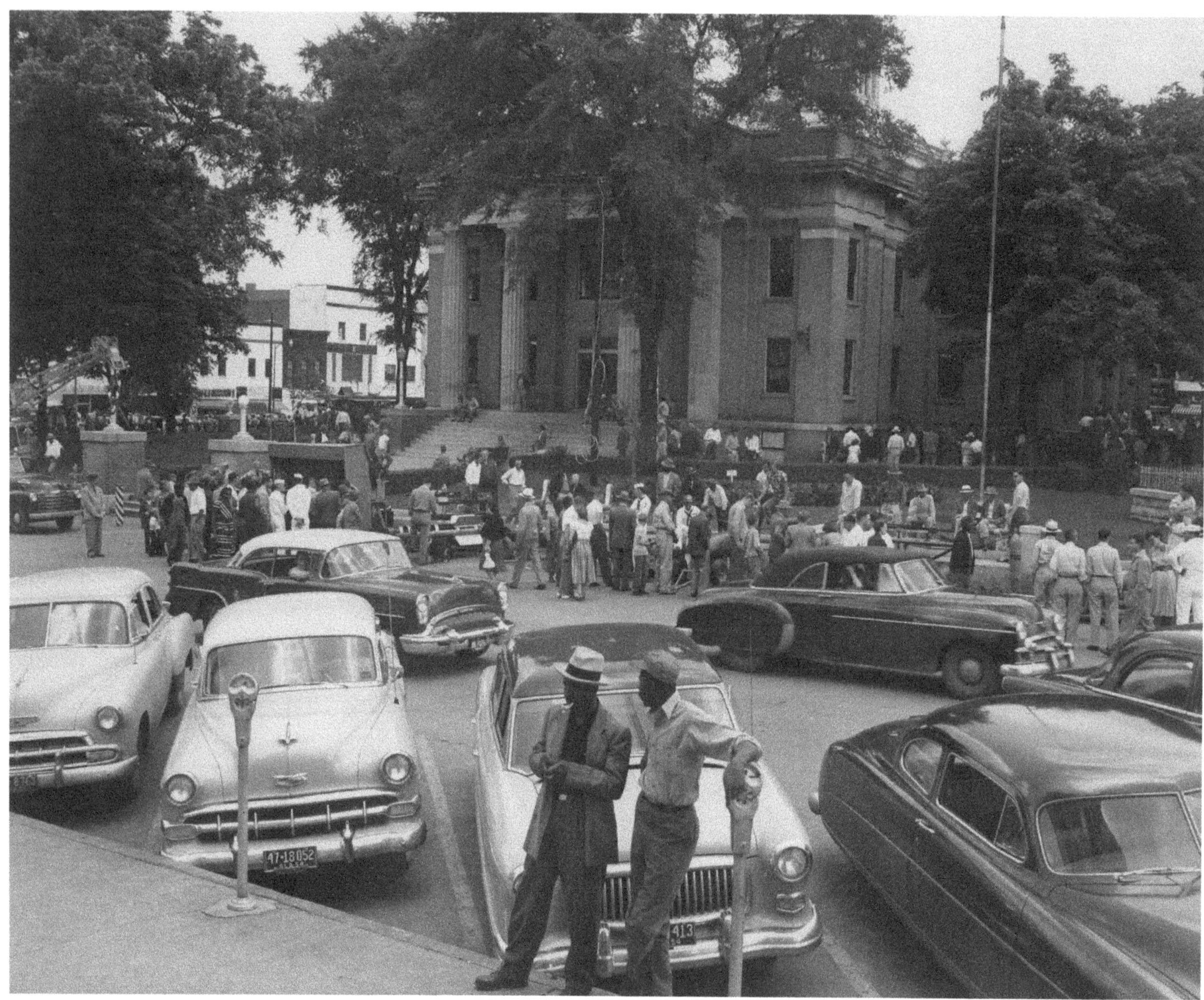

A parade to celebrate Huntsville's Sesquicentennial gave civilians a chance to cheer for members of the armed forces in September 1955. The photographer was facing North Side Square.

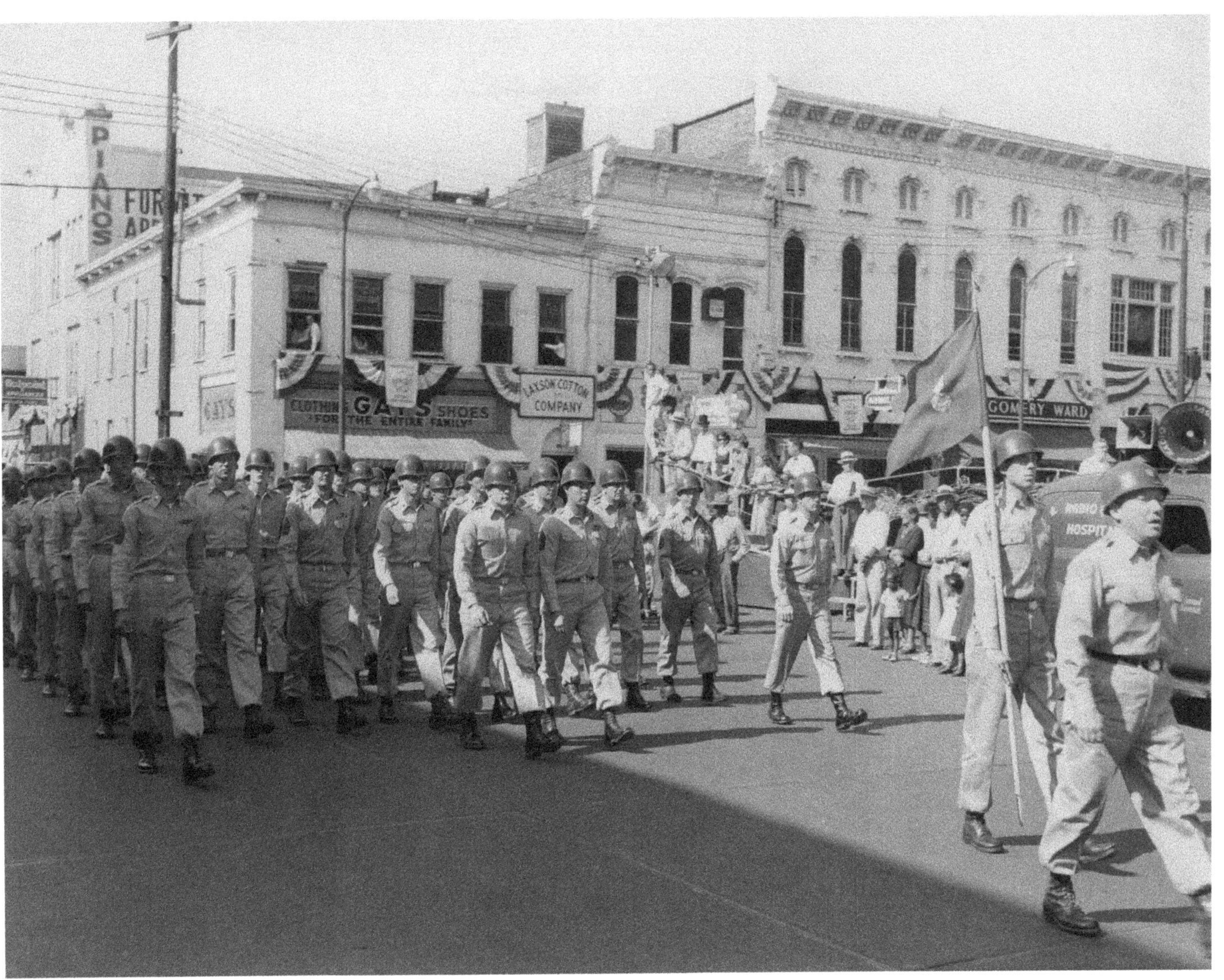

North Side Square is unusually quiet, an indication that this is probably a Sunday or holiday. Sno-Wite Hamburgers cost 12 cents. Next door was Arnold's, a record shop owned by Arnold Hornbuckle. The steeple of the Methodist Church rises at the far right.

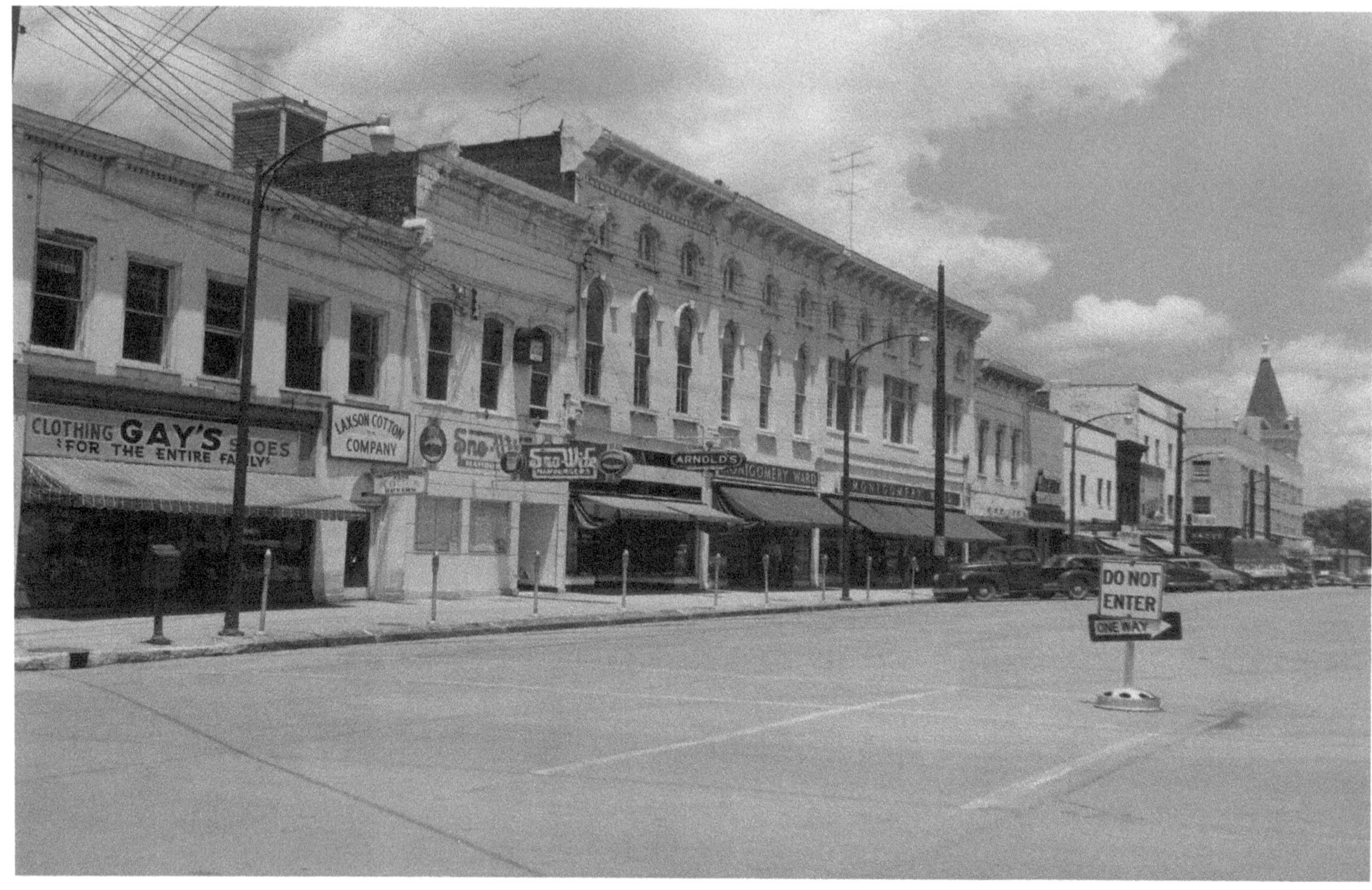

Mason's Furniture was one of many furniture stores in downtown Huntsville. Many businesses later moved out of downtown, leaving abandoned buildings.

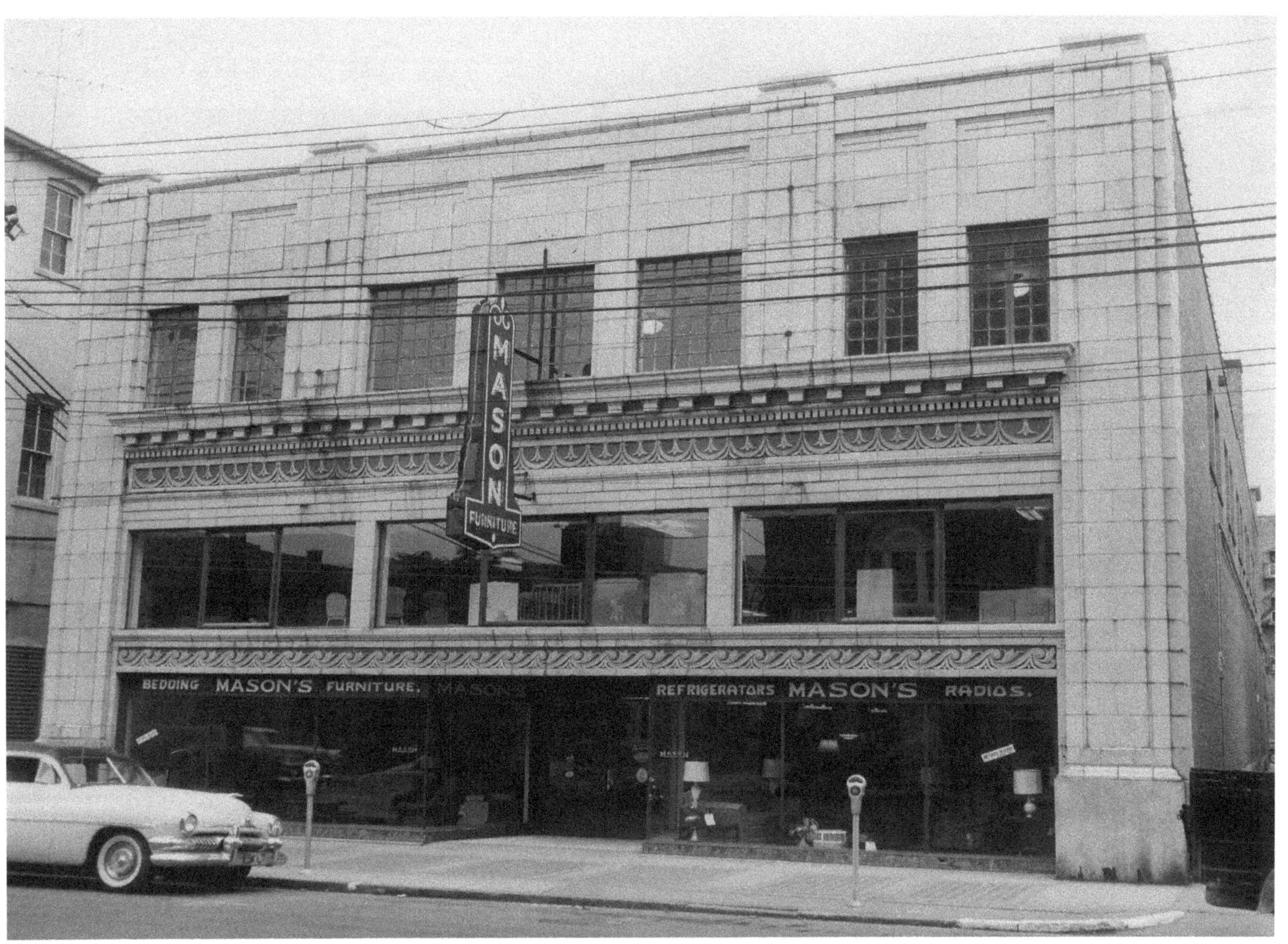

The V-2 Missile, developed by Germans in World War II, was studied by American scientists when von Braun and his team of rocket scientists came to America. This missile "as used for high altitude research firings at White Sands" was on display at the Courthouse Square.

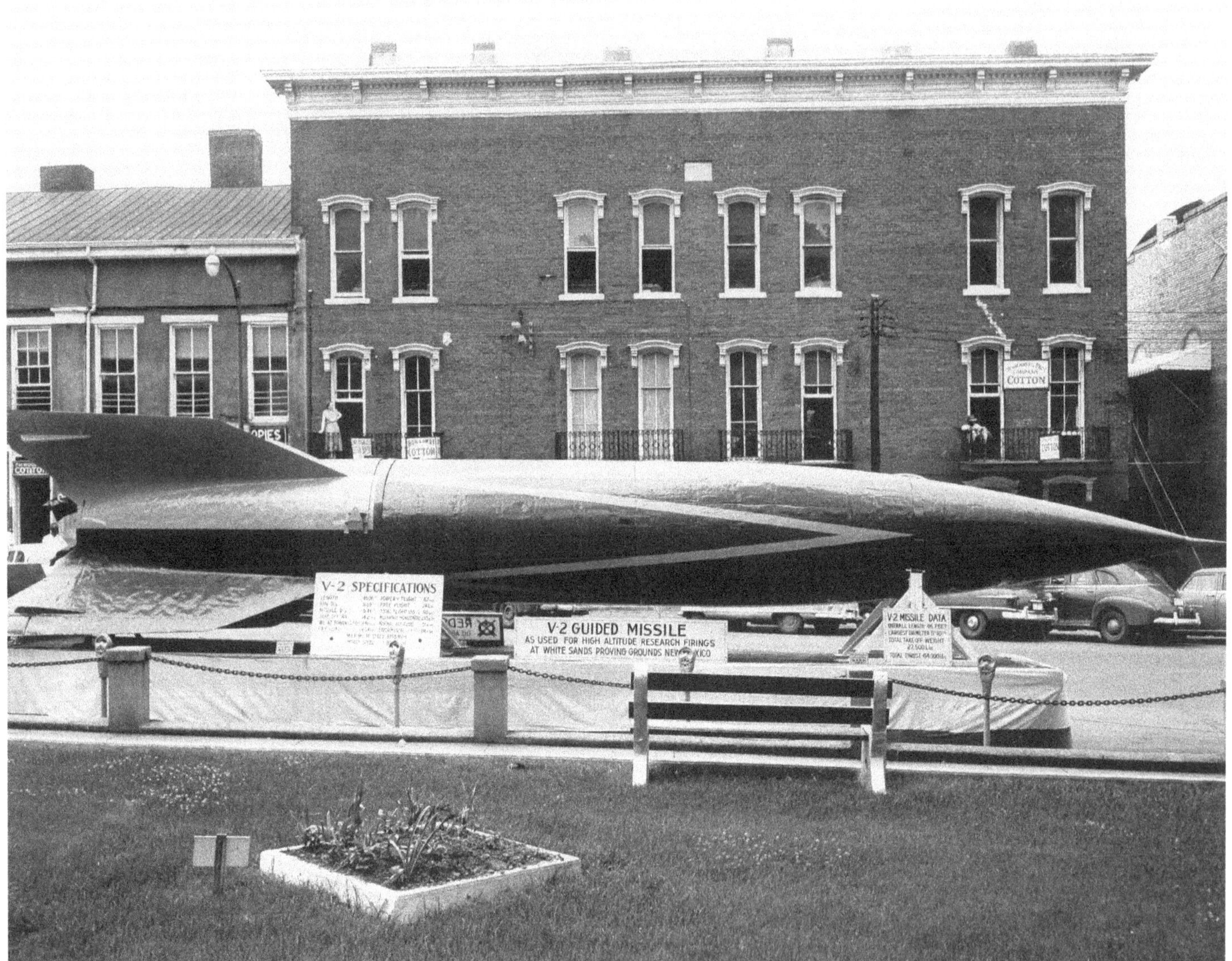

Stockton Motor Car Company was the place to buy a Buick or GMC. It was located on Greene Street, but eventually moved to University Drive as the need for larger inventory became crucial.

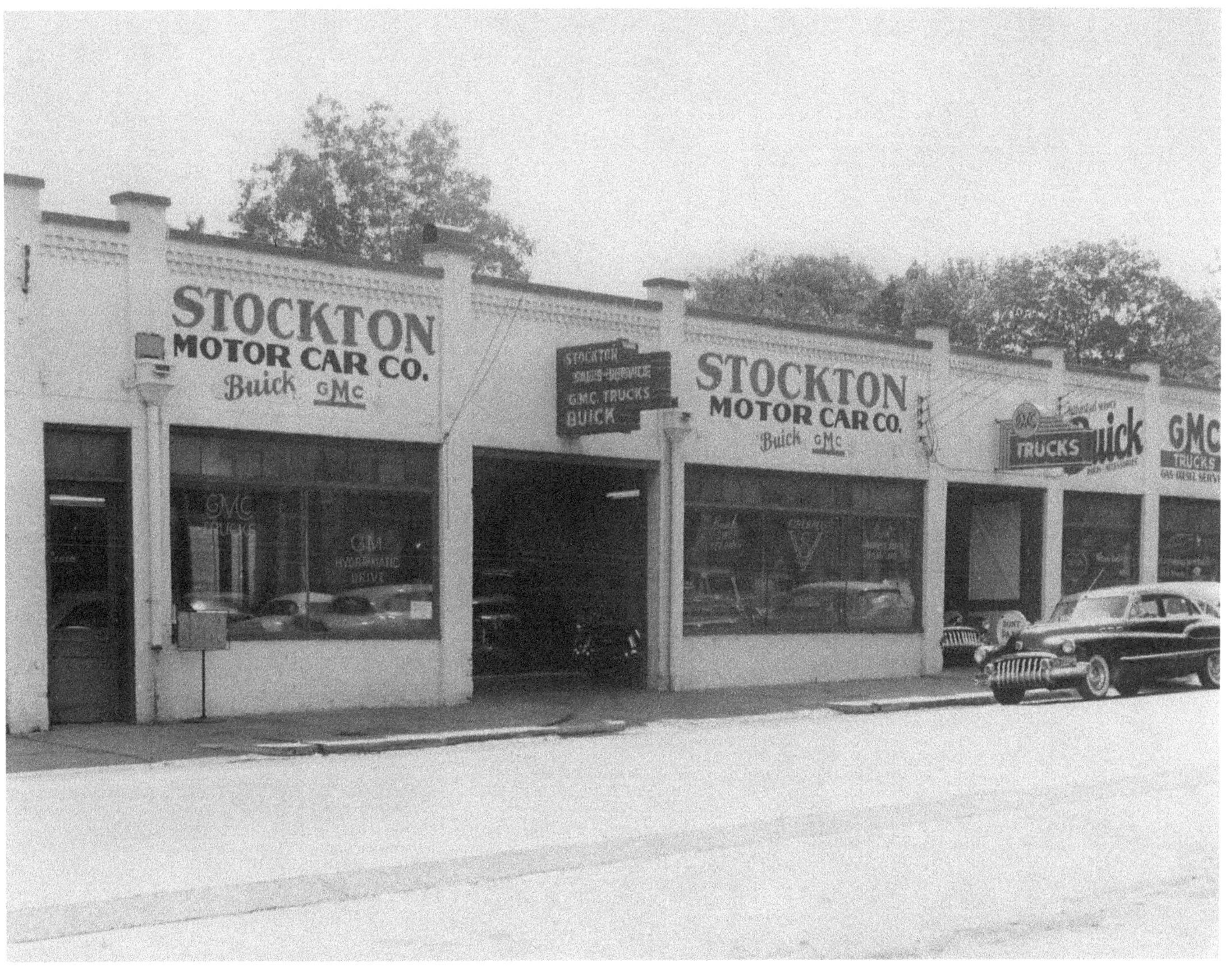

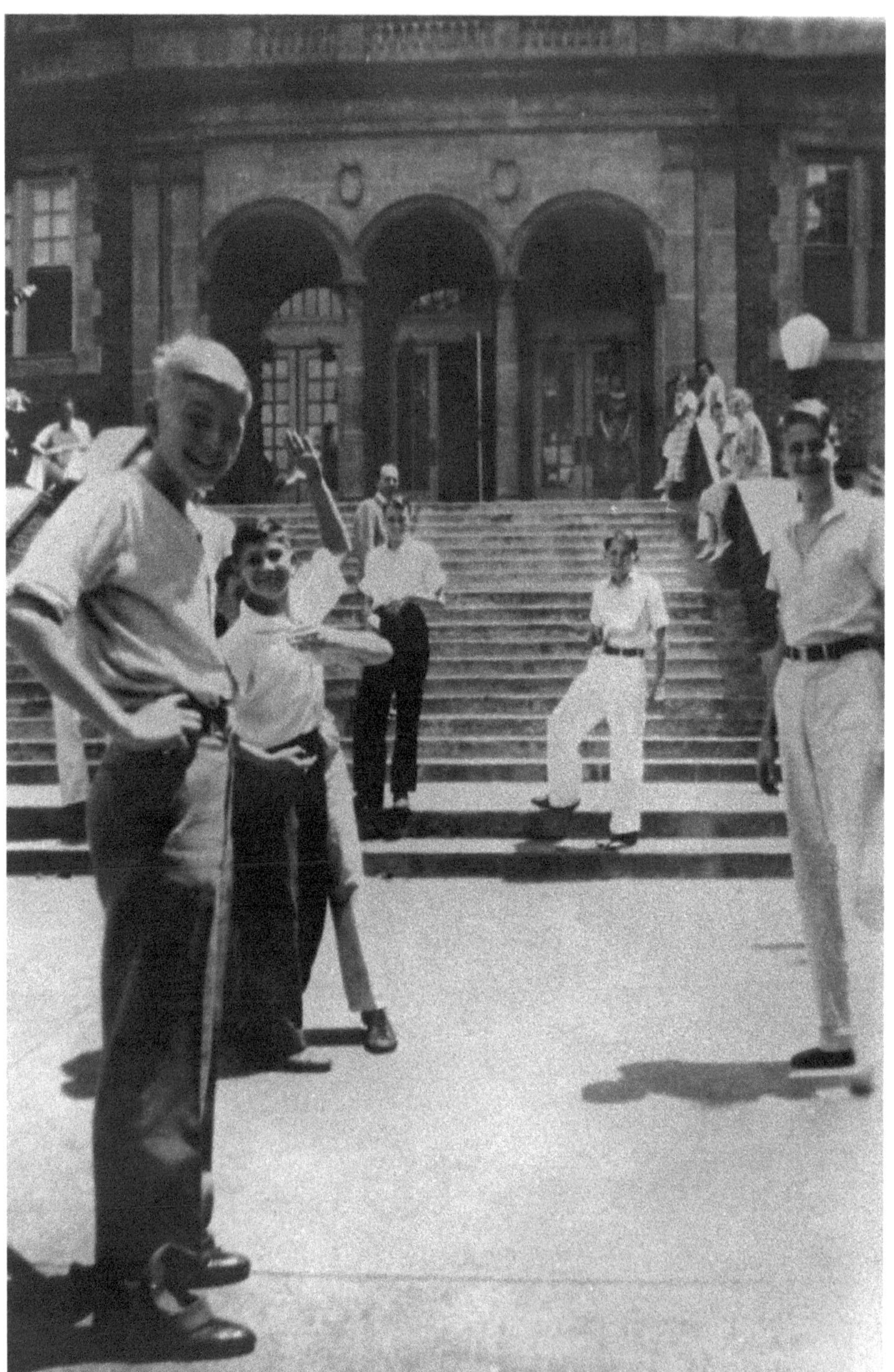

Huntsville High School once had a very different dress code for their students. The newest Huntsville High School building was opened in August, 2004.

The opening of Parkway Center, a modern strip mall, was a cause to celebrate on March 14, 1957.

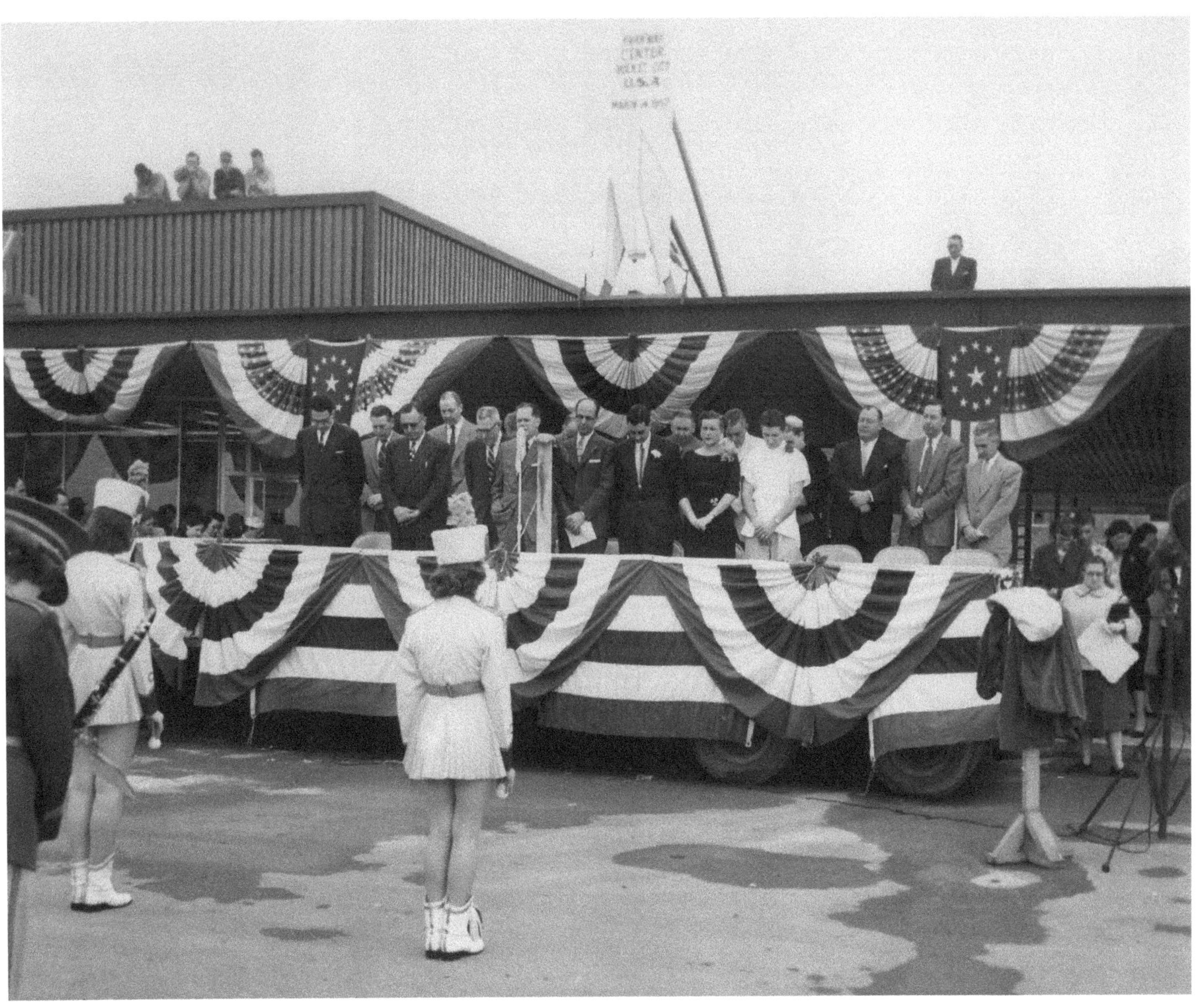

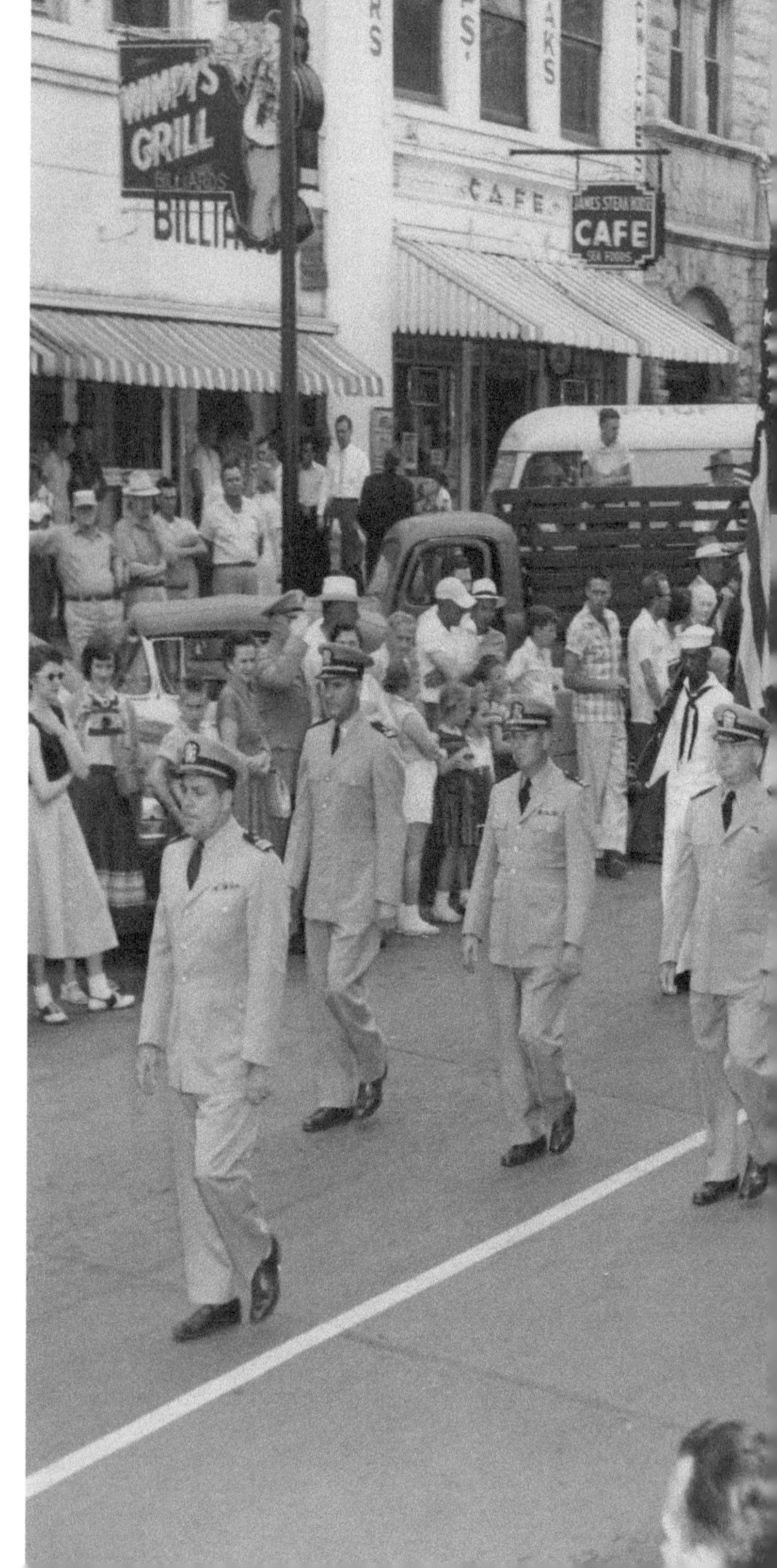
WIMPY'S
GRILL
CAFE
CAFE

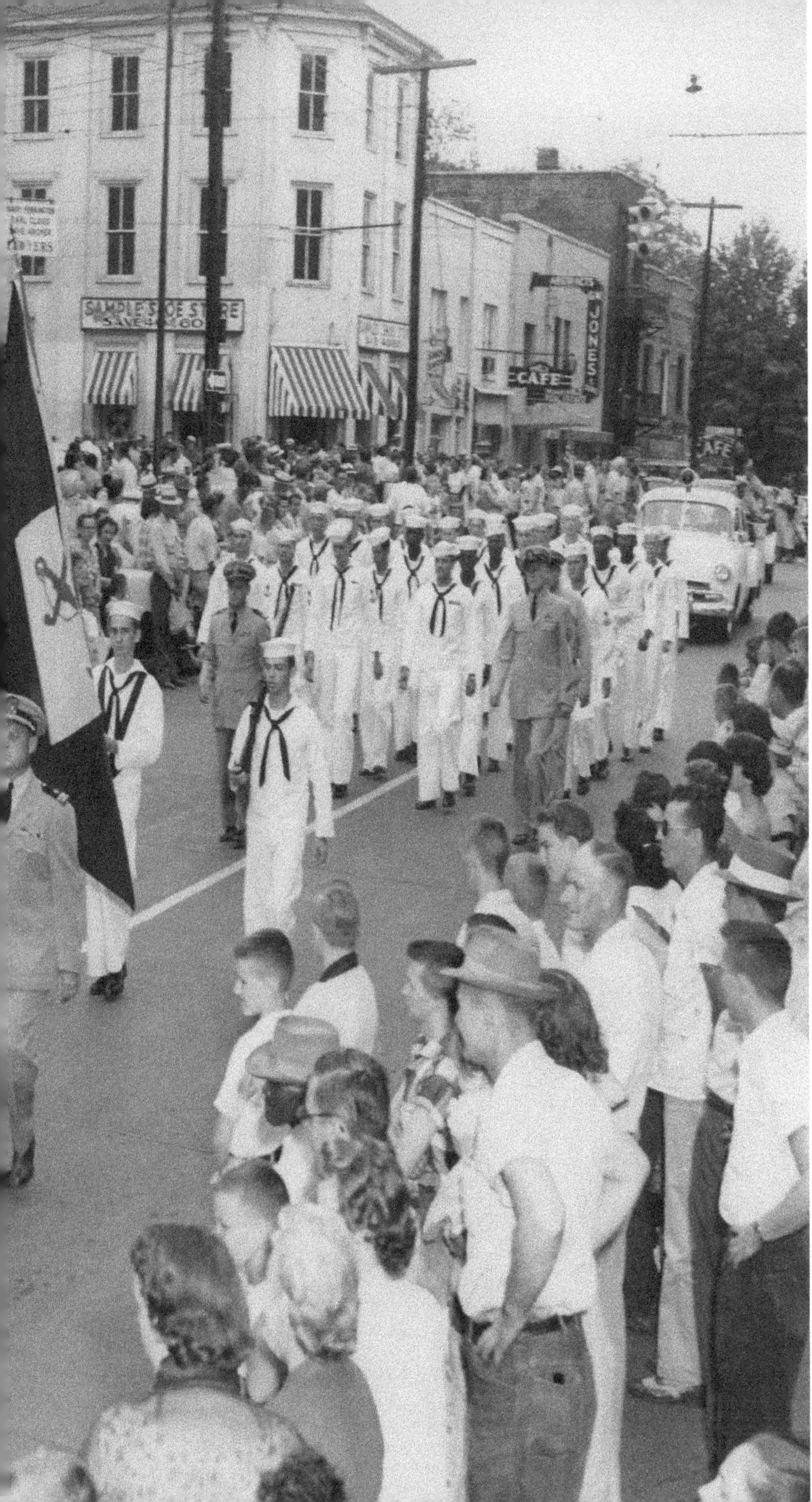

Spectators admire Navy men in summer "Cracker Jacks" uniforms during a patriotic parade in 1956.

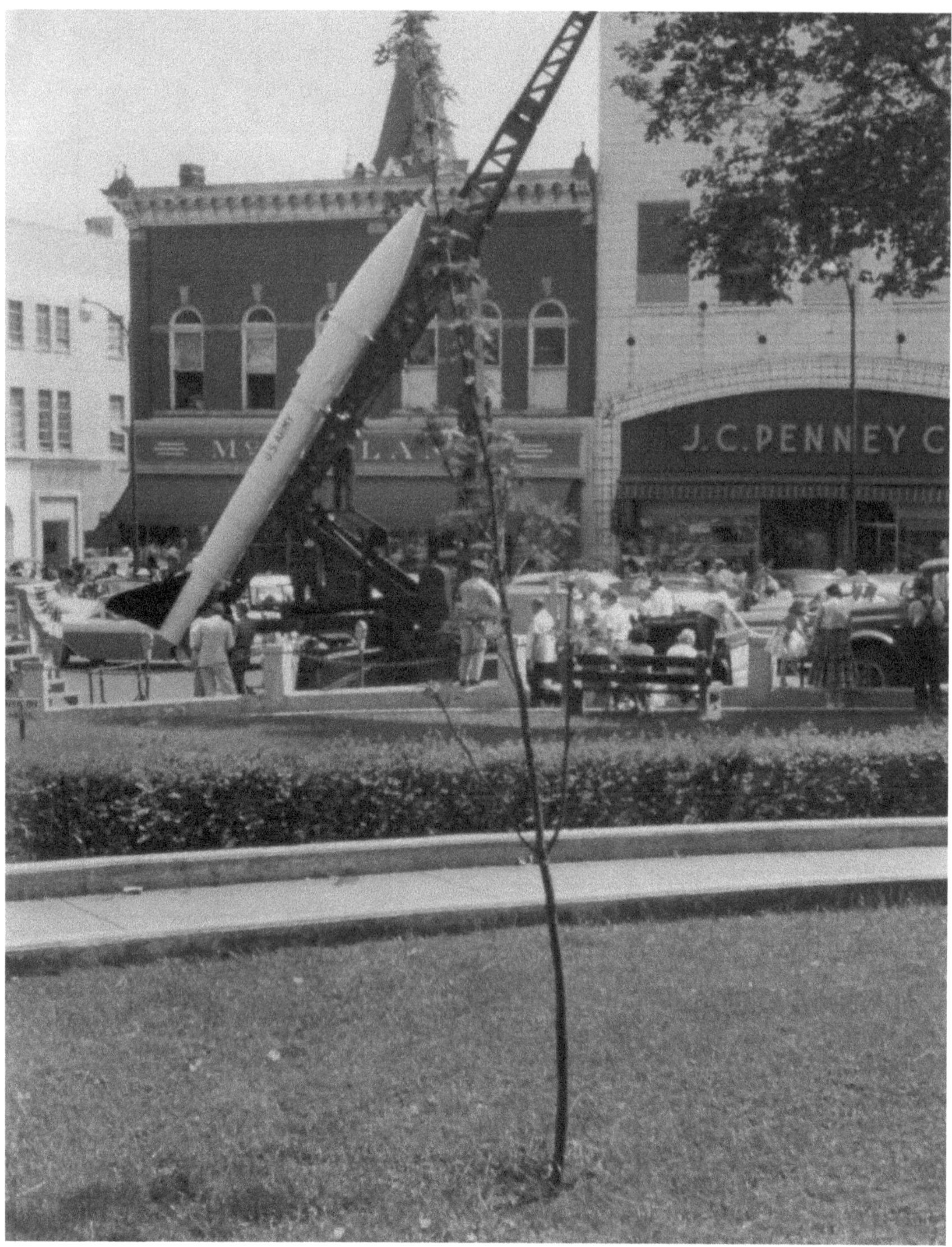

This is another of Redstone Arsenal's proud accomplishments, on display during Armed Forces Day, May 19, 1957.

This photograph was taken May 19, 1957, on Armed Forces Day. The celebration was an opportunity for the public to get more information on what was being developed at Redstone Arsenal.

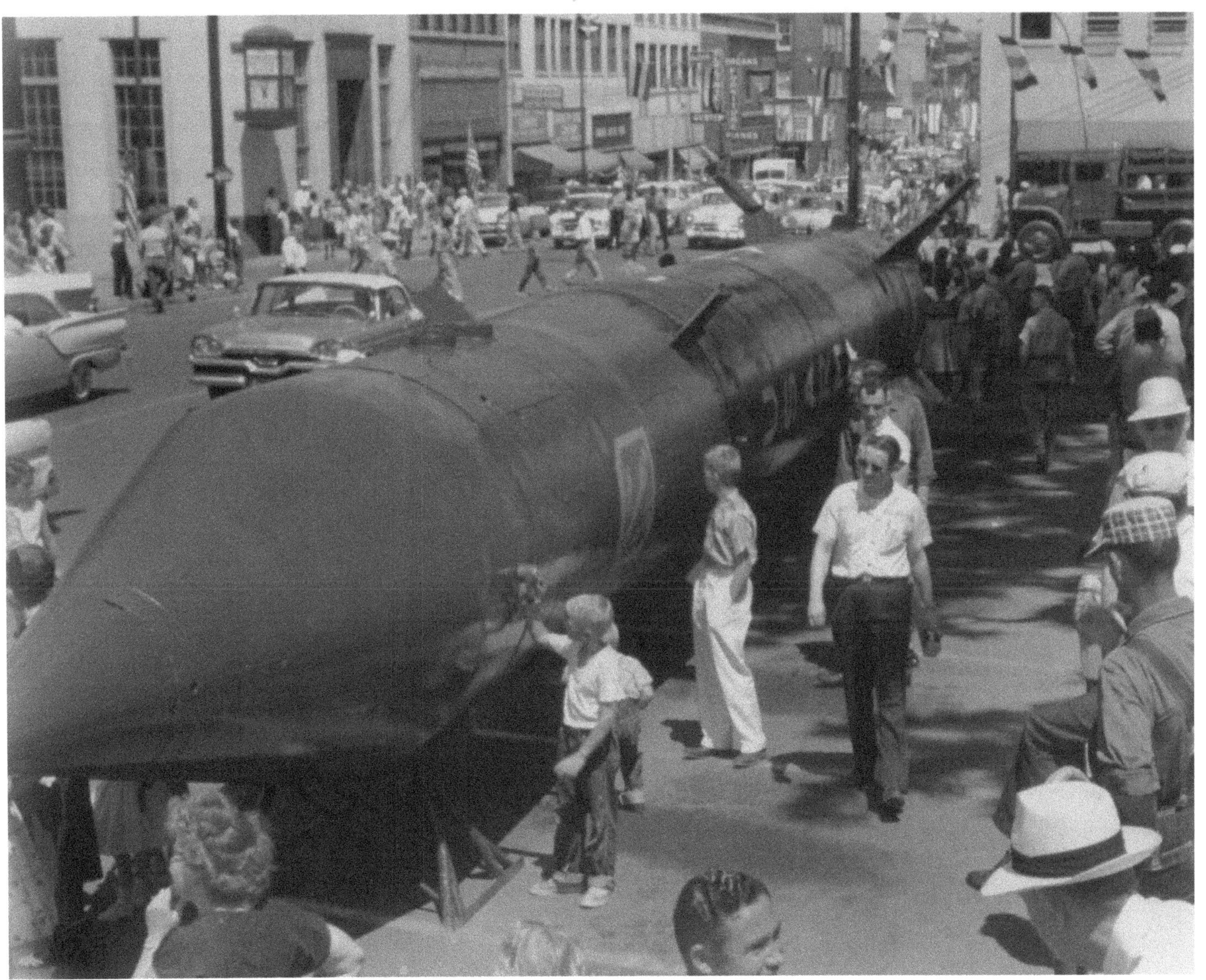

A banner on the back of the American Legion's mock locomotive in 1957 reflects the pride of these Huntsville residents.

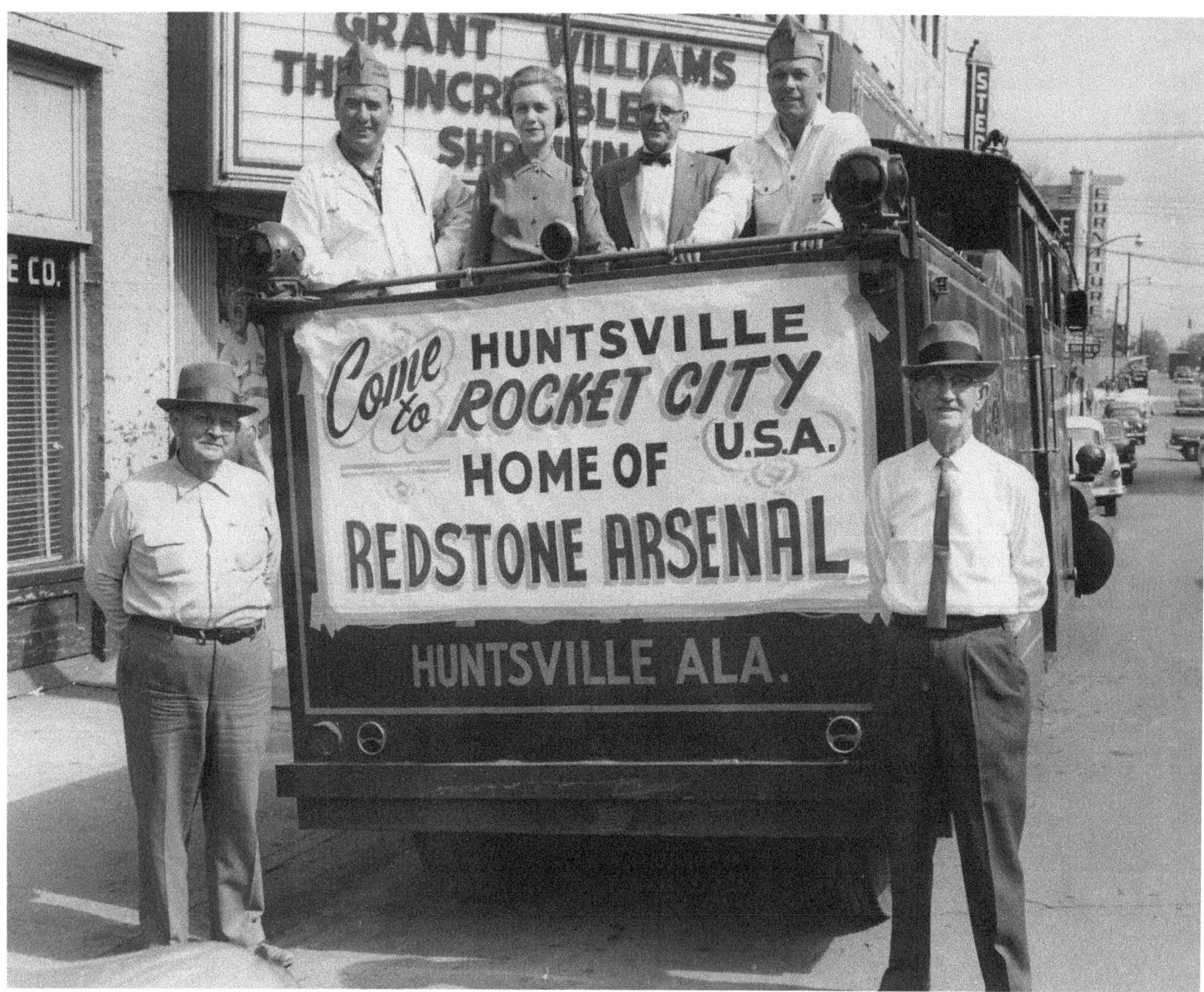

With the exception of the I. Schiffman building on the right, all other businesses on East Side Square have changed. Today, most are attorneys' offices and the Law Library.

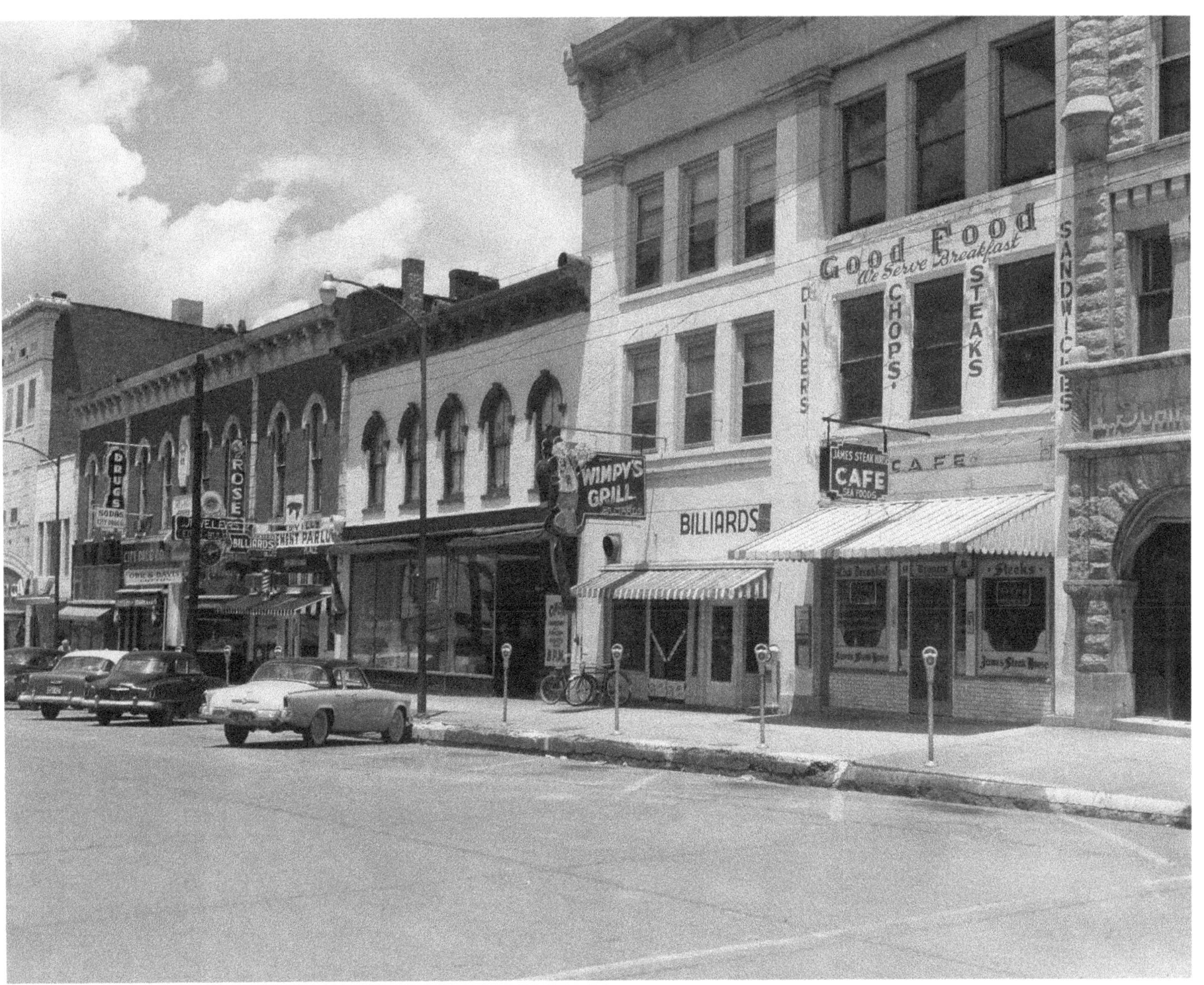

A car accident, involving a 1958 Chevrolet cab, brings the fire department out as water gushes from the hydrant. The Ritz Café was a popular place for local businessmen to have lunch. See the partial face of a boy peeking out from behind the street sign.

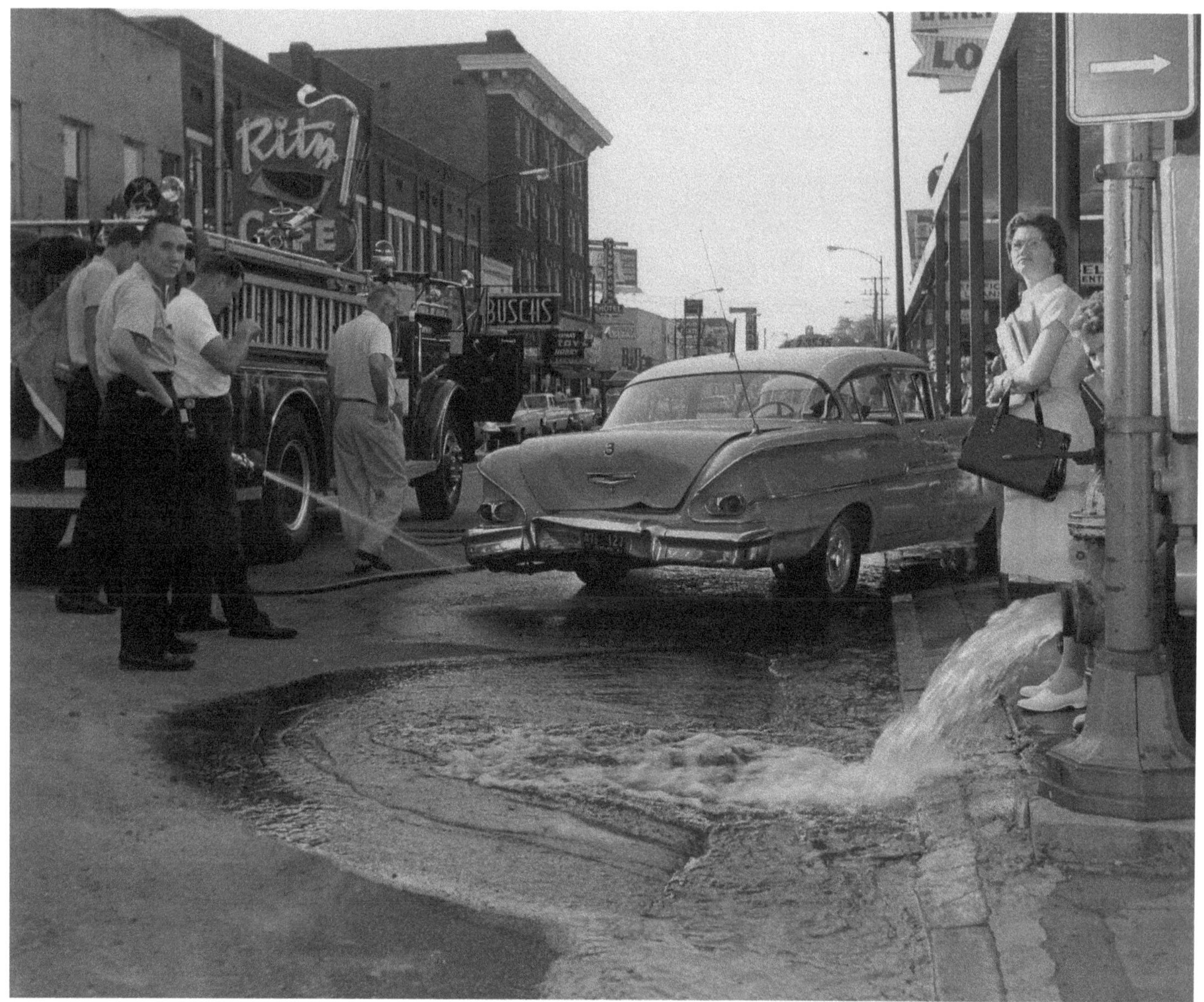

Visitors enter the Redstone Arsenal Headquarters during what appears to be an open-house day for the public at the restricted facility.

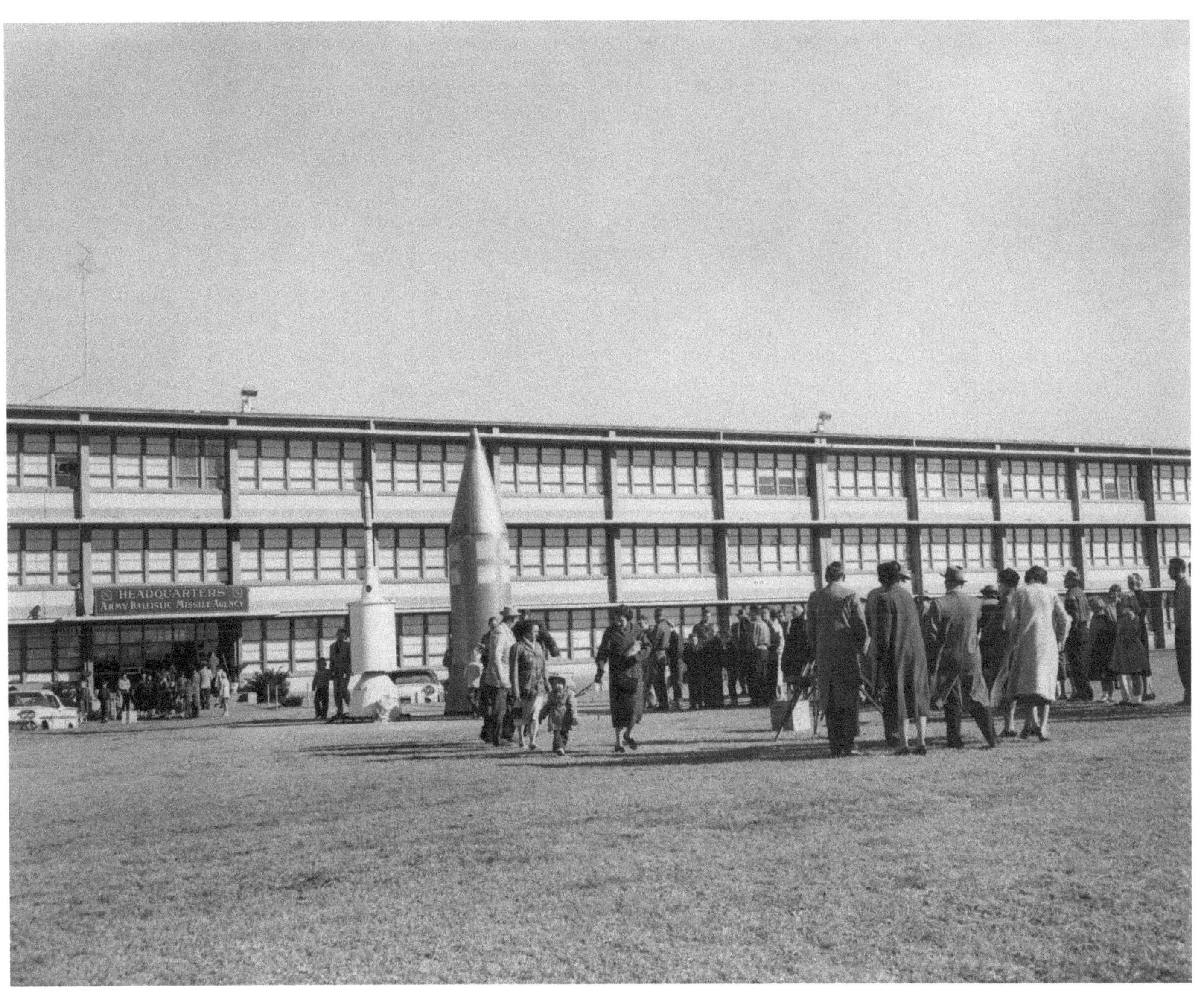

Jimmy Walker, Mayor R. B. Searcy, Stuart Jones, and Dorsey Uptain "launch" a symbolic rocket to celebrate the successful launching of the Explorer I Satellite in January, 1958.

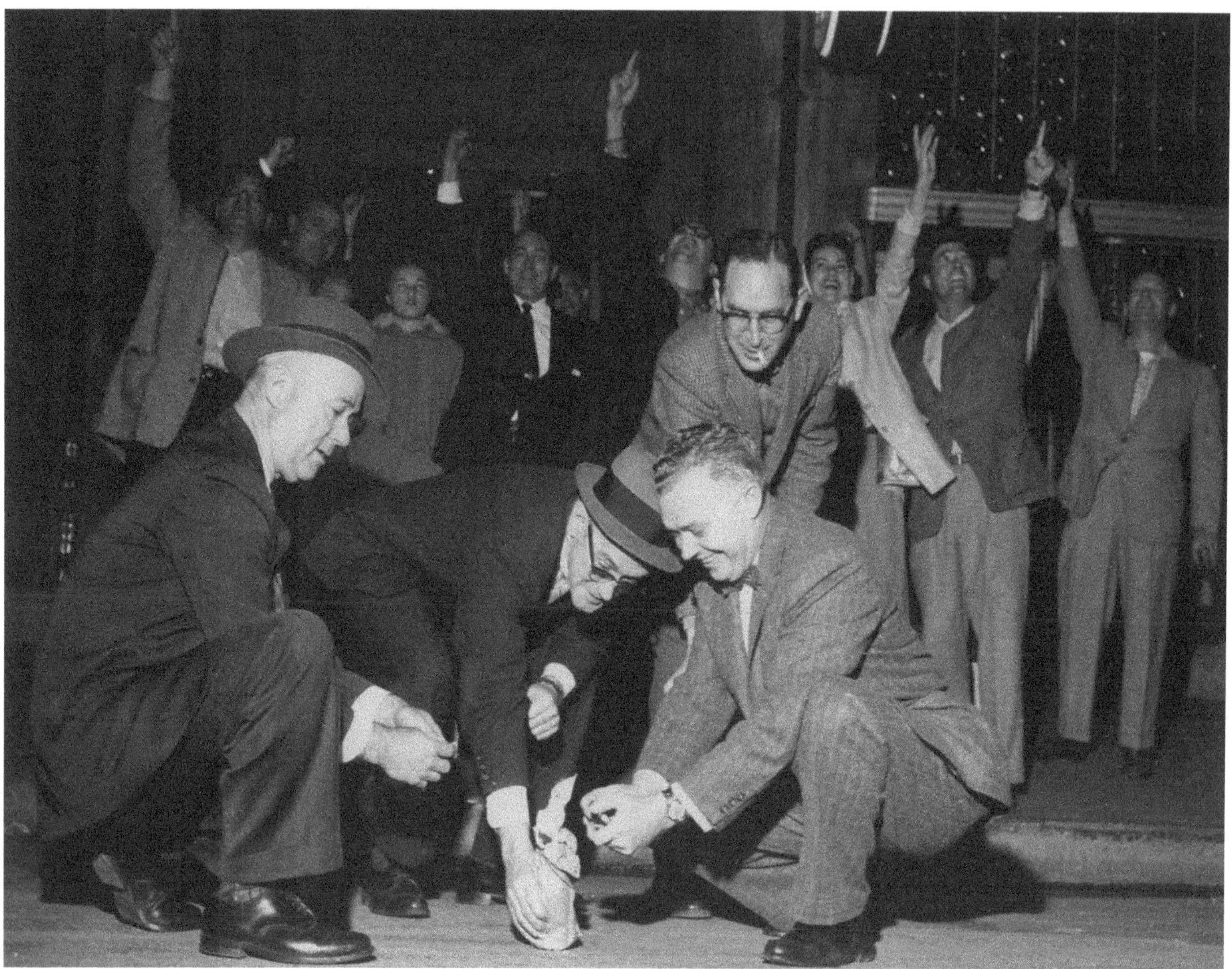

Locally made missiles ready for inspection. A Redhead Roadrunner target drone and Little John rocket stand alongside a display of the Zeus interceptor missile which was first launched in 1959.

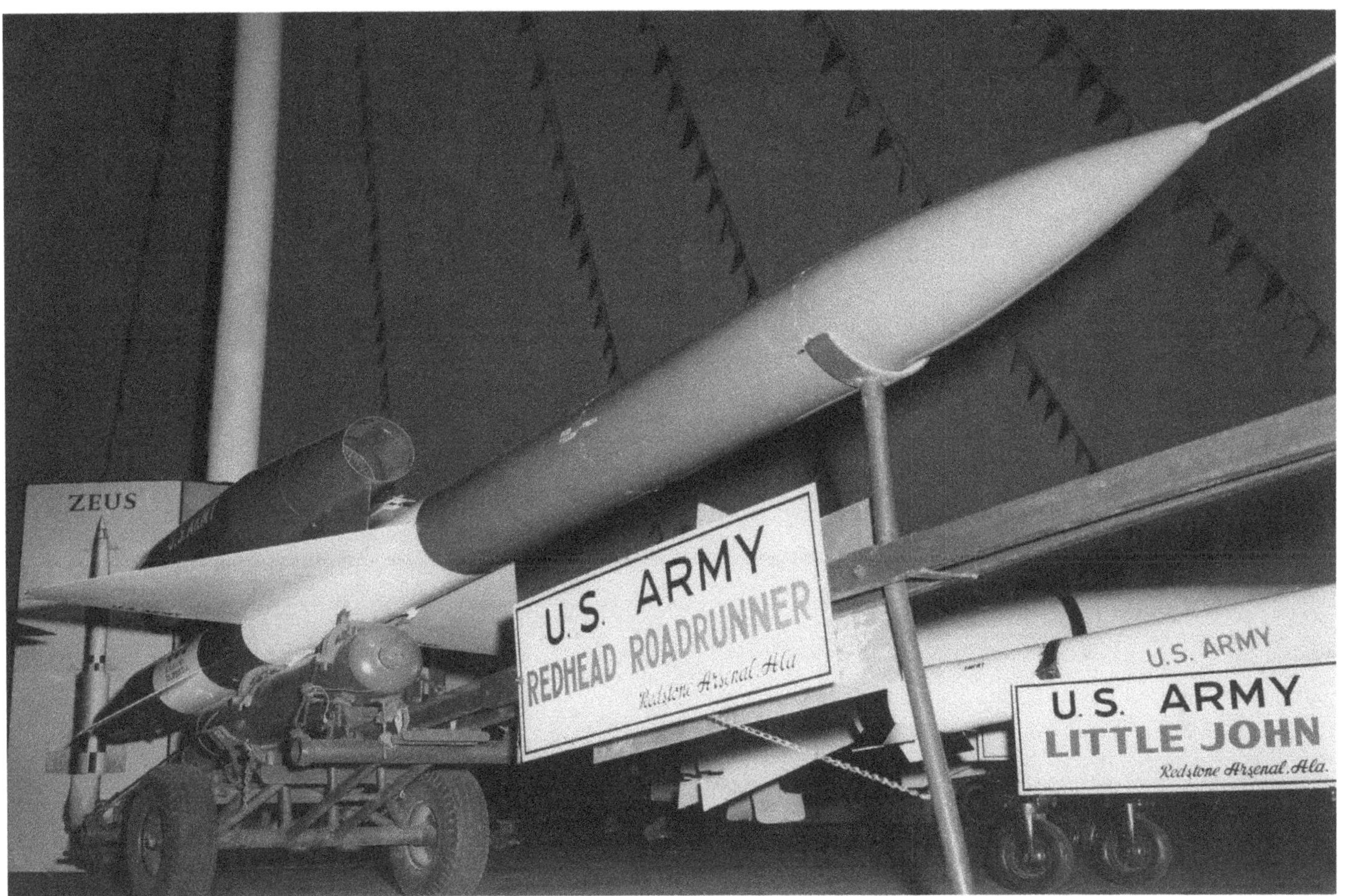

A nighttime celebration was held on March 5, 1959, to commemorate the success of the Pioneer IV Moon Probe. The Space Age made Huntsville the Rocket Capital of the World.

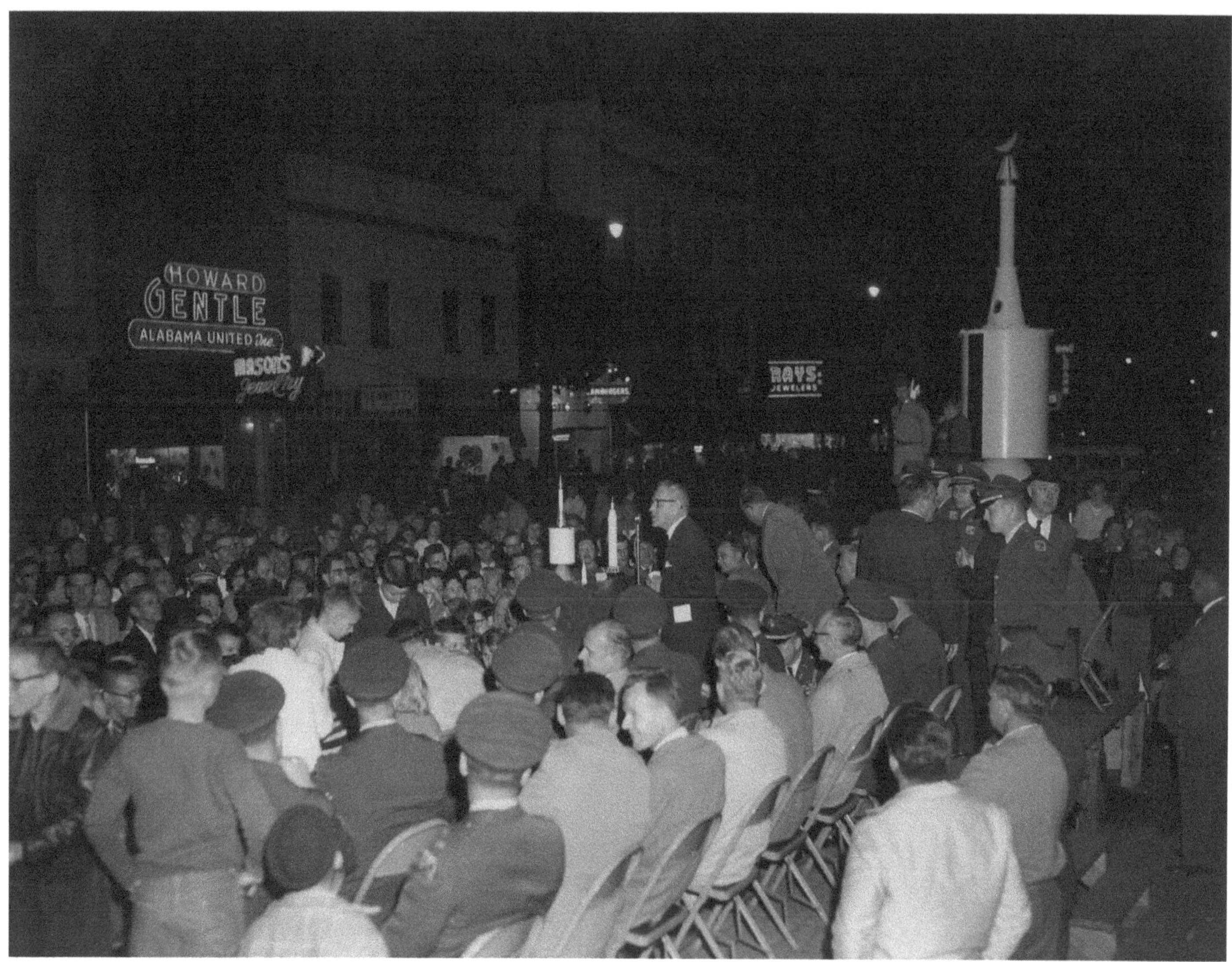

Monkeynauts Baker and Able rode into space on May 28, 1959. They survived the flight, but Able died on June 5 as technicians removed recording devices. Miss Baker lived for more than two decades after that historic flight.

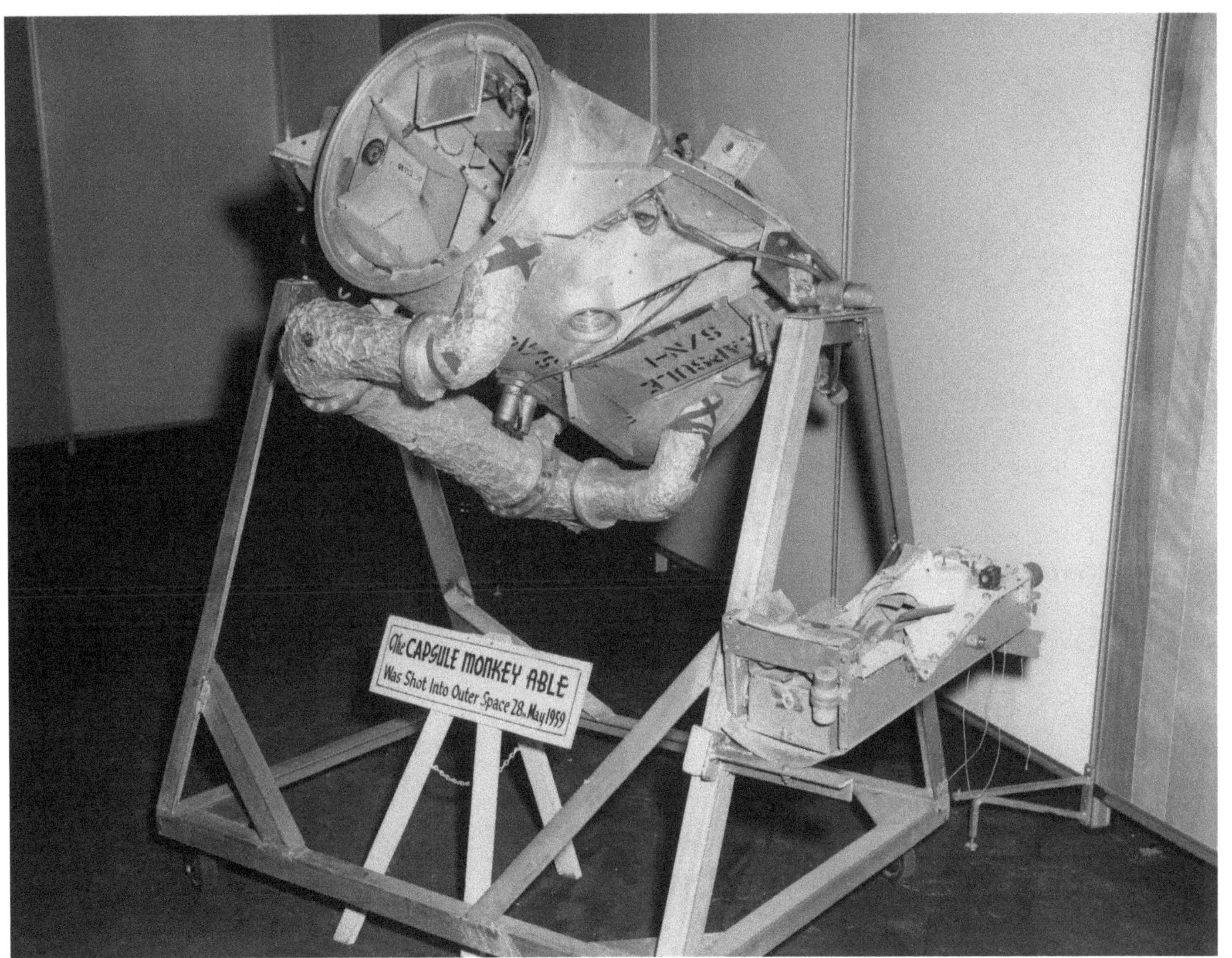

Miss Baker, the celebrity monkey, enjoyed her retirement at the U. S. Space and Rocket Center, where she is now buried.

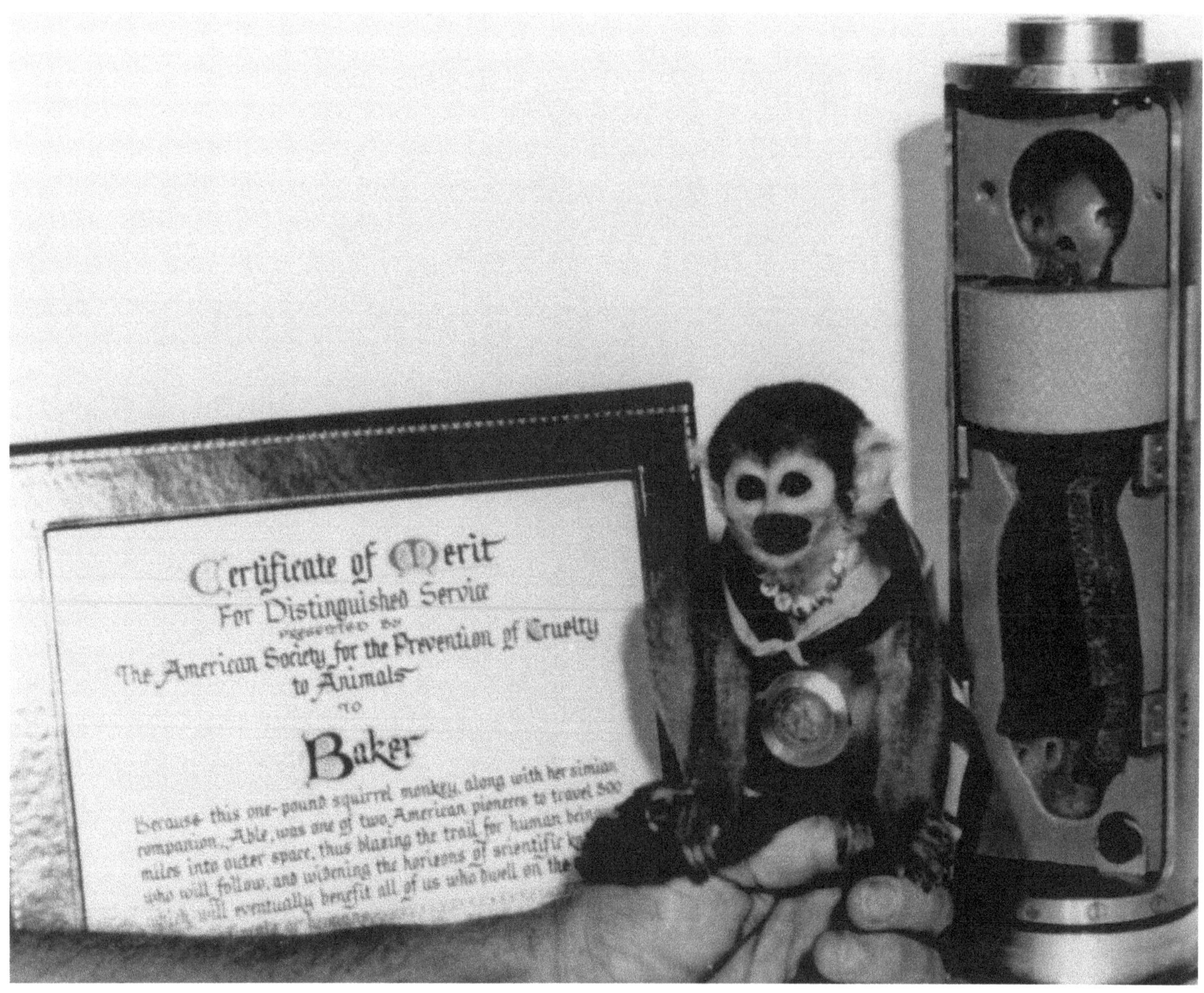

A few members of Dr. von Braun's team are gathered for a public event in 1959.

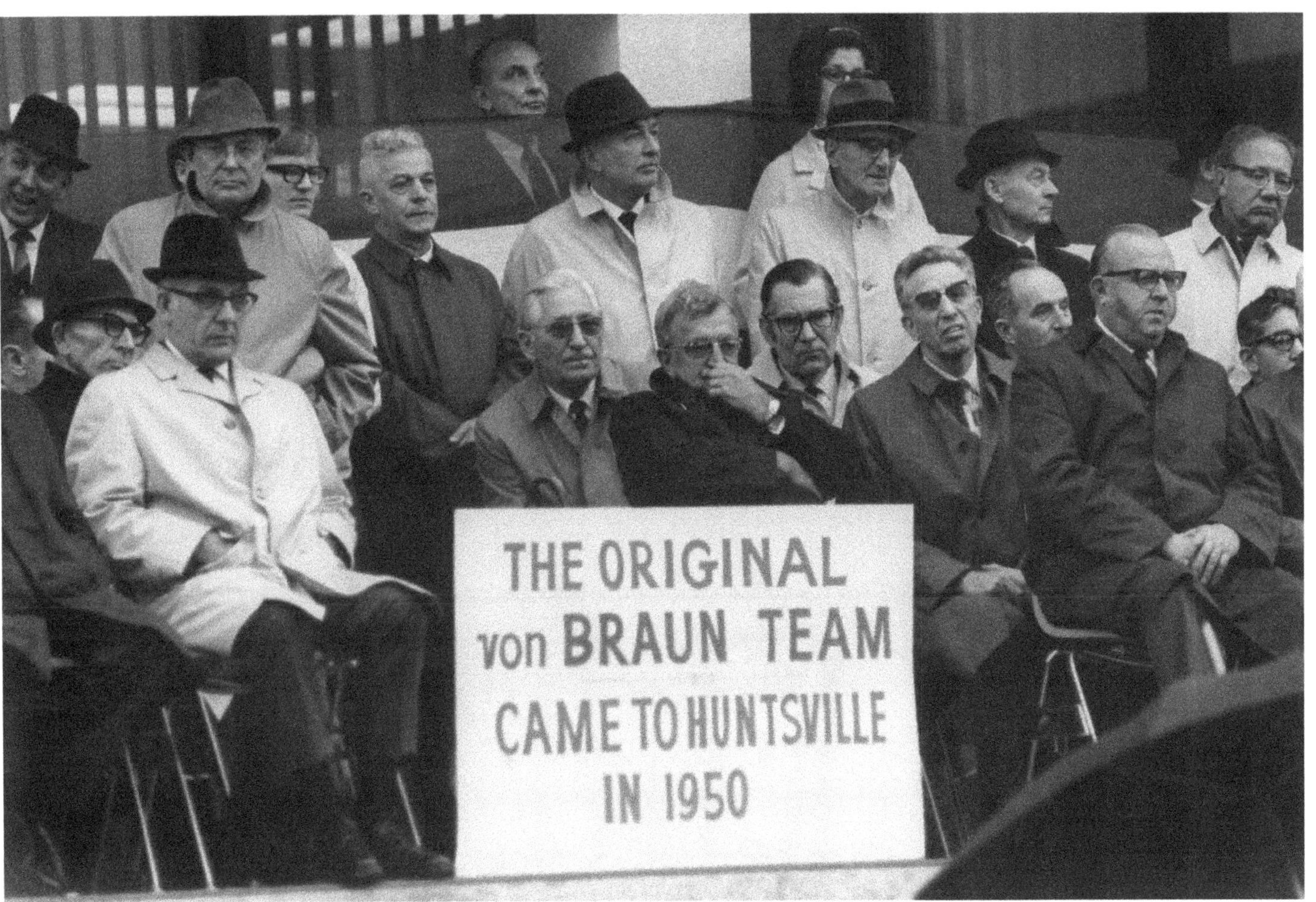

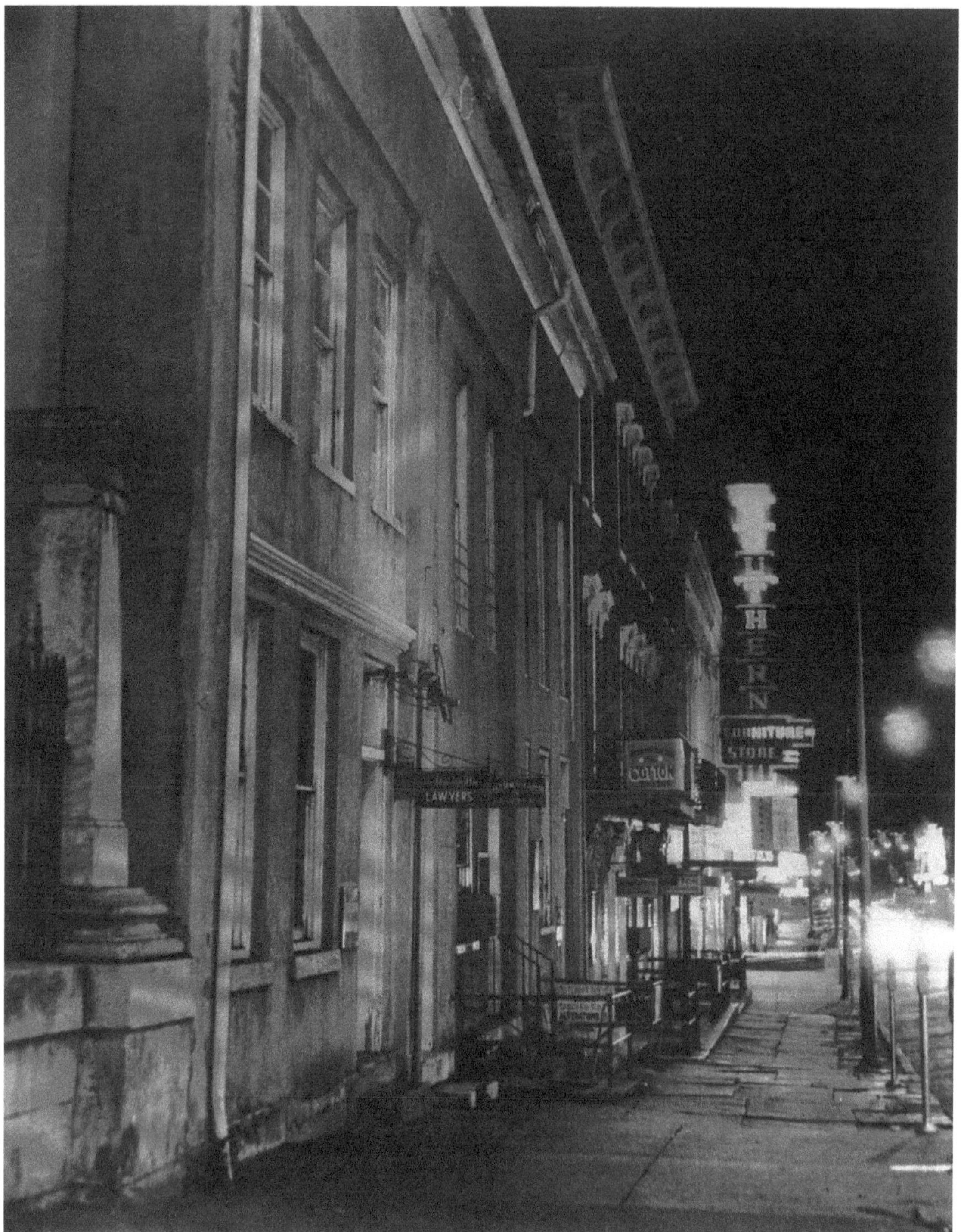

Southern Furniture Store pulled out all the stops to promote business. This evening scene invites window shoppers on West Side Square, once known as Cotton Row.

Wernher von Braun addressed a crowd gathered at the Courthouse Square to commemorate Astronaut Alan B. Shepard's 302-mile ride into space aboard the Redstone Rocket at a speed of 5,100 miles per hour. Huntsville was proud to boast that the rocket was designed and built locally. In addition, the mission was managed at Marshall Space Flight Center.

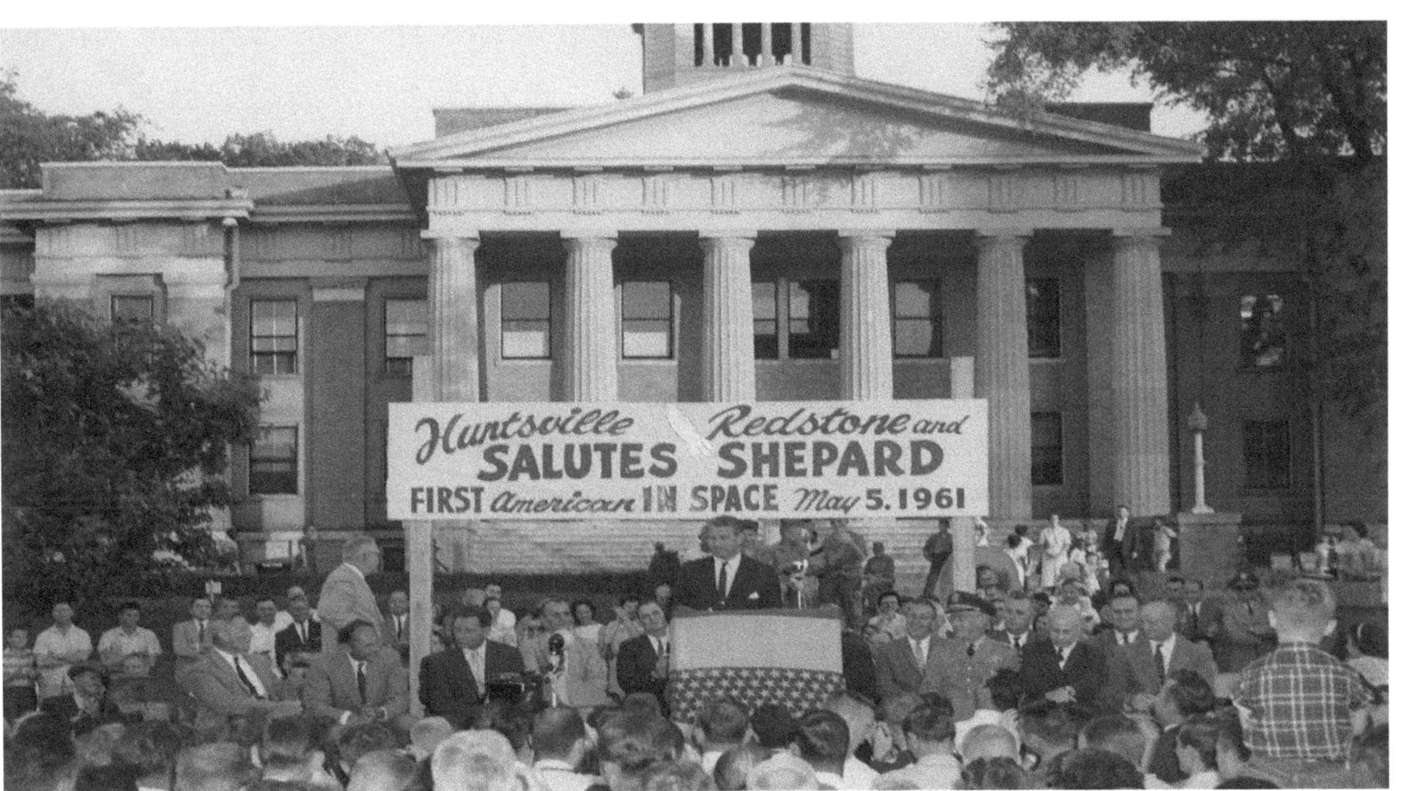

The third Madison County Courthouse is being demolished to make way for a modern skyscraper, a courthouse of steel and glass. Note the four solitary columns on the far left of the building in this 1964 photograph. Four more, still covered, are on the right.

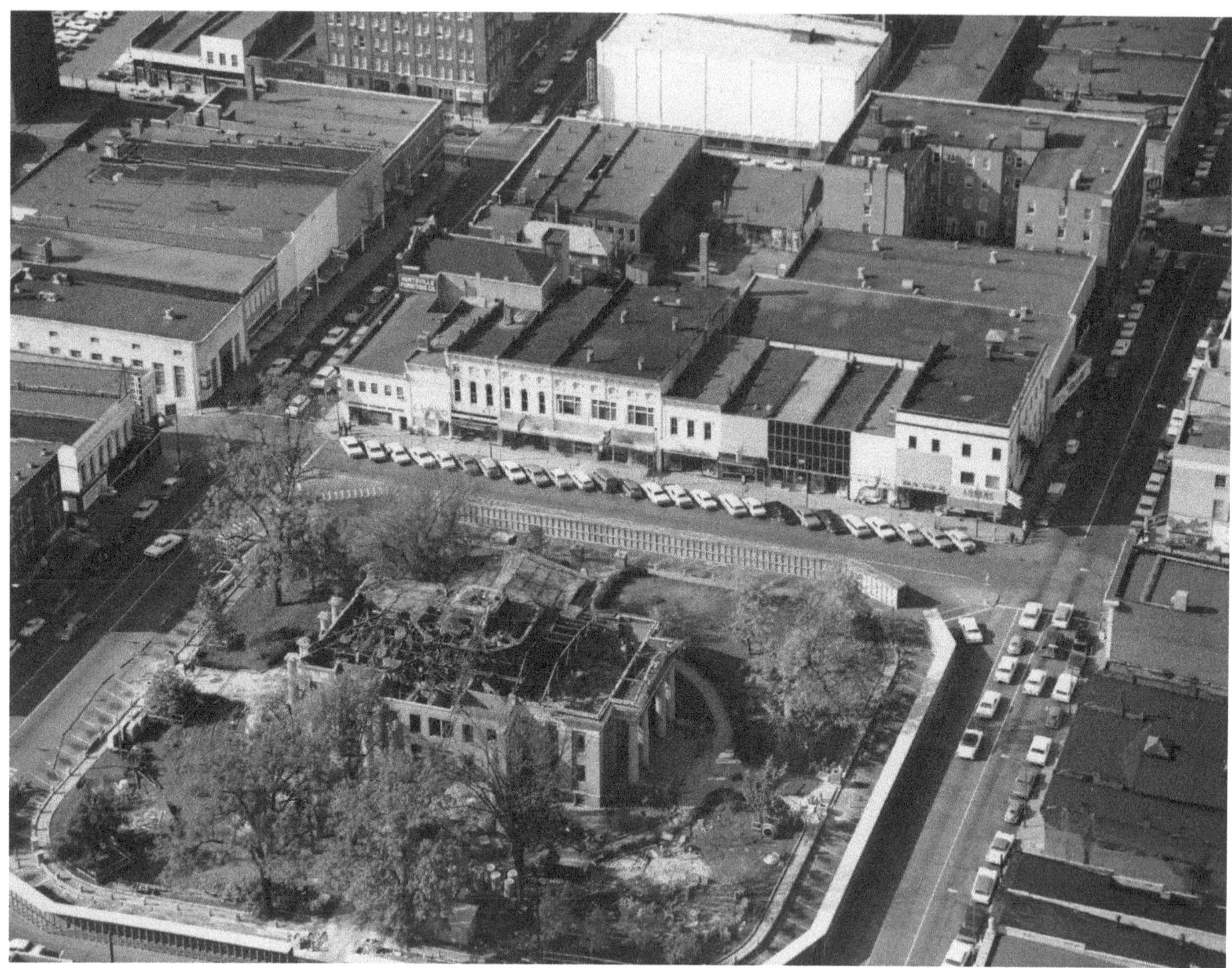

A few members of Dr. Wernher von Braun's original rocket team pose with city dignitaries.

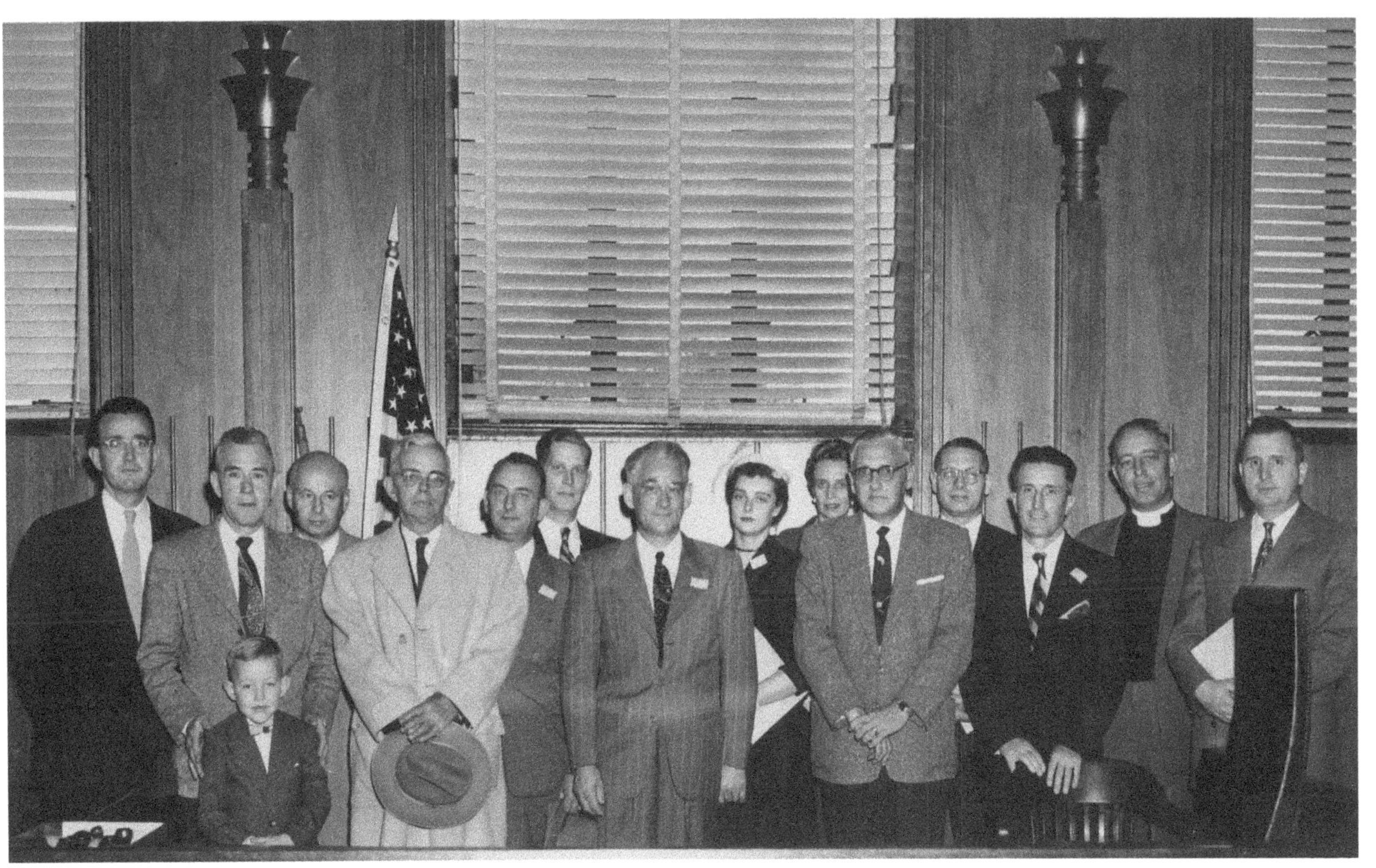

Park benches in front of the courthouse seem to be a natural place to sit and people-watch in this 1964 photo. Across the street, the Amusement Parlor offered billiards, next to Kennamer's Mill Ends Store. Posters on the fence announce Century 21 Shows will be in town Sept. 28 - Oct. 3.

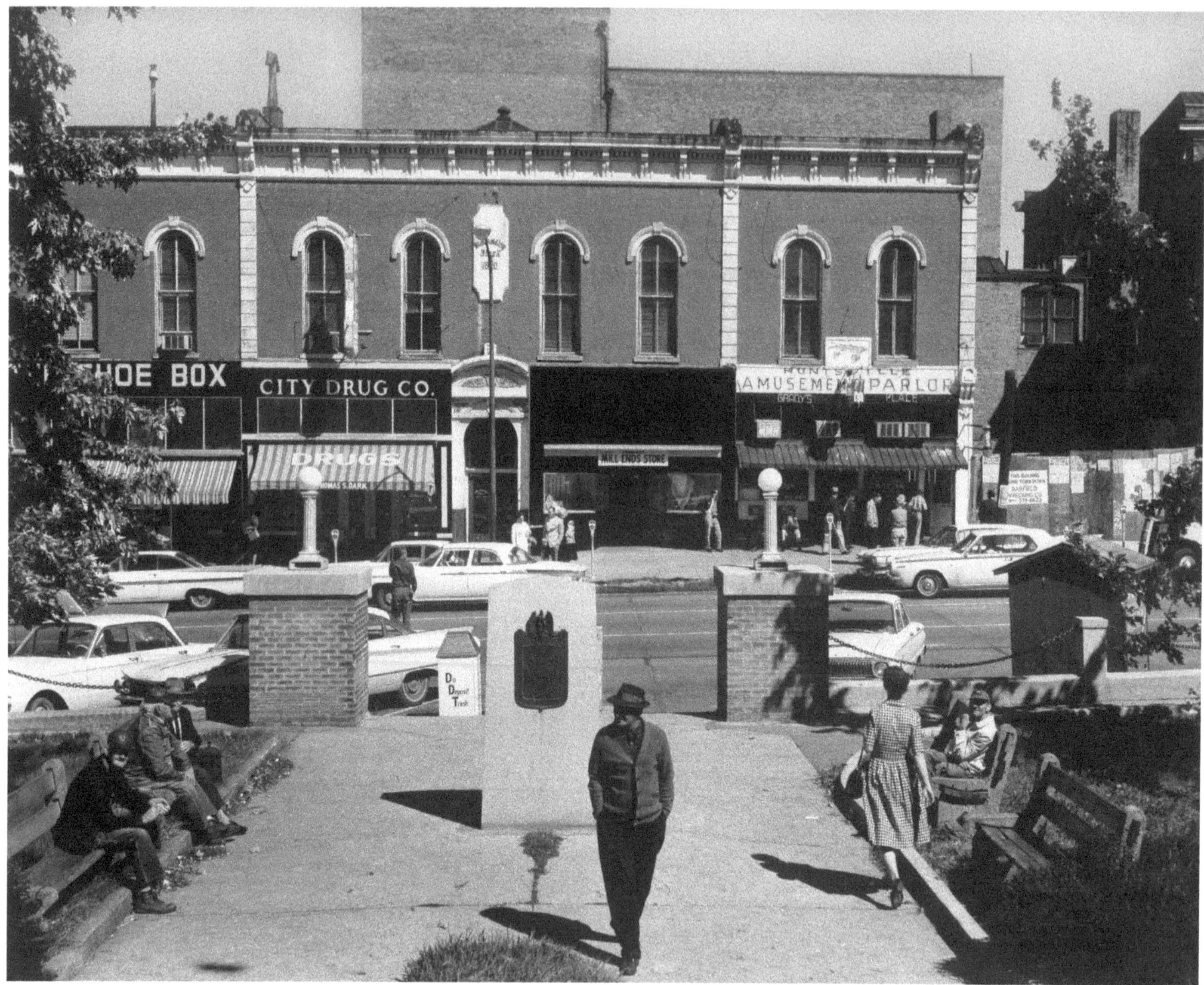

Glenn Hearn, candidate for Mayor of Huntsville, set up his headquarters on West Side Square. He won the election in 1964, and has been recognized by historians as a progressive leader.

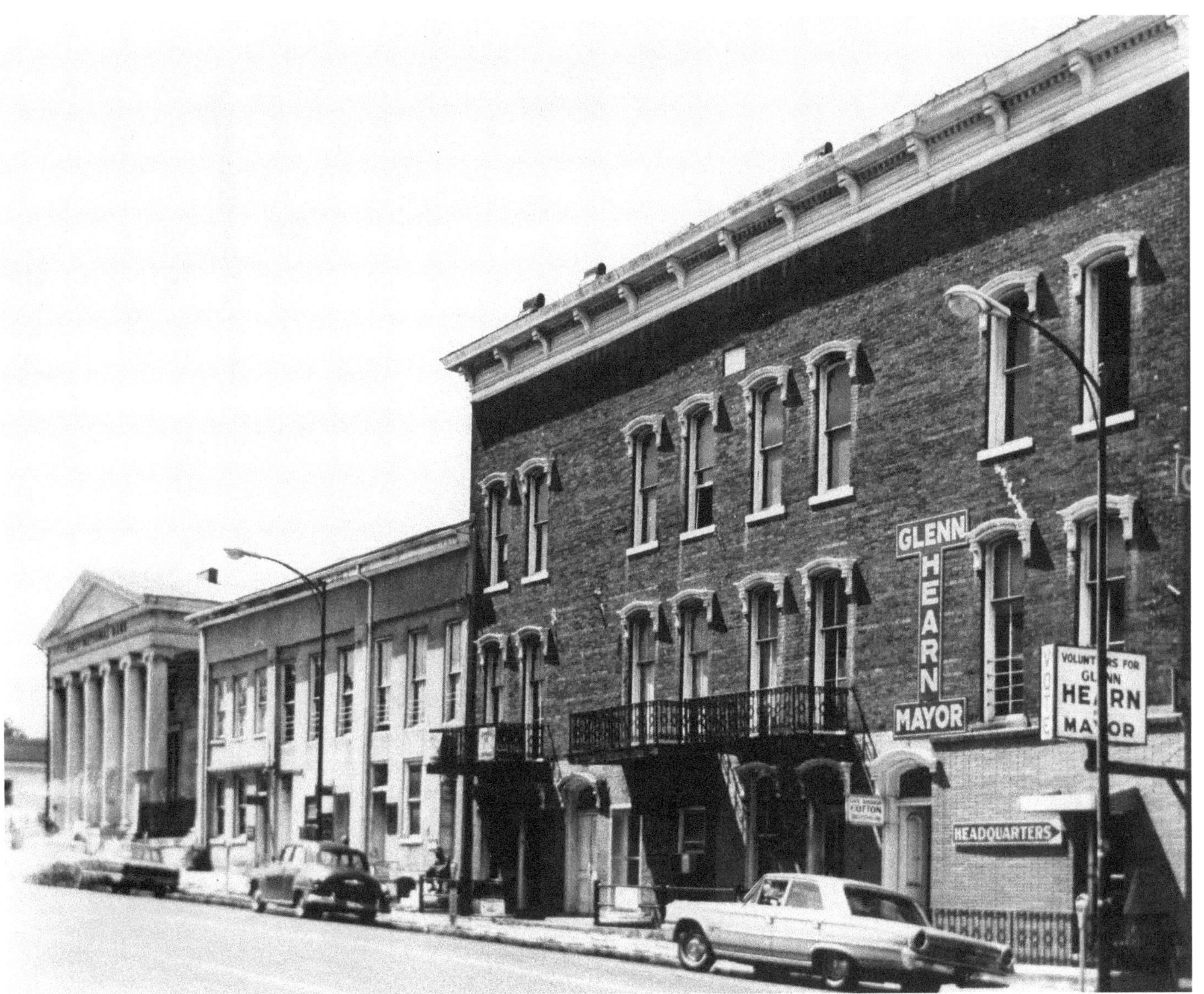

This scene of South Side Square in 1965 reflects the change of businesses in downtown Huntsville as family stores were moving to strip malls and closer to Memorial Parkway and University Drive.

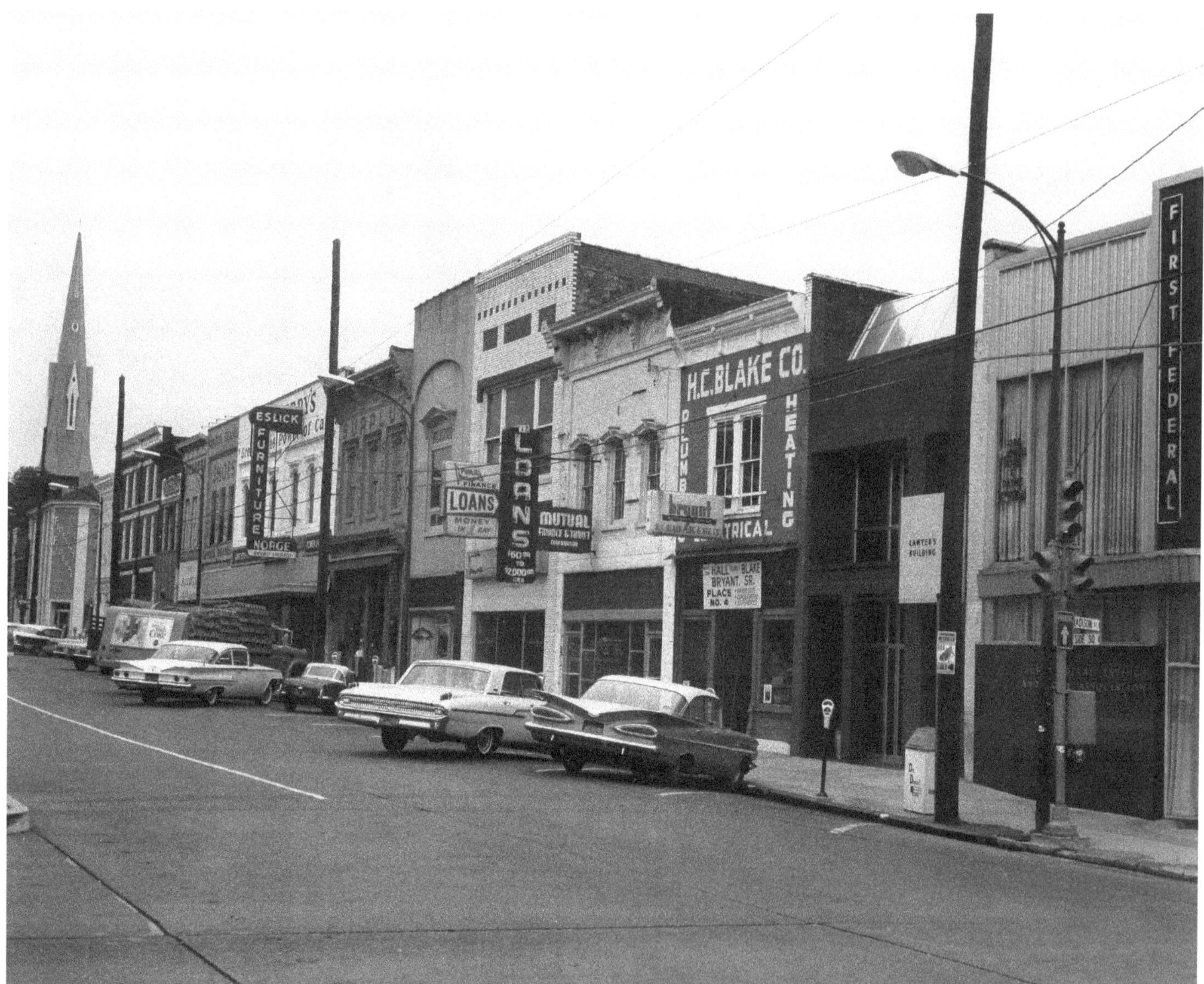

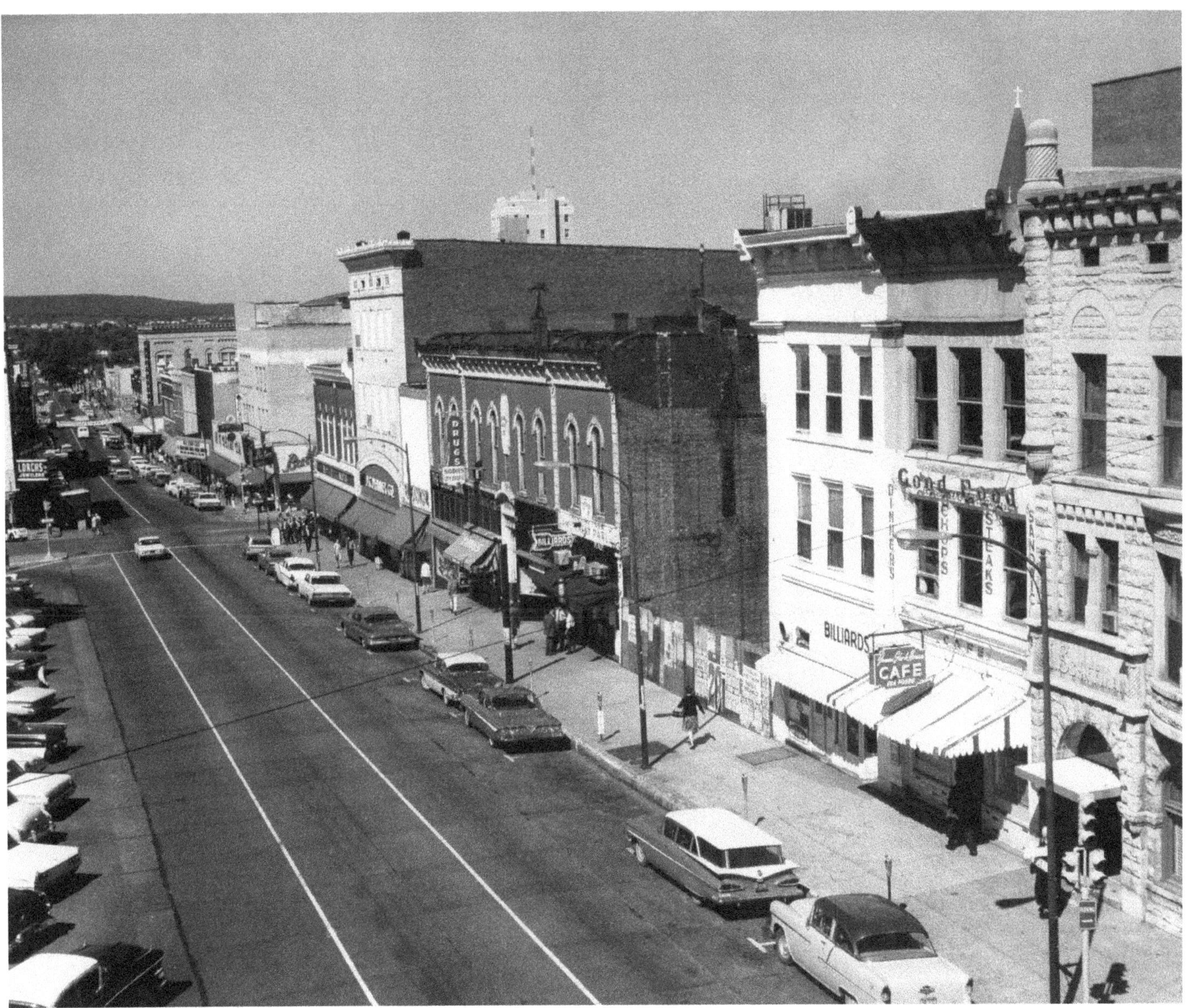

An aerial view of the east side of Washington Street looking north shows the Huntsville Times Building in the far background in this 1966 photograph.

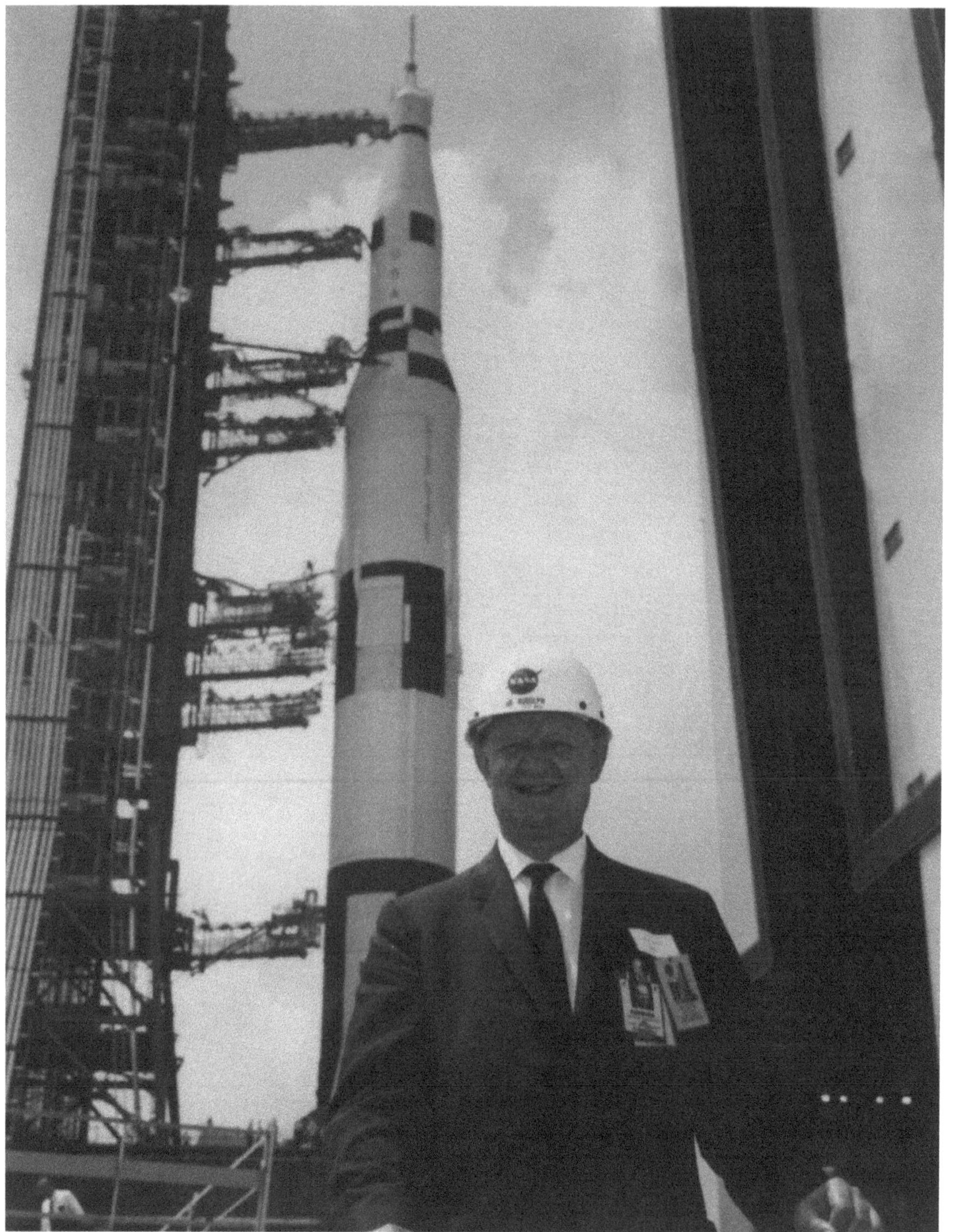

Arthur Rudolph, one of the original members of Wernher von Braun's team and project manager for the Saturn V rocket, was exiled to West Germany and threatened with prosecution for alleged Nazi war crimes if he returned to the United States.

Navy divers watch NASA/MSFC engineer Charles Cooper use a specially designed shepherd's hook in the Neutral Buoyancy Simulator.

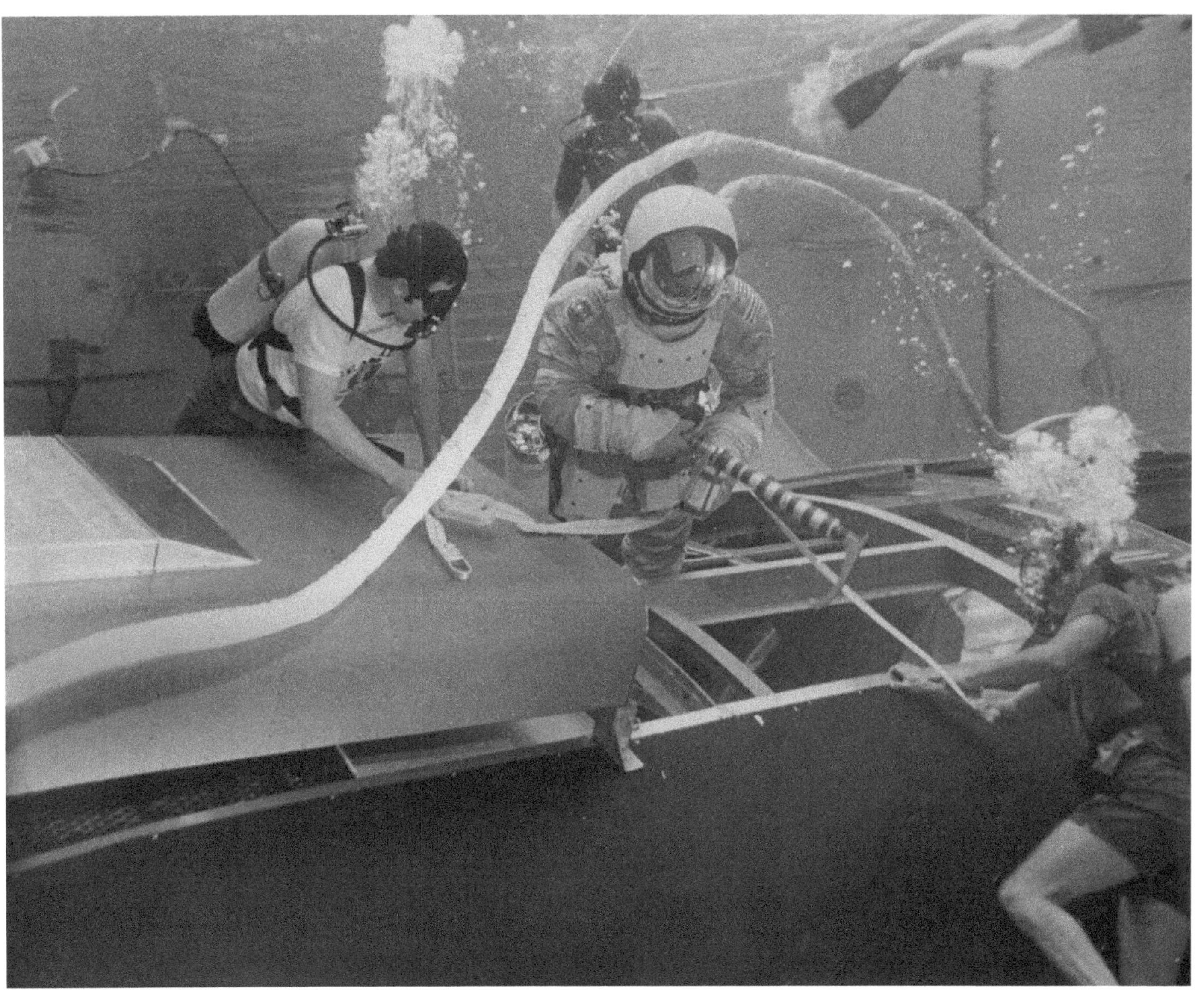

A miniature satellite hangs suspended from a globe above a model of the moon's surface. This 1968 photograph was taken at NASA.

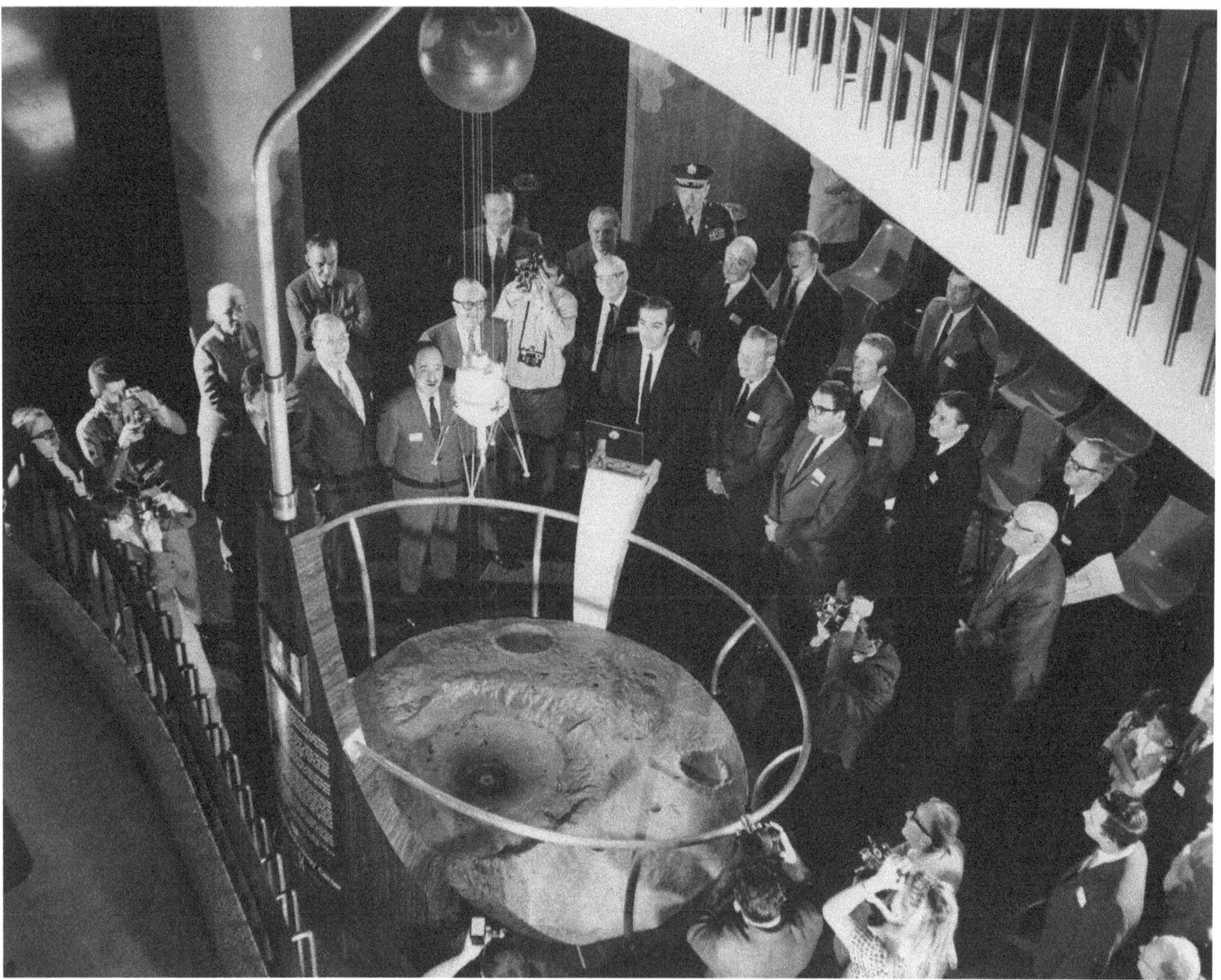

NASA scientists examine a model of a moon buggy on April 1, 1971.

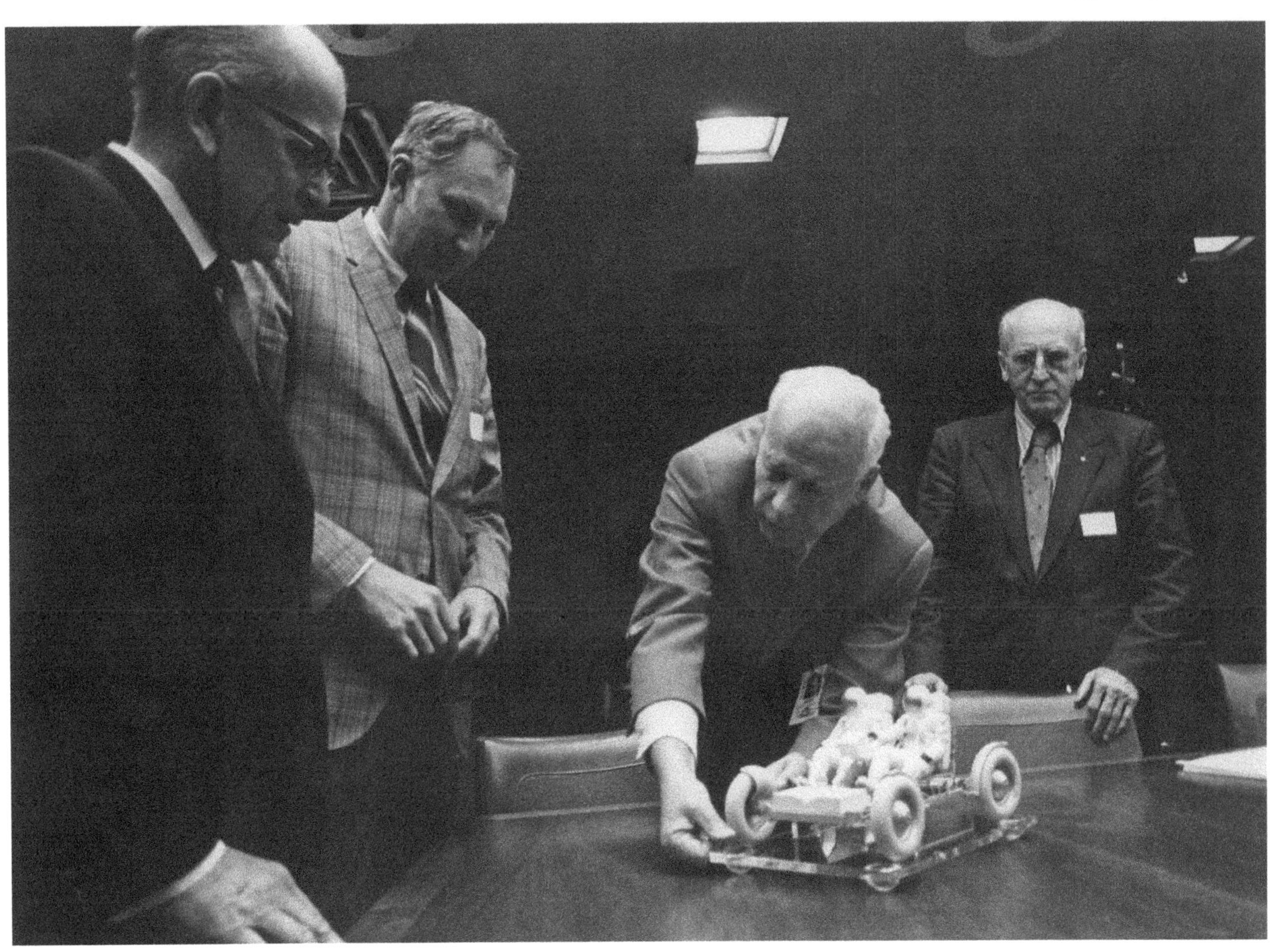

This aerial view of Propulsion and Vehicle Engineering Laboratory was taken in October 1965.

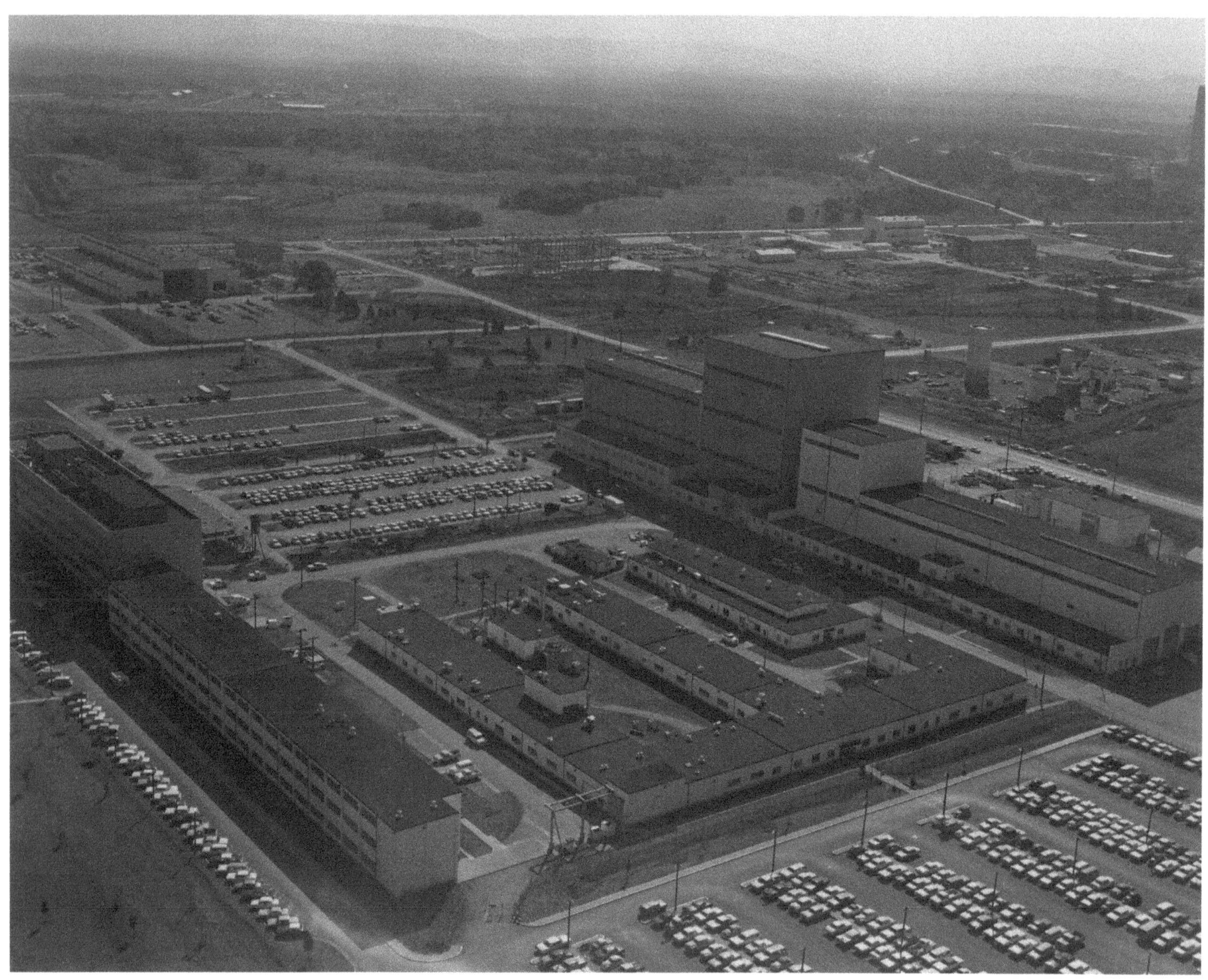

General Charles W. Eifler, 3rd from right, signed this photograph of local dignitaries. General Eifler served three tours of duty at Redstone Arsenal: Commandant of United States Army Ordnance Guided Missile School, Deputy Commanding General Lead Combat Systems for MICOM, and finally MICOM Commanding General. At the time of his death in Huntsville on September 20, 2005, he was the highest-ranking retired army general in the state. He is buried at Arlington National Cemetery.

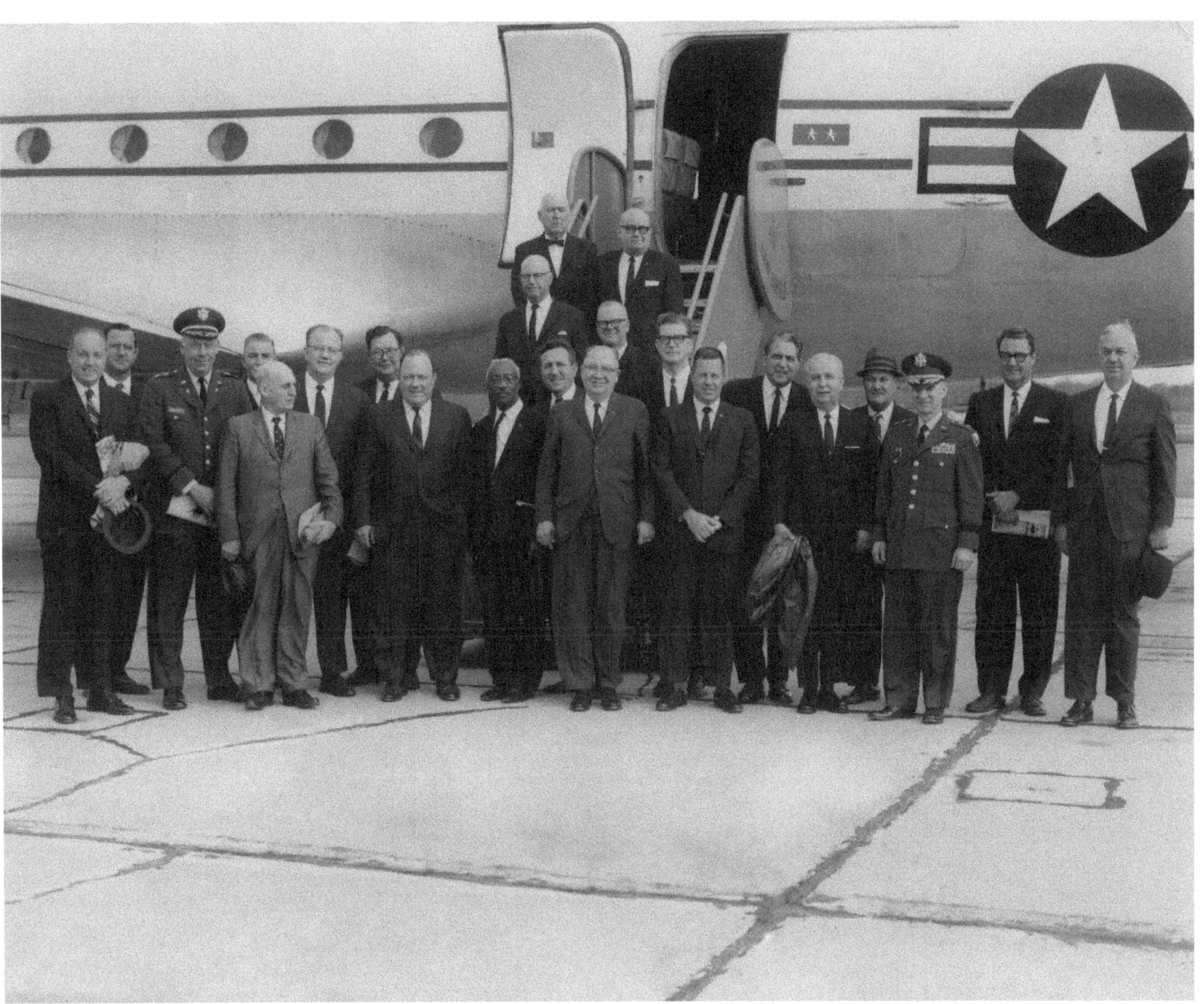

July 24, 1969, was a historic day for the entire world. Apollo 11 Astronauts returned safely to earth after their lunar landing and walk on the moon. Wernher von Braun, the leader of America's race to space, was carried on the shoulders of proud Huntsville residents as the citizens of the city rushed to the courthouse to celebrate.

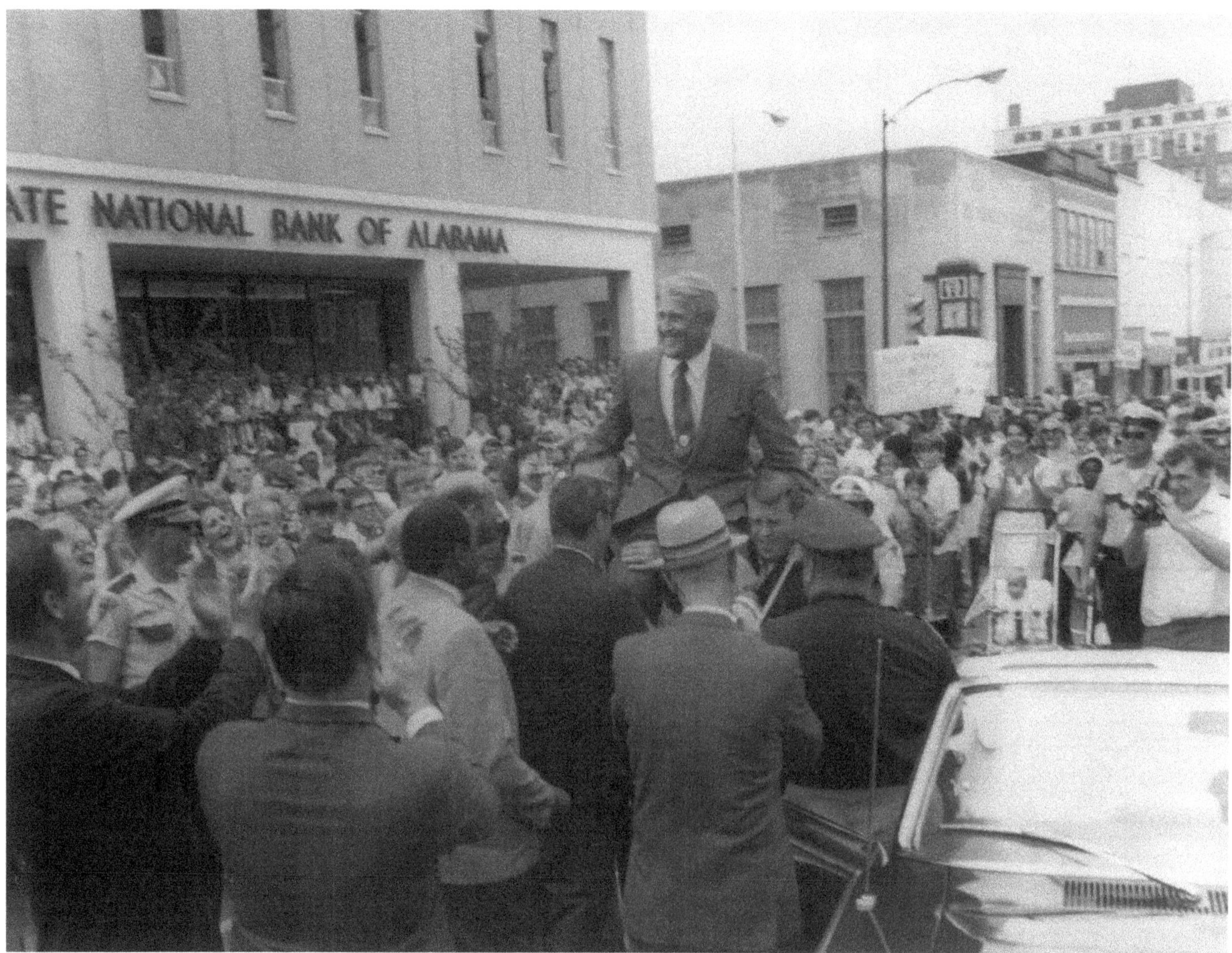

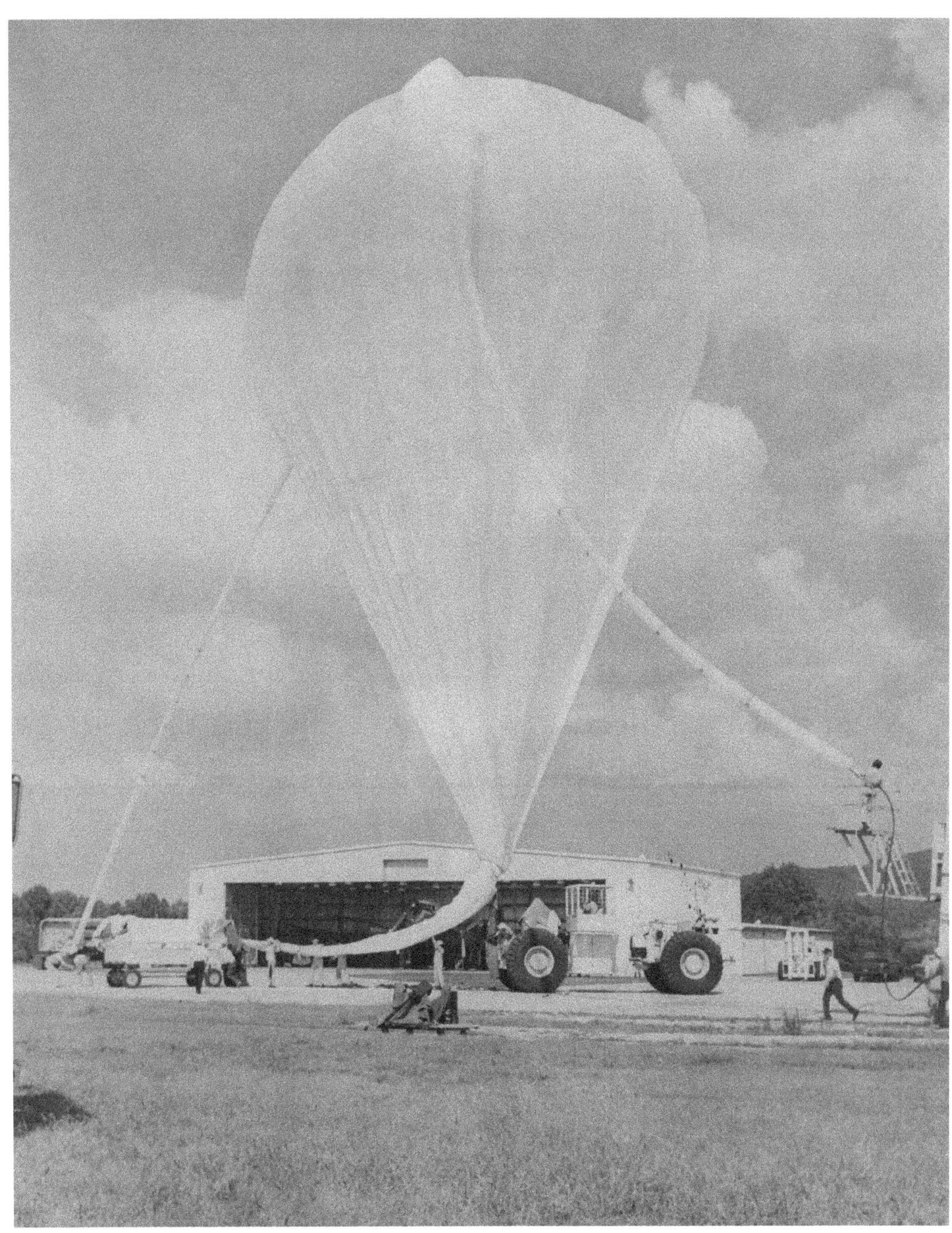

A balloon being inflated with helium at Redstone Arsenal, September 10, 1971.

Alabama's Governor George Wallace makes a stop in Huntsville with his wife Cornelia in June 1971.

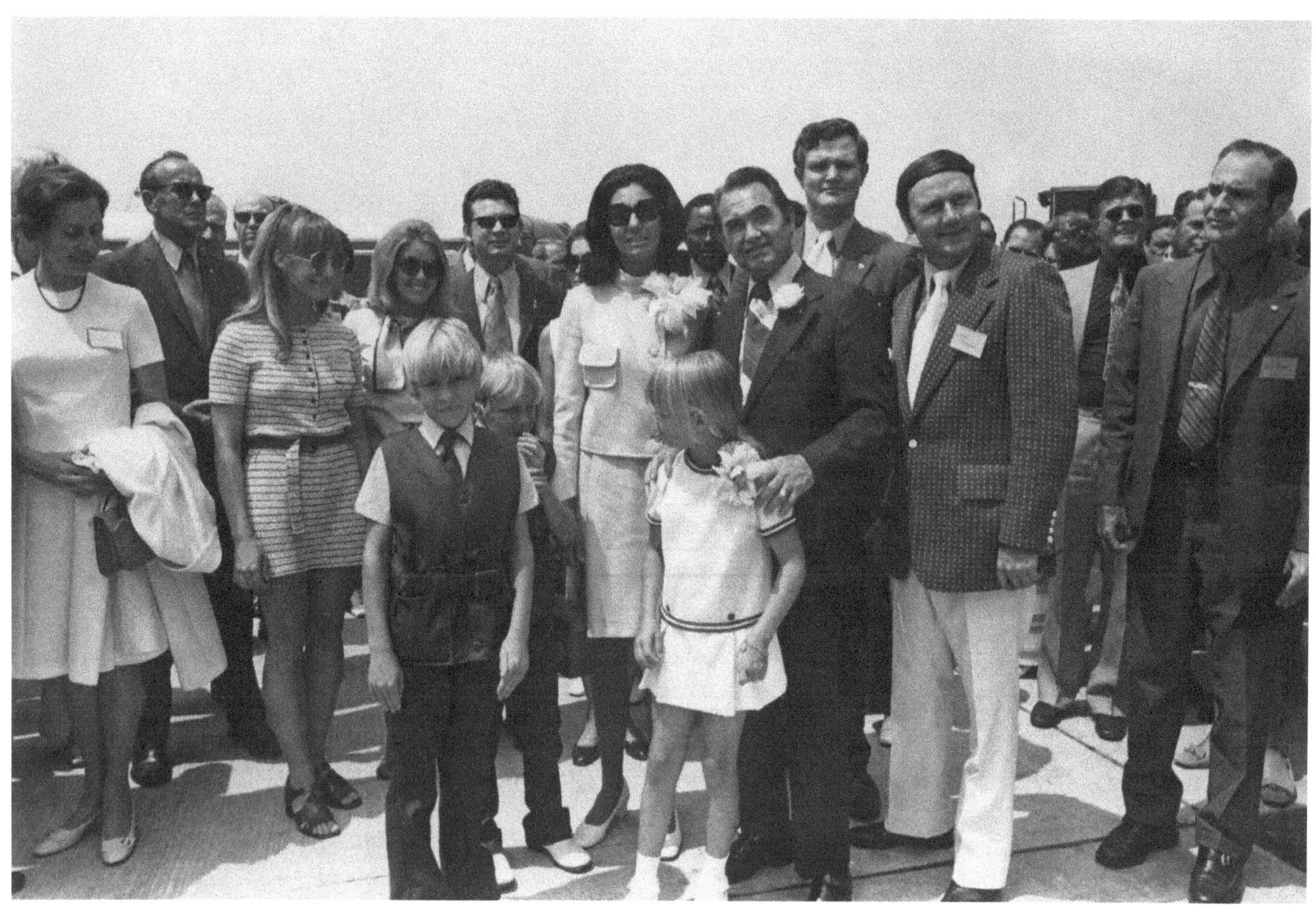

Dr. Ernst Stuhlinger; Dr. Brian O'Brien, Chairman of NASA's Space Council Program Advisory Council; Dr. George Bucher; and Dr. Harvey Hall inspect a model of the Skylab in 1971. Dr. O'Brien was given a briefing on the Marshall Space Flight Center's work on the space shuttle, space station, and future space flights.

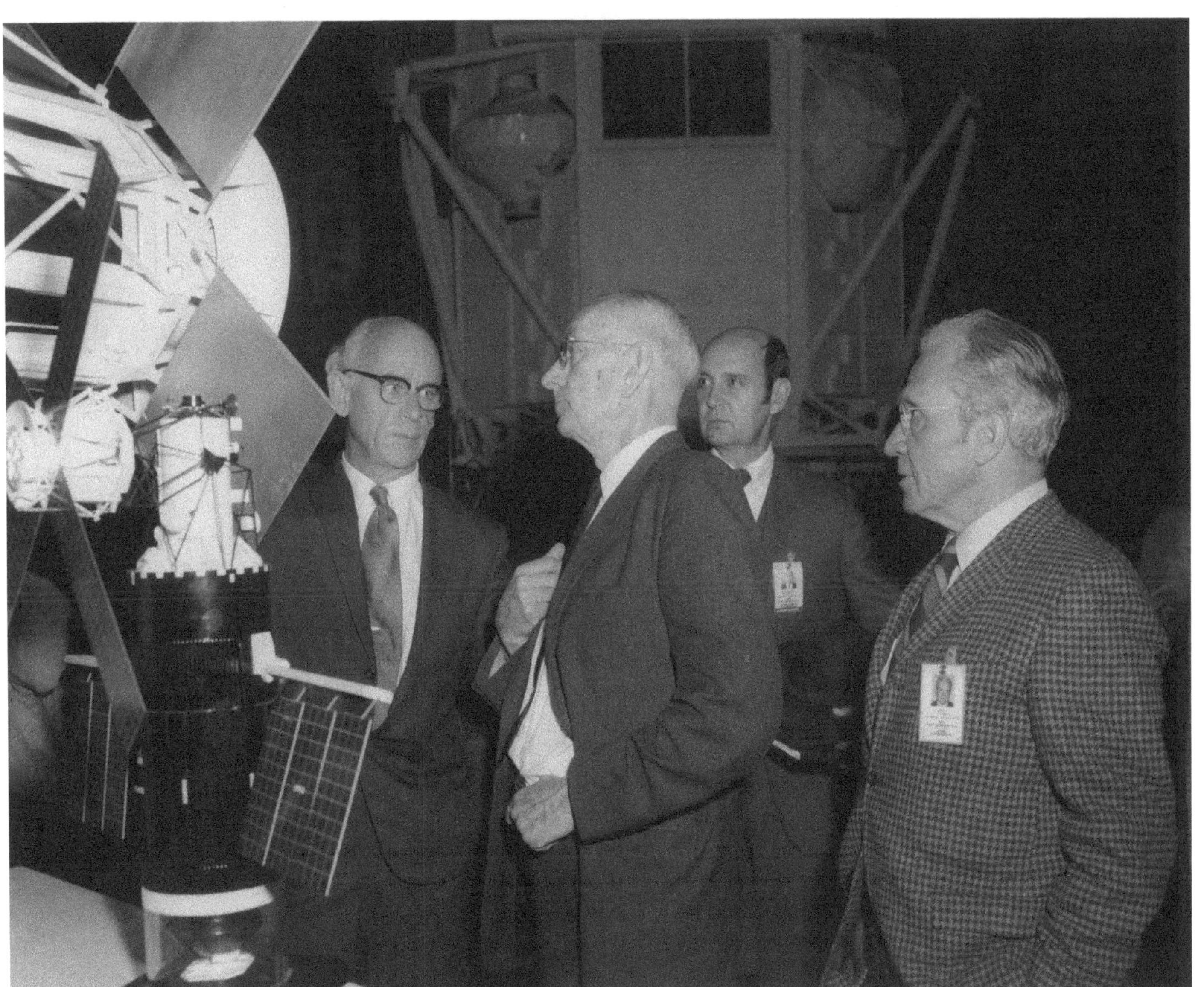

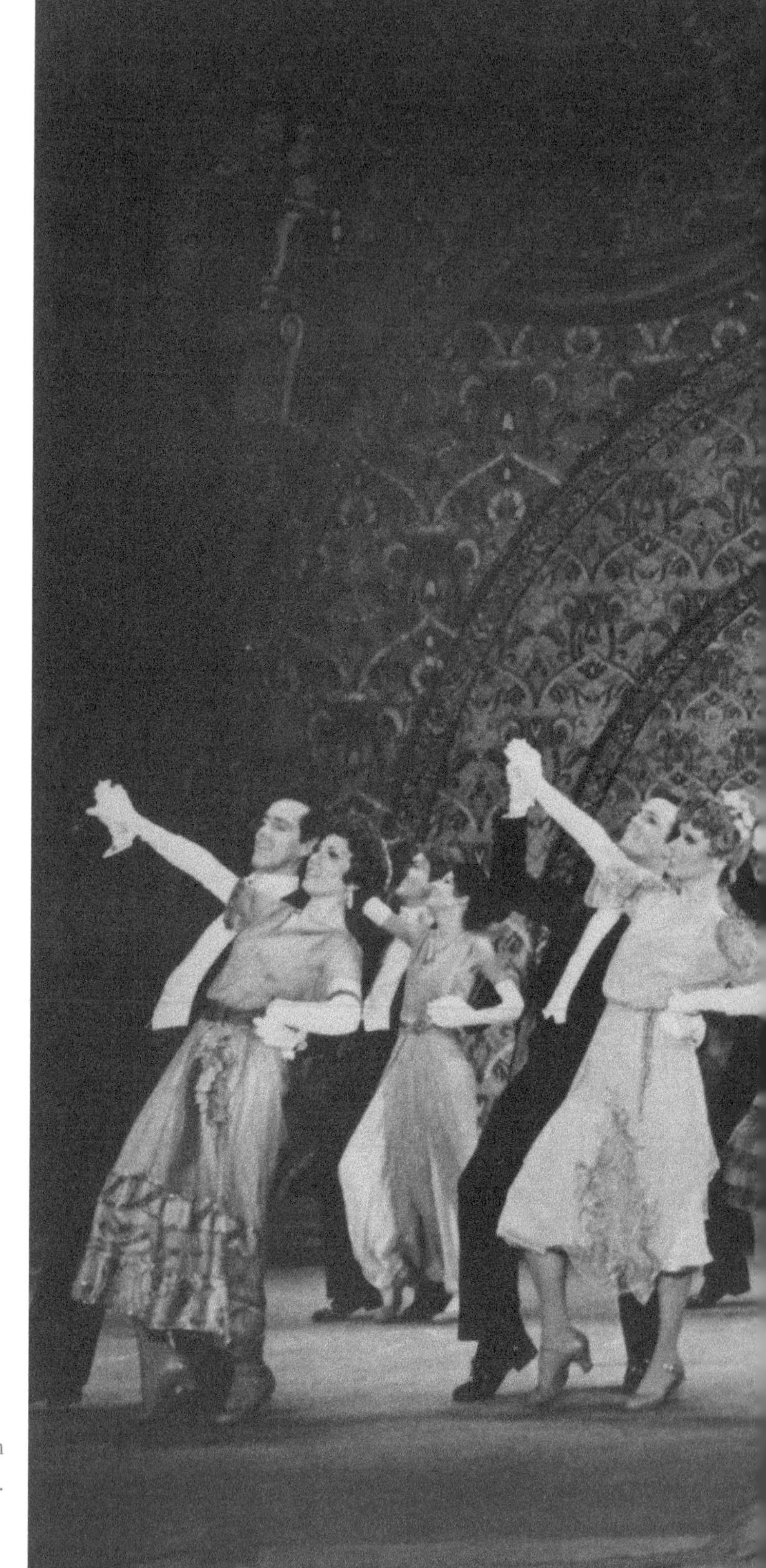

The hit Broadway musical *Irene* dazzled Huntsvillians at Von Braun Civic Center Concert Hall in February 1976.

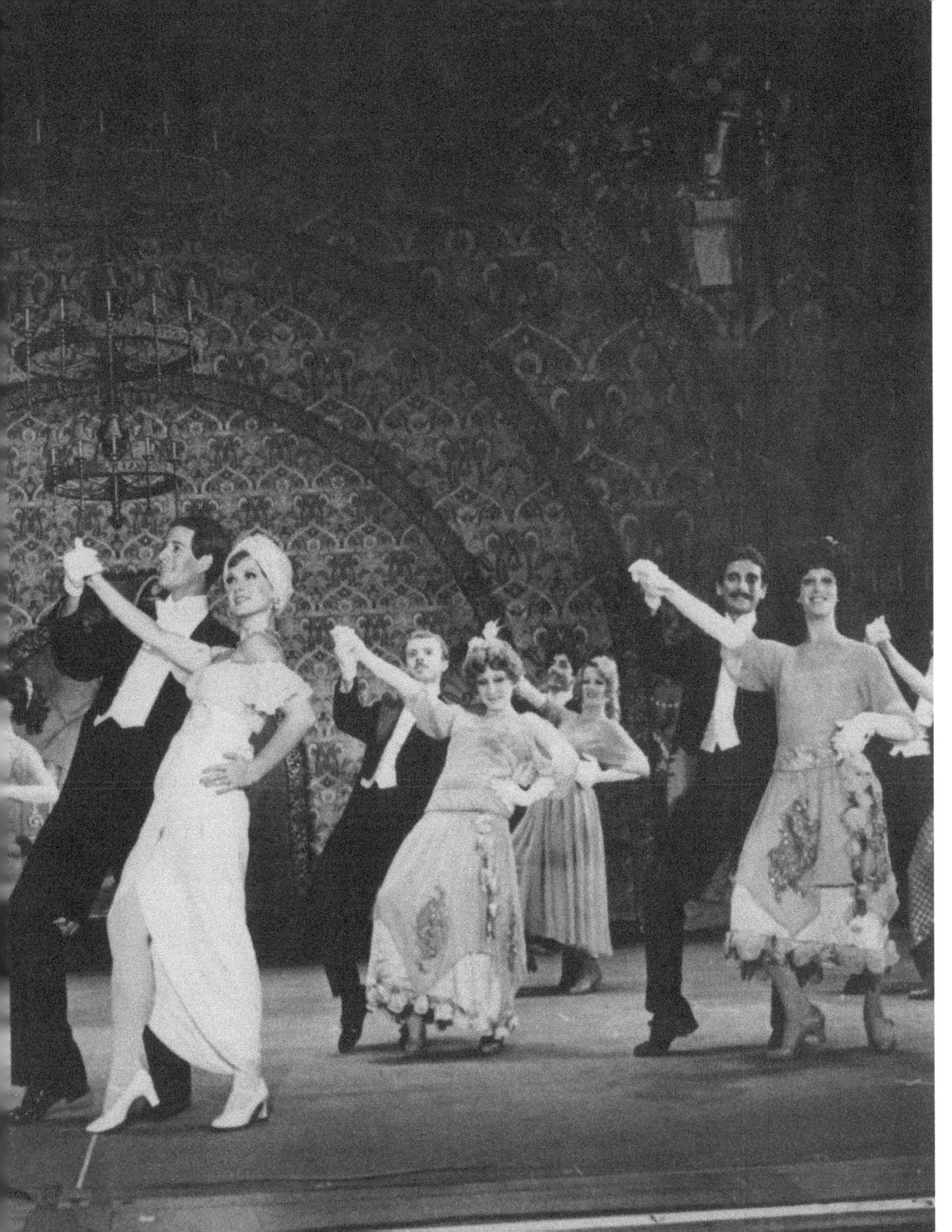

Cotton remained the staple of local farmers more than a century-and-a-half after Huntsville was first settled. These bales are stacked near the Dallas Mill warehouse to be graded and weighed.

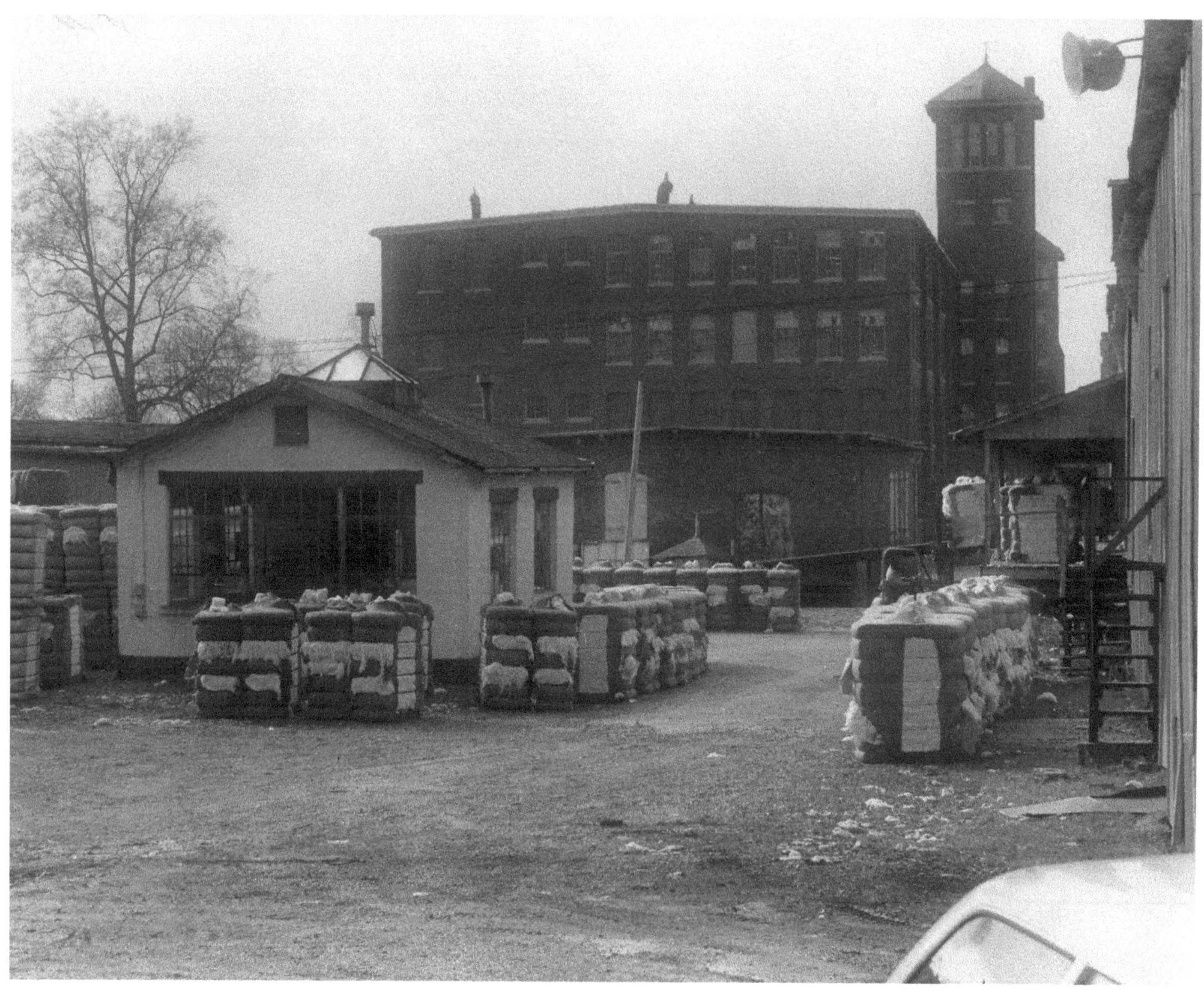

Legendary Alabama football coach Paul "Bear" Bryant carries his trademark hat as he walks a downtown street on "Honor America Day." County Commissioner James Record is at the extreme left. Huntsville's current mayor, Loretta Spencer, holds Bryant's arm.

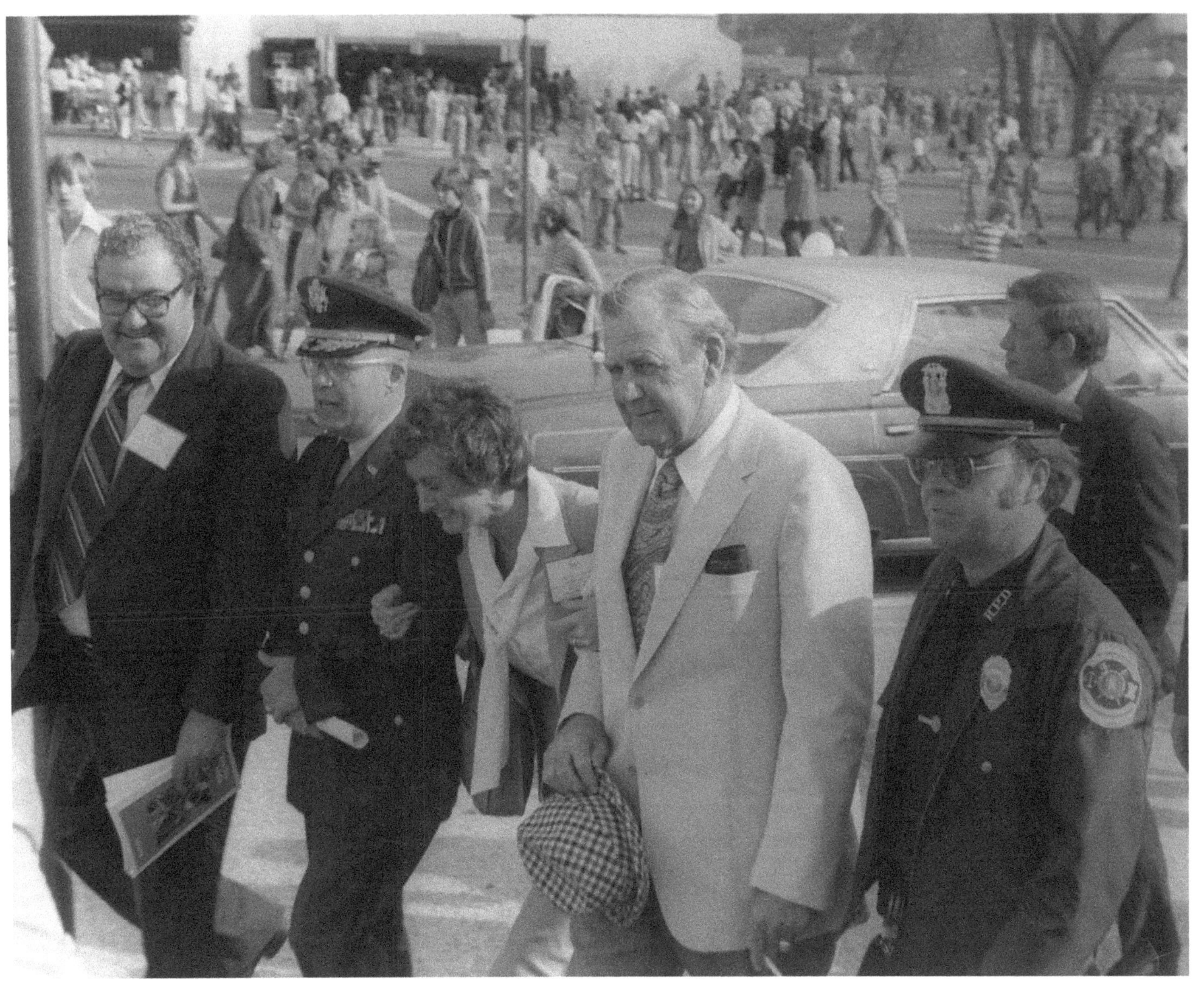

Notes on the Photographs

These notes, listed by page number, attempt to include all aspects known of the photographs. Each of the photographs is identified by the page number, photograph's title or description, photographer and collection, archive, and call or box number when applicable. Although every attempt was made to collect all available data, in some cases complete data was unavailable due to the age and condition of some of the photographs and records.

II **South Side Square**
Huntsville Public Library

VI **John Stallworth**
Huntsville Public Library

X **Oldest Bank**
Huntsville Public Library

2 **Courthouse**
Huntsville Public Library

3 **Bringing in Cotton**
Huntsville Public Library

4 **Church of Nativity**
Huntsville Public Library

5 **East Side Square**
Huntsville Public Library

6 **Union Tent City**
Huntsville Public Library

7 **Jefferson Davis**
Huntsville Public Library

8 **South Side Square**
Huntsville Public Library

9 **Market House**
Huntsville Public Library

10 **North Side Square**
Huntsville Public Library

11 **Timber Wagonloads**
Huntsville Public Library

12 **Wagons of Cotton**
Huntsville Public Library

13 **East Side Square**
Huntsville Public Library

14 **Presbyterian Church**
Huntsville Public Library

15 **East Side Square**
Huntsville Public Library

16 **Engine House No. 1**
Huntsville Public Library

17 **City Hall**
Huntsville Public Library

18 **Thompson Land & Investment**
Huntsville Public Library

19 **J. E. Payne & Co. Bar**
Huntsville Public Library

20 **Madison County Courthouse**
Huntsville Public Library

21 **Jefferson Street**
Huntsville Public Library

22 **Livery Stable**
Huntsville Public Library

23 **City Waterworks**
Huntsville Public Library

24 **Church of Nativity**
Huntsville Public Library

25 **Federal Courthouse**
Huntsville Public Library

26 **Grocery Store**
Huntsville Public Library

27 **Mill Workers**
Huntsville Public Library

28 **Cold Spring**
Huntsville Public Library

29 **Railroad Workers**
Huntsville Public Library

30 **Dummy-line Railway**
Huntsville Public Library

31 **Rock Crusher**
Huntsville Public Library

32 **Monte Sano Hotel**
Huntsville Public Library

33 **Dallas Cotton Mill**
Huntsville Public Library

34 **Dallas Mill**
Huntsville Public Library

35 **1892 City Hall**
Huntsville Public Library

36 **Gatekeeper's House**
Huntsville Public Library

37 **Carriage Factory**
Huntsville Public Library

38 **Schiffman Store**
Huntsville Public Library

39 **Schiffman Store**
Huntsville Public Library

40 **Southern Bell**
Huntsville Public Library

41 **Pump House**
Huntsville Public Library

42 **Merrimack Mill**
Huntsville Public Library

43 **Merrimack Mill**
Huntsville Public Library

44 **Barber Shop**
Huntsville Public Library

45 **Barbers' High Style**
Huntsville Public Library

46 **Big Spring Flood**
Huntsville Public Library

47 **Ice at Big Spring**
Huntsville Public Library

48 **Laxson & Kelly**
Huntsville Public Library

49 **Fire Department**
Huntsville Public Library

50 **Mill Workers**
Huntsville Public Library

52 **Lowe Mill**
Huntsville Public Library

53 **Woman in Carriage**
Huntsville Public Library

54 **Crowd Scene**
Huntsville Public Library

55 **Elks Picnic**
Huntsville Public Library

56 **Cotton Parade**
Huntsville Public Library

57 **Horses Pulling Carriage**
Huntsville Public Library

58 **Jail**
Huntsville Public Library

59 **General Repair Shop**
Huntsville Public Library

60 **Sparkman Marble and Granite Works**
Huntsville Public Library

61 **Spring City Mills**
Huntsville Public Library

62 **Building Dedication**
Huntsville Public Library

63 **Dunnavant's Store**
Huntsville Public Library

64 **Oddfellows at Dallas Mills Post Office**
Huntsville Public Library

65 **Monument Dedication**
Huntsville Public Library

66 **South Side Square**
Huntsville Public Library

67 **Cotton Wagonloads**
Huntsville Public Library

68 **Baseball Team**
Huntsville Public Library

70 **Huntsville Hotel**
Huntsville Public Library

71 **London Plumbing Co.**
Huntsville Public Library

72 **Fire Scene**
Huntsville Public Library

73 **Sunday School**
Huntsville Public Library

74 **Porters Grocery**
Huntsville Public Library

75 **People on Horseback**
Huntsville Public Library

76 **Grocery Store**
Huntsville Public Library

77 **Marble Works**
Huntsville Public Library

78 **Methodist Church**
Huntsville Public Library

79 **Elephant Walk**
Huntsville Public Library

80 **Elephant Walk**
Huntsville Public Library

81 **Huntsville High**
Huntsville Public Library

82 **Men with Axes**
Huntsville Public Library

84 **Big Spring**
Huntsville Public Library

85 **Clinton Avenue**
Huntsville Public Library

86 **Street Scene**
Huntsville Public Library

87 **Cumberland Presbyterian Church**
Huntsville Public Library

88 **Parade Car**
Huntsville Public Library

89 **Wagon in Big Spring**
Huntsville Public Library

90 **Probate Office**
Huntsville Public Library

91 **Fire Department**
Huntsville Public Library

92 **Courthouse**
Huntsville Public Library

93 **Jefferson Street**
Huntsville Public Library

94 **Fire Department**
Huntsville Public Library

96 **Street Scene**
Huntsville Public Library

97 **Parade Float**
Huntsville Public Library

98 **Business Supplies**
Huntsville Public Library

99 **Street Crowd**
Huntsville Public Library

100 **St. Mary's**
Huntsville Public Library

101 **Picnic**
Huntsville Public Library

102 **Road Dedication**
Huntsville Public Library

103 **American Legion**
Huntsville Public Library

104 **Weaving Machines**
Huntsville Public Library

105 **Steadman's Bar B Q**
Huntsville Public Library

106 **Clinton & Washington**
Huntsville Public Library

107 **Football Team**
Huntsville Public Library

108 **Washington Street**
Huntsville Public Library

109 **United Textiles**
Huntsville Public Library

110 **City Jail**
Huntsville Public Library

111 **Shoe Store**
Huntsville Public Library

112 **Central Church of Christ**
Huntsville Public Library

113 **Jefferson Street**
Huntsville Public Library

114 **Washington Street**
Huntsville Public Library

115 **DAR Monument**
Huntsville Public Library

116 **Temple B'nai Sholom**
Huntsville Public Library

117 **Park Dedication**
Huntsville Public Library

118 **Local Dance**
Huntsville Public Library

120 **1939 Parade**
Huntsville Public Library

122 **Building 7101**
Huntsville Public Library

123 **Women Mill Workers**
Huntsville Public Library

124 **Army Day Parade**
Huntsville Public Library

125 **Dude Ranch**
Huntsville Public Library

126 **Dude Ranch**
Huntsville Public Library

127 **Church of Christ**
Huntsville Public Library

128 **Veterans' Reunion**
Huntsville Public Library

130 **Randolph Street**
Huntsville Public Library

131 **Long Lines**
Huntsville Public Library

132 **Bicycles in Parade**
Huntsville Public Library

134 Cotton Ball
Huntsville Public Library

135 V-J Day Celebration
Huntsville Public Library

136 Band with Crowd
Huntsville Public Library

138 Russel Erskine Hotel
Huntsville Public Library

139 Woolworth Store
Huntsville Public Library

140 Lakeside Methodist
Huntsville Public Library

141 Southern Furniture
Huntsville Public Library

142 Dallas Manufacturing Office
Huntsville Public Library

143 "Bumper Lite" Tape
Huntsville Public Library

144 Strike Lines
Huntsville Public Library

146 Huntsville Manufacturing Co.
Huntsville Public Library

147 J. C. Penney
Huntsville Public Library

148 Big Spring Pool
Huntsville Public Library

150 Big Spring Park
Huntsville Public Library

151 Standard Loan Office
Huntsville Public Library

152 Swearing-in Ceremony
Huntsville Public Library

154 Christmas Parade
Huntsville Public Library

155 Booths at Square
Huntsville Public Library

156 Courthouse Square
Huntsville Public Library

157 Soldiers in Parade
Huntsville Public Library

158 North Side Square
Huntsville Public Library

159 Mason's Furniture
Huntsville Public Library

160 V-2 Missile
Huntsville Public Library

161 Stockton Motor Co.
Huntsville Public Library

162 Huntsville High
Huntsville Public Library

163 Strip Mall Dedication
Huntsville Public Library

164 Patriotic Parade
Huntsville Public Library

166 Rocket at Courthouse
Huntsville Public Library

167 Rocket at Square
Huntsville Public Library

168 "Come to Rocket City"
Huntsville Public Library

169 East Side Square
Huntsville Public Library

170 Car Accident
Huntsville Public Library

171 Redstone Arsenal
Huntsville Public Library

172 Symbolic Rocket Launch
Huntsville Public Library

173 Missile
Huntsville Public Library

174 Pioneer IV
Huntsville Public Library

175 Monkeynaut Capsule
Huntsville Public Library

176 Miss Baker
Huntsville Public Library

177 Von Braun Team
Huntsville Public Library

178 Night Scene
Huntsville Public Library

179 Redstone and Shepard
Huntsville Public Library

180 Courthouse Demolition
Huntsville Public Library

181 Dignitaries
Huntsville Public Library

182 East Side Square
Huntsville Public Library

183 West Side Square
Huntsville Public Library

184 South Side Square
Huntsville Public Library

185 Washington Street
Huntsville Public Library

186 Arthur Rudolph
Huntsville Public Library

187 Underwater Scene
Huntsville Public Library

188 Earth over Moon
Huntsville Public Library

189 Moon Buggy Model
Huntsville Public Library

190 Propulsion Lab
Huntsville Public Library

191 Army Plane
Huntsville Public Library

192 Von Braun Celebration
Huntsville Public Library

193 Helium Balloon
Huntsville Public Library

194 George Wallace
Huntsville Public Library

195 Model of Skylab
Huntsville Public Library

196 Stage Scene
Huntsville Public Library

198 Dallas Mills
Huntsville Public Library

199 "Bear" Bryant
Huntsville Public Library

HISTORIC PHOTOS OF HUNTSVILLE

Huntsville is an American city quintessentially founded upon change. From its birth to the present, Huntsville has consistently built and reshaped its appearance, ideals, and industry. Through changing fortunes, Huntsville has continued to grow and prosper by overcoming adversity and maintaining the strong, independent culture of its citizens.

Historic Photos of Huntsville captures this journey through still photography selected from the finest archives. From Huntsville's industrial revolution from the cotton fields, to being the birthplace of many technologies that would take man to the moon, *Historic Photos of Huntsville* follows life, government, education, and events throughout the city's history.

This volume captures unique and rare scenes through the lens of hundreds of historic photographs. Published in striking black and white, these images communicate historic events and everyday life of two centuries of people building a unique and prosperous city.

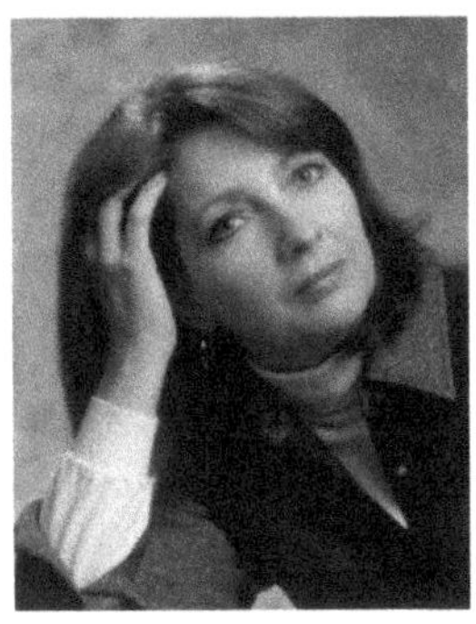

Jacquelyn Procter Reeves has written several books and numerous short stories, for which she has received several awards. She is editor of *Historical Huntsville Review, Valley Leaves,* and associate editor of *Old Tennessee Valley Magazine.* Jacque is the curator of the historic Donnell House Museum in Athens and teaches history via Distance Learning through Early Works Museum. Jacque is a native of Las Vegas, New Mexico, and a graduate of New Mexico Highlands University. Her ancestors were among the first settlers in Madison and Limestone Counties.

WWW.TURNERPUBLISHING.COM

www.ingramcontent.com/pod-product-compliance
Lightning Source LLC
LaVergne TN
LVHW060604110826
845154LV00003B/36

* 9 7 8 1 6 8 3 3 6 9 5 9 2 *